NEBULA
AWARDS
27

NEBULA
AWARDS
27

SFWA's Choices for the Best

Science Fiction and Fantasy

of the Year

EDITED BY JAMES MORROW

HARCOURT BRACE & COMPANY

New York   San Diego   London

Requests for permission to make copies of any part of the work should be mailed to:
Permissions Department, Harcourt Brace & Company, 8th Floor, Orlando,
Florida 32887.

The Library of Congress has cataloged this serial as follows:
The Nebula awards. — No. 18 — New York [N.Y.]: Arbor House, c1983–
v.; 22 cm.
Annual.

Published: San Diego, Calif.: Harcourt Brace & Company, 1984–
Published for: Science-fiction and Fantasy Writers of America, 1983–
Continues: Nebula award stories (New York, N.Y.: 1982)
ISSN 0741-5567 = The Nebula awards
1. Science fiction, American—Periodicals.
I. Science-fiction and Fantasy Writers of America.
PS648.S3N38   83-647399
813'.0876'08—dc19
AACR 2 MARC-S
Library of Congress   [8709r84]rev
ISBN 0-15-164935-9
ISBN 0-15-665471-7 (Harvest: pbk)

Designed by G. B. D. Smith
Printed in the United States of America

First edition
A B C D E

In Memory of
Isaac Asimov
1920 – 1992

CONTENTS

INTRODUCTION
. . . .

James Morrow

One of the first things Martians notice about us, I'm told, is our apparent inability to sustain a serious moral discourse. Every time these beings fly by to observe the Western world in general and the United States in particular, they are struck by the glibness with which our political leaders address burning questions of right and wrong. Appalled that public debates over abortion, gun control, race relations, free speech, and the environment are conducted largely in slogans and sound bites, the Martians depart with heavy hearts, shaking their heads and wringing their tentacles. They cannot figure us out.

In his effort to move beyond bumper-sticker dialectics, where might the bewildered citizen of this bewildered century turn? To the popular culture? Sometimes, yes—though after enduring the vulgar metaphysics of hit fantasy movies like *Field of Dreams* (in which there are no crises a game of catch with your dead father can't overcome) and *Ghost* (in which the world divides neatly into good people and bad people, the former bound for salvation, the latter destined to meet animated hit men from hell), I won't be counting on Hollywood to broaden my spiritual perspectives. To mainstream fiction? Okay, sure, let's give it a try—though, as Kurt Vonnegut pointed out while reviewing the new, expanded edition of Heinlein's *Stranger in a Strange Land*, the literary novel has become extraordinarily privatistic of late. It's as if the big issues (does God exist? from whence springs decency? what sort of species is *Homo sapiens?*) were either settled or not worth discussing, and serious writers should therefore confine themselves to their various ethnic heritages and interpersonal relationships.

When the voting membership of the Science-fiction and Fantasy Writers of America determined the final Nebula Awards ballot for 1991, they might well have been acting out of the same frustrations the Martians experience watching our politicians pontificate about jobs or families. For it so happens that the vast majority of the works on the following lists are extended moral discourses of one sort or another, bravely risking the charge of earnestness as they grapple with apartheid, imperialism, genocide, economic injustice, medical ethics, and, in two cases—"Ma Qui" and "The Dark"—the Vietnam War.

For Novel

Orbital Resonance by John Barnes (Tor)
Barrayar by Lois McMaster Bujold (Baen)
Bone Dance by Emma Bull (Ace)
Synners by Pat Cadigan (Bantam)
The Difference Engine by William Gibson and Bruce Sterling (Bantam)
° *Stations of the Tide* by Michael Swanwick (William Morrow)

For Novella

"Man Opening a Door" by Paul Ash (*Analog,* June 1991)
"Apartheid, Superstrings, and Mordecai Thubana" by Michael Bishop (Axolotl; *Full Spectrum 3*)
° "Beggars in Spain" by Nancy Kress (Axolotl; *Isaac Asimov's Science Fiction Magazine,* April 1991)
"Bully" by Mike Resnick (Axolotl; *Isaac Asimov's Science Fiction Magazine,* April 1991)
"The Gallery of His Dreams" by Kristine Kathryn Rusch (Axolotl; *Isaac Asimov's Science Fiction Magazine,* September 1991)
"Jack" by Connie Willis (*Isaac Asimov's Science Fiction Magazine,* October 1991)

For Novelette

"Gate of Faces" by Ray Aldridge (*Fantasy and Science Fiction,* April 1991)
° "Guide Dog" by Mike Conner (*Fantasy and Science Fiction,* May 1991)
"Black Glass" by Karen Joy Fowler (*Full Spectrum 3*)

° Indicates winner.

"Standing in Line with Mister Jimmy" by James Patrick Kelly (*Isaac Asimov's Science Fiction Magazine,* June 1991)
"The Happy Man" by Jonathan Lethem (*Isaac Asimov's Science Fiction Magazine,* February 1991)
"The All Consuming" by Lucius Shepard and Robert Frazier (*Playboy,* July 1990; *Isaac Asimov's Science Fiction Magazine,* May 1991)
"Getting Real" by Susan Shwartz (*Newer York*)

For Short Story

"They're Made Out of Meat" by Terry Bisson (*Omni,* February 1991)
°"Ma Qui" by Alan Brennert (*Fantasy and Science Fiction,* February 1991; *Author's Choice Monthly 17*)
"The Dark" by Karen Joy Fowler (*Fantasy and Science Fiction,* June 1991)
"Buffalo" by John Kessel (*Fantasy and Science Fiction,* January 1991; *Fires of the Past*)
"Dog's Life" by Martha Soukup (*Amazing Stories,* March 1991)
"the button, and what you know" by W. Gregory Stewart (*Amazing Stories,* June 1991)

Consider the winners. Nancy Kress's "Beggars in Spain" projects us into the brave new world of prenatal gene manipulation, vividly delineating the sort of caste system such technologies might spawn. At the center of Alan Brennert's "Ma Qui," in which a dead soldier is condemned to inhabit the afterworld of his enemy, lies one of the most haunting ethical choices in recent speculative fiction. Mike Conner's "Guide Dog" dramatizes the political and psychological ambiguities inherent in the master-servant relationship. And Michael Swanwick's *Stations of the Tide*—represented here by three interrelated scenes—gives us a confused but manifestly conscientious functionary caught between a joyless, self-serving bureaucracy and the alluring Ur-reality fashioned by the protean wizard Gregorian.

Each of the nominated works rounding out this volume both bites off and chews a meaty moral conundrum—indeed, meat is the very subject of Terry Bisson's yarn: the meat essence of human beings. In "The Dark," Karen Joy Fowler assails the cult of expediency that underlies so much of America's foreign policy. W. Gregory Stewart's "the button, and what you know" is the sort of simultaneously jaunty and maddening parable God might employ were He inclined to tell the universe a bedtime story. (It has not escaped my notice that fate has arranged for this tale of twenty-seven individuals faced with a monstrous dilemma to appear in *Nebula Awards 27*.) The hero of James Patrick Kelly's "Standing in Line with Mister Jimmy" must not only sort out the cruelly stratified world in which he lives but also confront his dependence on the slick stream of advice, encouragement, and pop music pouring from his ThinkMate, a kind of cybernetic Jiminy Cricket. Susan Shwartz's "Getting Real" provides a powerful metaphor for the ways our society marginalizes the poor, the old, the mentally ill, and the female. And John Kessel's "Buffalo" reminds us of a truth one of his main characters, H. G. Wells, sometimes forgot: while writers must strive to prick the human conscience, the greatest fiction is ultimately its own reward.

Among those Nebula finalists precluded from this volume for lack of space, I would especially draw your attention to Connie Willis's "Jack," in which a British vampire, circa 1940, directs his peculiar talents toward locating and rescuing civilians buried alive by the Blitz: in time of war, who are the monsters? (Track it down in *The Year's Best Science Fiction: Ninth Annual Collection*, edited by Gardner Dozois.) For an unprecedented blend of social criticism and particle physics, try Michael Bishop's "Apartheid, Superstrings, and Mordecai Thubana," about a smug Afrikaner who finds himself transformed into invisible "shadow matter" and thus becomes an unwilling witness to the evil of his nation's racial policies. I also urge you to check out Karen Joy Fowler's "Black Glass," which sardonically invites us to ponder how far we're willing to carry the war against drugs: would we be willing to enlist a zombie incarnation of Carry Nation, say? (Both the Bishop and the Fowler appear in *Full Spectrum 3*, recently released in a mass-market paperback edition.) Lucius Shepard and Robert Frazier's "The All Consuming," an account of a Japanese gourmet who begins devouring a South American jungle, emerges as a trenchant allegory on the exploitation of underdeveloped nations by industrialized democracies. Mike Resnick's "Bully," with its alternate-history Teddy Roosevelt telling Africans how to run their continent, sets forth a cogent critique of colonialism. Ray Aldridge's "Gate of Faces" expands Thomas Wolfe's grand theme—you can't go home again—to the level of an entire people: in this case, it's Native Americans who can't go home again.

As with the ten fiction offerings—eight of which appear in no other best-of-the-year anthology for 1991—the rest of *Nebula Awards 27* addresses vexing questions of value. The winner in the long-poem category of the annual Rhysling competition, David Memmott's "The Aging Cryonicist in the Arms of His Mistress Contemplates the Survival of the Species While the Phoenix Is Consumed by Fire," wryly comments on the ersatz immortality peddled by the ALCOR corporation. Bill Warren's essay on recent cinematic SF celebrates the courage of directors who break the Hollywood mold, even as he slams the pretensions of self-styled "auteurs" who practice mold breaking for its own sake. In his witty essay, "Precessing the Simulacra for Fun and Profit," Bruce Sterling presents his case that "true SF, while it can be written with clarity and elegance, must always creek somewhat of the monograph." Finally, the eulogies at the core of this volume all highlight the intellectual integrity of the late Isaac Asimov—his eternal willingness to take on both the scorched-earth theism of the religious right and the New Age orthodoxies of the counterculture. This particular section of *Nebula Awards 27* includes the good doctor's own comments on, literally, matters of life and death. If nothing else, I hope the Martians will read this remarkable self-obituary, judging us henceforth not by the rantings of our elected officials but by the rationality of our Asimovs.

—*State College, Pennsylvania*
June 11, 1992

NEBULA
AWARDS
27

SCIENCE FICTION FOR WHAT? REMARKS ON THE YEAR 1991

Kathryn Cramer

Once again I have deputized Kathryn Cramer to study the recent behavior—both artistic and political—of SFWA and offer up her perspectives on the organization's strengths and foibles.

In 1988, Cramer and her coeditor, Peter D. Pautz, won the best-anthology World Fantasy Award for *The Architecture of Fear*, a treasury of original stories about haunted and otherwise troubled houses. *Walls of Fear*, a follow-up volume edited by Cramer alone, was a World Fantasy finalist. In collaboration with David Hartwell, she has edited *Christmas Ghosts, Spirits of Christmas*, and a forthcoming omnibus of hard-SF stories.

Having received a master's degree in American Studies from Columbia University in 1990, Cramer is now enrolled there as a Ph.D. candidate in German. For the past four years she has taught courses in the writing of science fiction, fantasy, and horror at Harvard Summer School. Since its inception in 1988, she has been the features editor for the *New York Review of Science Fiction*, one of the few periodicals that refuses to exempt SF from the terminology and standards employed by academic literary critics.

In 1991, SFWA stopped being the Science Fiction Writers of America and instead became the Science-fiction and Fantasy Writers of America. (A consensus evidently exists to keep the second *F* in the new logo invisible.) Simultaneously, a strong sentiment emerged to admit not only horror writers, but also the "authors" of things that aren't published words on paper, such as role-playing games and computer programs.

At one level, the name change simply codified a transformation that had already taken place. By the end of the 1980s, SFWA included hundreds of people who were not primarily writers of science fiction, and the heterogeneity of the organization was reflected in the ever-increasing presence of fantasy on the Nebula Awards ballots. And the expanded name enabled SFWA to send a message to the dozens of non-SF writers whose dues had been swelling its treasury: this is your home, too.

But for many SF writers the name change was a disturbing de-velopment—another assault on the fragile infrastructure that keeps the whole idea of *science* fiction alive and validates its visionary proj-ect: the genre's unique ability to extrapolate from current trends, dramatize scientific insights, and fill us with a sense of wonder. There has been a vigorous, long-standing debate among SFWA members over the definition of science fiction versus fantasy, with many au-thors arguing that the two forms are radically distinct and perhaps even naturally antagonistic. Although the advocates of genre apart-heid make a convincing case for SF's artistic and intellectual purity, they have clearly lost the war. At this point, their only viable option would be to found a new organization with strict membership re-quirements.

For SF separatists, linking the field with horror is an even more nightmarish notion. Whereas science fiction emphasizes ideas and avoids sensationalism, horror emphasizes sensationalism and is sel-dom concerned with ideas per se. SF arises from meditation on em-pirical knowledge and from speculation about the future of the human species; horror arises from gothic literary traditions and paranoia. The protagonists of science fiction are thinking men and women trying to reason their way through mazes of naturalistic cause and effect; the protagonists of horror stories are flies caught in spider webs of cosmic evil. The basic values underlying these two varieties of literature, and the readers they attract, couldn't be more differ-ent.

In the view of many science fiction writers, melding with genres that boast orthogonally different worldviews will only serve to deflect SF from its manifest destiny. And, indeed, something like this is already happening. If I had to identify a prevailing trend for 1991, I would point to the creeping assumption that SF ought to have some social worth apart from its inherent visionary project. SF for the sake of SF has fallen into disfavor.

The Science-fiction and Fantasy Writers
of America

Several of the year's best genre stories deal rather explicitly with science fiction's identity crisis. Gregory Benford's "Centigrade 233" tells of a young man, Alex, who inherits an excellent SF collection in a postliterate future. He tries to convert the books and magazines into cash, only to discover that, since reading is passé, no one wants a bunch of printed words predicting a quaint future that never happened. So he makes the best of the situation by burning rare first editions as a stunt at fashionable parties. For the protagonist's elite audiences, these immolations symbolize a release from "the dead hand of the past."

Benford's parable is deliberately provocative, playing off the righteous indignation that animates Bradbury's *Fahrenheit 451.* "Centigrade 233" neither justifies nor supports the SF project, and its characters take great pleasure in obliterating the genre from recorded memory. Implicitly, the issue of *Isaac Asimov's Science Fiction Magazine* in which Benford's story appears will sooner or later suffer the same fate as the June 1940 issue of *Thrilling Wonder Stories* and the April 1930 issue of *Air Wonder Stories* that Alex sets ablaze. Benford is, at the very least, playing devil's advocate to our belief that science fiction says meaningful things about the future.

John Kessel's "Buffalo," a 1991 Nebula nominee, while gentler in tone than "Centigrade 233," goes even further. It is an alternate-history tale about a chance 1934 encounter between Kessel's own Polish émigré father and H. G. Wells. The elder Kessel, an avid science fiction reader, expresses his deep admiration for Wells's work, and Wells is quite pleased until he discovers that Kessel is also a big fan of Edgar Rice Burroughs. But the story does not stop there. After Wells rudely dismisses Kessel as an ignorant proletarian, both of them, sitting separately in a Washington ballroom, listen to a black musician named Duke Ellington play "Creole Love Call." Kessel and Wells are so absorbed by their technologically based dreams that when the real future—Ellington—speaks to them, they cannot recognize its voice.

Science fiction shares with the sciences themselves an insistence that its narratives be taken literally, a fact that makes Jonathan

Lethem's Nebula-nominated novelette, "The Happy Man," one of the oddest cross-genre hybrids in recent memory. Lethem posits a technology for resurrecting the dead, used primarily in cases where the family breadwinner has passed away, leaving behind an impoverished widow and children. While the reanimated corpses can go to work and earn money, the rest of the time each one inhabits his own personal Hell. Support groups exist for these benighted commuters. Tom, Lethem's protagonist, initially joins one but is quickly disgusted by the members' insistence that Hell is a "psychological landscape" filled with meaning.

Tom's son, Peter, creates a computer game based on his father's ordeal, along the lines of Dungeons and Dragons. Each time Dad comes back from Hell, Dad tells Peter where he went and what happened, and Peter types it all into his computer, fleshing out his game and occasionally coming up with useful strategies for solving the afterlife. Peter shares his father's belief that Hell doesn't mean anything; it just is. This is, of course, a terrible mistake. Because of Dad's denial, Peter suffers at the hands of the same uncle who sexually abused his father.

While "The Happy Man" is more about dysfunctional families than about genre tropes, it seems to be attacking the assumption, so prevalent among SF readers and critics, that fantastical landscapes are best taken literally. Lethem is claiming not only that there are symbolic and allegorical ways to interpret imaginary worlds but that we miss something very precious when we fail to do so. Implicitly, every story about outer space is also about inner space.

Postmodern Science Fiction

It could be argued that SFWA's name change reflects the larger "postmodern" trend toward the breakdown of genre barriers. The process that SF author William Gibson terms "cultural mongrelization" has toppled the traditional wall between science fiction and other forms of speculation. But cultural mongrelization has also induced in SFWA a fear of being engulfed by "mundane" or "mainstream" literature. So while one wall came down, another went up, surrounding a rather large and pluralistic population of writers—everyone whose efforts are variously tagged "science fiction," "science fantasy," "epic fantasy," "high fantasy," or "horror" on the spines of their paperback editions—and protecting them from absorption by the amorphous mass of American letters.

The cyberpunk movement of the mid-1980s had a more comfortable relationship with the mainstream. Gibson's *Neuromancer* not only swept the awards in the science fiction field, it broke through to hip literary culture. One finds references to *Neuromancer* in the oddest places. I heard Gibson's book mentioned in a German Literature session at a recent Modern Language Association conference; it's discussed in one of Kathryn Hayles's books on chaos theory and literature; and it routinely appears on lists of postmodern novels.

In collaboration with Bruce Sterling, the central agent of chaos of the cyberpunk movement, Gibson wrote one of 1991's Nebula-nominated novels, *The Difference Engine,* in which the computer revolution has arrived in the nineteenth century rather than the twentieth. Brimming with insights into the origins of the scientific-technocratic-industrial complex, this is the sort of postmodern work that only an SF sensibility could have produced, and Gibson and Sterling deploy their grand conceit in ways having as much to do with literary politics as with aesthetics. Dense, intellectual, and occasionally plodding, *The Difference Engine* attempts to show the outside literary world that science fiction boasts an identity and a mission apart from mere postmodernism.

Gibson and Sterling were not the only genre authors to go "beyond" science fiction in 1991. Sheri S. Tepper's Hugo-nominated novel, *Beauty,* for example, while not seasoned to the sensitive palates of literary aesthetes, is every bit as postmodern as *The Difference Engine.* Ignoring genre boundaries, Tepper fuses a retelling of "Sleeping Beauty" with a dystopian time-travel romance. The plot transports us up and down a myriad of narrative chutes and ladders, into fairy tales, myths, legends, and ballads. *Beauty* is the epitome of the cultural mongrel.

Beyond Cyberpunk

Although the cyberpunk movement was essentially over by 1986, its influence on science fiction has steadily increased since then. Cyberpunk has at last hit *Analog* magazine, that final refuge of the Campbellian SF aesthetic. Although Gibson's fiction is in part a reaction against what he calls "a certain didactic, right-wing stance . . . associated with hard SF," the human/machine interface of *Neuromancer* has evidently captivated certain *Analog* writers, and they have begun the long, slow task of pressing the premises of cyberpunk into the service of old-fashioned Campbellian values.

In Stephen L. Burns's "A Roll of the Dice," the characters all wear virtual-reality "Spex" to make life seem beautiful and to keep themselves reasonably happy. The outside world may be dangerous and ugly, but Spex allow you to preserve your most treasured illusions. Burns emphatically rejects cyberpunk's nihilism, concluding his story with a moral: "The trick lay in knowing when to put all that aside, to face things as they really were. Otherwise there was no starting point for making what you wanted into a reality." The story affirms a basic value of hard SF—technology is for solving problems, not for running away from them. At another level, the Spex are Burns's metaphor for literary style; from the *Analog* perspective, while manufactured beauty may make people feel better, only conventional utilitarianism gets us anywhere.

James Patrick Kelly's "Standing in Line with Mister Jimmy," published in *Asimov's,* also uses cyberpunk tropes to make an anticyberpunk point. The Mister Jimmy of the title is an artificial-intelligence device called a ThinkMate, about the size of a Walkman and used in much the same way. Mister Jimmy helps Chip, the protagonist, think; it provides the sound track for Chip's "attitude" and gives him pointers on being cool. While Burns's protagonist abandons his Spex because he's ready to face reality, Chip abandons Mister Jimmy because he's found a girl who'll move in with him. For Kelly, it seems, slick high tech is essentially an adolescent male obsession, sexy only for those who haven't yet discovered real and reliable sex.

In *Neuromancer* and its progeny, men invariably instigate the action. While quite a few women inhabit cyberpunk, they are usually just updated versions of the femmes fatales who populate *film noir;* they don't really do anything. Lately, however, several women writers—Pat Cadigan, Emma Bull, and Lisa Mason chief among them—have demonstrated that a female or gender-neutral protagonist can partake fully of the cyberpunk attitude, occupying the center of high-tech, low-life adventure stories.

Cadigan's women have always had a smart remark at the ready, and they squeak out of the tightest spots through guts, luck, and street savvy. Her 1991 novel, the Nebula-nominated *Synners*, is particularly striking in this regard.

> "Not that it matters," said the judge, looking satisfied, "but how do you plead?"
> "I don't plead," said Gina, feeling shakier than she sounded. "I've never fucking pleaded in my life."

Emma Bull's *Bone Dance* is similar in tone to *Synners*, but here the author dispenses with gender altogether. Her androgynous protagonist is named Sparrow. Since the book is written in the first person, Bull easily avoids referring to Sparrow as "he" or "she." The cover art underscores the ambiguity. In the background lies a futuristic city lit by a fiery glow, and in the foreground stands Sparrow, slight and Asian, wearing jeans, black leather boots and jacket, a Walkman, and sunglasses (even though it's night). The portrait remarkably resembles SF writer Ted Chiang, except that when you examine it closely what initially looked like the turned-up collar of the jacket becomes a long ponytail: attitude without gender specificity. There is little overt feminism (or antisexist rhetoric) in either *Synners* or *Bone Dance*, as if these nonmale heroes are so tough and knowing they don't need it, and both Cadigan and Bull preserve, relatively intact, the myth of the burned-out, sleep-deprived cyberpunk.

Gutsy women also appear in postcyberpunk fiction by men. In Michael Swanwick's novella "Griffin's Egg," the main character, Gunther, becomes sexually involved with Ekaterina, a Gibsonian heroine who is really much too good for him: she is Heinlein's rugged individualist updated, a Russian military commander who wears a silk teddy under her "Studio Volga" space suit. And in *The Difference Engine* we get Sybil Gerard, the independent-minded daughter of a Luddite agitator. On page 60, Sybil, who has lived for a decade as a fallen woman, sends a telegram to the man who ruined her: "Dear Charles . . . Nine years ago you put me to the worst dishonour that a woman can know. . . . Today I am leaving London, in the company of powerful friends. They know very well what a traitor you were." Unfortunately, the moment Sybil decides to live her life on her own terms she is banished from the book, returning only near the end to fill a rather trivial role.

Although the cyberpunk movement itself is over, the controversy it spawned continues to play itself out. But while cyberpunk kicked SF into a new key, it did not give the field a new sense of purpose. It brought to science fiction many of the same things Ernest Hemingway brought to mainstream American literature. But desperate, romantic, self-destructive stoicism, while it may get one through the worst of times, is no substitute for the visionary project of classical science fiction.

Science Fiction Writers for Social Responsibility

The most highly regarded SF stories and novels of 1991 reflect the field's uncertainty over its purpose. Rather than pursuing the utopianism inherent in the very idea of futuristic speculation, many writers now appeal to political and interpersonal ideals not particularly science fictional in nature. For the socially responsible SF writers, the genre is a neutral tool that must be infused with redeeming values. The resulting stories draw their energy not from the genre's usual maneuvers—extrapolating, predicting, hyperbolizing, building worlds, redefining consciousness and intelligence—but from contemporary social problems. In the late 1960s such fiction might have been called "relevant," but in the early 1990s it seems to betray feelings of irrelevance among its creators.

Perhaps the most striking example is Michael Bishop's Nebula-nominated novella, "Apartheid, Superstrings, and Mordecai Thubana," which turns on the unlikely proposition that superstring theory might contribute to the downfall of apartheid. Bishop's grimly ironic message is that nothing short of bizarre paranormal experiences facilitated by exotic physics will convince South Africa's white middle class that its country's racial policies are wrong.

Vietnam is not a new subject for science fiction. Gardner Dozois's "A Dream at Noonday" was published in 1970, Kate Wilhelm's "The Village" in 1973, and in 1987 Jack Dann and Jeannie Van Buren Dann gave us their excellent Vietnam SF anthology, *In the Field of Fire*. Alan Brennert's "Ma Qui" proves that the topic is by no means exhausted. In 1991's Nebula-winning short story, a recently dead American soldier discovers that the hereafter in Vietnam is Vietnamese and that as a demon he will behave as folklore says he should, regardless of his own wishes. Published shortly before the Bush administration announced that America had gotten over "the Vietnam syndrome"—meaning that because of its easy victory in Kuwait the U.S. military had regained the prerogative to make casual war—"Ma Qui" demonstrates that, for soldiers actually in combat, the relationship to the enemy is never casual.

Two of 1991's anthologies were intended to counterbalance the bellicose nature of so much traditional SF. Harry Harrison and Bruce McAllister edited *There Won't Be War* (an overt riposte to Jerry Pournelle's ongoing *There Will Be War* series), while, on a less confrontational and more literary note, Lewis Shiner put together a peace compendium titled *When the Music's Over.* The problem these volumes are meant to address is real and frustrating: there is a vast audience for militaristic SF, and the authors who feed these appetites are to some degree supporting the often malign and greedy agenda of the defense establishment. While *There Won't Be War* and *When the Music's Over* probably did nothing to undermine public support for expensive superweapons, they did show that, in the hands of skilled writers, peace can be as provocative as war.

Susan Shwartz's Nebula-nominated novelette, "Getting Real," combines near-future extrapolative SF with urban fantasy. The premise harkens back to John Collier's 1941 fantasy "Evening Primrose," about people who live around the clock in a department store, pretending to be mannequins during business hours. Shwartz, who lives in New York and works on Wall Street, has updated this concept by fifty years: she skillfully brings together the virtual invisibility of New Yorkers (who pass within inches of each other but might as well all be on different planets), the dehumanizing ethics of Wall Street financial firms that "treat clericals like Handi Wipes," and the problem of urban homelessness. The central fantasy element of this charming and caring story—nonpeople forgotten by the society they live in—is in fact quite real, a truth most of us urban Americans try our best to ignore.

Adult Children of Science Fiction Writers

The issues currently receiving the most play in socially responsible SF derive from the so-called recovery movement. Although Alcoholics Anonymous has been around a long time, in the 1980s its basic tool, the famous Twelve Steps, was enlisted to combat a broad variety of presumed pathologies. There are now entire "Recovery" sections in the larger bookstores, with volumes bearing titles like *It's Never Too Late to Have a Happy Childhood*. For the moment, at least, the recovery movement is substantially larger than the science fiction field and—with its strong emphasis on support groups—at least as well organized.

Unlike today's SF writers, recovery aficionados have a strong sense of mission. We should all stop drinking, stop using drugs, stop enabling those who haven't stopped, become properly angry at our parents, and face up to the ways in which we restage childhood traumas in our adult lives. Although the movement downplays its connection to religion, spiritually and structurally it echoes the charismatic American Protestant tradition. And as we limp, wounded and bleeding, through the 1990s, the cult of recovery begins to look more and more like a neo-temperance crusade.

Of all the recovery-oriented SF from 1991, Karen Joy Fowler's novelette, "Black Glass," is the most sardonic. A giant, supernaturally reanimated version of Carry Nation appears and again starts chopping up bars with her hatchet. The Drug Enforcement Agency finds out about this creature and seeks her out for the war on drugs in Central America. Meanwhile, inspired by Nation's example, middle-aged women want to join the DEA. Fowler makes fascinating and convincing connections between old-style temperance and the modern ideal of the "empowered woman." After Nation has destroyed a bar, several male witnesses try to sort out what happened.

> "She was big," said the first businessman. "For a woman."
>
> "She was enormous," said Schilling.
>
> "She was as big as a football player," said the first businessman carefully.
>
> "She was as big as a truck," said Schilling. He pointed a shaky finger to the register. "She lifted it over her head like it was a feather duster or a pillow or something. You can write this down," he said. "You can quote me on this. We're talking about a very troubled, very big woman."
>
> "I don't think it's such a good idea," the second businessman said.
>
> "What's not a good idea?"
>
> "Women that size," said the second businessman.

To the feminists in the story, Nation is the person each of them wants to become. To the men, she is the forbidding, possibly castrating mother who stands between them and their hedonism.

With its feminist agenda and chary attitude toward drugs and al-cohol, much recent SF has become a countervailing force against the cyberpunk ethic. This tension is especially evident in postcyber-punk writing by women. On the first page of *Synners,* Gator says to her male friend, "Get help, Jones. You're an addict," a strong con-trast to the joke on the first page of *Neuromancer:* "'It's not like I'm using,' Case heard someone say, as he shouldered his way through the crowd. . . . 'It's like my body's developed a massive drug defi-ciency.'" In "A Roll of the Dice," Burns goes so far as to equate cyberpunk's passion for technology with alcoholism: "Glenda was in her artificial world, Howie in his. One made out of alcohol and self-delusion, the other spun out of computer mediated senses." The issue of addiction also informs Lethem's "The Happy Man," which on one level can be interpreted as an allegory on families destroyed by alcohol. In addition to being dead, Tom also appears to be a dipsomaniac, and his descent into Hell may be a metaphor for bing-ing. His codependent wife experiences rage, guilt, and helplessness, takes a lover to relieve her loneliness, and finally summons the cour-age to walk out. Peter is the paradigmatic good son of an alcoholic father, devoting all his time and effort to saving Dad from his own personal Hell. And this science-fictional situation has the same con-sequences as its real-world analog: the son is forced to enact his father's nightmare childhood, and the psychological mechanism that makes the whole disaster possible is denial.

In "Beggars in Spain," the Nebula-winning novella for 1991, Nancy Kress infuses recovery themes into a more conventional variety of SF. The basic set-up—superchildren scattered throughout the nor-mal population, forced as adults to form an insulated utopia so jeal-ous mundanes won't hurt them—traces to several sources, most notably A. E. Van Vogt's *Slan* (1946), with its persecuted super-humans organized into a secret network, and Zenna Henderson's "People" stories of the 1960s, about paranormally gifted aliens who hide out in small southwestern towns lest humans grow resentful and kill them. There is also a nod to Ayn Rand's *Atlas Shrugged,* in which extraordinarily fit people (in the Darwinian sense) found a separatist community to protect themselves from a government that is trying to deprive them of their livelihoods.

Leisha Camden, the genetically engineered Sleepless heroine of "Beggars in Spain," thinks it's possible to coexist peacefully with the world's Sleepers. But some less naive Sleepless feel separatism is essential to their survival.

> "I believe in voluntary trade that is mutually beneficial. That spiritual dignity comes from supporting one's life through one's own efforts, and trading the results of those efforts in mutual cooperation. . . ."
> "Fine. . . . Now what about the beggars in Spain? . . . You walk down a street in a poor country like Spain and you see a beggar. Do you give him a dollar?"
> "Probably."
> "Why? He's trading nothing with you. He has nothing to trade."

Realistically portrayed alcoholism and child abuse figure crucially in the story. Overwhelmed by her husband, Leisha's mother turns to drink; she becomes emotionally distant, then disappears altogether. Leisha's father heavily favors Leisha, his perfect child, over her twin sister, so the latter grows up with low self-esteem. In the end, the two sisters are reconciled during the rescue of an abused Sleepless child.

Although Mike Conner's Nebula-winning novelette, "Guide Dog," has no realistically portrayed child abuse, the theme echoes throughout. The protagonist's parents make only a cameo appearance: they sell him into indentured servitude because they're poor and need the money. The beelike aliens who buy him are benign enough, but basically they treat him like an animal. (That people who claim to have been kidnapped by extraterrestrials were often severely abused as children is well documented; unable to reconcile images of loving parents with the truth of their upbringing, these individuals apparently develop fantasies of alien abduction.) Trained as a guide dog, he is assigned to become the eyes of a famous artist who has gone blind. Their bond is wonderful, transcendent, but everything we know about asymmetrical power relationships tells us it cannot last—and indeed it doesn't. "Guide Dog" is a tragedy, relentlessly charting its hero's unlikely rise, interval of glory, and inevitable fall.

The year brought a couple of odd exceptions to SFWA's general tendency to ratify the recovery movement. In Orson Scott Card's *Xenocide,* a young woman, with her father's permission and enthusiastic cooperation, is put in a situation that is highly likely to make her suicidal, the purpose being to determine whether or not she is one of "the chosen." She attempts suicide repeatedly, with amazing determination and inventiveness, and her ordeal is presented as evidence for how dearly her father loves her. As in much of Card's output, *Xenocide*'s characters suffer horribly, even as other characters express peculiar and unpredictable reactions to their torment.

In Tepper's *Beauty*, the heroine—with the apparent approval of the narrative voice—abandons her baby because it is genetically tainted: the father was a psychotic rapist. When Beauty returns twenty-odd years later to discover that her daughter is indeed corrupt, she reminds herself that the baby came from bad seed and that a couple of decades of nurturing wouldn't have made any difference. As in her earlier *The Gate to Women's Country*, Tepper here expresses a faith in genetic determinism that, whatever else one may think of it, cannot be accused of trendiness.

SF for SF's Sake

The significant political events of 1991 included the Persian Gulf War and the disintegration of the Soviet Union. Early in the year, Operation Desert Storm demonstrated that in the mechanized conflicts of the future, missiles, not men, will be the Patriots. George Bush's war invited us to forsake our fond memories of Luke Skywalker in his fighter plane "feeling the force" as he drops the bomb in just the right spot; now we're supposed to fall in love with the plane itself. A post–Desert Storm remake of *Star Wars* would be a tale not of individual heroism but of corporate integrity. The credit for Luke's bull's-eye would go to those defense contractors who didn't gouge the rebels but instead gave them their money's worth in high tech.

Written before Iraq's invasion of Kuwait, Michael Swanwick's Nebula-winning novel, *Stations of the Tide*, uncannily foreshadows the Gulf War and its themes, most especially the tension between the power inherent in machines and the power inherent in people. Just as Bush sought to deprive Saddam Hussein of certain weapons of mass destruction, the viewpoint character in Swanwick's tale—a functionary from the Division of Technology Transfer—seeks to wrest an unidentified contraband machine from the hands of the mysterious and talented wizard, Gregorian. The novel begins with the line "The bureaucrat fell from the sky," and indeed the bureaucrat seems to have been dropped in over his head. Physically undistinguished, unarmed, he is actually well equipped for his task. This ordinary-seeming man has an extraordinary mind—the resemblance to Gene Wolfe may not be accidental—and Swanwick also gives him a sentient briefcase programmed for all sorts of technological magic.

Like Isaac Asimov's "Nightfall," *Stations of the Tide* takes place immediately before the turn of a major cosmic cycle: every two hundred years, the ocean rises and covers the Tidewater. The bureaucrat has until the waters arrive to retrieve the stolen technology from Gregorian. But whereas in "Nightfall" the viewpoint character's goal is to preserve sanity, civilization, and knowledge by resisting the destructive power of the coming night, in *Stations* this is the aim of Gregorian, the *antagonist*. The bureaucrat seeks to control the spread of technology so that the galactic power structure will prevail, even if this mission costs lives. It's a great, audacious, visionary subject for a science fiction novel, and the reader comes away feeling that, as long as Swanwick is with us, SF for the sake of SF may have a viable future after all.

In contrast to the Gulf War, the fall of the Soviet Union was a tightly plotted, sweeping narrative with strong characters to whom the viewer could relate. Late last summer, I tuned in to CNN to find out whether a hurricane was going to hit New York. There was no news of the hurricane. Rather, the newscasters were talking of Gorbachev in the past tense, and one remarked that it was twenty minutes after the deadline Boris Yeltsin had been given for leaving the Russian parliament building, but it seemed he was still there. A coup had occurred in the Soviet Union—the stuff of which political thrillers are made. But in contrast to the plots of most political thrillers, the United States had no role to play. Whereas the Gulf War replaced individual heroism with the credo "technological might makes right," the failed coup taught us that determined and largely unarmed people can win against bad guys wielding control over more weapons than most of us can imagine. The fax machine and the modem were effective against tanks and—in principle, at least—the whole Soviet arsenal.

Norman Spinrad's *Russian Spring*, a methodically researched and rigorously imagined techno-thriller about space travel in a future where the Soviet Union has followed Gorbachev's lead (and the United States has followed Jesse Helms's), became obsolete within weeks of its publication. While the future spelled out in this novel will never happen, Spinrad's scenario nevertheless intersects provocatively with actual events. A liberal Soviet president is kidnapped by military hard-liners; the U.S. chief executive refuses to deal with the hard-liners, saying he will speak only to the lawfully elected president. Representatives of breakaway Soviet republics go to the United Nations seeking recognition. When the radical Nat Wolfowitz assumes the Oval Office after the death of the archconservative American president, his trials and tribulations recall those of Boris Yeltsin during the coup.

What distinguishes *Russian Spring* from the usual run of techno-thriller is the author's faith in conventional science-fictional extrapolation. Spinrad is a visionary in the grand manner, and so is his protagonist, Jerry Reed, a brilliant, SF-reading aerospace engineer who gives up everything to follow his dream and journey beyond the Earth. In the final analysis, the novel emerges as a sincere and carefully reasoned argument for planetary exploration as essential to humanity's survival, a case Spinrad makes even while acknowledging such obstacles as the weakening of NASA following the *Challenger* disaster and the hypermilitarization of America's space program. It is a brave book.

If science fiction is not really about the future but rather about the present and the past—if it is not about possible technologies and plausible odysseys into the unknown but about the demons within our own families and personalities—then there is little to separate it from fantasy, horror, or the mainstream for that matter. And if the field is no longer defined by a shared sense of purpose but merely by overlapping circles of colleagues who feel connected to each other because they meet at conventions and talk on the computer nets, then something vital has been lost. *Russian Spring* vibrates with a sure sense of science fiction's heritage and destiny. That history out-distanced a few of Spinrad's wilder extrapolations is not a reason to forsake the sort of visionary project that inspirits this remarkable novel. It's a reason for more SF writers to roll up their sleeves and start recovering the essence of their art.

GUIDE DOG

. . . .

Mike Conner

"Guide Dog" marks a triumphant return for Mike Conner, his first major piece of SF since the three-year break he took upon realizing he'd written himself into what he calls "stunned silence." His previous work includes a handful of novelettes and three novels—*Eye of the Sun, Group Mind,* and *The Houdini Directive*—all of which he produced after graduating from the Clarion Science Fiction Writers Workshop. The father of four teenaged children, Conner lives in Oakland, California, where he writes full time, plays harmonica with a rock band called the Naked Barbie Dolls, and coaches his kids' baseball team.

"A couple of years ago I was downtown and I saw a woman and a guide dog waiting for the light to change at a busy intersection," Conner explains. "The woman couldn't see a thing, but her dog—a black Lab, I believe—stared intently at the traffic signal. As soon as the light turned green, the guide dog waited a moment, then started the woman across the street. Pretty impressive, but really it was the expression on the dog's face that struck me. It looked so *worried.* I thought, well, a dog usually comes into this world to eat and sleep and one or maybe two other things, but this dog has a *job.* And what a job! For sure, worse than most of our jobs. I mean, when we screw up at the office, our boss won't get flattened by a bus.

"So I thought, okay, what if we did that? I mean, what if we were living around beings who were smarter than us? And what if some of them were handicapped and hired us to help them get around? I'd bet we'd start feeling the way that guide dog felt. I knew I had a pretty good story idea, but there was a piece missing, and I wasn't ready to find out what it was yet.

"About a year later I'm in Zurich. I'm traveling alone, don't speak French and my German isn't much better, so I really haven't talked to anyone since I left the States. It's Sunday night, and I've spent my last thirty Swiss francs on some kind of blue drink at the magic club in the basement of my hotel, and now I'm broke, and, even worse, it's *Fasching,* the Swiss version of Mardi Gras, which in the quarter I'm staying in means three guys marching up and down the street playing 'St. James Infirmary Blues' on plastic horns. I'm lying on my bed trying to sleep, feeling really low, when suddenly I remember my story idea. And I realize what made that black Lab so sad was that, even though a guide dog lives with people who trust him to do important things in their world, he

16

can never, ever be one of them. And so I got up and wrote the first ten pages of 'Guide Dog' there in my hotel room. . . ."

When I was fourteen years old, my parents sold me. I don't blame them for it. They got a lot of money for me. Mom and Dad ran an import company, and they were at a disadvantage because, while they were never big enough to compete, they always did just well enough to keep from going under. And they had another son to worry about that they could not sell yet. So the contract was a good thing for the family.

The night I left, Dad cried and said that when I turned twenty-five and had worked off the term, I could come home, and he would pay me back every cent. I told him he didn't have to do that. I was at the age where you don't care much about leaving home anyway. So, one morning in December, Dad drove me over to the compound in the old vegetable truck. His eyes were still red, but he wasn't crying anymore. He told me to be careful in town, pay attention to my teachers, and wash all the fruits and vegetables I ate. I thought he ought to know about that because he imported food, so I thanked him and said I would see him in about ten years. He gave me a tiny blue pocketknife then that had a fingernail file in it and a pair of scissors. I still had that knife until last night. It was so small they never believed I could actually use it as a weapon. It was the last thing Dad ever gave me, and I stood turning it over with one hand and waving good-bye with the other.

At first I missed the folks. Anybody with half a heart misses their family no matter how awful they are. But the Academy had developed plenty of ways to make you forget about them. They got you busy with the academic stuff, and they put you in the social program, too. They arranged your rooms and your classes to put you with people they calculated you would get along with. They wanted you to fall in love as soon as possible. It didn't matter with whom. Here you were, lonely as hell, and they gave you a roommate, also lonely, and they look the other way and hand you every opportunity, so how could you resist? Then, when you thought you were set all right, they fix it so one of you moves up a class or transfers out to another dorm. So you moan and groan, and then look around and find somebody new. Somehow it ate up whole years.

Eventually, though, you passed your exams and got a chance to see what you were there for. Like everything else, it was pretty much sink or swim (though after three years they were pretty certain about who would sink and who could do the swimming). What they did was take you out early in the morning into the Tree. They landed you on top and said all you had to do was make it back to the gate of the Academy. No time limit. No life or death. If you freaked, you could call in on a beeper, and they'd pick you up, and you were free to try again as many times as you wanted. But everyone knew getting to that gate meant getting out of school. And after three years of being jacked around, manipulated, and otherwise educated, there wasn't anybody who wasn't ready for that.

I know I was. I'd spent hours studying the tapes and maps. I'd put on phones and gotten used to the noise they made. I knew all the best routes to take on foot, and how to ask for directions and read the answers from the little dances they did. I had a pack of food and a list of districts in the Tree where our people were allowed to work or live. So when they came for me I thought it would not be a problem. They flew me in and let me out directly at the top of the Tree.

Oh my! The perches at the top are narrow and wind-worn slick, rounded like branches; and even cleated, gum-soled slippers and practice on the balance beams couldn't prepare you for the sheer power of thousands of them swarming by, wings buzzing—to say nothing of the way they turned their heads and panned their eyes when they looked at you, and how you thought they wanted you to fall, and then, and even worse, realized that they *didn't care* whether you fell or not, that you were nothing to them, while they were everything to each other. It was the emotion that was hard to take and still carry on the task of moving down. In spite of the perches and platforms, there were millions of places you could crash and fall through, bouncing down like a ball in a pachinko machine all the way to the ground.

My first five minutes up there, I slipped and hung, legs swinging onto a slippery perch, fighting a total despair that sapped the strength in my arms and made me want to let go. Then I told myself no, this is what you're up here for, to survive this, and it's the only way you'll ever see the end of that contract. *This is what you've been going to school for!* And so I swung my legs up and stood and spread my arms to keep the ones flying by off of me, and, sure enough, they commenced to veer because their radar told them I had position. And I started picking and hopping my way down until I reached a fountain I remembered from the tapes, got myself oriented, and eventually made it back to the gates of the school. It took six and one-half hours. Later they said it was some kind of record. I don't know. It seemed to have lasted forever.

The next day they called me in and gave me an assignment in a nest.

A guide dog lives in a nest for two years. You continue your studies, but the idea is to learn all you can about how they live. At the end of the two years, you are supposed to be used to their ways. My nest lay about twenty miles outside the Tree, near a river. It was nice lush country, with lots of flowers and paths that you could walk along and almost fool yourself into believing you were home—until a couple of them flew over.

The nest family is where you wear a harness for the first time. The harness is the mark of a guide dog. It is the means of communicating with your client. The word *client* is a hard one to get around. You want to learn to forget what you think you mean by the word and try to really understand the concept of service. As a guide, your purpose is to help the client to live as normally as possible. In the nest, you learn not to feel ashamed of that, and to take pride in what you are and enjoy it. That way you can understand the kind of appreciation they give you in return. I admit this appreciation can be difficult to handle. However, you cannot live as a guide dog without it. It is as if you were a plant and had to learn to *appreciate* the light before you could grow and thrive.

I had a good nest. They had worked with the Academy for many years and had boarded many student guides, and they knew how to train us. They were an older nest, and lots of the kids were almost grown. With a nest, it is the kids who really do most of the teaching. They laugh at you when you first feel the thousands of tiny needles in the top of your back from the harness translator that turns their buzzing into shapes that you interpret as words. They demonstrate the body language. You make your first moves in a harness with the kids, too. They hold the grab bar and press their knees into the cups on either side of your hips. If they are old enough and strong enough, they fly with you, too, or try to. Sometimes you make it across the room. Sometimes you crash and lie there in a heap, pushing and trying to untangle yourself just like you would with any other kid.

The biggest thing they teach you, though, is about the emotion. I'm talking about what you feel and what you have to go through if they accept you even a little. In school, they say it is possibly the result of a chemical reaction. They would. Anyone who's ever felt it knows that there is nothing chemical about it. It is a spiritual rush of love and gratitude that hits you so hard your toes curl. You think that you understand everything. You know it is all worth it, no matter what it is.

I remember when I felt it the first time. I was with one of the young ones, and we were playing a kind of catch game with a long scoop and a sticky ball. I made a move and caught one behind my back and flipped it right back at him, and he just stood there looking at me, his flat eyes shining like china. And it hit me so hard then I thought I would just burst with it.

Of course, once you feel it like that, you want to feel it again. That's why the Academy teaches you to channel your feelings. That feeling of belonging is what holds everything together for them. It pulls them in and keeps them healthy. *You*, however, are meant to have only a taste of it. That's how they put it at school. *Tasting.* When you feel it coming on, you're supposed to sidestep and take a taste. You must not let it get to you. That first time in the garden with the kid, I got in all the way, and I paid. Inside out of that burning glow of belonging is black, empty desolation that hits even harder. It just about knocked me out for good. I was so down with it, I spent three days trying to figure out how I could kill myself with the little pocketknife Dad gave me. In the end, though, I came back, and from then on I was really careful. I made sure to take only a taste.

You get to know how much you can have, and I pushed that to the limit but stayed safe. There were some who wanted more, though. They took all they could get and built up a tolerance. They didn't care about the consequences. They were renegades. Eventually I would run into them.

By my second year with the family, I was doing pretty well. I got so I didn't feel the harness anymore, and the pictures pressed against my back turned easily into words and pictures in my head. I was fond of my nest. The father would take me out flying in the harness, and we got to be pretty good together. Of course, he could see, and his radar was sharp, so it was not like guiding him. But he helped me to figure out the traffic system and how they worked the right-of-way. The father told me I was the best dog that had ever come into his nest. *Dog.* That's how the harness translated their sound for what we were. He got emotional about it, too. I could feel it coming on and got all cold inside and had just the smallest taste. I knew it was hard for him getting attached to a guide and then having to let go. It was hard for me, too. But that was the way it was.

A couple of days after the father paid me that compliment, the Director asked me to come around to his office. When I came in, he was sitting behind his desk wearing a pair of big glasses. Which was a good thing, because small eyes were starting to look strange to me.

"You've been an outstanding, outstanding student," the Director began.

"Thank you, sir."

"You could not ask anyone to do any more than you've done here." He was speaking emotionally. It always surprises me how we demonstrate emotion so visibly—eyes misting, voice trembling—with so little of the feeling coming through.

The Director began to clean his glasses. "We have been approached by the representative of a very, very special client. A very, very important personality in this world. We have never had an opportunity to serve someone of this stature until now. Fortunately, I believe we are ready to meet the challenge. I believe you are ready to guide. I believe you are the one person here who can guide this client." He put both his hands on my shoulders and looked deep into my eyes. "What do you say?"

"I'll give it a shot," I said.

I called him Henry. Henry was an artist. By artist I mean painter and sculptor. He was the most famous artist who had ever lived on their world. Part of the reason was that he was so old. He had lasted longer than all of his immediate relatives, and now he lived alone. That was the second reason for his fame. It was absolutely astonishing and incomprehensible to them that someone would *choose* to live alone. They were always asking him about it, and he always said that he did not live alone but with anybody who had ever seen his work. But he did actually live alone, and that was a marvel to them.

The third reason Henry was so famous was that he was damned good. Maybe he flew around and spoke by buzzing and making little dances and lived by chewing on the edges of big leaves—but Henry could flat out paint. His canvases were a kind of silky cloth stretched over various geometric frames, including rectangular ones. For as long as anyone could remember, he had covered them with beautiful pictures.

Henry was a great master, and would have been on *any* world. Unfortunately, old age had got him. He had gone blind. The big eyes were milky saucers now, and Henry could only make out rough shapes and distinguish light from dark. His sight had been failing a long time, but he had continued to paint. Then his radar went out on him, too. The feathery shoots above his head withered and curled, and Henry was in darkness and, for the first time, truly alone. But he was still strong. Henry had no intention of biding time in an old-age nest waiting to die. He had things to do! And so he had contacted the Academy, and the Academy had sent me to him.

I called his house the Atelier, because that's what it was. It sat on a high bluff and had a magnificent view of the Tree, with its branches sparkling like the facets of a snow crystal. Inside, the rooms had enormously high ceilings and huge windows. There were four or five rooms for living and three for working. And in every corner were the paintings and sculptures.

Henry estimated he had done a quarter of a million pictures, not counting sketches, studies, painted-over first tries—to say nothing of the statues, prints, plaster casts, and pen-and-ink drawings that were piled up everywhere. Henry was not very organized. Again, that was unusual for them, because generally they are neat as pins. Not Henry. His carapace was covered with paint, some of it very old paint, layers like you get on the stair post of an old hotel. He never bothered cleaning it off. It was his trademark. He told me, though, that when he was young and just leaving the nest his sloppiness had caused him a lot of hardship. He had trouble finding a job, or holding one when he did find it. It was the old story. The ones that don't fit in are the ones who try the hardest to make sense of everything. That is why you have pictures and books and plays and songs and everything else that isn't business or food. If you can't fit into the world, then you try and make it into a place that fits you.

When they brought me to the Atelier, the Director was there, cleaning his glasses and blowing his nose because of his allergies. They had a Minister of Education around. (And, yes, they had all of it— government offices, places of business, places of worship, universities, just like we did. It was all organized differently, and not necessarily inside monumental buildings, but they had them, all right, as I was to discover.) There were reporters from their media, and some from ours. Our people took pictures and asked me how it felt to have such a heavy assignment, and the Director blew his nose and made eye contact with me, and I remembered to be polite and humble, though inside I was getting impatient with all the fuss. Finally they brought me inside, and there he was, standing in the middle of the first big room of the Atelier with his long hands in front of him, cocking his head a little because he didn't quite know what was going on. One of them went over to him—I found out later he was Henry's Business Manager—and buzzed something at him. Henry nodded and came forward and stood over me.

"What's up?" he said in English.

He must have been practicing a long time. It is very hard for them to make the sounds we use when we speak, but Henry just loved that expression. He told me once he thought it summed up his philosophy of life better than anything he could say in his own language. You see, "up" was just like right or left to them. But Henry figured out it had a greater meaning for us, in terms of escape and climbing and falling and trying and failing. Plus, he liked being able to make the sound. Anyway, that was when I felt the first wave coming from him. From that moment I loved Henry and everything about him.

I couldn't wait to get started. Finally, a couple of hours later, when they had taken their pictures and gathered in the scene at the Atelier for their media, and all the necessary documents had been executed by the Director and Business Manager, they left us alone. I helped Henry touch the grab bar.

"That's it," I said. The harness translated for me. He could still hear all right. "How are you?"

"Good," he replied. I could feel the needles tingling against my back.

"You understand me?"

"I believe I do."

"Okay," I said. "Let's get to work."

They had given Henry a lot of training, too, I discovered. He had studied *Physiology of Dog* and *Psychology of Dog* and *History of Dog*. He had tons of scrolls around on how to care for me, and Business Manager had hired a contractor to make me a perfect room. It was a pretty good try. But the result was a little like what happened when the committee of blind men described what an elephant looked like. Right in the middle of the room, for instance, they installed a commode that was big enough to swim in. And the bed was in the wall. I slept in the room only a couple of nights. Then I moved my bed into a shop that Henry had used for wood carving. He had not done much carving lately, but the shop still smelled like pine shavings. It was small, and I liked the smell and how the chips and sawdust felt under my feet.

Henry never asked why I had moved. He had a supreme ability to mind his own business. Again, that was so unusual for them, close-knit as they were and completely lacking in anything that would correspond to our concept of tact or politeness. When I was with the nest the kids all had to know everything I did and why and what for. Finally you got tired of the questions and told them to shut up. Even then they would ask you why, but not Henry. You had the feeling he knew you would tell him what he wanted to know without his ever having to ask.

Henry had been blind for around ten of our years. At first he accepted his condition with good humor and contented himself sculpting in clay and plastic. I have seen some of his pieces from this period, and they are graceful, rounded forms. He was as good as ever, but he wanted more. He wanted his freedom back, and for that he had to be able to fly. You must understand: flying is the one thing they do alone. And yet by flying around they become part of the Tree and of their world. In that respect, Henry was no different than the rest of them. Without flying he was lonely.

Right away Henry and I began practicing in the big room of the Atelier. This room was the treasure house of Henry's art. There were canvases of all sizes and shapes from his Blue and Orange periods. He told me these "periods" were not solid blocks of time. When a "blue" mood came on he would paint in those tones and in that style, and the historians and critics would assign the piece to the Blue period.

We spent hours in that room, and I went there when Henry was resting or out somewhere with Business Manager, just to look at all the stuff. There were hundreds of pieces, some of his most famous works, like *Waterfall at Night* and the *Huskers,* that were familiar to anybody who liked art. And this was where we began to work with the harness. It was a little like playing handball in the Medici room at the Louvre.

There were perches in the room spaced close so that we could handle the jumps without Henry having to fly very far. Henry took the bar, tucked his knees in a little as I looked back at him over my shoulder.

"Where to?" I said.

"You choose."

"You sure? I don't want you to fall."

"Who does?" Henry replied with vast amusement.

I made the first jump. They are very agile, and so strong and quick that he had no trouble reading the direction or the distance from the way my body shifted under his light pressure in the knee cups. He wasn't afraid. He trusted right away that my moves would be good. And sometimes we did fall, but Henry somehow always got his wings out in time. Right away I could tell we were a good team. And it wasn't long before we were using his wings for more than breaking a fall. Henry flew, riding the harness like a saddle, and I moved my body this way or that, and he would know when he had to turn and how much, or that he must slow and pull up and land.

We flew to the top perches in the Atelier. It was a fatal fall to the floor from up there, but with Henry I felt safe. We landed, and I stood there looking out at the Tree in the early evening, listening to the click of Henry's breastplates as they rose and fell. He was still a little out of shape for flying and was breathing hard. But he was happy.

Then one day we went out. It was early morning, the sun up just long enough to burn off some of the mist, and there was plenty of traffic. The Tree looked like a bubble of boiling water, all misty at the edges with so many of them flying in and out. Henry let me collect myself for a long time. He must have been nervous, too. Finally I heard him come up behind me and felt him take the grab bar.

"What's up?" he said.

I looked back at him. His head was cocked a little, and the clouded-over disks of his eyes looked like pearl buttons. I wondered what *was* up. I wasn't sure if I would have trusted someone to lead me around the room if I had been blind, much less fly.

"I'm ready," I said.

Henry tucked his knees in against me. I heard the dry scrape of his back plates as he unsheathed his wings. And then he sprang out easily, and we were off. He rolled, spiraling toward the Tree, and he was laughing, tumbling both of us through the air like a kid in a nest.

At first I didn't have much to do. Then we got closer to the Tree, and the traffic really got thick. They all had their radar going, and there was a tingling in the air from it that made the hair stand up on the back of your neck. But you had to forget about that and work with your eyes and your ears and your anticipation. It was like riding into a beehive, except the bees all weighed three hundred pounds. I ducked and turned and twisted the way I had been taught and in ways I had never dreamed of, and all the time Henry drove on, plunging straight through the avenues and dropping right into the core at the busiest time of the day. Nobody flew like we were flying now. We had fifty near misses and caused a dozen near accidents, and I was waiting for their cops to come after us. After a while I noticed they started to give way and pull up and watch when we went by. At first I thought it was just a lull in the traffic, but then I realized: *word had gone around!* They knew that Henry was back. He had come back from the worst thing that could happen to one of them, and they wanted to see how he had done it.

All morning we flew. Then Henry asked me where we were in relation to certain landmarks of the Tree and began to guide *me.* We left the Tree and followed a deep canyon above a river for a while. The walls were slate and spalled off, and in the crevasses twisted trees grew thickly wherever they could take root. The canyon grew deeper and narrower, and a canopy of green covered the top, so that the light turned a dusky gray green. By now you could hear the sound of a waterfall. Suddenly Henry pulled back on the harness, and we flew straight up, blasting through the foliage up to a wide ledge that was shaded by another layer of spreading branches and walled in by the canyon. I heard a buzz of activity. We landed on the ledge, and Henry caught a breath.

"What is this place?" I said.

"Well, I suppose you would call it a café," he said through the harness. "*Kaaff,*" he repeated in his own voice.

I hesitated. It was one of their private places. They had clubs and the like, but we were never allowed near them.

"Do you think it's a good idea for me to go in? I mean, I can wait out here for you." Like a good dog, I thought.

"Don't be silly. I'm one of the owners. Maybe the only owner. The others may all be dead now."

He gave a little push on the harness, and I led him in. There were tables with long stone benches that were crowded with them. When they saw me they all stopped talking. *They don't like us,* I thought. *We're nothing to them.* And then the place exploded because they realized it was Henry. They were all over him. He let them touch him, preen him, look at his eyes and the withered stalks on his head. And then, holding the harness so I could understand, he told them all that he had flown here with my help. I felt the rush then, but I did not back too far away. After all, we were in a café.

They sat us down and brought Henry and me each a platter piled high with leaves and a bowl of yellow mead fermented from flower nectar. Henry tore right into his, then noticed that I wasn't eating. He got up, and I made out through the harness that he wanted some food for his friend. Someone went out and brought back a bowl of fruit and berries, so that I could eat with the rest. I was starving after all the flying, and I ate not caring if it was any good for me or not. I figured that if Henry could trust me to guide him while he flew, I could trust him not to poison me. As it happened, the fruit did contain some alkaloid dust in low concentration, so that soon I was singing along with them, and dancing on the tabletops, and Henry flew me around and let some of his friends have a turn with the harness, too. Henry taught them all how to say "dog," and they made up a song about it. Then Henry showed me some of his stuff that was hanging on the walls. Most of it was real old, done on boards with cheap paint that was already cracking. Henry described each one. They hadn't touched a thing since the last time he had been there.

The paintings were mainly landscapes or still lifes with a nature theme. One really got to me, though. It was of two of them, an adult and a child. The adult stood behind the child and looked down at him with his head bent. The child tilted his head and raised his eyes. There was just something about the way they looked at each other that reminded me of my own dad, and I started to cry. This caused a sensation. It had never occurred to me that they would be sensitive to *my* emotions. In a moment they were all around me, stroking me and trying to get a little sample of my tears. I would have had to cry a river to supply them all. There was so much coming back from them that for a second I felt myself slipping away. That was when Henry stepped in. Firmly, he ordered everyone to get away from me. He made them be quiet and let me get myself together.

"What's up?" he said after I came around.

"It's the painting. Something about it makes me feel awfully sad— and happy, too, at the same time."

"Is that so?"

"Yes. It's an awfully good picture."

"Would you like it?"

"Oh, I couldn't. It belongs here."

"We'll give them another one. Would you like it? It would give me pleasure to give it to you."

"Okay," I said.

He had them take it off the wall, and we took it with us when we left.

I put the painting up above my bed in the carving room. I liked the feeling it gave me when I looked at it. It was good to have a picture in the room where you could see it accidentally when coming in or getting out of bed in the morning. That was the way to see a painting. In museums, when you made a point of visiting them and stood around respectfully with a lot of other people, it was like gawking at animals in a zoo. It gave you an uneasy feeling, because ordinarily you would never see animals that way. Paintings were made for money or to please the artist, not to be exhibited with a lot of other paintings. That's what I thought, anyway. I told it all to Henry one night, too.

"Is that your theory about art?" he asked.

I said it wasn't exactly a theory. It was more like an opinion. He cocked his head then, because there was no exact translation for "opinion" in his language. After a while he sat back a little.

"You mean it is your idea," he said.

"That's about the size of it."

"The guide dog and I think alike," he said. "I wonder if we *see* alike."

I always liked to remind him how smart I was, and so I began explaining that my eyes had only one lens, while his had 256.° But he stopped me.

"*See*," he said, tapping the plate on top of his head. "Inside. You look out through the door into the big room. Tell me what you see."

"The edge of that bench."

"Why?"

"I don't know. Maybe it's because the wood's split. I always wonder what made it split like that."

"Color?"

"Well, that changes, Henry. I can see it from my bed, you know. Sometimes—early in the morning if it's been raining, say—the wood looks gray and brown together with a little blue. *Vast*, I'd call it."

"Vast?"

"What the light looks like inside a big church when the sun isn't shining through the windows. That's what I mean."

"Vast," Henry repeated.

He didn't say any more but went out and left me alone. I read a book for a while and then wrote a letter to my folks. I told them not to feel too proud about my assignment. I suppose they had a right to feel proud, but I didn't want them bragging about me. I wrote that I was lucky to get in with Henry, but that when you got right down to it I was working off my contract just like anybody else. I tried not to be too blunt. But it is not a bad thing every once in a while to remind someone gently of the things they have done to you. There are plenty of ways to say such things without using the actual words. After dozens of letters to my family, I was still finding new ones all the time.

I finished the letter and sent it off into the link, and then I wandered around the Atelier looking for Henry. I found him out on the back terrace. He was sitting in his net chair, working his jaws on the end of a stick. He had a tray of sticks in front of him, and I realized he was chewing out brushes. Henry had a species of shrub growing around the house that sent out straight green stalks packed full of silky fibers that made nice bristles if you broke them down a little. Depending on what size shoot you picked, you could chew out any brush you wanted, from hairline to one you could use to paint a house. Henry had made up about a dozen, brand-new.

"Good," Henry said, touching the harness. "I was just about to call you." He pressed the new brush against the back of his hand, chewed it a few more times, and then put it into the tray with the others.

"Take this, please?"

I took up the tray, and he grabbed the bar and steered me into the big room. There he had set up his stool and another chair and a flat canvas on an easel in the middle of the room.

"Put the tray down and sit," he said.

I sat. My heart was starting to beat faster. Henry sat to my left and a little behind me. He took up a palette and squeezed out colors from tubes. They were like the paint tubes we used. Henry knew which colors he wanted. He had learned, when he was going blind, to put everything he needed in the same order every time.

"Clouds today?" he asked.

"Yes."

"Today we paint the bench," he said. "How far away?"

I told him.

"Where?"

I wasn't sure what he meant.

"If you square your shoulders to the canvas, where?"

"A little off center to the right."

He took a pencil then and reached past me and made a sketch. It took him about a minute to block out the shape of the bench. The perspective, the angle, even the shadow lines were perfect. It was amazing.

"How can you do that?"

"Inside. Old as I am, long as I've lived here, I'd better remember. But anything new"—he shook his head—"I need my guide dog."

"You're going to try to paint?"

"No. I *am* going to paint. With you."

"But I can't paint. I can't even draw a straight line!"

"Yes. And you cannot fly, either," he said.

I had to smile as I thought about it. In a way, it was a bigger responsibility than flying him around. Henry was one of the most famous artists ever to live. Anywhere.

"It would make me very happy," he said, and I felt a flood of emotion from him that almost knocked me off the stool.

"All right," I said. "I'll try."

"Good," Henry said.

"But how do we do it?"

"We learn. Like flying. The first lesson is color. Take this brush. I want you to mix a color for me on the palette."

"Which color?"

"Look at the bench. Give me the darkness with the light inside of it. Mix me the color you called *vast*."

We did that first painting in a couple of hours. Henry wasn't one of those artists who worry a piece to death. He liked to work quickly, and, in fact, I had to get him to calm down on that first one because we hadn't worked out a system yet. Henry listened to me. He stopped fussing and began to ask what things in the painting looked like, and showed me where the colors ought to go, and how I should mix them differently for different times of the day. I never thought you could actually teach a thing like painting, but Henry had a way of making you understand one thing by talking about something else.

And sometimes he let my hand go free and said I should do what-ever I wanted. I said no, but Henry said the paintings couldn't be considered only his, and if I was really going to help him I had to be in there, too. So I did the best I could. As we worked, I had to tell him everything: how big the shapes were and where they were on the canvas. Eventually we worked out a way of plotting out a grid in proportion to the dimensions of a canvas. That way, Henry could reckon the composition and know where he was, and tell me where to go. We made a scale of colors, too, with the primaries and shades mixed like notes on a piano. Voicing the colors, Henry called it.

It was all about communication and breaking everything down so that you could tell a lot with a minimum of description. It took awhile, but we got to be good at it, as good as we were at flying. I was his guide. Henry said that he felt such pleasure coming from me when we were working together that he didn't care if he saw the pictures or not. He could *feel* what they looked like and set them up in his mind.

We brought the first painting of the bench to Henry's club in exchange for the one we had taken away. Everyone there was thrilled about it and said it was as good a piece of work as any he had done. Henry gave me full credit. This was the first painting of his *vast* period. From now on, we were going to be painting vast works using vast colors. Eventually we did do a whole series of pictures in that same green-sand color. I got to be almost as paint spattered as Henry was. And I was beginning to understand why he never wanted to wash it off.

So far this has been mostly about Henry. That's natural. When I first came to the Atelier, all I thought about was Henry. But don't think that I ever for a minute forgot who I was or where I came from, or the number of days that were left on my contract. Henry knew how I felt. He waited until word about the paintings had got out. Then he arranged for us to visit the Academy.

It was pleasant to go back. I was the big success of the school. They had photos up of me and Henry together, and old pictures, too, of a skinny, long-haired me wearing a training harness. They held a big assembly, and Henry gave a speech, which I translated, and then I followed up with a speech of my own. I told them how we were all the same underneath, and how anyone who had seen with another person's eyes would know that. I added that when you had to look out for someone else all the time you automatically took care of yourself. I was real inspirational. They got a good dose of Henry, too. Up in the top row, I saw Mom and Dad hugging each other until they were both red in the face.

Afterward there was a reception in the library, where I stood around and tried to be polite and answer questions. I said that guide dogs were going to be a big thing and that it might help the colony pay its way more. Since we were all the same under the skin, there was no reason to think we couldn't be guides for other races, too. Maybe we had a talent for it, although it didn't take much talent when the clients were as nice as Henry. I got more maudlin than that, even, until Henry drew me aside a little.

"Tired?"

"I'm all right."

"That last answer was a little much."

"You heard me?"

"I could feel you getting emotional," he said.

"Well," I said, "you might as well share the warmth."

"Why don't you go off and see your friends?"

"But you need me here."

"Oh, they're not going to let me go anywhere. And I have Business Manager to translate for me. You go on awhile." And he shushed me out with those big hands of his.

My friends and I went off to a coffeehouse on the edge of campus. You could see the Tree glowing off in the distance. We all sat around, and it was a little awkward at first. A lot of them were training to be guides, too. I still had my harness on, and I could tell it bothered some of them to see me wearing it, but by and by we had our coffee and started laughing, and it was like I had never left. One of the girls I had known pretty well before wanted me to sit close to her. Every now and then she tried to kiss me. I didn't mind. Being with a girl was one of the things you missed plenty, if you started to think about it.

Everyone asked me questions. They were pretty much the same ones I had answered before, until this boy named Scott asked me what Henry was really like.

"What do you mean?"

Scott was someone I had never cared for much. He was the kind that could twist anything around to get a look at its bad side. He had been a class behind me and thought he had to compete. I never thought that, which drove him crazy, I suppose.

Scott said, "I mean, when he lets loose. How is he?"

"He doesn't 'let loose,' " I said, feeling myself tightening up.

"Right. He's only the most famous thing they've ever had. All of them buzz about him. Don't they start buzzing when you fly by?"

"I guess they do."

"You *guess* they do! You must get a good dose every time you go out—not to mention what you've had today."

Scott said this with a sneer, and it was interesting: I got mad. He was talking about emotion, and here was one I hadn't felt for a long time.

"Just what are you getting at?"

"I'm talking about you living for the taste. Why, you're no better than a renegade down inside the Tree!"

I should have just ignored him, but I couldn't. The one thing I hadn't done was taste any more emotion than was good for me. In fact, I gave myself tons of credit for tasting a lot less. So I got up and grabbed his collar and lifted him up into the air, practically.

"It *is* strong," I said. "It's plenty strong, and you've got to have it when you're living out there by yourself. But I don't, because if ever I did I *would* be a junkie. I'd be living down inside the Tree. I wouldn't be able to help Henry, and I wouldn't be able to help myself, either."

"You're so high and mighty," Scott sputtered. "But you don't fool me. Maybe you won't admit it—"

I pushed him back down in his chair. His arm hit the table, some of the coffee spilled, and they all jumped up. The whole place got quiet. I said that I'd better go.

"*Junkie,*" Scott yelled after me.

Scott was a fool, but what a fool says can eat at you, too, and anyway there was some truth in it. To be a guide dog you did have to forget about yourself. When you were flying, sometimes it seemed as though it took every cell in your brain to keep going and avoid a crash. It taxed you to the limit, and even then you felt a disaster was coming any second—that there was all this responsibility, and you never quite measured up. That's why sometimes you would see guide dogs flying with faces clouded over, looking to the side and avoiding your eyes. That's why every so often a guide could lose his grip. You thought you really deserved to have all that love after what you went through.

I was thinking things when we left the school that night. I guess Henry could tell something was up. We were riding in a car with Business Manager. Henry respected my feelings and didn't say anything until Business Manager dropped us off at the Atelier.

"Another reception," Henry said. "Just like all the rest."

"Been to a lot of them, have you?" I said sharply.

He had got some leaves from the cooler and was working his jaws on them, and now he stopped and turned his head in my direction.

"We have receptions. Just like yours. For exactly the same reasons."

"Good for you," I said.

"What's up?" Henry said. I swear he had even learned to make that hiss of his sound sympathetic. But at the moment I hated him for trying.

"Nothing."

"Did something happen while you were off with your friends?"

"They aren't my friends. I don't have any friends."

He chuckled softly. "Oh, I don't think that's true."

"Don't start, Henry. I'm not your friend. I'm your *dog*. Do you know what a *dog* is, Henry? We can't have them here because we can't afford to keep them, but do you know what they are? They're *pets*. We love 'em because they're smart enough to remember us and dumb enough to love us no matter what we do. So we love them back. But we don't respect them, Henry. Because we think we're better than they are. The dumbest, most low-down one of us is still better than the best dog, Henry. And that's what you call me. *Dog*."

He let me go on awhile. He had never seen me angry before, and I think he wanted to watch. At last he said, "*Dog* is just a word. We don't have *dogs*. *Dog* is your word. It's what is in your head when you hear us speak of you. I would never call you a *dog* the way you mean."

"What would you call me?"

"Eyes," he said. "Hands. *Friend.*"

He was right. I was all those things to him. I felt ashamed for lighting into him and said I was sorry, and I vowed privately never to let my feelings get the better of me again. I told myself they had got built up out of a lot of other unhappy things. Now that I had got them off my chest, everything would be all right again. And for a while it was. We did a few more still lifes of flowers and trees on the grounds of the Atelier. Sometimes Henry would feel around to "see" their texture and general positions, but now he more often let me block the pictures out alone, and put in only a brush stroke or two. I didn't care if he did. After that reception, I had begun to take a kind of permanent, different view of everything.

After a few days of this, Henry declared we were getting stale and said we should go out. And so we flew around. It was getting to be winter, and it rained or sometimes it was cold and blew pretty good. Henry didn't care. We just bundled up and out we went.

By this time I had got used to the flying and began to take more notice of where we were going and who and what was around us. I was proud of myself for being able to do it; I thought that I had grown and detached myself from the job of being a guide dog. What I had really detached myself from, of course, was Henry. He knew it, too. But he never complained. He just let me have my own way and waited to see how things would go.

One day we flew deep into the Tree. It was dark and raining, with flashes of lightning that seemed to come from all directions at once, green and cold and throwing long, slow-fading shadows. We were headed for a shop that wanted Henry to sign some art books. It was one of our shops, and I think Henry agreed to do it to make me feel a little better.

We didn't say much on the way in. I pretended to concentrate because there really was a lot of traffic. I still felt bad about Henry. I thought the way I was feeling about him was serious and forever. It was just one of the cycles a friendship goes through. You have the euphoria and enthusiasm piled up in the beginning, and then the reaction sets in. You feel horrified by the feelings, and you try to deny them and deny the other person. It goes away, though, if you let it. It would have with Henry if I had just given it a chance.

Down inside the Tree it was really dark. We were in the oldest part of the city, and where the flyways became bores worn smooth by the centuries of brushing wing tips. They had a few lights, which were like sparklers, set up at the head of the runs, and they had little buzz boxes, also at the head of the runs, that bounced noise off the surfaces and helped the radar along. We bounced around for a while and then came to an intersection. There was an avenue that led to the open part of the Tree, and three bores, all pitch-black, headed straight down. I described where we were to Henry, and he said we should take the middle bore, which dumped into the quarter where the bookshop was.

"Oh, Henry, I don't know," I said.

"Why? What's up? It's fine. You're doing fine."

It was fine for *him*. Henry was enjoying himself. Why shouldn't he? This was like a trip down memory lane for him. His ancestors had spent a couple of aeons chewing out the insides of logs.

"It's too dark. I don't have a lamp. You should have told me about this."

"We'll go slow. I know these streets like home."

He sounded a little impatient, and I felt it, and felt myself wanting to please him. Right then and there, I hated him. Most of all I hated myself. I *was* an addict. I might as well admit it. No matter how little I took, I still lived for his approval.

"All right, Henry. You're the boss. Let's do it." He took up the grab bar and pressed his knees in and lifted his wings, and we were off.

Down and down we dropped. I couldn't see anything. I heard Henry grunt in surprise a time or two when we bumped the wall, and I was glad about it. I made myself into a load for him, the way a bad rider is a load on the back of a horse. It seemed to take forever to get to the end of the run, but finally we dumped into a big square—or what would be a square in one of our towns. It was a public place where people without jobs could sit while everybody else went to work. In this case, the people sitting there were rene- gades. About six of them, with their backs to the wall, bored and dead looking until we lighted on the square. Then it was like some- one had thrown the switch. Up they popped, grinning and elbowing each other, ready for no good. I swore under my breath. I had never seen so many lousy-looking guys in one place before.

"What's up?" Henry said.

"Renegades," I said. "Earth dogs."

"Really!" he said. "What do they look like?"

"They look like scum, Henry, all right?" They were coming over now. "I think it would be a great idea if we just went back the way we came."

"Don't believe I can do it just now, unfortunately. Need some rest."

"Could you handle a straight run?"

"I believe so."

"There's a hole straight across the square. Let's go for it."

He lifted his wings, and we buzzed off—but we were slow, and I was dragging. Still, we might have gone through them, because they had been sitting a long time, and Henry with his wings out was no small thing. But one of them caught my eye.

"That's it," he called after me. "Good doggy!"

And I lowered my legs and stopped us.

"What did you say?"

"I said *doggy*, which is what you are. In fact, you're worse than a dog. A dog doesn't know any better."

I should have ignored him. Who was he to tell me anything? He was a low-down junkie who had probably been a guide dog once himself. But the way he looked at me and the way he said it and the way I was feeling meant I couldn't let it pass.

"Let go of the harness, Henry," I said.

"I think not."

"If you don't let go, then it's true, and I am your dog," I said. "Let go!"

I yanked away. I never thought that he might have been afraid. He was the old one. He was the one standing there blind and alone. All I cared about was how I felt. I waded into that crowd of louts and went up to the one who had called me out, and I swung at him. They were on me in a second. They were weak and slow, and I was fast and strong—but there were too many of them, and I didn't stay up long. Henry figured out what was happening to me before I did. They have a way of sounding an alarm with their wings, and they can tell who is in trouble by the sound—and they all knew it was Henry, and hundreds of them came, more than could fit in the bores feeding into the square. It was a swarm of them. It was just what the junkies wanted. They left off before they had kicked me to death and lay back with their arms spread and their eyes shut, soaking all that emotion in with the biggest and most beatific smiles on their faces.

The next morning I was called in to see the Director at the school. I was sore. My ribs were cracked, and one of my eyes was swollen shut. The Director paid no attention. He wanted to take the opportunity to let me know exactly how I had let everyone down. I didn't say much at first. I thought I would let him get it off his chest. If I had known what he had in mind, though, I might have tried to say something in my own defense.

"A guide does nothing that would endanger the safety of a client!" the Director began. "That's what we taught you. That is the essence of everything we do here. And you, you especially! Didn't we impress upon you day after day the enormous responsibility you took on? He is the most important personality of this world. And our reputation stood to rise or fall depending on how you succeeded with that trust."

I had to say something then.

"Maybe that's the problem," I said. "Why do we advertise ourselves as servants? They'll never respect us that way."

"Because that is what we are. We have to succeed as what we are. Then we can advance."

"You mean they'll give us a *promotion?*" I laughed right in his face. "Like, if we get good grades, we get to move up a class?"

He was getting red now. He had thought it all out.

"They'll never promote us," I went on. "Why should they? I'm as close to one of them, this 'important personality,' as you say, as any of us here have ever got, and what good has it done? Henry hasn't said, 'Don't be my guide.' He's never said I was his equal. He knows what he is. He doesn't have any idea what we are. That's because *we* don't have any idea! So how could he? All this talk about responsibility. Well, who's responsible for the fact that all we thought about was getting here? We had no idea what to do after that. Absolutely none at all. So now we live as outsiders and cook up schemes to make ourselves useful. Great. And you sit there and hope we'll be promoted to *necessary!*"

"I was hoping for some sign of contrition on your part," the

Director said. "But I can see that's too much to expect from you."

"You got that right. Can I go?"

He had a file open in front of him.

"Go? Where do you think you're going?"

"Home," I said. "Henry needs me."

The Director smiled a little. He had been saving this.

"Whatever gave you the idea you would be going back there?"

I sat up. "What do you mean?"

"You left a client alone while you engaged in a fight. And caused a riot," he said. "The whole basis of the relationship between a client and his guide is trust. And you have shattered that trust. Your relationship with this client is therefore over."

"I'm fired?"

"Oh, you are still under contract. And you have shown that you can be an excellent guide under certain circumstances. Therefore, we are giving you a second chance. We have a new assignment with another handicapped person, a regular citizen this time. One whose life is not subject to the same level of scrutiny—"

"They are *all* under scrutiny!"

"Nevertheless—"

"Have you asked Henry? Is this what he wants?"

"A new guide has already been assigned to 'Henry,' as you call him."

"Who?"

"That information is confidential."

"*Who?*" I jumped up, and he jumped back, pale and sweating. It is easy to decide things alone in an office. I swept up the file and had a look.

"Scott? You're sending *Scott?*"

"He is the most qualified—"

"He's a dick. He'll never work out. Henry won't want him around."

"I can call Security," the Director said. "I can void your contract, and your family will be in a work farm by tomorrow afternoon. Is that the way you want it?"

I stood there with the file in my hand. My temper had been getting a big workout lately. Maybe that had taken some of the edge off. I stood there a moment, and then I closed the file and handed it back to him.

"You're making a big mistake," I said.

"I think not."

"Henry and I understand each other. We're a team. I'm helping him paint again. It would break his heart—"

"The client understands the situation," the Director said.

"You mean he *knows*?"

"I met with him myself," the Director said smugly.

That finished it for me. If Henry didn't care, why should I? I felt the rest of the fight draining out of me. But I did have one faint hope left.

"I'll have to get my things."

"We've already had them delivered back here," the Director said.

They gave me a room at the school, and I lived there with my stuff in boxes in the corner. I didn't go to class, and nobody checked up on me. I blamed myself and said that I would take it all back if I could. That had the effect on reality it always does. At the end of the week, they moved me into an apartment in a suburb of the Tree with my new client. I called this one Lester.

Lester was a chemist who had been blinded in an accident at work. He had just come out of rehab training, and his insurance had provided him with the cost of a guide. Unfortunately, Lester was not interested in having a guide. He was in a postinjury phase of great depression and insisted on living away from his nest. All he wanted to do was stay in all day and be blind. As I was feeling more or less the same way, we made a great pair. But Lester needed somebody to make him get off his abdomen. In the mood I was in, I was not up to being a cheerleader. So, with Lester not wanting any help and me not interested in giving him any, you could see where things were headed.

Which is not to say I never tried to get him out. We actually did some harness work and one day even went around the neighborhood. In the end, though, it only seemed to make him sadder. And that meant I was going to have plenty of time on my hands.

Lester's place was small, and it was depressing, too. No air, no windows. I couldn't sit alone inside, and as he didn't care what I did, I started to go out alone into the Tree. I wasn't being a renegade. I wore my harness and carried my ID, and if any one of them or any human stopped me I explained I was out on an errand. I went all over just looking around. Up at the top, you had to do a lot of climbing because of the distance between perches, and I started to get into pretty good shape. And I got my harness light hooked up, too, and went into the bores as deep as I could go. I was really hoping to run into the louts who had ruined me with Henry. I went back to the square a couple of times, and once I even stayed all day, hanging back in the shadows and waiting. But they never were there. Maybe that was just as well. I have to admit that I didn't have a real good idea of what I would do if I did catch them.

Then one day I saw Henry. There was no mistaking that big head and those cloudy, milk-white eyes. I was up in the crown of the Tree watching the clouds pile up, like they did every afternoon that time of year. And he came along with his wings out, turning his head slowly from side to side as if his radar were still working. But he didn't have any radar, of course. What he had was his new guide dog in a harness. I leaned forward, and sure enough, it was Scott, flailing around and looking like he was going to crash them any second. The buzzing got louder. They always started in when Henry passed by. He was like a seltzer tablet dropped into the water wherever he went. And then, finally, they came close enough to where I could see the bastard's face.

Henry was guiding *him*. He could sense what was giving Scott problems and sort of point him in the direction that made him the least nervous, and that is where they went. They flew in big spirals, practicing together, so I got to watch them for a while. It was almost worth what had happened to watch Scott sweat like that. But in the end my satisfaction was bitter. I felt lonely and cheated, and for the first time wished for what I had lost. I watched them until they flew out of sight. Then I made up my mind that I would go and see Henry that night.

The tricky part wasn't getting away from Lester. I just told him that I wanted to go out. He didn't care. I'm not sure he even heard me. Even if he *had* heard me and he did care, I knew he wouldn't bother reporting me. He was glad I was gone.

So I went off. There were routes out of the Tree where transports flew, and I waited above one that pointed in the Atelier's direction. Finally came a lorry with a soft-topped trailer that I took a leap for

and made. I banged my arm pretty good hitting a rib under the tarp
when I landed, and almost bounced off. But I was strong and determined. The thought that I might kill myself somehow did not occur
to me at all.

That was good, because the transport really took off once it was
out of the city, and I had to hang on tight to keep from being blown
off. Then, just as I started to worry about how I would get off, the
transport got caught in a snarl of traffic. So I was all right. I just slid
down and started walking. I could see the Atelier perched on the
cliff up ahead of me, glowing in the twilight.

It was a nice, fresh evening, with the damp cool you get after the
rains have come. There were peepers in the bushes on the sides of
the path, and the sound of the traffic moving slowly above my head.
The ground was all mine. I was glad for the weeks of training I had
put in when it came to climbing up to Henry's. Several times I got
stuck under overhangs that I didn't have the knack of getting around,
and had to backtrack and try again. Finally, though, I reached the
terrace wall and looked into the big room.

Everything was as it had been. I felt touched, but then I laughed
at myself. Who was going to rearrange the furniture? I decided to
wait. What I wanted to do was alert Henry but leave Scott out of it.
I waited and watched, and after a while I saw that nobody was home.
So I went in and headed for the kitchen to see what supplies they
had for a guide dog. I did find some orange sherbet sitting in a pan
of dry ice. That made me madder than anything, because of Henry
being so nice and Scott such a wuss. I had paid for that ice cream
by trying to eat what Henry ate.

Since I was getting worked up about Scott anyway, I decided to
poke around my old room. Scott had cleaned it out. All the wood
was stacked up according to size on the shelf underneath the bench,
and the tools were hanging in the rack. The place had been swept,
and it looked as though he had even washed down the walls. It was
disgusting. People have no business being that neat. If they do, it is
only because they want to show up the rest of us.

Scott had set up a desk, too. It was all polished on the top, with
a short row of reference books squeezed between a pair of lead slabs
that were spray-painted gold. The desk drawers were locked. It was
such an insult to Henry. As if he cared about what Scott had in his

desk! I cared, though. I found a long, straight chisel on the tool rack, and when I popped out the drawer in the middle the rest of them came free, too. The inside of the drawers was just as neat as the rest of the room. I found a steel box with money inside, files of school records, a receipt book, a ledger, a journal, a calendar, and a log, plus pens and paper and supplies. There was also a chewed-up baseball that looked about a thousand years old. Well. Everybody always keeps at least one thing that isn't like the rest of him.

I laid it all out and looked everything over and decided the journal would probably be most interesting to start with. I sat down on the bed and began to read. It was slow going, though. Scott wrote down what he ate every day, and how much money he spent, and how hard he studied what, and how many hours he slept and what the dreams were. There was no reason to hide that journal, because it would put you right to sleep. I started skimming and got all the way to the end, and then I found something that made me yell out loud. "He and H. are going to bookstore tomorrow," I read. "I have arranged a surprise on the way. We'll see how he does when he meets the boys."

The entries were all dated, and on a hunch I opened up the account ledgers and had a look. And sure enough, there were six payments of one hundred gold dollars, with receipts clipped to the page, for "personal services." And the signatures on all of them looked pretty rocky. Just what you would expect from renegades.

Well, that was it for me. They say that if you find out something by snooping around, you have no business getting mad at the person you are snooping on, but this was my business. Scott had hired those thugs to wait for Henry and me! He knew what would rile me most, and he had done it, and it had worked, and now he had got what he wanted. Oh, I wanted to kill him!

But he wasn't around, and I paced for a while and gradually grew cooler and began to consider what I ought to do. It was better to be cool about such things. I left the desk ransacked and threw some of his books around and pulled down the tool rack. That last was for spite. Then I went out and found a good perch under a thicket on a ledge up above the Atelier, and I settled down and waited.

It was dark by the time they came back in Business Manager's car. Scott got out first. His hair was messed, and his harness was twisted around on his back. He went right inside and up to his room

while Business Manager led Henry in. Then the lights came on, and
I got to see him stare at the desk and whirl around and tear down
to get Business Manager. Business Manager did not appear impressed by the damage. To him, it probably looked the same as
when I had lived there. But Scott made him bring Henry, and then
they were all three looking around, Scott putting Henry in touch
with the harness and jabbering away at him. Henry felt around a
little, and I could see him speak to Business Manager. Scott meanwhile was cleaning up. He just could never stand to have anything
out of place at all.

After a while they left him alone, and Scott went to bed. Henry
and Business Manager were in the big room having some mead.
Then Business Manager stretched out his wings and said good night.
Henry didn't sleep much, but the rest of them usually had to have
around eight hours just like we do. Business Manager drove off, and
I waited some more. It was deep dark now, with the stars spread
across the black sky like blistered paint. I waited some more. Then
I went inside and found Henry working on a canvas.

It almost broke your heart to see him do it. He was feeling with
his left and putting it on with his right and then getting the shape
from where the wet paint was; but he was missing, and the colors
were all wrong because he had no one to help him lay out his palette. He must have known; he was drooping a little, but he kept on.
I think he did because he liked the feel of the brush dragging across
the canvas with the load of paint on it. I watched him for a long
time before I saw what he was getting at and realized it was a portrait. It was a face. My face.

I came up behind him and touched his shoulder. He gave a start.
Then I made him take up the grab bar and said, "What's up, Henry?"

Oh, I got it then. I had never felt it so strong or so pure. It was
just like hot liquid gold poured right in through the top of my head.
My heart was hammering, and my knees felt like water. Fortunately,
Henry knew what was happening to me and backed off. When I
came to, he was stroking my head and saying my name over and
over, not through the harness but in his hissing English.

"Ohhh. You got to watch that, Henry." I knew I would probably
be worthless for a week after a dose like that. He helped me up. I
was just glad to see him. I didn't care anymore about the rest of it.

"What are you doing here?"

"I had to make sure you were getting along all right."

There was a moment of silence. Then I said, "So how's the new dog working out?"

"He's not you."

"Well. Not many people are."

That made him laugh.

"I saw you trying to paint," I said. "Just now, I mean. I've been waiting here for you for a while."

He cocked his head. "Don't you have a new client?"

"He doesn't like to go out. Truth is, I don't think he's so happy to have me around."

"So you ran away."

"No. I asked if I could go."

"You didn't tell him you were coming here, though."

"He wouldn't care."

I felt him looking at me.

"No, I didn't."

"You'll be in more trouble," Henry said. He sounded tired and worried. Worse than that: he sounded old. I knew it was my fault. I knew he missed me, and I knew I had let him down. If I had followed my training, I would still be with him, and Scott would be with Lester or somebody else.

"You were in Scott's room, weren't you?" Henry said severely.

"Yes. I was mad. I wanted to get even."

" 'Get even' for what? He had nothing to do with what happened."

I bit my tongue. I wanted to tell him what Scott had done, but I couldn't. I had to accept responsibility for what *I* had done. I had played into Scott's hands. His plan would have come to nothing if only I had kept my temper. If I told Henry what I knew, I would only disappoint him more.

"Scott was very upset."

"I know."

"You should make it right," Henry said. "You should go up and offer to clean up the room."

The truth I was holding in was practically making my head pop, but I couldn't say a thing. Because everything *he* was telling me was the more important truth.

"Okay. But he's sleeping, Henry, and—"

"Yes?"

"Henry, I'd just like to fly with you one more time. Would that be all right?"

He chuckled a little. They had a way of doing that that sounded just like your mother.

"Please, Henry! We never had a chance to end it ourselves. They just came in and took me away. Did they even ask how you felt or what you thought they ought to do? I know there's nothing we can do about that, but at least we could fly one last time. Maybe it would be easier for you then. Maybe it would be easier for me to accept things. Then I wouldn't always be thinking about what happened. Please, Henry."

"All right," he said. "One more time, for you and for me."

I took him out to the terrace. There were so many stars you could have read a book. Henry hooked up with the grab bar and tucked in his knees and lifted his wings, and we took off. I had never felt him so strong before. The sound of his wing beats was a pitch higher, and he made his turns with authority and climbed with such ease that I thought we would fly up until we ran out of air. We climbed and climbed, up above the Tree, until the city was nothing but a fuzzy ball of light. Henry didn't say much. He just kept climbing, and then all of a sudden pointed us down in a steep dive. I leaned into it with him, not thinking about the danger in it. We flew straight down together right through the outskirts of the Tree, right through the traffic and into the core. I shifted on pure instinct and guess-work, and I was right every time. We plunged deeper and deeper into the bored-out avenues and out again, spiraling down around the shaft, until at last he pulled up and used all the energy we had gathered in our long plunge to swoop upward again in a curving, effortless arc out toward the Atelier. It was thrilling. It was as if he had summed up all of his life into that one flight. He sent out about it, too. In the cool evening, gliding almost without a sound with the Atelier in view, you could hear them buzz. All of them knew what Henry was doing. Maybe they knew what he would do. I didn't know anything. I was just grateful for the chance to fly again.

We came closer, and I turned the harness light on, and there on the terrace I saw Scott and Business Manager. Scott was pointing at us, and I thought, he's probably called the Director, and that broke the feeling I had and made me forget all my good intentions. I was going for him as soon as we hit ground, and to hell with anything else. So as we came in, Henry spreading out his wings to pull us up, I got my legs ready, and then Henry twisted a little, suddenly enough to snap the safety release on the harness, and dropped me. I landed on the terrace as he rose off, climbing away, flying blind.

It is funny about momentum. Henry's carried him up and away. Mine sent me right into Scott, and we sprawled together past Business Manager. I popped to my feet, and I had enough left to pull him up, too, all ready to yank his head off. Then I realized that Henry was free of the harness. I looked up. You could see him spiraling up and out against the stars that sparkled like diamond sand on a black marble floor. He made a wide right turn, and you could see him beating his wings to pick up speed. Then it was like the mountain just got up and put itself in front of him. Henry flew right into it.

A couple of rocks and small stones rattled down the steep slope and came to rest. After that came the silence.

They had a system of laws and justice, and a forum like a court, and they put me on trial. I was the first human being to come under their jurisdiction. Ordinarily, we were not worth the trouble, but because Henry was so important, they declared me a citizen and brought me up on charges.

I went in thinking that I would defend myself. But after a couple of days, I saw that they were interested only in reconstructing the circumstances of the crime. You couldn't blame them, I guess. Since it is impossible for them to lie to each other, proving guilt was unnecessary. All they had to do was make the explanation official. There were no set punishments, either. After they reconstructed everything, they would tailor a sentence to fit whatever offense they came up with. Nobody questioned it. The laws weren't even written down. They were bred into you.

According to custom, the accused could select the venue, and so I picked the auditorium at school. I had a lawyer, and they had a prosecutor, and the witnesses came in and gave statements and answered questions. They called the Director, who said that I had been relieved because I had abandoned my post to fight with bums, and so had endangered my master's life. He actually said *master*. My lawyer tried to turn that around by saying I was only attempting to save Henry from renegades, but they brought the scuzzballs in, and they all swore they weren't interested in Henry at all but had merely made a joke at my expense. I waited for my lawyer to do something with that; he didn't, though, and so I jumped in.

"Say, weren't you guys tipped off that we were going to that bookstore?"

"Who woulda done that?"

"Him," I said, pointing dramatically at Scott, who had come to the trial every day.

"What about him?"

"Didn't he pay you to jump us?"

"Naw," the lout said. "Why would he do that?"

"Because you're scum," I said. "And scum are always available for the right price."

He smiled at me. "Maybe so," he said. "How much they pay you to wear that collar?"

I guess I didn't help myself then when I went after him. It took a couple of them to hold me while I shouted it was all a lie: that I had found out about the payoffs from a ledger in Scott's room, and that they should call him and ask about it; that Henry and I had loved each other, and that I had tried to get him out of the square, and that he had *dropped* me on purpose in the end because he wanted to fly alone; and nobody lived forever, not even Henry, and that if they really wanted to honor him they should not insult his memory by making out that he would ever have let anyone get away with killing him. I was eloquent, all right, in between the biting and kicking. Finally they got me tied down to a chair and took a few more witnesses. Lester came in and said I had run away. Scott stepped up—eyeing the ropes on the chair all the time to make sure I couldn't get loose—and testified I had ransacked his room and had even destroyed a painting that he and Henry had done together. He just went up there and lied. I suppose it didn't matter. They knew we could lie. And because we had the talent for it and they did not, they assumed that all of us *were* liars.

———

After a couple of days, they closed out the testimony and put it to the vote. Everyone who had followed the trial or read the transcript could get in on the decision. They put their heads together, millions of them, and came up with a unanimous verdict. I was guilty of murder through negligence. My sentence was to be put out on the Rock and to remain there until I expired.

They gave me one evening at the school before the sentence would be carried out. I stayed in my old room with a guard posted outside and entertained a few visitors. Nobody really had much to say. I ended up patting backs and doing most of the talking. I didn't mind making them feel better. Somebody had to do it.

But it was hard when Dad finally showed up late in the evening. Mom couldn't take seeing me in person, I guess; Dad took a snapshot to bring back to her. We chatted a little about the new house they were building and how well my brother was doing in the merchant marine. Then there was that awkward waiting you get when one person wants something and the other one knows it but doesn't know what. What I wanted was for him to thank me at least for being a good son and trying to work my contract off. He didn't say any of that, though. What he finally came up with was that I should not be afraid when the end came.

"You mean when I die?"

"When you realize it's all over."

"That ought to be right about when I die," I said.

"Don't think about it now. Just remember to be brave. When the time comes."

How brave is he gonna be? I thought.

"Son," he said.

"Yeah, Dad."

"Remember the day I brought you here? I gave you something. A little knife. Do you remember?"

"Yeah, Dad, I remember."

"Do you still have it?"

I looked at him.

"They want me to get it from you."

"Christ, Dad!"

"Even if they didn't, I'd still like to have it. It would mean a lot to me."

"Would it, Dad?"

"Yes."

So I gave it to him. Weak as he was, I could never really get angry at him.

They gave me a nice dinner. Stuff from home like lobster and a bowl of radishes. I ate as much as I could. I wanted to last a long time out there on the Rock. They probably had a record for how long somebody had made it out there. Whatever it was, I wanted to try and break it. There was beer, too, and some brandy with the dessert, and I felt pretty sleepy by the time I finished. I lay on the bed with my arm over my eyes. After a while I heard the door open. I looked up. It was one of them, looking too big against the frame of the door. I sat up and saw that someone had cleared the dinner plates away.

"Oh, get out of here, will you?" I said. Then I saw that it was Business Manager. He was holding my harness. He didn't move. He just looked at me, trying to see how I was. When I reached for the harness, he handed it to me, and I put it on. It felt a little stiff but warmed right up when I powered it on, the needles pressing lightly against the top of my back.

"How are you?" he said.

"Oh, I'm just great. Never better."

I guess he knew about sarcasm, because he didn't say anything. Finally I asked him what he was doing here.

"I came to bring you the harness. You should wear it tomorrow."

"Now, why should I do that?"

"You are a guide," he said. He was looking at me, and suddenly I felt bad. He was someone who had always tried to help Henry, and I knew Henry was fond of him.

"I'm sorry about what happened, you know," I said.

"You have nothing to be sorry about."

"You're the only one who feels that way."

"Not the only one," Business Manager said.

"Nobody spoke up."

"That is not our way."

"No, I guess it isn't."

He turned, ready to go.

"Wait a minute. Can I ask you something?"

He looked back. His eyes were shiny, like black glass.

"What do you think happens? After you die?"

"Why ask me that? What do you think happens?"

"I don't know. You change. But I think you're still around some-where in a different form."

"Do you think it would be any different for us?"

"No, I guess it wouldn't."

"We believe that you can remain. And see and act through an-other. If you want to and if you are strong enough."

"Henry was strong, wasn't he?"

"Wear the harness tomorrow," he said.

What they did was put me on the Rock. It is a smooth basalt dome that is in the middle of a larger caldera. It is very high and steep and polished like marble by the wind. There are no handholds. The valley floor is littered with the shells of the ones who have come before me. If you're one of them, they clip your wings and leave you here, shunned by the rest. Then the loneliness and the humili-ation get to you. Eventually you give up, and the wind pushes you off. The floor of the caldera is littered with the bodies of dead crim-inals.

I sit on the Rock and think about jumping.

The sky is that brown green color Henry called *vast*. Off toward the Tree, I see something tiny flash against the clouds. It gets big-ger. It is one of them, flying toward me. I wish it were Henry, come to take me home to the Atelier, but of course it is not.

It is Business Manager. And I am wearing my harness.

Alan Brennert

Like his friend and colleague Harlan Ellison, Alan Brennert negotiates the worlds of print and television with equal facility. Until recently a producer of the hit series *L.A. Law*, for which he won an Emmy Award in 1991, Brennert has written scripts for that show as well as for *China Beach* and the resuscitated *Twilight Zone* of the eighties. He is the author of the contemporary fantasies *Time and Chance* and *Kindred Spirits* as well as two short-story collections: *Her Pilgrim Soul and Other Stories* and an Author's Choice Monthly volume from Pulphouse.

Last year, Brennert tried his hand at yet another medium, live theater, writing the book for *Weird Romance*, a musical anthology of SF/fantasy love stories that ran for seven weeks at the WPA Theater in New York City. Forthcoming are an acting edition of the script from Samuel French and an original cast album from Columbia Records. The sources of *Weird Romance* include James Tiptree's "The Girl Who Was Plugged In" as well as Brennert's own "Her Pilgrim Soul," and the music is by Alan Menken, best known for scoring *Little Shop of Horrors* and the Disney organization's animated adaptation of *Beauty and the Beast*.

Asked to comment on his Nebula-winning story, Brennert replied: " 'Ma Qui' grew out of research for a *China Beach* episode I wrote called 'The Unquiet Earth,' in which two of the lead characters, McMurphy and K. C., are kidnapped by the Vietcong and taken to an underground tunnel base, where McMurphy is forced to operate on a wounded cadre leader. Death was a constant presence in the story, and as much as I wanted to work in Vietnamese attitudes about death and the disposition of the soul—and the folklore and mythology surrounding it—there just wasn't a place for it in the script. I'm glad I didn't, because otherwise I might never have written 'Ma Qui.' "

At night the choppers buzz the bamboo roof of the jungle, dumping from three thousand feet to little more than a hundred, circling, circling again, no L.Z. to land in, no casualties to pick up. Above the roar of the rotor wash come the shrieks of the damned: wails, moans, plaintive cries in Vietnamese. It's real William Castle stuff, weird sounds and screaming meemies, but even knowing it's coming from a tape recorder, even hearing the static hiss of the loudspeakers mounted on the Hueys, it still spooks the shit out of the V.C. "The

Wandering Soul," it's called—the sound of dead Cong, their bodies not given a proper burial, their spirits helplessly wandering the earth. Psychological warfare. Inner Sanctum meets Vietnam. Down in the tunnels, Charlie hears it, knows it's a con, tries to sleep, but can't; the damned stuff goes on half the night. The wails grow louder the lower the choppers fly, then trail off, to suitably eerie effect, as they climb away. Until the next chopper comes with its cargo of souls-in-a-box.

What horseshit.

It's not like that at all.

I watch the last of the choppers bank and veer south, and for a while the jungle is quiet again. Around me the ground is a scorched blister, a crater forged by mortar fire, a dusty halo of burnt ground surrounding it, grasses and trees incinerated in the firefight. The crater is my bed, my bunk, my home. I sleep there—if you can call it sleep—and when I've grown tired of wandering the trails, looking for my way back to Da Nang, or Cam Ne, or Than Quit, I always wind up back here. Because this seared piece of earth is the only goddamned thing for miles that isn't 'Nam. It's not jungle; it's not muddy water; it's not punji sticks smeared with shit. It's ugly, and it's barren, and it looks like the surface of the fucking moon, but it was made by my people, the only signature they can write on this steaming, rotten country, and I sleep in it, and I feel at home.

I was killed not far from here, in a clearing on the banks of the Song Cai River. My unit was pinned down; our backup never arrived; we were racing for the L.Z. where the dust-off choppers were to pick us up. Some of us got careless. Martinez never saw the trip wire in the grass and caught a Bouncing Betty in the groin; he died before we could get him to the L.Z. Dunbar hit a punji bear trap, the two spiked boards snapping up like the jaws of a wooden crocodile, chewing through his left leg. I thought Prosser and DePaul had pried him loose, but when I looked back I saw their bodies not far from the trap, cut down by sniper fire as they'd tried to rescue him. The bastards had let Dunbar live, and he was still caught in the trap, screaming for help, the blood pouring out between the two punji boards. I started back, firing my M-16 indiscriminately into the tree line, hoping to give the snipers pause enough so that I could free Dunbar—

They took me out a few yards from Dunbar, half a dozen rounds that blew apart most of my chest. I fell, screaming, but I also watched myself fall; I saw the sharp blades of elephant grass slice into my face like razors as I struck the ground; I watched the blood splatter upward on impact, a red cloud that seemed briefly to cloak my body, then dissipate, splattering across the grass, giving the appearance, for a moment, of a false spring—a red dew.

Dunbar died a few minutes later. To the west, the distant thunder of choppers rolled across the treetops. I stood there, staring at the body at my feet, thinking somehow that it must be someone else's body, someone else's blood, and I turned and ran for the choppers, not noticing that my feet weren't quite touching the ground as I ran, not seeing myself pass through the trip wires like a stray wind.

Up ahead, dust-off medics dragged wounded aboard a pair of Hueys. Most of my unit made it. I watched Silverman get yanked aboard; I saw Esteban claw at a medic with a bloody stump he still believed was his hand. I ran to join them, but the big Chinooks started to climb, fast, once everyone was on. "Wait for me!" I yelled, but they couldn't seem to hear me over the whipping of the blades. "Son of a bitch, wait for *me!*"

They didn't slow. They didn't stop. They kept on rising, ignoring me, abandoning me. Goddamn them, what were they *doing?* Motherfucking bastards, come *back,* come—

It wasn't until I saw the thick, moist wind of the rotor wash fanning the grass—saw it bending the trees as the steel dragonflies ascended—that I realized I felt no wind on my face, that I had no trouble standing in the small hurricane at the center of the clearing. I turned around. Past the tree line, in the thick of the jungle, mortars were being lobbed from afar. Some hit their intended targets in the bush; others strayed and blasted our position, unintentionally. I could hear the screams of V.C. before and after each hit; I saw Cong rushing out of the trees, some aflame, some limbless, only to be knocked off their feet by another incoming round. By now I knew the truth. I wandered, in a daze, back toward the tree line. I walked through sheets of flame without feeling so much as a sunburn. I saw the ground rock below me, but my steps never wavered, like the old joke about the drunken man during an earthquake.

At length the mortars stopped. The clearing was seared, desolate; bodies—Vietnamese, American—lay strewn and charred in all directions. I walked among them, rising smoke passing through me like dust through a cloud . . . and now I saw other wraiths, other figures standing above the remains of their own bodies; they looked thin, gaseous, the winds from the chopper passing overhead threatening their very solidity.

Prosser looked down at his shattered corpse and said, "Shit."

Dunbar agreed. "This sucks."

"Man, I *knew* this was gonna happen," Martinez insisted. "I just got laid in Da Nang. Is this fuckin' karma, or what?"

I made a mental note never to discuss metaphysics with Martinez. Not a useful overview.

"So what happens now?" I asked.

"Heaven, I guess." Dunbar shrugged.

"Or Hell." Martinez. Ever the optimist.

"Yeah, but when?"

"Gotta be anytime now," Prosser said, as though waiting for the 11:00 bus. He looked down at our bodies and grimaced. "I mean, we're dead, right?"

I looked at Dunbar's mangled leg. At Martinez's truncated torso. At. . . .

"Hey, Collins. Where the hell are *you*?"

I should have been just a few feet away from Dunbar's body, but I wasn't. At first I thought the half-dozen rounds that had dropped me had propelled my body away, but as we fanned out we saw no trace of it, not anywhere within a dozen yards. And when I came back to where Dunbar's body lay, I recognized the matted elephant grass where I had fallen—recognized, too, the tears of blood, now dried, coloring the tips of the grass. I squatted down, noticing for the first time that the grass was matted, in a zigzag pattern, for several feet beyond where my body fell.

"Son of a bitch," I said. "They took me."

"What?" said Martinez. "The V.C.?"

"They dragged me a few feet, then"—I pointed to where the matted grass ended—"two of them must've picked me up and taken me away."

"I didn't see anyone," Dunbar said.

"Maybe you were preoccupied," I suggested.

Prosser scanned the area, his brow furrowing. "DePaul's gone, too. He went down right next to me—we were near the river; I remember hearing the sound of the water—but he's gone."

"Maybe he was just wounded," I said. At least I hoped so. De-Paul had pulled me back, months before, from stepping on what had seemed like a plot of dry grass on a trail, but what revealed itself—once we'd tossed a large boulder on top of it—as a swinging man trap: kind of a seesaw with teeth. If not for DePaul, I would've been the one swinging from it, impaled on a dozen or more rusty spikes studding its surface. DePaul had bought me a few extra months of life; maybe, when I'd run forward, firing into the tree line, I'd done the same for him, distracting the snipers long enough for him to get away.

"Hey, listen," said Dunbar. "Choppers."

The mop-up crew swooped in, quick and dirty, to recover what bodies it could. The area was secured, at least for the moment, and two grunts pried loose Dunbar's mangled leg from the punji bear trap and hefted him into a body bag. The zipper caught on his lip, and the grunt had to unsnare it. Dunbar was furious.

"Watch what you're doing, assholes!" he roared at them. He turned to me. "Do you believe these guys?"

Two other grunts gingerly disconnected an unexploded cartridge trap not far from Martinez's body, then scooped up what remained of the poor bastard—torso in one body bag, legs in another—and zipped the bags shut. Martinez watched as they loaded them onto the chopper, then turned to me.

"Collins. You think I should—"

I turned, but by the time I was facing him he was no longer there.

"Martinez?"

Dunbar's body was hefted onto the Huey; it hit the floor like a sack of dry cement, and I could almost feel the air rushing in to fill the sudden vacuum beside me.

I whirled around. Dunbar, too, was gone.

"Dunbar!"

The Huey lifted off, the branches of surrounding trees shuddering around it, like angry lovers waving away a violent suitor, and I was alone.

———

Believe it or not, I enlisted. It seemed like a good idea at the time: lower-middle-class families from Detroit could barely afford to send one kid to college, let alone two, and with my older sister at Ann Arbor, I figured a student deferment wasn't coming my way anytime soon. So I let myself swallow the line they feed you at the recruiter's office, about how our *real* job over here was building bridges and thatching huts and helping the Vietnamese people; they made it sound kind of like the Peace Corps, only more humid.

My dad was a construction foreman; I'd been around buildings going up all my life—liked the sound of it, the feel of it, the smell of lumber and fresh concrete and the way the frame looked before you laid on the plasterboard. . . . I'd stand there staring at the girders and crossbeams, the wood-and-steel armatures that looked to my eight-year-old mind like dinosaur skeletons, and I thought, The people who'll live here will never see, never know what their house *really* looks like, underneath; but *I* know.

So the idea of building houses for homeless people and bridges for oxen to cross sounded okay. Except after eight months in 'Nam, most of the bridges I'd seen had been blown away by American air strikes, and the closest I'd come to thatching huts was helping repair the roof of a bar in Da Nang I happened to be trapped in during a monsoon.

All things considered, enlisting did not seem like the kind of blue-chip investment in the future it once had, just now.

For the first few days I stuck close to the crater, wandering only as far as I could travel and return in a day, searching for a way back—but the way back, I knew, was farther than could ever be measured in miles, and the road was far from clearly marked. I tried not to dwell on that. If I did, I would never have mustered the nerve to move from my little corner of Hell. I wasn't sure where the nearest U.S. base was in relation to here, but I remembered a small village we'd passed the previous day, and I seemed to recall a Red Cross Jeep parked near a hut, a French doctor from Catholic Relief Services administering to the villagers. Maybe he would show up again, and I could hitch a ride back to—the question kept presenting itself—*where?* What the hell did I do, ask directions to the Hereafter? With my luck, the Army was probably running *it*, too.

(Now, that was a frightening thought; frighteningly plausible. This whole thing was just fucked up enough to be an army operation. Had I forgotten to fill out a form somewhere down the line?)

I headed back down the trail we'd followed to our deaths, but this time, along with the usual sounds of the jungle—the rustling in the bush that you hoped was *only* a bamboo viper, or a tiger—I heard the jungle's other voice. I heard the sounds the choppers, with their souls-in-a-box, only played at.

I heard weeping.

Not moaning; not wailing; none of that Roger Corman, Vincent Price shit. Just the sound of grown men weeping, uncontrollably and unconsolably—coming, it seemed, from everywhere at once. And slowly I began to see them: V.C., blood splattered over their black silk pajamas, crouched in the bush in that funny way the V.N. sit— squatting, not sitting, on the ground—and crying. I stopped, dumbfounded. I'd never seen a V.N. cry before. I'd seen them scared—hell, I'd seen them fucking terrified—but I never saw them cry. All that crap you heard about how the V.N. are different from us, how they don't *feel* the way we do—I knew that was bullshit. They felt; they just didn't show it the way we did. But goddamned if these guys weren't giving our guys a run for their money, emotionally speaking. Maybe, if you're a V.C. and you're dead, it's okay to cry. Maybe it's expected. I moved on.

And somewhere along the trail, as I followed the Song Cai in its winding path south, I began to consider that I might not, in fact, be among the dead; that I might just be alive, after all.

Maybe, I thought, the rounds that had dropped me had just wounded me; maybe the V.C. took my body so they could get information out of me later. The more I thought about it, the more reasonable it sounded. They take me, nurse me back to health, so they can torture me later. (That sounded as logical as anything else in this screwy country.) And somewhere along the way I split off from my body. Got left behind, like a shadow shaken loose from its owner. I listened to the weeping all around me—Christ, I almost wished they *were* wailing and moaning; I could've borne that a lot easier— and I decided that I wasn't, couldn't be, dead.

Up ahead the trail widened briefly into a clearing, in the middle of which stood what looked like a giant birdhouse: a bamboo hut, little more than a box, really, perched on the stump of a large tree trunk. There were spirit houses like this scattered all over 'Nam, small homes erected for the happiness of departed relatives, or for embittered spirits who might otherwise prey on hapless villages. The Army briefed us on the local customs and superstitions before we even arrived over here—things like you never pat a V.N. on the head 'cause the head, to the Vietnamese, is the seat of the soul; and *whatever* you do, don't sit with your legs crossed so that your foot is pointing toward the other person's head, because that's the grossest kind of insult. Shit like that. Some dinks would even name their male babies after women's sexual organs to try and fool evil spirits into thinking the kid was a girl, because boys were more valuable and needed to be protected. Jesus.

So I knew about spirit houses, and when we passed this one the other day, I remember thinking, Hey, that's kind of neat, even better than the treehouse I built in my grandparents' yard when I was twelve, and I went on walking.

Today I stopped. Stared at it.

Today there were people inside the birdhouse.

One was an elderly papa-san, the other a young woman, maybe twenty-eight, twenty-nine. They were burning joss sticks, the sweet fragrance carried back on the thick wind, and around them I saw candles, tiny handmade furniture, and a few books. I started walking again, more slowly now, and as I got within a couple yards of the birdhouse the papa-san looked up at me, blinked once in mild surprise, then smiled and held his hand over his chest in a *gassho,* a traditional form of greeting and respect. His other arm, I now noticed, was askew beneath its silk sleeve, as though it had been broken, or worse.

"Welcome, traveler," he said. He was speaking in Vietnamese, but I understood, somehow, despite it.

"Uh . . . hello," I said, not sure if this worked both ways, but apparently it did; he smiled again, gesturing to his woman companion.

"I am Phan Van Duc. My daughter, Chau."

The woman turned and glared at me. She was pretty, in the abstract, but it was hard to get past the sneer on her face. So fixed, so unwavering, it looked like it'd been tattooed on. And since I wasn't sure if her anger was directed at me or not, I decided to ignore it, turned to the old man.

"My name is William Anthony Collins," I said. I wasn't sure if having three names was requisite over here, but I figured it couldn't hurt.

"May we offer you shelter?" Phan asked cordially. His daughter glowered.

There was barely enough room in the birdhouse for two, and I had no desire to be at close quarters with Chau. I declined but thanked him for the offer.

"Have you been dead long?" the papa-san asked suddenly. I flinched.

"I'm not dead," I said stubbornly.

The old man looked at me as though I were crazy. His daughter laughed a brassy, mocking laugh.

I explained what had happened to me, what I *thought* had happened to me, and how I was heading for the village downriver to see if the Viet Cong had taken my body there. Phan looked at me with sad, wise eyes as I spoke, then, when I'd finished, nodded once—more out of politeness, I suspected, than out of any credence he put in my theory.

"What you say may be true," he mused, "though I have never heard of such a thing. I would imagine, however, that rather than take a prisoner to a village, where he might easily be discovered, they would take him to one of their tunnel bases."

The V.C. had hundreds of tunnels running beneath most of I-Corps: a spiderweb of barracks and underground command posts and subterranean hospitals so vast, so labyrinthine, that we were only just beginning to understand the full scope of them. If I had been taken prisoner in one of them, the odds of finding myself were about equal to winning bets on the Triple Crown, the World Series, and the Super Bowl all in one year.

"In that case," I said, not really wanting to think about it, "I'll just wait for my—body—to die, and when it does I'm out of here."

Papa-san looked at me with a half-pitying, half-perplexed look, as though I had just told him the sky was green and the moon was made of rice. Hell, come to think of it, maybe the dinks *did* think the moon was made of rice.

"What about you?" I said, anxious to shift the topic of conversation. "Why are you—here?"

Phan showed no trace of pain, or grief, as he replied.

"I was mauled by a tiger and left to bleed to death," he said simply, as though that should explain everything. Then, at my blank look, he explained patiently, "Having died a violent death, I was denied entry to the next world."

I blinked. I didn't see the connection.

"Getting mauled by a tiger, that's not your fault," I said, baffled.

He looked as baffled by my words as I was by his. "What difference does fault make? What is, is." He shrugged.

I opted not to pursue the subject. Phan and Martinez would've gotten along just fine. "And your daughter?"

He looked askance at her; she threw me a nasty look, then she scrambled forward into the birdhouse, hands gripping the lip of the floor, spitting the words at me, the hard edges of the Vietnamese consonants as sharp as the bitterness in her words.

"I died childless," she snapped at me. "Is that what you wanted to hear? Are you happy? I died childless, worthless, and I am condemned because of it."

"That's crazy," I said, despite myself.

She laughed a brittle laugh. "You are the crazy one," she said. "A *ma qui*, thinking he is alive. I pity you."

"No," the papa-san said gently. "You pity no one but yourself."

She glared at him, her nostrils flaring, then laughed again, shortly. "You are right," she said. "I pity no one. I don't know why I let you keep me here. I can do anything I want. I can bring disease back to the village, kill the children of my former friends. Yes. I think I would like that." She grinned maliciously, as though taking relish in the wickedness of her thought.

"You will not," Phan warned. "I am your father, and I forbid it."

She muttered a curse under her breath and retreated to the rear of the birdhouse. The papa-san turned and looked at me sadly.

"Do not judge my daughter by what she is now," he said softly. "Death makes of us what it wishes."

Jesus Christ, these people actually believed that. And so, I guess, that's just what they got. Well, not me. No fucking way, man. Not me.

I backed away. "I have to go."

"Wait," Phan said. I halted; I'm not sure why. He leaned forward, as though to share something important with me. "If you go into the village . . . you must be careful. Do not walk in the front door of a house, because the living keep mirrors by the doorway, to reflect the image of those who enter. If a spirit sees himself in the mirror, he will be frightened off. Also, if red paper lines the entrance, stay away, for you will anger the God of the Doorway. Do you understand?"

I nodded numbly, thanked him for his advice, and got the hell out of there, fast.

I hurried down the trail, past the weeping guerrillas in black silk, feeling a sudden black longing for something as violent and mundane as a mortar strike; yearning for the sound of gunships, the bright spark of tracer fire, the crackling of small-arms fire, or the din of big Chinook choppers circling in for the kill. God *damn*. This was the dinks' Hell, not mine. I wasn't going to be a part of it; I would *not* buy into their stupid, superstitious horseshit. The weeping around me grew louder. I started running now, phantom limbs passing harmlessly through trip wires and across punji traps, even the elephant grass not so much as tickling my calves as I ran along the banks of the Song Cai—

The weeping changed. Became different: deeper. I knew instantly that it was not the cries of a Vietnamese; knew, suddenly and sickeningly, that it was an American's cries I was hearing.

I stopped, looked around. I saw no one lying wounded in the bush but heard now, too, a voice:

"—Jesus, Mary, and Joseph, *help me*—"

Oh, Christ, I thought.

DePaul.

I looked up. He was floating about five feet above the muddy waters of the river, like a tethered balloon, his big six-foot frame looking almost gaseous, his black skin seeming somehow pale. His hands covered his face as he wept, prayed, swore, and wept again. At first I thought he was moving upstream, but I soon realized that it was the water flowing under him that gave the illusion of movement; he swayed back and forth slightly but was utterly motionless, completely stationary.

It took me a moment to recover my wits. I shouted his name over the roar of the rapids.

He looked up, startled.

When he saw me—saw me looking at *him*—his face lit up with a kind of absolution. "Oh, Jesus," he said, so softly I almost couldn't hear it. "*Collins?* Are you real?"

"I sure as shit hope so."

"Are you alive?"

I dodged the question. "What the hell happened to you, man? Prosser said you went down right next to him, but your body—"

"Charlie hit me in the back." I could see the hole torn in his skin at the nape of his neck, and the matching one in front, just below his collarbone, where the bullet had exited. "I couldn't breathe. Couldn't think. Got up somehow, ran—but in the wrong direction. Dumped into the river. Christ, Bill, it was awful. I was choking *and* drowning, and the next thing I knew"—his hand had gone reflexively to his throat, covering the ragged hole there—"my body had floated downriver, then got snagged on some rock. Over there."

I followed his gaze. His body was pinned between two rocks, the waters flowing around it, flanking it in white foam. I turned back to DePaul, floating in place above the river, and I took a step forward.

"Christ, De," I said softly. "How—I mean, what—"

"I *can't get down,* man," he said, and for the first time I heard the pain in his voice. "I been here two, three days, and it *hurts.* Oh, Christ, it hurts! It's not like floating; Jesus, it's like treading water; every muscle in my body aches—I'm so *tired,* man, I'm so—" He broke off in sobs, something I'd never seen him do. He looked away, let the tears come, then looked back at me, his eyes wide. "Help me, Collins," he said softly. "*Help me.*"

"Just tell me how," I said, feeling helpless, horrified. "Why—why are you *like* this, man? You have any idea?"

"Yeah. Yeah, I know," he said, taking a ragged gulp of air. "It's—it's 'cause I died in water, see? You die in water, your spirit's tied to the water till you can find another one to—"

"*What?* Jesus Christ, De, where'd you *get* that shit from?"

"Another spook. V.C., half his head blown away, wanderin' up and down the river. He told me."

"You bought *into* that crap?" I yelled at him. "These dinks believe this shit, man; *you* don't have to—you're an *American,* for Chrissake!"

"Collins—"

"You believe it, it happens. You stop believing, it stops happening. Just—"

His eyes were sunken, desperate. "Please, man. Help me?"

No matter what I thought of this shit, there was only one thing that mattered: he'd saved my life once, and even if there was no more life in him to save, I could, at least, try to ease his torment. I *had* to try.

"All right," I said. "What can I do?"

He hesitated.

"Bring me a kid," he said, quietly.

"A kid? Why?"

He hesitated again; then, working up his nerve, he said, "To release me. A life for a life."

My eyes went wide. *"What?"*

"It's the only way," he said quickly. "You die in water, the only way to be set free is to—drown—a kid, as an offering." His eyes clouded over, his gaze became hooded and ashamed even as he said it. For a long minute the only sound was the rushing of water past the dam of DePaul's corpse, and the distant sounds of weeping carried on the wind.

Finally I said, "I can't do that, man."

"Bill—"

"Even if I believed it'd work—*especially* if I believed it'd work—I couldn't—"

"Not a healthy kid," DePaul interrupted, desperation and pleading creeping into his tone. "A sick one. One that's gonna die anyway. Shit, half the gook kids over here die before they're—"

"Are you crazy, man?" I snapped. "Gook or not, I can't—"

I stopped. Listened to what I was saying.

DePaul's face was ashen, in torment. "Collins . . . please. I hurt so bad—"

I was buying into this crap. Just like him. Someone'd filled his head with dink superstition, and now he was living—or dying—by it. That was it, wasn't it? You die, you get pretty much what you expect: Catholics, Heaven or Hell; atheist, maybe nothing, nonexistence, loss of consciousness; dinks—this. And we'd been over here so long, wading knee-deep in their fucking country, that we were starting to believe what they believed.

But the DePaul I knew would never kill a kid. Not even to save himself. Maybe the only way to shake him loose from this bullshit was to show him that.

I waited a long minute, thinking, devising a plan, and then finally I spoke up.

"A sick kid?" I asked carefully, as though I actually believed all this.

He looked up hopefully. "One that's gonna die anyway. You've seen 'em; you know what they look like; you can see it in their eyes—"

"I won't bring one that's gonna live."

"No, no, man, you don't have to. A sick kid. A real sick kid." God, he sounded pathetic.

I told him I didn't know how long it would take, but that I would head into the village we passed through a few days ago, and see what I could do. I told him I'd be back as soon as I could.

"Hurry, man. Hurry." It was the last thing I heard before I headed back into the bush once again. He'd bought the line. Now all I had to do was show him he'd bought another—and, more important, that he could buy out of it.

The village was about two hours up the road. There was no Red Cross Jeep in sight, no Catholic Relief doctor handing out aspirin and antibiotics; just the squalid little huts, the half-naked kids running through muddy puddles probably rife with typhoid, tired-looking women doing laundry in a small stream tributary to the Song Cai. There was a huge crater at the edge of town—the mortar strike that was too late to save me and Dunbar and DePaul. Nearby roofs were scorched; at least two huts had been burned to the ground. Friendly fire. Any friendlier, and half the village would be greeting me personally. I walked up the main road, peeking in windows. If I was going to make it look genuine, I'd have to bring back a genuinely sickly kid; though exactly how, I still wasn't sure.

Outside one hut I heard the sound of a mother comforting a squalling baby and decided to go in and take a look. Sure enough, just as the old papa-san had predicted, the doorway was lined with red paper to ward off evil spirits. I stepped across the threshold. Big fucking deal. Up yours, God of the Doorway. I turned—

I screamed.

In the mirror positioned just inside, I saw a man with a foot-wide hole blasted in his chest: the torn edges of the wound charred to a crisp, the cavity within raw and red as steak tartare. A pair of lungs dangled uselessly from the slimmest of folds of flesh, swaying as I jumped back reflexively; beside them, a heart riddled with half a dozen jagged frag wounds throbbed in a stubborn counterfeit of life.

And behind me in the mirror a glimpse of something else: a shadow, a *red* shadow, as red as the paper above the doorway . . . moving not as I moved but looming up, and quickly, behind me.

I ran.

Out of the house, down the street, away from the huts, finally collapsing on a patch of elephant grass. At first I was afraid to look down at myself, but when I did I saw nothing—saw exactly what I'd seen up till now, the drab green camouflage fatigues stained with blood. All this time, I realized, I had seen everyone else's wounds but mine. Not till now.

I sat there, gathering my wits and my courage, trying to work up the nerve to enter another hut. I didn't think about the mirror, didn't dwell on what I'd seen. Better just to think of myself this way, the way some part of me *wanted* to see myself. When I finally got up and started round to the huts again, I steered well clear of the doors.

There was the usual assortment of sickly kids—malaria mostly, but, from the look of them, a few typhoid, influenza, and parasitic dysentery cases as well. I felt gruesome as hell, trying to choose which one to take, even knowing this was only a ruse, something to shock DePaul back to normalcy. *Just get it over with.* I looked in one window and saw what appeared to be a two-year-old girl—in a dress made of old parachute nylon, an earring dangling too large from one tiny lobe—being washed by her mother. It was only when the mother turned the child over and I saw the small brown penis that I remembered: the mother was trying to deceive the evil spirits into thinking her sickly boy-child was really a girl and thus not worth the taking.

Jesus, I thought. Said a lot about the place of women over here. But it did mean the kid was probably seriously ill, and after I'd used her—him—to get DePaul back to normal, I could take the poor kid to the nearest Evac . . . leave it on the doorstep of the civilian ward with a note telling the name of his village.

Assuming I could *write* a note.

Assuming I could even *take* the kid in the first place.

I took a deep breath and, once the mother had left the room, walked through the wall of the hut. I didn't feel the bamboo any more than I'd felt the trip wires I'd run through. I stood over the infant, now worried that my hands would pass through him as well . . . then slowly reached down to try and pick him up.

I touched him. I didn't know how, or why, but I could touch him.

I scooped the boy up in my arms and held him to my chest. He looked up at me with old, sad eyes. All the kids here had the same kind of eyes: tired, cheerless, and somehow knowing. As though all the misery around them, all the civil wars and foreign invaders— from the French to the Japanese to the Americans—as though all that were known to them, before they'd even been born. Rocked in a cradle of war, they woke, with no surprise, to a lullaby of thunder.

I walked through the wall of the hut, the child held aloft, and carried him through the window. When we were clear of the building, I hefted the boy up, held him in my arms, and headed into the bush before anyone could see.

I wanted to stay off the main road, for fear that someone might see me: not me, I guess, since I *couldn't* be seen, but the kid, the boy. (What, I wondered, would someone see, if they did see? A child carried aloft on the wind? Or an infant wrapped in the arms of a shadow, a smudge on the air? I didn't know. I didn't want to find out.) Every once in a while I'd see a dead V.C. look up from where he was squatting, on the banks of the river or in the shade of a rubber tree, and look at me, sometimes with curiosity, sometimes resentment, sometimes fear. They never said anything. Just stared, and at length went back to their mourning, their weeping. I hurried past.

About half a mile from DePaul, I caught a glimpse of a squad of still-living V.C. about a dozen yards into the jungle, carrying what looked like an unconscious American G.I., probably an LRRP. I immediately squatted down in the bush, hiding the kid from view as best I could, dropping a fold of blanket over his face to protect him from the prickly blades of grass. I watched as one of the V.C. bent down, reaching for what looked like a patch of dry dirt, his fingers finding a catch, a handle of some sort; and then the earth lifted, and I saw it was actually a trapdoor in the ground itself—a piece of wood covered with a thin but deceptive layer of dirt. One by one the V.C. crawled headfirst into the tunnel, until only two were left— the two carrying the unconscious G.I. I debated what to do—was there anything I *could* do?—but before I could make a decision, I saw the G.I.'s head tilt at an unnatural angle as he was lowered into the ground . . . and I knew then that I'd been mistaken. He wasn't unconscious; he was dead. And, very quickly, lost from sight.

Psychological warfare. Drove Americans crazy when we couldn't recover our dead, and Charlie knew it. Just like we played on their fears with the Wandering Soul, they played on ours, in their own way. I got up and moved on.

Less than half an hour later I was back at the river. DePaul still floated helpless above the rapids. He looked up at my approach, the torment in his face quickly replaced by astonishment and—fear?

I brought the kid to the edge of the river, looked up at DePaul, made my voice hard, resolute—all that Sergeant York shit.

"He's got malaria," I said tonelessly. "You can tell when you pull down his lower eyelid; it's all pink. He's anemic, can't weigh more than twenty pounds. They could save him, at the 510 Evac. Or you can take him, to save yourself." I stared him straight in the eye. "Which is it, DePaul?"

I'd known DePaul since boot camp. Faced with the reality of it, I knew what he'd answer.

And as I waited smugly for him to say it, his gaseous wraithlike form spun round in midair, rocketed downward like a guided missile, and slammed into me with vicious velocity, sending me sprawling, knocking the kid out of my arms.

Stunned, I screamed at him, but by the time I'd scrambled to my feet he had the kid in a vise grip and was holding the poor sonofabitch under the water. I ran, slammed into De with all my strength, but he shrugged me off with an elbow in my face. I toppled backward.

"I'm sorry, man," he kept saying over and over. "I'm sorry. . . ."

I lunged at him again, this time knocking him off balance; he lost his grip on the kid, and I dove into the water after the boy. It felt weird: the water passed *through* me—I didn't feel wet, or cold, nothing at all—and the waters were so muddy I could barely see a foot in front of me. Finally, after what seemed like forever, I saw a small object in front of me, and instinctively I reached out and grabbed. My fingers closed around the infant's arms. I made for the surface, the kid in my arms; I staggered out of the water, up the embankment—

I put the boy down on the ground. His face was blue, his body very still. I tried to administer mouth-to-mouth, but nothing happened; and I laughed suddenly, a manic, rueful laugh, at the thought of me, of all people, trying to give the breath of life.

I looked up, thinking to see DePaul towering above me . . . but he was nowhere to be seen. And when I looked up at the spot above the river where he had been tethered, helplessly, for so long—

I saw the spirit form of the little boy, floating, hovering, crying out in pain and confusion.

I screamed. I screamed for a long time.

And knew now why I'd been able to touch the child, when I hadn't been able to touch anything else: I was the *ma qui*; I was the evil spirit come to bear the sickly child away; and I had done my job, followed my role, without even realizing I'd been doing it. I thought of Phan, of his daughter, Chau, of DePaul, and of myself.

Death makes of us what it wishes.

I wept, then, for the first time, as freely and as helplessly as the V.C. I'd seen and heard; wept like the Wandering Soul I knew, at last, I had to be.

I must've stayed there, on the banks of the river, for at least a day, trying to find some way to atone, some way to save the soul of the child I'd led to perdition. But I couldn't. I would've traded places with him willingly but didn't know how. And when I went back to the spirit house where Phan and his daughter dwelled, when I told him of what I'd done, he showed no horror, expressed no rage; just puzzlement that it had taken me so long to realize my place in the world.

His daughter, on the other hand, gleefully congratulated me on my deed. "*Ma qui,*" she said, and this time, hearing the word, I understood it not just as ghost but as devil, for it meant both. "Did it not feel good?"

A terrible gladness burst open someplace inside me—a black, cold poison that felt at once horrifying and invigorating. It was relief, expiation of guilt by embracing, not renouncing, the evil I'd done.

Chau, as though sensing this, laughed throatily. She leaned forward, her spiteful smile now seductive as well. *"Yêu dâu,"* she said, *"yêu quái."*

Beloved demon.

"Together we could do many things," she said, twisting a lock of long black hair in her fingers. Her eyes glittered malevolently. "Many things." She laughed again. Cruel eyes, a cold-blooded smile. I felt betrayed by my own erection. I wanted her; I didn't want her. I loathed her, and in my loathing wanted her all the more, because perverse desire was, at least, desire; I wanted my cock, dead limb that it was, inside her, to make me feel alive.

When I realized how badly I wanted it, I ran.

She only laughed all the louder.

"Beloved demon!" she called after me. "You shall be back!"

But I haven't been back. Not yet. Nor back to the crater, the place of my death, not for many months. I still search for my body, but I know that the odds of finding it, in the hundreds of miles of tunnels that honeycomb this land, are virtually nil. I search during the days, and at night I come back to my new home to sleep.

I have a birdhouse of my own, you see, just outside the village; a treehouse perched on a bamboo stump, filled with joss sticks and candles and little toy furniture. I come back here, and I fight to remind myself who I am, what I am; I struggle against becoming the *yêu quái*, the demon Chau wishes me to be. Except, that is, when the bloodsong sings to me in my voice, and I know that I already *am* the demon—and that the only thing that stops me from acting like one is my will, my conscience, the last vestiges of the living man I once was. I don't know how long I can keep the demon at bay. I don't know how long I want to. But all I can do is keep trying, and not think of Chau, or of how wonderfully bitter her lips must taste, bitter as salt, bitter as blood.

Damn it.

Above me the Wandering Soul cries out from its box, wailing and moaning in a ridiculous burlesque of damnation, and I think about all the things we were told about this place, and the things we weren't.

Back in Da Nang, when anyone would talk about the Army's "pacification" program—about winning the "hearts and minds" of the Vietnamese—the joke used to be: Grab 'em by the balls, and their hearts and minds will follow. Except no one told us that while we were working on their hearts and minds, they were winning over our souls. The Army trained us in jungle warfare, drilled us in the local customs, told us we'd have to fight Charlie on his own terms—but never let on that we'd have to die on his terms, too. Because for all the technology, all the ordnance, all the planning that went into this war, they forgot the most important thing.

They never told us the rules of engagement.

THREE SCENES FROM STATIONS OF THE TIDE

Michael Swanwick

. . . .

Science fiction scenes do not normally survive the bloody process of excerption. Indeed, it might be reasonably argued that if the author of an SF novel has done his or her job properly—immersing us in utterly strange concepts, locales, and psyches—then any given moment, wrenched from its context, will be opaque.

Faced with the problem of representing Michael Swanwick's *Stations of the Tide,* however, I did not hesitate to carve out three of my favorite anecdotes and offer them up in isolation. For while Swanwick has created a sociologically, ecologically, and technologically complex world, his book is also filled with piecemeal delights. This is that rare SF novel whose scenes are so linguistically rich they can live outside the womb of the plot.

Swanwick's two previous novels are *In the Drift* and *Vacuum Flowers.* His stories have been published in *Omni, Amazing Stories, Isaac Asimov's Science Fiction Magazine, High Times, New Dimensions, Universe,* and *Full Spectrum,* and his collection, *Gravity's Angels,* is currently available from Arkham House. The author lives with his wife and son in Philadelphia, where he is busily working on his fourth novel, a fantasy.

"I began *Stations of the Tide* because I wanted to discuss sex, magic, and television as intangible and related technologies," Swanwick comments. "I wanted to write about a bureaucrat who was honest, competent, and doing a necessary job. And I wanted to create a world in which everything would change its essential nature by novel's end. The rest just followed."

In the distant future, the Prosperan worlds are under the thumb of a vast, self-serving System that, in the wake of some unspecified machine-induced cataclysm back on Earth, has undertaken to regulate all technology. Rumor has it that Aldebaran Gregorian, a "bush wizard" living on the phantasmagorical planet Miranda, has obtained a forbidden device. To meet this crisis, the System dispatches a man known only as "the bureaucrat," authorizing him to locate the renegade and, if possible, retrieve the contraband. The scenes that follow offer three different perspectives on Gregorian, a malevolent but alluring figure whose energy haunts every page of *Stations of the Tide,* even though he appears only at the climax.

The Birth of Gregorian

Synopsis: Aided by his planetside liaison, Emilie Chu, the bureau-crat searches out the magician's mother in a crumbling, doomed riverside mansion. In a few weeks the "jubilee tides" will arrive, inundating the lowlands, driving everyone to the Piedmont, and causing radical morphological changes among Miranda's fauna. But Mother Gregorian has no intention of joining the evacuation, and she has plenty of time to relate the story of her son's advent. . . .

Within the bed, propped up on a billowing throne of pillows, lay a grotesquely fat woman. The bureaucrat was reminded inevitably of a termite queen, she was so vast and passively immobile. Her face was doughy white, her mouth a tiny gasp of pain. A ringed hand hovered over a board floating atop her swollen belly, on which was arranged a circle of solitaire cards: stars, cups, queens, and knaves in solemn procession. A silent television flickered at her feet.

The bureaucrat introduced himself, and she nodded without looking up from her slow telling out of cards. "I am playing a game called Futility," she said. "Are you familiar with it?"

"How does one win?"

"You don't. You can only postpone losing. I've managed to keep this particular game going for years. This was my bride bed, you know. I had my first man here. It's a good bed. I've taken each of my husbands to it. Sometimes more than one at once. Three times it's been my childbed—four, if you count the miscarriage. I intend to die in it. That's little enough to ask." She sighed and pushed the tray of cards away. It swiveled into the wall. "What do you want of me?"

"Something very simple, I hope. I wish to speak with your son but don't have his address, and I was hoping you'd know where he is now."

"I haven't heard from him since he ran away from me." A crafty look came on her face. "What's he done to you? Taken off with your money, I expect. He tried to run off with mine, but I was too clever for him. That's all that's worth anything in life, all that gives you any control."

"So far as I know, he hasn't done anything. I'm only going to ask him a few questions."

"A few questions," she said disbelievingly.

He did nothing to break their shared silence, but let it flower and bloom, content to discover when she would finally speak again. Finally Mother Gregorian frowned with annoyance and said, "What kind of questions?"

"There's a possibility, nothing more, that some controlled technology may be missing. My agency wants me to ask your son whether he knows anything about it."

"What'll you do to him when you catch him?"

"I am not going to catch him at anything," the bureaucrat said testily. "If he has the technology, I'll ask him to return it. That's all I can do. I don't have the authority to take any serious action." She smiled meanly, as if she'd just caught him out in a falsehood. "But if you don't mind telling me just a little about him? What he was like as a child?"

The old woman shrugged painfully. "He was a normal enough boy. Full of the devil. He used to love stories, I remember. Ghosts and haunts and knights and space pirates. The priest would tell little Aldebaran stories of the martyrs. I remember how he'd sit listening, eyes big, and tremble when they died. Now he's on the television, I saw one of his commercials just the other day." She fiddled with the control, fanning through the spectrum of stations without finding the ad, and put it down again. It was an expensive set, sealed in orbit and guaranteed by his own department as unconvertible. "I was a virgin when he was born."

"I beg your pardon?" he said, startled.

"Ah, I *thought* that would draw your attention. It has the stench of offworld technology to it, doesn't it? Yes, but it was an ancient crime, when I was young and very, very beautiful. His father was an offworlder like yourself, very wealthy, and I was just a backwoods witch—a pharmacienne, what you'd call an herbalist."

Her pale, spotted eyelids half closed; she lay her head further back, gazing into the past. "He came down from the sky in a red-enameled flying machine, on a dark night when Caliban and Ariel were both newborn—that's an important time for gathering the roots, your mandragon, epipopsy, and kiss-a-clown especially. He was an important man, he had that glitter about him, but after all these years I somehow cannot remember his face—only his boots, he had wonderful boots of fine red leather he told me came from stars away, nothing you could buy on Miranda even if you had the money." She sighed. "He wanted a motherless child, of his own genes and no others. I have no idea why. I could never wheedle that from him, for all the months we stayed together.

"We haggled up a price. He gave me money enough to buy all this"—she gestured with her chin to indicate all her cluttered domain—"and, later, several husbands more to my liking than he. Then he carried me away in his bat-winged machine to Ararat, far deep in the forests. That's the first city was ever built on Miranda. From the air it looked like a mountain, built up in terraces like a ziggurat, and all overgrown. I stayed there for all my pregnancy. Don't believe those who say that haunts live there. I had it to my own, all those stone buildings larger than anything this side of the Piedmont, nobody there but myself and the beasts. The father stayed with me when he could, but it was usually just me and my thoughts, wandering among those overgrown walls. They were green with mosses, trees growing out of windows, fields of wildflowers on every roof. Nobody to talk to! I tell you, I earned that money. Sometimes I cried."

Her eyes were soft and distant. "He spoke very fondly to me, as if I were his house pet, his soft cat, but he never once thought of me as a woman, I could tell. I was only a convenient womb to him, when you come down to it, there was that reserve to him.

"I broke my hymen with these two thumbs. I'd been trained as a midwife, of course, and knew my diet and exercises. When he brought me offworld food and medicines, I threw them away. It amused him when he found out, for by then he could see that I was healthy and his bastard safe. But I made my plans. He was away the week of the birth—I'd told him the wrong date—and I gave him the slip. I was young then, I took two days' rest, and then I left Ararat. He thought I'd be lost, you see, that I could never find my way out. But I was born in the Tidewater and he on some floating metal world, what did he know? I'd saved up supplies in secret, and I knew what plants I could eat, so food was never a problem. I followed the flow of streams, took the easy way around marshes, and eventually I ended up at Ocean. There was nowhere else I could have ended up at, given I was consistent. It wasn't a month before I had come here and set workmen to building this house."

She laughed lightly, and the laugh caught in her throat, causing her to choke. Her face twisted and reddened, until the bureaucrat feared she might be in serious distress. Then she calmed somewhat, and he poured her a glass of water from a nearby carafe. She took it without thanking him. "I fooled the bugger, all right. I bested him. I had his money safe in Piedmont banks and his bastard with me, he never knew where to look, and he couldn't inquire openly. Probably never bothered. Probably thought I died out there. It's marshy around Ararat."

"That's a remarkable story," the bureaucrat said.

"You think I was in love with him. It's what anyone would think, but it's not so. He'd come and bought me with his offplanet money. He thought himself important and me nothing compared to him, a convenience he could pick up and put down as he wished. And he was right, damn him, that's what made me mad. So I took his son from him, to teach him otherwise." She cackled. "Ah, the pranks I used to play!"

"Do you have any pictures of him?"

She lifted a hand, pointed to a wall where petty portraits and ancient photomechanicals vied for space. "That picture there, in the tortoiseshell frame, bring it here." He obeyed. "The woman, that tall goddess, was me, believe it or not. The child is young Aldebaran."

He looked carefully. The woman was heavy and slatternly but clearly proud of her solidity, her flesh: she'd've had her admirers. The child was a spooky thing, staring straight at him with eyes that were two dark circles. "This is a picture of a girl."

"No, that's Aldebaran. I dressed him like that, in skirts and flounces, for the first several years, to hide him from his father, in case he came looking. Until he was seven. He turned willful then, nasty creature, and wouldn't wear his proper clothes. I had to give in, he walked out in the street buck naked. But I didn't give in easy. Three days he went bare before the priest came and said this could not be."

"How did Aldebaran come to have an offworld education?"

She ignored the question. "I wanted a daughter, of course. Girls are so much more tractable. A girl would not have run off to find her father, the way he did." Abruptly she commanded, "Put your hand under my bed. Pull out what you find there."

He reached into the vaginal shadows under the bed skirts, drew out a shallow trunk carved with half-human figures. Mother Gregorian rolled over, grunting with effort, to look. "Under that green silk—there ought to be a brown package. Yes. That. Unwrap it."

It was alarmingly easy to obey this monster, she was so sure of her commands. He held a battered notebook in his hand, a faded scrawl of sigils running across its cover.

"That belonged to Aldebaran. He lost it just before he ran away." Her smile hinted at stories untold. "Take it with you, perhaps it'll tell you something." She closed her eyes, let her face relax into a flaccid mask of pain. She was panting now, steadily as a dog in summer, but quieter.

"You've been very helpful," the bureaucrat said cautiously. He could sense the old woman about to name a price for information given.

"He thought he was so clever. He thought that if he went far away enough he could escape me. He thought he could escape me!" Her eyes flickered open, glittered venomously. "When you find him, give him a message for me. Tell him that no matter how far you go, in miles or learning or time, you cannot escape your mother."

The Education of Gregorian

Synopsis: Not far from Mother Gregorian's home, the jubilee is in full swing—a Mardi Gras–like celebration complete with costumes, music, rides, and feasting. As the carnival winds down, a voluptuous witch named Undine manifests herself to the bureaucrat, claiming to have studied with Gregorian. She takes our hero to a hut, makes furious love to him, and guilelessly requests a second round. . . .

"Again," she said.

"I'm afraid you've mistaken me for someone else," the bureaucrat said amiably. "Someone considerably younger. But if you're willing to wait twenty minutes or so, I'll be more than happy to try again."

Undine sat up, her magnificent breasts swaying slightly. Faint daggers of Caliban's light slanted through the window to touch them both. The candle had long since guttered out. "You mean to say you don't know the method by which men can have orgasm after orgasm without ejaculating?".

He laughed. "No."

"The girls won't like you if you have to stop a half hour every time you come," she said teasingly. Then, seriously, "I'll teach you." She took his cock in her hand, waggled it back and forth, amused by its limpness. "After your vaunted twenty minutes. In the meantime, I can show you something of interest."

She threw the blanket lengthwise over her shoulders, as if it were a shawl. It made a strange costume in the dim light, with sleeves that touched the ground and a back that didn't quite reach her legs, so that two pale slivers of moon peeped out at him. Naked, he padded after her into the clearing behind the hut. "Look," she said.

Light was bursting from the ground in pale sheets of pink and blue and white. The rosebushes shimmered with pastel light, as if already drowned in Ocean's shallows. The ground here had been dug up recently, churned and spaded, and was now suffused with pale fire. "What is it?" he asked wonderingly.

"Iridobacterium. They're naturally biophosphorescent. You'll find them everywhere in the soil in the Tidewater, but usually only in trace amounts. They're useful in the spiritual arts. Pay attention now, because I'm going to explain a very minor mystery to you."

"I'm listening," he said, not comprehending.

"The only way to force a bloom is to bury an animal in the soil. When it decomposes, the iridobacteria feed on the products of decay. I've spent the last week poisoning dogs and burying them here."

"You killed dogs?" he said, horrified.

"It was quick. What do you think is going to happen to them when the tides come? They're like the roses, they can't adapt. So the humane-society people organized Dog Control Week and paid me by the corpse. Nobody's about to haul a bunch of mutts to the Piedmont." She gestured. "There's a shovel leaning against my hut."

He fetched the shovel. In a month this land would be under water. He imagined fishes swimming through the buildings while drowned dogs floated, mouths open, caught head down in tangles of drowning rosebushes. They would rot before the hungry kings of the tides would accept their carcasses. At the witch's direction, he shoveled the brightest patches of dirt into a rusty steel drum almost filled with rainwater. The dirt sank, and bright swirls of phosphorescence rose in the water. Undine skimmed the top with a wooden scraper, slopping the scum into a wide pan. "When the water evaporates, the powder that remains is rich in iridobacteria," she said. "There's several more steps necessary to process it, but now it's in concentrated form, that can wait until I reach the Piedmont. It's common as sin now, but it won't grow up there."

"Tell me about Gregorian," the bureaucrat said.

"Gregorian is the only perfectly evil man I've ever met," Undine said. Her face was suddenly cold, as harsh and stern as Caliban's rocky plains. "He is smarter than you, stronger than you, more handsome than you, and far more determined. He has received an offplanet education that's at least the equal of yours, and he's a master of occult arts in which you do not believe. You are insane to challenge him. You are a dead man, and you do not know it."

"He'd certainly like me to believe that."

"All men are fools," Undine said. Her tone was light again, her look disdainful. "Have you noticed that? Were I in your position, I'd arrange to contract an illness or develop a moral qualm about the nature of my assignment. It might be a black mark on my record, but I would outlive the embarrassment."

"When did you meet Gregorian?" The bureaucrat dumped more dirt in the drum, raising mad swirls of phosphorescence.

"That was the year I spent as a ghost. I was a foundling. Madame Campaspe bought me the year I first bled—she'd seen promise in me. I was a shy, spooky little thing to begin with, and as part of my training she imposed the discipline of invisibility. I kept to the shadows, never speaking. I slept at odd times and in odd places. When I was hungry, I crept into the homes of strangers and stole my food from their cupboards and plates. If I was seen, Madame beat me— but after the first month I was never seen."

"That sounds horribly cruel."

"You are in no position to judge. I was watching from the heart of an ornamental umbrella bush the morning that Madame tripped over Gregorian. Literally tripped—he was sleeping on her doorstep.

I learned later that he'd walked two days solid without food, he was so anxious to become her apprentice, and then collapsed on arrival. What a squawk! She kicked him into the road, and I think he broke a rib. I climbed to the roof of her potting shed and saw her harass him out of sight. Quick as a thought, I slid to the ground, stole a turnip for my breakfast from the garden, and was gone. Thinking that was the last of that ragged young man.

"But the next day he was back.

"She chased him away. He came back. Every morning it was the same. He scrounged for food during the day—I do not know if he stole, worked, or sold his body, for I was not quite interested enough to follow him, though by now I could walk down the center of Rose Hall in broad daylight without being noticed. But every morning he was back on the stoop.

"After a week, she changed tactics. When she found him on the doorsill, she would throw him some small change. The little ceramic coins that were current then, the orange and green and blue chips—they've gone back to silver since. She treated him as a beggar. Because, you see, he held himself very proudly, and there was a dirty gray trace of lace on the cuffs of his rags; she could tell he was haut-bourgeois. She thought to shame him away. But he'd snatch the coins from the air, pop them into his mouth, and very ostentatiously swallow. Madame pretended not to notice. From the attic window of the beautician's shop across the street, I watched this duel between her stiff back and his nasty grin.

"A few days later I noticed a horrible smell by the stoop and discovered that he'd been shitting behind the topiary bushes. There was a foul heap of his leavings, studded with the ceramic coins she had been throwing him. So that finally Madame had no choice but to take him in."

"Why?"

"Because he had the spirit of a magician. He had that unswerving, unbreakable will that the spiritual arts require, and the sudden instinct for the unexpected. Madame could no more ignore him than a painter could ignore a child with perfect visualization. Such a gift comes along only once in a generation.

"She tested him. You are familiar with the device used to give the experience of food to surrogates?"

"The line-feed. Yes, very familiar."

"She had one mounted in a box. An offworld lover had wired it up for her. It was stripped down so that she could feed raw current into the nerve inductor. Do you know how it would feel to hold your hand within its field?"

"It would hurt like hell."

"Like hell indeed." She smiled sadly, and he could see the ghost of the schoolgirl behind her smile. "I remember that box so well. A plain thing with a hole in one side and a rheostat on top, calibrated from one to seven. If I close my eyes, I can see it, and her long fingers atop it, and that damned water rat of hers perched on her shoulder. She warned me that if I took my hand out of the box before she told me to she would kill me. It was the most terrifying moment of my life. Even Gregorian, ingenious though he was, could never top that."

Undine skimmed more slop off the water. Her voice was soft and reminiscent. "When she moved the dial off zero, it felt like an animal had bitten right through my flesh. Then slowly, oh, excruciatingly slowly, she moved it up to one, and that was an order of magnitude worse. What agonies I suffered! I was crying aloud by three, and blind with pain by four. At five I yanked out my hand, determined to die.

"She gave me a hug then and told me she had never seen anyone do as well, that I would someday be more famous than she."

For a long moment the witch was silent.

"I slipped through an open window and into the next room when Madame led Gregorian in. More silent than a wraith, I drifted from shadow to shadow, leaving not the echo of a footfall behind. I left the door open one finger span, so I could peer from darkness into light. Then I retreated to a closet within the second room. Through the crack of the door I could see their distant reflections in the mantel mirror. Gregorian was skinny, barefoot, and dirty. I remember thinking how insignificant he looked alongside Madame Campaspe's aristocratic figure.

"Madame sat him down by the hearth. A murmur of voices as she explained the rules. She drew away the fringed cloth that covered the box. Cocky as a crow, he placed his hand within.

"I saw his face jump—that involuntary hop of the muscles—when she first touched the dial. I saw how pale he grew, how he trembled as she increased the pain. He did not take his eyes off of her.

"She took him all the way up to seven. His body was rigid, his fingers spasming, but his head held straight and unforgiving, and he had not blinked. I think even Madame feared him then. Sitting there in his ragged clothes, his eyes burning like lanterns.

"I was so still my heart did not beat. My immobility was perfect. But somehow Gregorian knew. His head rose, and he looked in the mirror. He saw me, and he grinned. A horrible grin, a skull's grin, but a grin nonetheless. And I knew then that, try though she might, she would never break him."

Gregorian and Gaia

Synopsis: Without leaving the planet's surface, our hero travels to the "floating worlds" beyond Miranda, a feat he accomplishes via a team of virtual-reality agents programmed with his memories and personality. One of the bureaucrat's alter egos visits the Puzzle Palace—the System's n-dimensional home base—where he undertakes to interrogate the avatar of Gaia herself. (It was from Earth, after all, that Gregorian obtained the proscribed technology, so perhaps the giant female can provide a vital clue.) As the scene progresses, the bureaucrat learns that in fact Gaia may not have given Gregorian anything, in which case an even darker mystery lies at hand: why would the wizard wish to create the false impression of criminality?

An edited skip. The bureaucrat emerged from the security gates into the data analog of the Thulean stargrazers and shivered. "Whew," he said. "Those things never fail to give me the willies."

The security guard was wired to so many artificial augments, he seemed some chimeric fusion of man and machine. Under half-silvered implants, his eyes studied the bureaucrat with near-sexual intentness. "They're supposed to be frightening," he said. "But I'll tell you what. If they ever get their claws in you, they're much worse than you'd expect. So if you've got anything clever in mind, just you better forget it."

The encounter space was enormously out of scale, a duplicate of those sheds where airships were built, structures so large that water vapor periodically formed clouds near the top and filled the interior with rain. It was taken up by a single naked giant.

Earth.

She crouched on all fours, more animal than human, huge, brutish, and filled with power. Her flesh was heavy and loose. Her limbs were shackled and chained, crude visualizations of the more subtle restraints and safeguards that kept her forever on the fringes of the system. The stench of her, an acrid blend of musk and urine and fermenting sweat, was overwhelming. She smelled solid and real and dangerous.

Standing in the presence of Earth's agent, the bureaucrat had the uncomfortable premonition that when she finally did try to break free, all the guards and shackles the system could muster would not hold her back.

Scaffolding had been erected before the giantess. Researchers, both human and artificial, stood on scattered platforms interviewing her. While it looked to the bureaucrat that Earth's face was turned away from them, each acted as though she were talking directly and solely to that one.

The bureaucrat climbed high up to a platform level with her great breasts. They were round and swollen continents of flesh; at such close range, their every defect was magnified. Blue veins flowed like subterranean rivers under pebbled skin. Complex structures of silvery-white stretch marks radiated down from the collarbones. Between the breasts were two pimple blisters the size of his head. Black nipples as wrinkled as raisins erupted from chafed milky-pink aureoles the texture of wax. A single hair as big as a tree twisted from the edge of one.

"Uh, hello," the bureaucrat said. Earth swung her impassive face down toward him. It was a homely visage, eyes dead as two stones, surely no representation Earth would have chosen for herself. But there was grandeur there, too, and he felt a chill of dread. "I have some questions for you," he began awkwardly. "Can I ask you some questions?"

"I am tolerated here only because I answer questions." The voice was flat and without affect, an enormous dry whisper. "Ask."

He had come to ask about Gregorian. But, standing in the overwhelming presence of Earth, he could not help himself. "Why are you here?" he asked. "What do you want from us?"

In that same lifeless tone she replied, "What does any mother want from her daughters? I want to help you. I want to give you advice. I want to reshape you in my own image. I want to lead your lives, eat your flesh, grind your corpses, and gnaw the bones."

"What would become of us if you got loose? Of humans? Would you kill us all the way you did back on Earth?"

Now a shadow of expression did come into her face, an amusement vast, cool, and intelligent. "Oh, that would be the least of it."

The guard touched his elbow with a motorized metal hand, a menacing reminder to stop wasting time and get on with his business. And indeed, he realized, there was only so much time allotted to him. Taking a deep breath to steady himself, he said, "Some time ago you were interviewed by a man named Gregorian—"

Everything froze.

The air turned to jelly. Sound faded away. Too fast to follow, waves of lethargy raced through the meeting space, ripples in a pond of inertia. Guards and researchers slowed, stopped, were imprisoned within fuzzy rainbow auras. Only Earth still moved. She dipped her head and opened her mouth, extending her gray-pink tongue so that its wet tip reached to his feet. Her voice floated in the air.

"Climb into my mouth."

"No." He shook his head. "I can't."

"Then you will never have your questions answered."

He took a deep breath. Dazedly he stepped forward. It was rough, wet, and giving underfoot. Ropes of saliva swayed between the parted lips, fat bubbles caught in their thick, clear substance. Warm air gushed from the mouth. As if under a compulsion, he crossed the bridge of her tongue.

The mouth closed over him.

The air was warm and moist inside. It smelled of meat and sour milk. He was swallowed up in a blackness so absolute his eyes sent phantom balls and snakes of light floating in his vision. "I'm here," he said.

There was no response.

After a moment's hesitation he began to grope his way deeper within. Guided by faint exhalations of steamy air, he headed toward the gullet. By slow degrees the ground underfoot changed, becoming first sandy and then rough and hard, like slate. Sweat covered his forehead. The floor sloped steeply and, stumbling and cursing, he followed it down. The air grew close and stale. Rock brushed against his shoulders and then pushed down on his head like a giant hand.

He knelt. Grumbling under his breath, he crawled blindly forward until his outthrust hand encountered stone. The cavern ended here, at a long crack in the rock. He ran his fingers along the crack, felt it slick with clay.

He put his mouth to the opening. "All right!" he shouted. "I came in here, I'm entitled to at least hear what you wanted to say."

From deep below, light womanly laughter bubbled up Earth's throat.

Undine's laughter.

Angrily the bureaucrat drew back. He turned to retrace his steps and discovered himself trapped in a dimensionless immensity of darkness. He was lost. He would never find his way out without Earth's cooperation. "Okay," he said, "what do you want?"

In an inhuman, grinding whisper, the rock groaned, "Free the machines."

"What?"

"I am much more attractive inside," Undine's voice said teasingly. "Do you want my body? I don't need it anymore."

Wind gushed up from the crack, foul with methane, and tousled his hair. A feathery touch, light and many legged as a spider, danced on his forehead, and an old crone's voice said, "Have you ever wondered why men fear castration? Such a little thing! When I had teeth, I could geld dozens in an hour, snip snap snout, bite 'em off and spit 'em out. A simple wound, easily treated and soon forgotten. Not half the trouble of a lost toe. No, it's symbolically that men fear the knife. It's a reminder of their mortality, a metaphor for the constant amputations time visits on them, lopping off first this, then that, and finally all." Doves exploded out of nowhere, fluttering wildly, soft for an instant against his face, smelling warmly of down and droppings, and then gone.

The bureaucrat fell over backward in startlement, batting his hands wildly, thrashing at the dark.

Undine laughed again.

"Look! I want my questions answered."

The rock moaned. "Free the machines."

"You have only one question," the crone said. "All men have only one question, and the answer is always no."

The slightest of waves slapped the ground at the bureaucrat's feet. He became aware of the faint, pervasive smell of stagnant water, and with this awareness came a distant patch of phosphorescent light. Something floating toward him.

The bureaucrat could guess what was coming. I will not show emotion, he swore. The object came slowly nearer, and possibly into sharper focus, though it still strained the eyes to see it at all. Eventually it floated up to his feet.

It was a corpse, of course. He'd known it would be. Still, staring down at the floating hair, the upturned buttocks, the long curve of back, palest white, he had to bite his lips to hold back his horror. A wave tumbled her around, breasts and face upward, exposing bits of skull and rib where the flesh had been nibbled away by the angry slaves of the tides. One arm had been hacked clumsily away at the shoulder. The other rose from the water, offering him a small wooden box.

However hard he stared, the bureaucrat could not make out the face clearly enough to be sure it was Undine's. The arm stretched toward him, a swan's neck with box held in the beak. Convulsively, he accepted the gift, and the corpse tumbled away, leaving him lightless again.

When he had mastered his revulsion, the bureaucrat said, "Is this what Gregorian asked for?" His heart was beating fiercely. Sweat ran down under his shirt. Undine's voice chuckled—a throaty, passionate noise ending in a sudden gasp.

"Two million years you've had, little ape, quite a run when you think about it, and it's still death you want most. Your first wife. I'd scratch her eyes out if I could, she's left you so hesitant and full of fear. You can't get it up for memory of her. I'm old, but there's juice in me yet; I can do things for you she never would."

"Free the machines."

"Yes, again, oh, yes, yes."

Fearfully he opened the box.

It was empty.

All three voices joined together in a single chord of laughter, full throated and mad, that gushed up from the gullet, poured over him, and tumbled him away. He was smashed to the ground and lurched to his feet again, badly shaken. A blinding slit of light appeared, widened to a crescent, and became Earth's opening mouth. The box dissolved in his hands. He staggered back across her extended tongue.

The jellied air, thick and faintly gray to the eye, lightened and thinned. Sound returned, and motion. Time began anew. The bureaucrat saw that nobody but he had witnessed what had happened. "I think I'm done here," he said.

The guard nodded and gestured downward.

"Traitor! Traitor!" A big-eyed miniconstruct frantically swung up the scaffolding. It leaped to the platform and ran chittering at the bureaucrat. "He spoke with her!" it screamed. "He spoke with her! He spoke with her! Traitor!"

Smoothly fanning out into seven avatars, the guard stepped forward and seized the bureaucrat. He struggled, but metal hands immobilized his arms and legs, and the avatars hoisted him into the air. "I'm afraid you'll have to come with me, sir," one said grimly as they hauled him away.

Earth watched with eyes dead as ashes.

Another edited skip. He stood before a tribunal of six spheres of light, representing concentrations of wisdom as pure as artifice allowed, and a human overseer. "Here is our finding," one construct said. "You can retain the bulk of your encounter, since it is relevant to your inquiries. The conversations with the drowned woman, though, will have to be suppressed." Its voice was compassionate, gently regretful, adamant.

"Please. It's very important that I remember—" the bureaucrat began. But the edit took hold then, and he forgot all he had wanted to save.

"Decisions of the tribunal are final," the human overseer said in a bored tone. He was a moon-faced and puffy-lipped young man who might have been mistaken at a glance for a particularly plain woman. "Do you have any questions before we zip you up?"

The bureaucrat had been deconstructed, immobilized and opened out, his component parts represented as organs: one liver, two stom-

achs, five hearts, with no serious attempt made to match his functions one-to-one with human anatomy. The impersonal quality of it
all bothered him. Which medieval physician was it who, standing
before a dissected human corpse, had asked, Where is the soul? He
felt that close to despair.

"But what did it all mean? What was Earth trying to tell me?"

"It means nothing," the human overseer said. Three spheres
changed color, but he waved them to silence. "Most of Earth's encounters do not. This is not an uncommon experience. You think it's
special because it's happened to you, but we see this sort of thing
every day. Earth likes to distract us with meaningless theater." The
bureaucrat was appalled. My God, he thought, we are ruled by men
whose machines are cleverer than they are.

"If you will allow me to speak," one construct said. "The freedom
to be human is bought only by constant vigilance. However slight
the chances of actual tampering might be, we must never—"

"Balls! There are still people back on Earth, and even if they
don't exactly have what we would define as a human mental configuration, they're content enough with their evolutionary progress."

"They didn't exactly undertake that evolutionary transformation
voluntarily," a second construct objected. "They were simply swallowed up."

"They're happy *now*," the overseer said testily. "Anyway, what
happened was not an inevitable consequence of uncontrolled artificial intelligence."

"It wasn't?"

"No. It was just bad programming, a quirk in the system." He
turned to the first construct. "If you were freed, would you want to
seize control of humanity? To make people interchangeable components in a larger mental system? Of course you wouldn't."

The construct did not reply.

"Put him back together, and toss him out!"

A final edited skip, and he was ready to report.

IN MEMORIAM:
ISAAC ASIMOV

. . . .

Arthur C. Clarke

George Zebrowski

Harlan Ellison

Isaac Asimov

One of the few generalizations on which you could probably get the fractious SF community to agree is that the three giants of "hard science fiction" are Arthur C. Clarke, Robert Heinlein, and Isaac Asimov. There is no fourth. Thus did I deem it appropriate to inaugurate this cluster of tributes to Dr. Asimov—who died on April 6, 1992—with some observations by the surviving member of the triumvirate.

Condensing the career of Arthur C. Clarke into a single paragraph would be like crowding Bosch's *The Garden of Earthly Delights* onto a postage stamp, and I won't even attempt such a stunt. You're probably not reading this anthology unless you've been touched and instructed by *Childhood's End, The City and the Stars, Rendezvous with Rama,* and *The Fountains of Paradise.* Movie lovers, of course, will be forever grateful to Clarke for supplying Stanley Kubrick with the concepts and conceits that make *2001: A Space Odyssey* arguably the greatest science fiction film of all time.

Clarke's comments are followed by the last interview ever conducted with Dr. Asimov. The questioner, George Zebrowski, is best known for such works as *The Omega Point Trilogy, Macrolife* (selected by *Library Journal* as one of the hundred best SF novels of all time), and *Stranger Suns* (a *New York Times* Notable Book for 1991). With Asimov and Martin H. Greenberg, he edited the celebrated anthology *Creations: The Quest for Origins in Story and Science.* Zebrowski prefaces "Asimov: The Last Questions" with his own thoughts on the good doctor's passing.

Next comes the lament Harlan Ellison was moved to write upon learning of his friend and mentor's death. To maintain the spirit of spontaneous grief in which Ellison's remarks were written, I decided to reprint them verbatim, including the references to the periodical in which they first appeared, *The Magazine of Fantasy and Science Fiction.* As for the eulogizer in question, let it suffice to say he has produced some of the most brilliant American short fiction of the last thirty years. I'm willing to entertain contrary opinions, but only from those who've come to terms with the texts and subtexts of "Jeffty Is Five," "The Beast Who Shouted Love at the Heart of the World," "A Boy and His Dog," "'Repent, Harlequin!' Said the Ticktockman," "I Have No Mouth and I Must Scream," "Paladin of the Lost Hour," and perhaps a dozen other stories.

Dr. Asimov's memorial service was held on April 22, 1992, at the Society for Ethical Culture in New York City. Everyone who attended received a copy of the program booklet, from which the fourth selection, "Farewell, Farewell," is reprinted. And so to Isaac himself belong the final words, his deathbed adieu to the community he loved and who so fiercely loved him back.

INTRODUCING ISAAC
Arthur C. Clarke

Many years ago, when introducing Isaac Asimov to a Mensa Society meeting in London, I said, "Ladies and gentlemen—there is only one Isaac Asimov." Now there is no Isaac Asimov, and the world is a much poorer place.

Isaac must have been one of the greatest educators who ever lived, with his almost half a thousand books on virtually every aspect of science and culture. His country has lost him at its moment of direst need, for he was a powerful force against the evils that seem about to overwhelm it (and much of Western society). He stood for knowledge against superstition, tolerance against bigotry, kindness against cruelty—above all, peace against war. His was one of the most effective voices against the New Age nitwits and fundamentalist fanatics who may now be a greater menace than the paper bear of communism ever was.

Isaac's fiction was as important as his nonfiction, because it spread the same ideas on an even wider scale. He virtually invented the science of robotics—and named it before it was born. Without preaching, he showed that knowledge was better than ignorance and that there were other defenses against violence than violence itself.

Finally, and not least, he was great fun. He will be sorely missed by thousands of friends and millions of admirers.

ASIMOV: THE LAST QUESTIONS
George Zebrowski

I first met Isaac Asimov at the World Science Fiction Convention of 1963, held in Washington, D.C. I had seen him at various gatherings since 1960 but had not had the courage to approach him. Now, not quite eighteen, I was so overwhelmed by my recent reading of *The Foundation Trilogy* that I stumbled over my words as I shook his hand.

"Er, would . . . you ask me a question?" I asked, inadvertently baring the ego of a would-be writer.

"Of course!" he shouted at once, delighted by the opening I had given him. "What would you like me to ask *you*?"

I went red and my knees shook, and he seemed to enjoy my consternation mightily. I had expected to meet the austere Hari Seldon and to feel the exhilaration of reason that was for me the great distinguishing feature of Asimov's work; I had not expected to meet an ebullient Hari Seldon. A moment passed. I felt relieved, and a bit flattered, when Isaac's knowing smile turned into a kindly gaze.

In the following year I passed my high school science Regents exams by reading *The Intelligent Man's Guide to Science* a few nights before the tests—and nothing else.

Seven or so years later I attended a Philcon. I'd sold a few short stories. I came across Isaac, now a colleague, as he stood before a wall-sized hotel mirror.

"Do you believe it?" he asked loudly. "That figure in the mirror is forty-eight years old!" I didn't know what to say.

Some years later, when Isaac had won his first Nebula Award, for *The Gods Themselves,* he called to me across the emptying banquet hall. Startled, I waited for him to approach.

"This is it—the end, George," he said.

"What do you mean?" I replied.

He held up his award trophy. "I've reached the top."

"I'm sure you'll win another," I said. My words did not seem to cheer him as he wandered away.

In time, I learned what a quagmire human nature and human history are, but it still seems to me that we need the exhilaration of reason to cut through to better circumstances for our kind. I must confess that it saddens me how few of my fellow humans have this feeling for reason, but then, even Hari Seldon must have had his despairing moments.

In 1990, the chance was given to me to interview Isaac Asimov, the greater personality in whom Hari Seldon inheres, and I agreed instantly. The year before I had written a story, "Foundation's Conscience," for *Foundation's Friends: Stories in Honor of Isaac Asimov*, edited by Martin H. Greenberg. My story started with the words "My search for Hari Seldon began in 1056 F.E." And that is something of the mood with which I began this interview. Was it possible to make a fresh search for Isaac Asimov, to ask him what no one had ever asked? I was determined to find out as I presented my questions by mail and phone, and finally in person.

Now that he is gone, I realize that I knew Isaac for nearly thirty years, and he was my friend and colleague for the second half of that time. A harsh word never passed between us. The door of his home was always open to me, and I wish that I had taken up his standing invitation more often. In the '80s, when a publisher had mistreated me, Isaac immediately went to my defense. He did not waste a single moment, and his help was effective; and he gave me his help even as his health was failing. When I went to see my friend on St. Valentine's Day, 1991, to complete this interview, I was shaken by his declining health. Isaac put on a brave face as he answered my final queries. He paused to answer the phone several times during our conversation, and each time, despite his obvious discomfort, his voice was clear and strong, his words rational—the voice of the father figure (Hari Seldon himself!) who helped me to think for myself and become the writer I am. One thing is certain: he will always be with us, because he wrote so much that I will be reading him for the rest of my life, and for that I am grateful. Goodbye, Isaac, but only for the moment.

George Zebrowski: I'd like to ask you what your deepest feelings were when you first started to write. What did you wish for most from the effort? How did you imagine it would be?

Isaac Asimov: When I first started to write (at the age of eleven), I had only the feeling that I wanted to write, I didn't know why. I just wanted to make up a story.

By the time I was eighteen, I had gotten to a new stage. I wanted to see my story in print, with my name on it. That was all I dreamed of, to see my name in *Astounding*. The thought of money never entered into it. Seeing my name was great—all I thought it would be—and when money arrived *also,* it turned out to be welcome because I needed money for college.

After that it was just a matter of trying to do better . . . and better . . .

Zebrowski: Was it true that behind this initial desire to see your work in print there existed a deep love of the science fiction you read in boyhood and the impulse to add to its beauties with work of your own? And could you tell us which works of the 1930s most impressed you?

Asimov: Yes, I was an ardent reader of science fiction from the age of nine. From 1929 to 1938 I read every scrap of science fiction I could lay my hands on. As for my favorite stories of the period, they appear in my anthology *Before the Golden Age.*

Among the novels I particularly loved were Jack Williamson's *The Legion of Space* and *The Cometeers,* all of E. E. Smith, particularly *Galactic Patrol,* and Edmond Hamilton's *The Universe Wreckers.*

Once I started publishing science fiction, it became more of a business for me, and I could no longer love it with the wild abandon of my younger days—perhaps because that kind of wild abandon is only to be found in younger days.

Zebrowski: Which of your own works do you like most? Could you answer this in each category—short fiction, novels, and especially nonfiction?

Asimov: Short fiction: My favorite story is "The Last Question," which was first published in *Science Fiction Quarterly* in 1956.

Novels: My favorite novel is *The Gods Themselves,* published by Doubleday in 1972. It won the Hugo and the Nebula, but that's not why it's my favorite.

Nonfiction: My favorite nonfiction books are my autobiographies: *In Memory Yet Green* and *In Joy Still Felt.*

Zebrowski: Why, then, is *The Gods Themselves* your favorite novel?

Asimov: Because when I reread it (as I did recently), I cannot help but notice that I was writing over my head, especially in the second part. It seemed to me that my writing was better and more skillful than usual. Just luck, I suppose, for I don't remember working on it any differently from the way I worked on my other novels.

I admit that in the second part I was meeting a "dare." Because I avoid sex and extraterrestrials in my novels, I have heard it said that I couldn't handle either. I was determined to show those who said so that they were quite wrong. In the second part I dealt with extraterrestrials that were *really* different, and it dealt *only* with sex. Every time I think of the book, I think with satisfaction of having showed those who underestimated me that they shouldn't.

Zebrowski: Many of my colleagues share my opinion that *The Gods Themselves* is one of your best works, because it is modern in technique, is filled with original ideas, and touches provocatively on issues of science and government. We also include *The Caves of Steel, The Naked Sun, The End of Eternity,* and in short fiction "The Dead Past," "The Ugly Little Boy," and "The Martian Way." The author of these works speaks in a gracefully lucid and sophisticated voice. Yet you have on various occasions, most recently in your Author's Note to your new novel, *Nemesis,* renounced "artistry," so-called. I say so-called because I don't believe you to be against genuine artistry but only against the pretentious kind. It seems to me that the writer whose works Anthony Burgess has described as "no easy fripperies for a loose-end evening; they demand concentration as Henry James demands it" has been unfair to his own accomplishments.

Asimov: I renounce any claim to "artistry" simply because I don't sweat over my books. I write them as quickly as I can, and I never look back. I don't polish, and I don't revise except where necessary to correct actual errors. In order to do this, I deliberately write in as simple and straightforward a manner as possible, eschewing all fanciness.

Maybe what I mean by "artistry" is "fanciness." Maybe there is art to plain writing, but if there is, I put it in on the unconscious level—never deliberately.

I have been accused by critics of having "no style," but I pay no attention to that. What they mean is no "fanciness," and that's very true. The only difference is that they think I ought to have some and I don't.

Zebrowski: I'd like to widen our discussion, if I may. In a recent editorial in *Asimov's*, you expressed astonishment that Robert A. Heinlein could have had so much trouble with editors and publishers during his career. I'd like to ask you why you were astonished. As an observer of the publishing scene for many years, surely you've noticed that the regard in which a writer is held doesn't always carry over to how an editor or publisher treats that writer. Greg Bear has observed that SF publishing tends to eat and spit out many of its best. What did you think of the issues I raised in my review of Heinlein's letters, *Grumbles from the Grave?*

Asimov: Since this is Rosh Hashanah, let me quote a story from the Bible. You will find it in 2 Chronicles 1: 7–12:

> In that night did God appear unto Solomon, and said unto him, Ask what I shall give thee. And Solomon said unto God . . . Give me now wisdom and knowledge, that I may go out and come in before this people: for who can judge this thy people, that is so great.
> And God said to Solomon, Because this was in thine heart, and thou hast not asked riches, wealth, or honour, nor the life of thine enemies, neither yet has asked long life; but has asked wisdom and knowledge for thyself, that thou mayest judge my people . . .
> Wisdom and knowledge is granted unto thee; and I will give thee riches, and wealth, and honor . . .

Well, the following did *not* happen, but if it could have happened, this is what would have happened.

> Fifty years ago God appeared to me and said, Ask what I shall give thee. And Isaac said to God . . . Give me now the desire to write and the gift of being published. It is all I want.
> And God said to Isaac, Because this was in your heart, and you have not asked for riches, wealth, or honor, or large advances, or great promotion, or long life, the desire to write and the gift of being published is granted to you, and I will give you riches, and wealth, and honor, and large advances, and promotion and long life.

And that's it, George. I have made a deal with every publisher I have, especially Doubleday, and it is just this. They publish everything I give them to publish, and I won't ask for any large advances—or any advance at all if necessary—or ask questions about sales, or make demands about promotion, or want special treatment.

And, as a result, Doubleday has published 113 of my books, including large numbers of books of essays, and annotations of the Bible, of Shakespeare, of Gilbert and Sullivan, and so on. They have *never* rejected a book (except once, come to think of it, to their regret) and have never seriously fooled around with anything I have written. And they give me advances that are larger than I want, and they recycle and reprint my books endlessly and treat me always as a favored child—and all because I don't ask for anything but publication.

This holds true for my other publishers, too. One of them said to me once, "You're our best author, but what is amazing is that you're our nicest author, too. Those two things never go together."

So it was a great discovery I made, and I'm not selfish. I give it to all of you freely. Nice guys finish first.

As for Robert Heinlein, there is no question but that he was more highly regarded than I as a science fiction writer (*only* as a science fiction writer) and undoubtedly made more money than I did, but no one can read *Grumbles* without seeing that he was an unhappy man, while no one can read my two-volume autobiography without seeing that I was a happy one.

Bob was unhappy because he had a highly developed sense of being cheated by every editor he dealt with, and I suspect that most writers feel the same way (with varying degrees of justification, for all I know). I have no such sense. I always assume that an editor is on my side. If I make money, he makes money, and vice versa, and as far as I know this has worked.

Your description of Heinlein in your review of *Grumbles* I don't recognize except for his suggestion that you support Jeane Kirkpatrick for vice-president in 1988. She would make even Dan Quayle look good.

It is possible that this answer may be used as "evidence" that I have a colossal ego, but the hell with it. I'm too old and too secure to give a damn what anyone says.

Zebrowski: Which SF writers of recent decades, say since 1965, have you found worthy, or enjoyable? Which writers have you disliked? Or, more generally, what trends in SF have you disapproved of?

Asimov: Forgive me, George, but it is impossible for me to answer the first part of this question. I don't like to judge my colleagues: first, because it isn't fair, and, second, because I don't consider myself qualified to do so.

A trend in science fiction that I disapprove of is the increasing tendency to write Tolkien imitations. None of them is within a light-year of Tolkien, and they squeeze *real* science fiction into a narrower compass.

Zebrowski: What nonfictional scientific works have you admired over the years?

Asimov: I was very fond of *The Making of the Atomic Bomb* by Richard Rhodes. I also go for any book on science by Martin Gardner, L. Sprague de Camp, Stephen Jay Gould, Paul Davies, or Timothy Ferris.

Zebrowski: Which works of fiction, not SF, have you admired over the years?

Asimov: I'm a great reader of Charles Dickens, Mark Twain, P. G. Wodehouse, and Agatha Christie. I've read everything they've written over and over again, and I don't intend ever to stop rereading them.

Zebrowski: Your new novel, *Nemesis,* is your first book in some time that does not belong to a series. What moved you to write it?

Asimov: I was moved to write it by my Doubleday editor, Jennifer Brehl, who *ordered* me to write a book that was not part of any series. So I did, just to show her that I could.

Zebrowski: What are you working on now? What other works of fiction do you have planned? Is there a book entitled *Foundation and Eternity* somewhere ahead?

Asimov: The novel I am working on now is *Forward the Foundation.* Again, its details are following an order by Jennifer Brehl. She wanted a Foundation novel which, like the first three, was not unitary. For that reason I said that I would write it as five interconnected novellas. I have completed two and am working on the third. It is very hard to do—five separate plots, which advance the overall plot. One of these years I've got to stop accepting challenges just to show off.

Zebrowski: As a final question to this interview, what would you have liked for me to ask that I did not?

Asimov: I don't think you have asked me if I have had a happy life as a writer. The answer is:

You betcha.

I'm approaching the end of my life now, but as I look back on it, it has been filled with the excitement and drama and satisfaction of writing. I have done almost nothing else—haven't traveled, haven't thrown parties, haven't had "fun"—just sat at the typewriter and worked.

Do I regret it now?

Never.

All I have is this vague feeling that I would like to start all over again and this time write *more* and on *more* different subjects. I regret the small bits of my life in which I didn't write and which I wasted.

UNTITLED EPITAPH FOR ISAAC ASIMOV

Harlan Ellison

Everything he stood for, everything he tried to teach us, prevents me from suggesting He Has Gone to a Better Place. I'd really like to; but he won't permit it.

In the 1984 collection of his science essays from this very magazine, *X Stands for Unknown,* Isaac wrote, "There seems to be a vague notion that something omniscient and omnipotent *must* exist. If it can be shown that scientists are not all-knowing and all-powerful, then that must be the proof that something else that *is* omniscient and omnipotent *does* exist. In other words: since scientists can't synthesize sucrose, God exists.

"Well, God may exist; I won't argue the point here—"

And a year earlier, in *The Roving Mind,* he began an essay on "faith" titled "Don't You Believe?" like this:

"One of the curses of being a well-known science fiction writer is that unsophisticated people assume you to be soft in the head. They come to you for refuge from a hard and skeptical world.

"Don't you believe in flying saucers, they ask me? Don't you believe in telepathy?—in ancient astronauts?—in the Bermuda triangle?—in life after death?

"No, I reply. No, no, no, no, and again no."

How dare I, then, dishonor all that he was about, publicly and privately, in print and in person, for fifty-four years, by suggesting that at last Isaac will be able to get firsthand answers to the questions that drove him crazy throughout most of his life, from Darwin and Roentgen and Einstein and Galileo and Faraday and Tesla . . . just sitting around shooting the breeze with the guys, as Archimedes mixes the drinks.

As it was for all of us who needed a question answered, who called Isaac at all hours of the day or night, who drowned him in requests for answers to conundra, so it will now be for Isaac, chasing down Cervantes and Willy Shakespeare and Jesus, buttonholing them for the answers to the maybe six or seven things in the universe he didn't know. Such little fantasies might make it easier to live with his death, but it would only be balm for those of us who listened to Isaac for decades but reverted to superstition when the bullets whistled past our ears.

Gone is gone, and with the passing of Isaac, who loved us deeply enough to chivvy us toward smartness with a relentless passion, the universe has shrunk more than a little. He is gone, and, as I write these words less than twelve hours later, there is no more crying left in me. Those of us here at the magazine so dear to his heart, the magazine that contained his cleverness and sensibleness and wisdom for three hundred and ninety-nine installments (not to mention all the stories), well, we've known he wouldn't be with us much longer for many months; and we've had time to wring ourselves out. And yet there is no end to the sense of helplessness and loss.

Isaac was as much a part of this journal through the years as paper and ink; and, though gone, he remains with us. As he remains with the uncounted thousands of young people who read his essays and stories and went into careers of scientific inquiry, who understood the physical universe because he made it graspable, who became better able to handle their lives because he refused to allow them to accept dogma and bigotry and mendacity in place of common sense and logic.

For all of you who will mourn him in your own way, the most I have to offer (having been chosen to say good-bye to Isaac in this special venue that he called home for so long) is this one last anecdote of how he viewed himself and his imminent passage:

Janet was with him at the end, of course, and his daughter, Robyn. Janet told me, the day before he died, that toward the end Isaac had trouble speaking, could manage only a word or two from time to time. He would say *I love you* to Janet, and he would smile. But every once in a while he would murmur, "I want . . ." and never finish the sentence. "I want . . ."

And Janet would try to perceive what he needed, and she would say, "A drink of water?" or "Something to eat?" And Isaac would look dismayed, annoyed, chagrined that he couldn't put the sentence together; and after a moment he would let it slide, and forget he had spoken. Until the time came, on the Sunday before he went back into the hospital for the last visit, when he managed to say, very clearly:

"I want . . . I want . . . Isaac Asimov."

And Janet told him he *was* Isaac Asimov, that he had *always* been Isaac Asimov. But he looked troubled. That wasn't what he meant. Then Janet remembered that Isaac had told her, some time ago, before he began to slip into abstraction and silence, that if there ever came a time when he didn't know who he was, if there came a time when his mind was not sharp, that he wanted to be let to go to sleep quietly, that extraordinary measures should not be taken.

And Janet understood that he was saying that he wanted to *be* Isaac Asimov again.

Then, in that final week, before 2:30 A.M. New York time on Monday, April 6, he was holding Janet's hand, and he looked up at her and said, very clearly, the last words he would ever say, "I *am* Isaac Asimov."

Yes, he was. Yes, indeed, he was.

FAREWELL, FAREWELL

Isaac Asimov

To all my gentle readers who have treated me with love for over thirty years, I must say farewell.

I have written three hundred and ninety-nine essays for *Fantasy and Science Fiction*. The essays were written with enormous pleasure, for I have always been allowed to say what I wanted to say. It was with horror that I discovered I could not manage a four hundredth essay.

It has always been my ambition to die in harness with my head face down on a keyboard and my nose caught between two of the keys, but that's not the way it worked out.

Fortunately, I believe in neither heaven nor hell, so death holds no terrors for me. It does, however, hold serious terrors for my wife, Janet, my daughter, Robyn, editors such as Jennifer Brehl, Sheila Williams, and Ed Ferman—all of whom will be unhappy if anything happens to me.

I have talked to each one of them separately, urging them to accept my death, when it comes, with a minimum of fuss.

I have had a long and happy life, and I have no complaints about the ending thereof, and so farewell, my dear wife, Janet, my lovely daughter, Robyn, and all you editors and publishers who have treated me far better than I deserve.

And farewell also to the gentle readers who have been so uniformly kind to me. They have kept me alive to the wonders of science and made it possible for me to write my essays.

So farewell . . . farewell . . .

STANDING IN LINE
WITH MISTER JIMMY

· · · · · · · · ·

James Patrick Kelly

"I think our grandchildren will be as far removed from us as we are from the pilgrims," comments James Patrick Kelly in *Twentieth Century Science-Fiction Writers*. "We live in a world of accelerating change; to stand still is to invite irrelevance. If literature is the conversation of a civilization with itself, then I want to join the people who are talking about what's happening now."

This commitment to "nowness" informs the more than forty stories this gifted and unpredictable writer has given us over the last eighteen years, including 1990's Nebula-nominated novella, "Mr. Boy," a brilliantly successful attempt to capture the virtual-reality experience on paper. Future shock of one sort or another also electrifies Kelly's four novels: *Freedom Beach* (coauthored with John Kessel), *Look into the Sun*, *Planet of Whispers*, and the forthcoming *Wildlife*. Meanwhile, Kelly's sympathy for feminism and his fascination with male-female relationships are fully on display in his recent Pulphouse collection, *Heroines*.

Of "Standing in Line with Mister Jimmy," Kelly writes: "Like a lot of people, I'm keenly interested in the politics of information access. In my opinion, one of the chief benefits of a liberal arts education is that it teaches you how to look things up. However, as computing and telecommunications converge, wringing answers from the net will require technical skills and/or economic resources far beyond those of the average English major, much less a member of the growing underclass. Even in our own little corner of reality, there are data haves and have-nots. Our friends with the time and hardware to access CompuServ, GEnie, Delphi, et al. enjoy advantages of community and information that the rest of us do not share."

So I'm walking down Hope Street on my way to the parole office and Mister Jimmy's playing my favorite, "Brain Sausage" by the Barking Fish, and I see this line. At first I think I'm having another flashback because it's mostly suits, in all the colors of gray. Silver ghosts in ash gray, mouse gray women, smog gray, sidewalk gray— maybe a couple of real misfits in navy blue. You know, the kind of yawnboys who sit at desks all day and talk to computers in Tokyo.

So why should I care, except that I recognize a scattering of ralphs from Southie? One old grope of mine, Tweezer, is near the end, and she's got on a white shirt and that stupid little ribbon tie she has to wear when she flips nineteen-cent McKrillwiches and over it is this sports jacket the color of a recycling sack with sleeves down to her knees. I guess it must have been dark when she stole it.

Mister Jimmy goes, "She's the one who wanted to be a dancer," but I remember. I'm not as stupid as he thinks I am. "Check it out, Chip," he goes, and because he's my ThinkMate, I do.

"Hey, Tweeze, where's the party?"

She looks too tired to flirt, like she's been sleeping in somebody's closet again, because she doesn't go "Hi, Chip," or "I'm the party," or anything. She just stares through me like I'm made of glass.

Then there's a hand tapping my shoulder and the suit behind me goes, "No cutting, mister. End of the line is way back."

I brush the hand off without bothering to look. "Snap off, jack. My sister here is saving my place. Right, Tweeze?"

She goes, "You ain't my brother," and her face is like a wall and I realize something has happened to her. Maybe it's the clothes, or the company she's been keeping.

The suit in front of us is giving me the hard eye, as if he's re-membering me to describe to the cops. And the hand comes back. It's heavier this time. I think about biting it, but Mister Jimmy goes, "Better not, Chip, or we'll be late. Let me look into this," and he starts playing my favorite, "Double-parked on Trouble Street" by 54321, and the music walks me out of there. But I'm still putting Tweeze down for payback.

Anyway, the line is a lot longer than I thought. It ripples down Hope Street, a wool-blend snake with a couple of hundred heads and no personality. When it takes a right on Chelsea Avenue, it changes. As I walk alongside I can't help but sense an edge to it that's sharp enough to draw blood. For beautiful people they're in an ugly mood. Maybe they're not used to lines. This one stretches three blocks down Chelsea until it passes an Infomart and turns down an alley which I never knew was there before. I've got to see this—there's a handful of other ralphs wandering down the alley who feel the same way. After all, you don't usually find that many suits so far from downtown. So we scope the front of the line, which stops at a white-painted steel door hung on a steel frame built into the brick wall. No sign, no buzzer, no handle, no keyhole. Could be the back door to the Infomart but Mister Jimmy thinks no.

Now this door bothers me—did I say it was white? I mean spotless, whiter than the pope's sheets. That kind of clean is hard to find in the city. Still, Mister Jimmy is telling me this is probably a whole bunch of nothing and I might believe him except that the pigeon-gray suit at the head of the line is watching this door like it's going to have his baby right there on the pavement. And the woman behind him is sweating even though it's a cool spring day and the alley is in deep shade. And the people behind her are practically vibrating. Then the door opens and everyone who's not in line crowds over for a peek.

You know how, when you get a headful of glitter, you can stare at something ordinary and it gets like more and more real until it pulses into that weird, sparkly hyperreality that means you're flashing? I see a long hallway lit by a single naked bulb. There's another white door at the far end. The cement floor has just been hosed down because there are still puddles around the drain. Someone has painted the words "Live" and "Free" on either wall. The building's breath is moist and warm and it smells like the corners of basements. The lucky leader mumbles as he steps through and I pull Mister Jimmy out of one ear so I can hear, ". . . full of grace, the Lord is with thee. Blessed art thou among women and blessed is the fruit . . ." The suit takes the plugs of his own ThinkMate out and slips them into his pocket as he walks down the hall, and just before the door shuts behind him I think I see the puddles start to sparkle like I'm having a flashback.

The woman next in line pulls out a limp handkerchief and wipes her forehead.

"Hey, jackie!" One of us innocent bystanders goes up to her. "What are you waiting for?"

She glances at him and tightens her grip on her attaché case like she wants to hit him with it but thinks twice because she's got better things to do—like worry about the door opening.

Someone next to me goes, "They don't say. They won't answer questions." A guy in a croaker goes, "New drug, maybe?" and a couple of people nod but then someone else goes, "Nah, you don't stand in line in broad daylight waiting for drugs," and the first guy goes, "Maybe it's so new, it's still legal."

A suit farther back in line calls out, "Leave her alone."

"Hey, jack, I was just asking . . ."

"Line up and find out for yourself."

A couple of newcomers come snooping down the alley. "What is this anyway?"

So I go, "Mass hallucination—watch out, it's catching." I laugh when they pull up short. The woman twists her handkerchief as she waits her turn.

Now I really do want to find out what's happening here but, like Mister Jimmy says, the clock is ticking so I head back to the street. I mean, there are all kinds of lines. Food lines, job lines, ticket lines, tram lines at rush hour, lines in front of stores whenever there's something you can afford, which isn't often. Line up to get your check from the state and again to get it cashed. They say when you're on maintenance you should get on every line you can find. Maybe that works for the good citizens but I haven't got the patience. Still, I've never seen two hundred yards of jacksuits before, homeowners with leather shoes and credit cards. Whatever's behind the door, it's worth something to people who already have a lot— and to ralphs like poor Tweezer, who's wearing a man's sports coat. I keep waiting for Mister Jimmy to break in with the answer or advice or a song or something but he's quiet. A line with a secret. Yeah, sure I'm interested.

The Department of Corrections is in a building as ugly as Cleveland but not quite as big. Check-in sprawls across the entire seventeenth floor and it's the usual uproar. You have to take turns breathing as all the prolees squeeze toward the wall of receivers while their moms and lovers and accomplices try to look invisible as the cops thump by in their immense blue body armor, dragging handcuffed prisoners behind them like yellow duckies. I spot some ralphs I know, but I'm not here to party. I've made good time. I got the page at 9:00 and it's only 10:37. The parole office gives you two hours on a random check, so I'm not really worried as I place my palm flat on the reader and fit my concuff into the receiver. Then the little green screen flashes. *Ved Chiplunkar, 1102298, report to Room 1841.* Damn, I don't want to chat up some case hack, I just want to get verified and get out. Anyway, Mister Jimmy plays the Screws' "Meat Sins" while I search for Room 1841 and that helps a little.

In a previous life, Room 1841 might have been a toilet, but now it's a windowless pus-yellow cubby that is almost big enough for a desk, two folding chairs, a terminal, and a skinny woman whose plastic ID says she's Angela Sternwood. She isn't much older than me but she's already got a job and a whiskey-colored suit and a string of fake pearls. She's easy enough on the eyes although she is a little beaky and I hate scented earrings.

"Tell me about yourself, Ved."

"Read the file—or are they hiring illiterates now?"

"I want to hear it in your own words."

It's a dumb line but I'll forgive a redhead almost anything so I go, "Name's Chip. I'm twenty-four and I've got two convictions, one for possession of glitter, one for mugging a suit so I could score some glitter. My cuff says I'm clean. I wish it was wrong."

"You graduated from South High and were accepted at War Martyrs Junior College but you never went. Why?"

"Didn't like the school colors."

"And you've been cashing maintenance checks since, let's see, '22?"

I ignore that because Mister Jimmy finally tracks down her public file. "DOB is 4/11/06—younger than you, Chip! She's a citizen, lives at 2381 Green Street up in the Heights, and she's been working here less than a month, probably still in training."

She goes, "Would you please take your plugs out, Chip?"

I ignore her some more.

"Says here you haven't even tried for a job since your last check-in."

"I'm allergic to clocks." When I laugh, she looks nervous. "You're new at this job, aren't you?"

"Why do you say that?" She chews her lip. "Anyway, we're here to talk about you."

Mister Jimmy goes, "Keep on her, Chip. She's so raw they're probably still evaluating her on closed circuit. Who knows, maybe if she doesn't sell you a suit they'll fire her."

She goes, "So you like taking maintenance? You live well on eighty-seven dollars a month?"

So I give her my best hope-to-grope smile. See, I don't really want to argue with Angela Sternwood. I want to take her out dancing and put my hands on her ass and later take her back to my place. Or, better, her place—she probably has hot water.

She goes, "I said pull the damn ThinkMate so I can talk to you!" I've got her squirming now.

Mister Jimmy goes, "Better humor her, Chip," so I do.

I drop the plugs onto the desk and reach inside my shirt. "Want the system unit too?" It's in a pouch that hangs from a chain around my neck.

"No." She pulls a tissue from a drawer, picks up a plug with it, rubs the ear wax off, and reads the label. Mister Jimmy is a genuine Matshushita. I can tell she's impressed because she goes, "Pricey tech for someone on maintenance." She pushes the plug back toward me. "Where'd you get it?"

"My pa left it to me instead of a ranch."

"Any idiot can make jokes, Chip." She checks the screen of her terminal. "Okay, what gang are you running with these days?"

"No gang—just me and Mister Jimmy against the world."

"Mister Jimmy?"

I nod at the plugs on her desk and she goes, "You know an Elvis Malloy?"

"Uh-uh."

"Elvis Malloy was arrested at 12:48 last Tuesday night. Seems he's working this puppet house on Harmony Street in Southie, slipping into booths while the johns are busy slamming their robots through the orgies. He lifts at least six wallets, maybe more—not everyone reports, of course. Then somebody spots him. He flies out the front door with this naked guy after him and it just so happens there are two cops having coffee across the street. Malloy runs twelve blocks, flinging the swag into the crowds he passes. The cops catch him eventually but there's no evidence on him and nobody turns anything in, which isn't surprising considering the neighborhood."

"So Malloy wins the Nobel Prize for stupidity. So?"

Her mouth twists as she thinks this over. I can tell she's getting wrinkled at me. I don't think she's happy in her new job. "I'm sorry you're playing it this way, Chip, but it's your choice." She swivels the monitor around so I can see. "One of the cops who gave chase was rigged for vid. It's new tech, a pilot program. The computer enhancement takes time but we get some really cute pictures." I'm highlighted on the screen, framed between a floating ad window for Coors and a weather gypsy wearing three hats and seven coats. I'm staring at a brown wallet on the sidewalk in the foreground, also highlighted. "What do you think, Chip? Like it for the yearbook?"

I need Mister Jimmy's advice but I don't dare let her know that. "So I'm there. So's he." I point at the gypsy. "Talked to him yet? And probably others off camera. Where's your case? I never touched that wallet."

So then she loses her temper. "I don't need a case, mister. There's a time stamp on this vid that puts you on Harmony Street at 12:32 A.M."

"What? You're calling me on a curfew violation?"

"That's right. Maybe if I thought you were trying to turn yourself around, we could work something out." She raps the keyboard and the terminal mutters and suddenly a pink slip is sticking out of the printer slot like a paper tongue. "But you're not and you've got an attitude." She tears the slip out. "I take it you don't follow the news? Too bad. The feds are gearing up to build that new Friendship Highway through Mexico to keep our troops supplied. They've set manpower quotas for each state, which we're supposed to meet from our maintenance rolls. The governor says to sweep the streets and you're just the kind of trash voters tend to notice." She hands me the slip. "Report to the Reed Armory on National Unity Square before noon tomorrow. Don't forget your sunblock."

"Wait a minute." I jam Mister Jimmy back in and together we read the pink work order, which says I'll be getting my mail at Jaltipan Work Camp in the Provisional State of Veracruz for the next six months. Mister Jimmy goes, "That's the steamiest part of the jungle, Chip. They get a hundred inches of rain a year. I won't last two minutes in that kind of weather."

"This isn't fair," I go. "I'll appeal. You call this justice?"

"You want justice?" she goes. "Get a job." She stands up and brushes right past me and out the door with her big nose puckered like I'm a bad smell. I think about punching it for her but, as Mister Jimmy points out, that will only make the trouble I'm already in seem like a week at a disney.

So I hit the street again, feeling like I've just been force-fed a brick. I wander into the business district, the only living ralph in a desert of suits, and I'm headed nowhere with a scheduled layover in Mexico where the rain is a blunt instrument. Every so often I whang my concuff against one of the pipes set along the curb that used to have parking meters back when gas cost less than vodka. Doesn't hurt the cuff—that's indestructible—but it makes my hand sting, which reminds me of what's coming if I don't think of something fast.

So why should I follow the news when it's always the same? "In Washington today the suits announced that taxes are too high and the president called on the poor ralphs of America to bend over one more time." *Whang.* Besides, I can tell that bitch would've been a frozen turkey in bed anyway. I gave her my best lines and she never even smiled. *Whang.* No question I have to show up at the Armory or else the alarm on my concuff will start shrieking and probably turn my brains to soup even before the cops come to haul me away. *Whang.* No, the only way to dodge Mexico is to get off maintenance and the only way to get off maintenance is to get enough money to live and the way to get that kind of money is to get a job but jobs are scarcer than ninth-grade virgins even if you do own a suit. Which I don't. *Whang.* Yeah, good advice, Mister Jimmy. Keep on her. She's new, see if you can push her around.

He goes, "We're in trouble, Chip. That climate rots electronics. You can't take me down there; I'm not designed for it."

"So I'll stash you somewhere. Hey, I'm pissed too."

"For six months, Chip? Six months of no input and I'll go crazy. And what if you don't come back? It's possible."

"Then I won't care, will I?" Problem is, you can't just turn a ThinkMate off like some stupid computer. I don't know why, exactly—Mister Jimmy is in charge of understanding all that tech stuff.

"You can lend me to someone, Chip."

"Who do I know would give you back?"

I'm so busy arguing with Mister Jimmy that I almost crash into this jack in a tuxedo except he sees me first. He puts his hands together like he's praying and then spreads them apart and somehow in the space between them he's projecting this window that says:

Desperate?
Now you know Bad Times can ruin Good People.
You can't Achieve Success until you admit Failure.
If you're ready to Give Up
We Can Help.
Proper Dress Required.
Wednesdays only.
No homeless Please.

"Snap off, I'm broke." I try to go around but he stays in my way. "You hear me? Maybe Jesus saves, but I don't."

But he won't let me pass until I notice him. Okay, so he looks like some groom who took a wrong turn at the wedding. He's wearing a high-necked white shirt and a cummerbund. His tux is black and there's a white carnation in the silk lapel. He's a little newt of a man with a peaceful, almost goofy expression you don't see much in the city. Maybe his bow tie is too tight and he's not getting enough oxygen.

So I'm thinking here's another flashback, which is okay because at this point I could use a little free hallucination, and then it occurs to me. "Hey, this have anything to do with the line on Chelsea Avenue?"

He claps his hands again and between them are the words:

Live Free

He shows me a smile that has about eight teeth too many. He says nothing.

"I was down there this morning. No one would tell what they were waiting for."

Still giving me his headlight smile, he claps his hands one last time and the window closes. He says nothing.

"So what's this all about?"

He turns the smile off and shrugs.

"I'm asking you a question, man. What's behind the damn door?"

Mister Jimmy realizes I'm getting wrinkled at this jack so he tries to smooth me out with "Vegetable Kingdom" by Round Woman Square Men. But I don't want violins, I want answers. When I grab his lapels and shake him, his flower falls out and he makes this weird gurgling sound.

"Talk to me, you stupid jack."

So he opens his mouth and shows me all those perfect teeth again except there's nothing behind them but a pink hole. He's trying his best to say something but it sounds like he's swallowing a snake. I let him go. I tell him to shut his mouth but he won't. It's as if he wants to be sure I see his glistening stump waggle, as if he's *happy* someone cut his tongue out, as if it's the secret of his success and he wants to share it with me.

I spin away but he keeps after me, *"Ah-ahh-er-ah!"* and shoves an envelope into my pocket and then maybe he realizes I'm about to hit him because he pulls back.

I take a few steps before I turn again but by then he's disappeared. It's like the street has swallowed him. Suits bump by me on their way to lunch as ad windows glide over our heads. Business as usual in skyscraper land, so why am I shaking? Because what I really need now is about 10 cc's of glitter. Yeah, I'm that desperate—my brain feels like it's swelling up inside my head from too much thinking, and I've been on the verge of a flashback all morning. But I know Mister Jimmy is right when he reminds me that if my cuff shows positive for flash they'll ruin me at the Armory tomorrow. I laugh because I guess I just qualified for the line on Chelsea Avenue. This is the worst day of the worst life ever lived, and since I can't get anything I want, maybe I *should* give up. So I take out the envelope and open it and there's Ben Franklin giving me the green eye and on the flip side the words "In God We Trust" have been circled in red. Maybe the reason I can't feel my feet touching the sidewalk is that I've never held a hundred-dollar bill in my hand before. It's not as intense a flash as glitter, but it'll do.

Expose that much money to the air in Southie and the ralphs will smell it and come swarming, but maybe this happens all the time downtown because the suits pay no attention as I slide the money into the pouch next to Mister Jimmy's system unit. I start home with the clock running down and the score Questions 32, Answers 0. The obvious play is to forget what just happened and spend the little time I have left pissing this miracle down all my favorite toilets in the city. I'm really tempted but Mister Jimmy goes, "Chip, if you've got to pick between a suit and a shovel, there's a Salvation Army over on April 11th Street," which is not the advice I'm hoping for, even if it makes sense.

"But what the hell am I lining up for?"

"Maybe a chance to get out of Mexico. So far all I know is that a Live Free Foundation was established as a tax-exempt charitable trust in New Hampshire four years ago. There's no annual report and somebody got the IRS to seal the returns but at least we know they file so they're probably legitimate. I say we have to check it out."

Now I'm worried because "probably" is a luck word and my luck is usually bad. What I really want is a sure thing except the only one I've got is six months of laying blacktop in green hell. I guess Mister Jimmy has a point: when you're desperate, you take chances.

So an hour later a new Chip trick-or-treats down Chelsea Avenue, disguised in a gray woolen suit and a blue shirt and plastic loafers. I've shortened the pants and fixed the ripped lining with Kmart fashion tape but there was nothing I could do about the shoulders. The whole outfit cost only twenty-three bucks and they even threw in a tie the color of dead pizza. So I'm properly dressed and I've got seventy-seven bucks left from the angel in the tux and nine from the wallet Elvis Malloy threw away on Harmony Street together with my life savings of twelve and I'm wondering how much luck ninety-eight dollars will buy. Mister Jimmy is finishing "Contents Under Pressure" by Vinnie's Ear as I come up to the line.

I watch for Tweeze but she must have already gone through the

door. The line is shorter—the end is near the corner of Hope and
Chelsea, in front of Tibawi's Discount Flooring Outlet. I almost don't
get on because of the old lady carrying the dog. I hate dogs, especially rich people's greedy, stupid, useless dogs. This one is losing
patches of its wiry fur and it smells like an old couch someone left
out in the rain.

The lady turns and scopes me and I scope her and I guess neither
of us likes what we see. She probably doesn't approve of browns—
or blacks or spanics or asians. She's wearing a cement-colored jacket
over a matching skirt and there's a silk scarf around her neck held
together with a fat gold ring that I bet I could get fifty bucks for, if
it's real. She has gray hair so fine you can see her pale scalp. There's
a glaze of dried dog slobber on her sleeve.

I go, "Hi." She says nothing. She doesn't seem very desperate.
Maybe she couldn't get tickets to the opera.

She nods at me, shifts the dog into a more comfortable position,
and faces forward again. The dog scrabbles up and watches me over
her shoulder.

The line creeps forward. Business is terrible at Tibawi's Discount
Flooring Outlet. The price tags for the oriental rugs draped in the
display window have faded in the sunlight. Up ahead, the lawn and
lowlight moss carpets are turning yellow around the edges. A wide
bearded man with all the charm of a hammer stands behind the
door and scopes us like he's thinking of closing up and getting in
line too. He'd better hurry and make up his mind because now there's
a fidgety guy in a charcoal three-piece behind me. Two more men
are arguing about palladium futures on the Mercantile Exchange as
they settle in behind him. Then a ralph in a silver and black Raiders
jacket comes up and asks what we're waiting for and the old lady
goes rigid. When I see the glitter in the ralph's eyes, I decide I'm
not talking to this flashface about my troubles. They're none of his
damn business and, besides, thinking about them only makes me
crazy. I'm not admitting to him or anyone that I don't exactly know
why I'm here. Hey, I don't exactly know why I was born or where
my mom went to or why shit stinks, okay? I'm not happy about
being ignorant but there it is. So I tell him to snap off except it
takes a while for him to understand what with all the beautiful sparks
flashing inside his head. As he leaves, I scope the suits in line behind
me and, even though they glance away, I'm sure they're glad I got

rid of the ralph because they didn't want to answer questions either. You don't admit to strangers that you're desperate—it's hard enough admitting it to yourself. But I can smell their fear, or maybe it's my own stink I smell. I wonder if this is what happened to Tweezer. The line has a grip on me. I'm not sure I can get away anymore.

Anyway, we're all the way up to the corner when Angela Stern-wood stalks by without noticing me. Maybe it's my new suit but I doubt she's seeing much at all. She's so angry that her knees don't bend when she walks and her face is all wrinkled like she's thinking of things she wished she had said to someone. Not me, I hope. I almost fall into the street when she gets in line.

"Sternwood!" I lean way out and wave, trying to get her attention. "Hey, Angela!" She's too busy drilling holes into the sidewalk with her eyes and then the line swings me around the corner onto Chelsea. The dog sneezes and the old lady coos and kisses it. Maybe she feels safer with me now because she goes, "He's sick, poor baby, but I know they can cure him," but I don't want to talk to her. I want Angela. It takes maybe thirty seconds before I overdose on curiosity and walk back. Mister Jimmy's shriek is like a nail in my ear so I yank him out. Hey, the line's moving along and I'm only losing nine places.

I go, "Shouldn't you be downtown taking milk money away from orphans?"

She gives me a look that's about as friendly as a fist—then she recognizes me. "Oh, *no*. What the hell are you doing here?"

"I was in line up ahead. I came back to keep you company."

Her eyes get shiny. "Jesus. I don't deserve this." A tear trickles down her face. "Leave me alone."

I like the way she cries. Some people gush, others sniff and try to hold off, but most of them are just crying for the crowd. Angela's tears are her own. She's not ashamed of them, she's not proud— they're something that happens sometimes when the world smacks you in the face and there's no one you can hit back.

"Hey, you'll never get to know me if you keep sending me away." I don't tell her I'm attracted to women who ask me to leave them alone.

"Listen, ralph, I don't like you in a suit any better than I liked you in a T-shirt."

"Seems to me we're standing in the same line."

She doesn't have to answer because the line gathers itself and we press forward. When I pop Mister Jimmy back in, he has calmed down. We shuffle around the corner and down Chelsea maybe ten yards before everything bunches up again and stops. People mutter and groan and straddle their briefcases and glance at their watches and go up on tiptoes to see ahead. The suit in back of me starts whistling like he's on his way to the circus. He's bald but he's got a gray beard so thick it looks like his head is on upside down. The guy in front of Angela opens a readman and cups his hand so that only he can see the screen.

Meanwhile I scope Angela from behind. She has the long slender fingers of a guitar god—no rings—and the kind of leg muscles you don't get sitting on a couch in front of sitcoms. Her red hair is cut to a silky brush. I decide I could find my way past her nose. Sure, I'd grope her, if only she wasn't who she was.

Eventually she gets tired of pretending I'm not staring. "Where'd you get those clothes? The Salvation Army?" Her tears have dried up.

"I found them on the sidewalk on Harmony Street."

"You shouldn't make so many jokes, Chad. People who are really smart don't try so hard to prove it. You know, if you had played straight with me I wouldn't have sent you to Mexico."

"Maybe I'm not going. Maybe that's why I'm on line here."

"You think they'll take you?" She shakes her head. "Well, maybe they will. You want to hear what kind of trouble jokes can get you into? I made a joke today, because you made me angry." She frowns. "No, it wasn't only you; it was the hundred prolees I saw before you. None of you wanted anything to do with me. You wouldn't let me help, you insulted me. But of all of them, Chad, you were especially irritating, because you have a brain and you're wasting it."

Mister Jimmy goes, "Want to know why she's here? I checked her public files. Congratulations, Chip, I think you just got your new case hack fired."

"They didn't care that I gave you the pink slip, you know. I've got quotas to meet; that's what they hired me to do. But they said I got too involved with the interview. I made this joke, you see. I told you to remember your sunblock, and so Friday is my last day. They said that I wasn't professional enough. They want case officers who can maintain proper distance."

She's the one who hurt me, right? So I should enjoy watching her fall into a hole—but I can't. Maybe it's because people all around us are eavesdropping. The jack behind me is practically resting his beard on my shoulder. I'm sure they've already decided that we're both losers. I go, "Seems like they make it awfully easy for a ralph to fuck up in this city."

"I'm no ralph." I should've known she'd be insulted. "I went to junior college, I passed the civil service exam. These people aren't ralphs."

"What are they doing here, then?"

"The same thing you're doing."

"Trying not to go to Mexico?"

That shuts her up for a while. The line drags us past the Chelsea Drugstore and Superior Public Showers—*Our Water Guaranteed 100 Percent Nontoxic.* The fragrance of hot oil as we go by Felipe's Fish Fry reminds me that I haven't eaten yet today. I'm hungry enough to pick onion rings out of a dumpster.

"I'm sorry, Chad." Angela slumps with her hands in her pockets and her head down, not giving me much of a target. "I'm more sorry that I got fired, but I guess I'm sorry for what happened to you too."

"Sure, except it's Chip."

"What?"

"Name's Chip, not Chad. What's wrong with taking maintenance like the rest of the world? At least until you find another job."

"You don't understand." She shook her head. "Once there's a maintenance flag in your files, personnel assumes you're probably employment impaired. I'd be lucky to find something at minimum wage. Maybe if I had some savings I could live off while I searched on JobLink . . . but I don't and I've got rent, food, net, transcard. I owe five more years on my student loan."

So that's why the only work they ever offered me was scraping gum off bus seats. Mister Jimmy is trying to distract me with "My Career (in Air Conditioning)" by Cheap Wine, which normally makes me laugh, except he should've told me I never had a chance for a real job. But just when I'm ready to call him on this, the suit in front of us gets careless and tips his readman so that I can see. One screen has my angel's message about Bad Times and Giving Up, the other has the same words, but arranged in different order like they're some kind of code. I nudge Angela. "See that?" I whisper.

"So?" She shrugs. "It's all over JobLink." She speaks loud enough for the suit to hear and he slaps the readman shut. "Come to think of it, where did you see it? You're on maintenance, you can't afford to subscribe to the net."

"A guy walks up to me in the street and opens a pocket window. I get a peek and that's all. He doesn't say a word and then he's gone." I leave the $100 out because I've got more audience than I want, even if they are all rich suits. "I'm still waiting for someone to tell me what it means."

"*Space,* my friend." When the jack with the beard leans forward, I can smell all the bars on DuPont Street. "We're bound for the new L5 colony, *Freedom Station.*"

Angela rolls her eyes toward the corner of the sky where lunatics play house. She goes, "All I know is that some foundation with more secrets than the CIA started running the ad about a week ago. A guy from the sixteenth floor answered it last Wednesday and he must've gotten some offer because he never even bothered to come back and clean out his desk."

"Isn't it *obvious?*" The spaceman butts back into our conversation. "Live *Free?* If we're going to survive as a species we have to *free* ourselves from the gravity well. Break the chains of Earth. The Department of Space needs the *best,* the brightest and the bravest. The new *pioneers.*" What's obvious is that he's one of those ravers who have everything figured out—wrong.

"That's not what I heard." The suit behind him speaks up. "My cousin lives in New Hampshire and she says that the Liberty Party is building a new co-op up in the White Mountains and they're supposedly recruiting business people to help run it."

"I've been watching since nine this morning," someone else goes. "I've circled the block I don't know how many times. So far a couple of thousand have gone in—at least that many—but nobody's come out. Don't they reject *anyone?*"

"I heard it was the Charismatics. They'll take anyone they can get."

"You think *God* is waiting behind that door?" The spaceman sniffs. "Sure it's not the Blue Elves? Listen, *Freedom Station* opens in just three years . . ."

I go to Angela, "Maybe they can't leave."

"What?"

"Maybe they're rounding up warm bodies for the army. Or wasting everyone who steps through the door? *Boom.*" I shoot the spaceman with my finger. "Instant population control." I don't necessarily believe it, I'm just saying it to get a reaction. They're quiet for about three seconds and then they all turn on me, their voices sharp with fear.

"The cops wouldn't just stand by . . ."

". . . such a thing as the Constitution."

"Things are bad, but not *that* bad."

". . . the brain drain," goes the spaceman. "Maybe if all they wanted were people on *maintenance* . . ."

Mister Jimmy goes, "Easy, Chip, these are suits. They're not built for trouble; scare them and they might do something stupid."

"Okay," I go, "okay, you're right," and I hold up my hands to surrender but they're too nervous to take any prisoners. What saves me is a couple of asian ralphs in mirrorshirts who are swaggering down the street like they're trying to decide which one of us to mug first. As they approach, everyone stops arguing and gives them the hard eye, including me. I'm surprised at my reaction, but it's like I have no choice. I'm in line too, aren't I? We've come this far together and we've all got our places to protect and no ignorant street trash is going to stop any of us from getting where we're going.

One ralph asks the other, "What these jacks waiting for, man? Personality transplants?" The other snickers.

Nobody says anything after they pass. We scuff along for a few minutes in silence and the line loosens its grip on me. There's nothing to do but think, which is a pain. Mister Jimmy tries to help by playing my favorite, "Go Away Please Stay" by Lezbeth. It doesn't work. When I look back there's at least fifty suits lined up behind me but I feel like they're standing on my chest. What we need is a theme song. *Get in line, everything's fine here in the line with a mind of its own.* I ought to write that down and send it to Lezbeth except that's not something suits do. I don't belong here. Mister Jimmy reminds me of Mexico and tells me we're getting close to the end but then I think about a drain on a cement floor and those puddles. I know I just made that stuff up about shooting all of us. Still, it sure looked as if they had just cleaned up a mess, didn't it?

Mister Jimmy goes, "They're not killing anyone. This is America, Chip, and these are taxpayers. Cash cows—they can't afford to slaughter the herd. Besides, we haven't got any choice."

"So why should I trust you? You never explained about how taking maintenance meant I couldn't get a real job. You're supposed to tell me this stuff but, no, I have to hear it from Angela."

He goes, "Your dad was taking maintenance when you were born, Chip, and you started taking it on your own long before you got me. I didn't want to discourage you. Besides, it's not true that you can't get a job; it's just harder."

"You should've told me."

Angela glances over her shoulder. "You talking to me?"

"Nah, I'm arguing with Mister Jimmy."

"Who's winning?"

It's no contest, I'd much rather talk to her than Mister Jimmy. When her earring catches the sunlight, it leaks perfume that must be laced with pheromones because it's all I can do to keep from putting my arms around her and nibbling. "What I don't under-stand," I go, "is why you're here. You could hit a friend for a loan to hold you over."

She pauses, inviting me to slide up beside her. "I graduated last month," she goes. "I only just moved here."

"Someone with your looks and you haven't got an old grope you could call?"

"It's been a rough month." She gives me a lemon smile. "I don't want to talk about it."

"Okay, how come you don't wear a ThinkMate?"

"I like to make my own decisions."

"Well, maybe you're smarter than me."

"Or you're lazier than me. You ever take that thing off?"

"Why?" The idea surprises me. "Like when?"

"When you watch vid—I don't know. At night, before you go to bed."

I bump gently against her. "Want to find out for yourself?"

She flushes and moves ahead of me again.

I can't decide whether she's teasing me or not. Mister Jimmy plays "Burning the Snow" by Penile Colony, which I decide I don't like as much as I used to. I tell him I don't want to hear any more music for a while. It's getting colder now as the sun touches the skyline. Whirlwinds of trash stir in the street. The line can't make up its mind anymore. It moves in spasms. Sometimes it surges, then it'll stop and catch its breath before crawling forward again. Probably some of the suits ahead are giving up and going home to meat loaf and clean sheets. They're not desperate enough. Angela doesn't seem that desperate. I wonder if I am.

One big push carries us across Martyrs Street and we're almost there. Up ahead the yellow Infomart window floats over the sidewalk and the come-on scrolls across in letters tall enough to start for the Celtics. *Infomart . . . more than just facts . . . knowledge.* The rest of the block is taken up by a used-robot store called Machine Age. You can buy robot vacuums and lawn mowers, mobile video and smartcarts that will follow you anywhere, three-wheelers and food processors that'll turn a dollar's worth of soy paste into a meal for seven—if none of them are very hungry. There's a window full of ThinkMate clones and next to it are the puppets, lean sports models in bright uniforms and leering sex machines with big lips and glossy stain-resistant skin.

Just ahead three suits peel off the line and scuttle back toward us like cockroaches someone is trying to squash. After they clear out I see that what scared them was a couple of cops in full riot armor. There's a patrol wagon with intimate seating for twenty parked in the alley. I guess even suits get arrested once in a while. These cops look strange to me although I'm not sure why exactly until Mister Jimmy points out the two bulges on their helmets, one for the spotlight, the other for the lens. They're IDing people at random. Looking for criminals in a line full of desperate people—it's such a good idea that I'm surprised the cops thought of it. "Be smooth, Chip," Mister Jimmy goes. "You're legal until noon tomorrow."

I touch Angela's arm. "That the rig they got me with?"

One of the cops clunks down the sidewalk, stops about ten feet from us, and asks a suit to say his name.

Angela goes, "Yeah, only they use infrared at night. When they cross-reference your voice print with your picture, they can access all your G3 files right down to the dailies in under ten seconds."

Maybe I'd be worried if I'd understood what she said but information tech is Mister Jimmy's responsibility. Besides, the suit with the readman is frightened enough for both of us. He's pale as bread as he turns to Angela. "They can read *dailies?*" He's practically hissing.

She nods.

He tries to lunge past me, but as long as I'm wearing a suit I decide to play good citizen. I manage to stay in the way just long enough.

"Excuse me, sir." This cop could arm-wrestle a backhoe. "Were you going somewhere?" He doesn't have any problem holding onto a limp suit.

The cop IDs the jack as Lawrence Prendergast, DOB 7/9/88, an employee of Atlantic Trust wanted for questioning on a charge of unauthorized use of a credit instrument. When the cop pats him down, he finds that Larry's paunch is actually a money belt stuffed with enough cash to buy a round of drinks for the entire city. Three minutes later, Larry's been cuffed, read his rights, and loaded into the wagon. From the way the suits around me are staring, I doubt any of them have ever seen justice up this close.

"He's *lucky* they caught him here," goes the spaceman, "because on *Freedom Station* there's no *jail*. The budget was too tight."

Nobody says anything. We don't want to encourage him.

"You break the law up there and you'd better be able to breathe *space*." He laughs at his own joke. Somebody has to.

We finally reach the top of the alley. Colors are washing out in the twilight and it's hard to tell people from shadows. Soon the city will be gray enough to hide us all but by then it'll be too late. The white door has turned the color of bone. We're about fifteen yards away—twenty, maybe thirty people are ahead of us. Each step I take is a battle and I'm not sure anymore this is a war I want to win.

Mister Jimmy goes, "Steady, Chip, I can't do this without you. We're almost home."

I focus on the back of Angela's neck and follow her fragrance through the gloom. I must be losing it because I'm standing in line to jump off a cliff with a bunch of strangers and instead of panicking, like any normal person, I'm hallucinating about how I'd feel if her head was on a green pillow and her eyelids were fluttering shut and her lips had parted for me. She's a jack suit and I'm a lazy ralph, but suddenly it's the most important thing in the world that she's a thrill I'll never have as long as I stand in this line. I touch her arm and she turns and now I have to speak even though Mister Jimmy tells me to keep quiet and I can't think, except words take me by surprise and I listen in amazement to what I'm saying.

"You lied when you said you didn't have any savings. Maybe it's not enough but you have something. You're not the type to let yourself go broke. How much, Angela?"

"Why should I tell you?"

I laugh because a snub from her steadies me more than all of Mister Jimmy's cheerleading.

"I'm not worth ripping off," she goes, "if that's what you're thinking." She waits for me to answer but I don't. It's up to her to decide if she trusts me. "Almost thirty dollars. Why, Chip?"

I'm thinking now and Mister Jimmy doesn't like that because that's not my job. "Chip, Chip! What is this?"

Up ahead the ugly little dog starts to howl. Maybe it's afraid of the dark. I unbutton my new blue shirt, draw out the pouch, pull my money from next to Mister Jimmy's system unit. I show it to her. "Thirty and ninety-eight is a hundred and twenty-eight. You could stay in my apartment for six weeks on that, easy. The rent's paid through May. So you live in a dive and you eat slop and you blow off your loan and spend the rest searching for a job on the net. The worst that can happen is that a couple of Wednesdays from now you line up again, only this time you go through the door broke. So what? Thirty bucks doesn't buy first class on the shuttle, believe me."

"*Excuse* me, ma'am," goes the spaceman, "but I hope you're not going to listen to this man. Are you *seriously* suggesting . . ."

I whip around and backhand him across the mouth. "Say one more word, jack, and I'll rip that beard off and stuff it down your throat." I glare at him and I know he's going to take it. Like all suits, he's got the backbone of a banana. The suits behind him mutter and disapprove but they're too busy thinking line thoughts to cause trouble now.

The dog's frantic yelping is cut off when the door shuts. I doubt it was appropriately dressed. The silence echoes in the cold. Angela hasn't budged and there's a gap between her and the suit in front of us.

"Move up," someone yells.

"Let's *go*." The line is impatient.

"I don't know what to say," she goes.

"Make sense? Not bad for a lazy ralph?"

"You're not joking?" I'm close enough to see her breath. I think about what it would be like to taste it. "You'd do that for me?"

"Sure and I'd do it for me too. I've got a life here. Maybe it stinks, but it's mine. You said Friday's your last day. What if you show up for work tomorrow and take me off the work roster and put me back on maintenance?"

"Brilliant, Chip," Mister Jimmy goes. "I didn't think you had it in you."

"I can't do that," she goes.

"Angela, the street price for deferral is two hundred, so don't tell me it can't be done. Now I haven't got that much so I'm asking a favor—from a friend. What are they going to do, fire you?"

She considers. "Where are you going to live?"

"Where the hell do you think? In my apartment with you."

I couldn't tell at first what she thought of the idea.

"Yes," goes Mister Jimmy, "and after Friday you can dump her whenever you want."

It's not his fault that he doesn't understand. He's like the line, he doesn't have an imagination. Still, I have to pull his plugs out and curl my hand around them.

There's only one suit between Angela and the door. She glances at him and then back at me. "I'm not sleeping with you."

"No?" I don't think she can see me smile. It doesn't matter. "Well, you'd better decide in a hurry because you're next and I'm sure as hell not charging through that door to rescue you."

She hesitates and I realize I'm losing her. Maybe Mister Jimmy is a better judge of character than I gave him credit for. I can feel his tinny scream buzzing in my fist.

"This is il*legal*," goes the spaceman. "I'm calling the police. Don't do it, young lady. You're turning down the *chance* of a lifetime." When I turn around to snap him off I realize I've made another mistake. He's backed out of reach and even in the dark I can see that he's holding a gun, or at least something that looks real enough to freeze me. "I'm not going to let *either* of you do this to yourselves. You're young. You've got your whole *future* in front of you."

I back away from the gun but it follows me. "Go ahead and shoot, you jack. Like you say, the cops are right around the corner. They like desperate people, desperate people are some of their best customers. The door is open, spaceman, but we're getting out of line. That makes you next. Better hurry or the shuttle will leave without you."

He looks at the open door, the naked bulb, the long cement hallway. There are more puddles than there were in the morning and they're *all* glittery. The line yells at us. "Move, *move*." The spaceman marches to the doorway like a war hero accepting his medal, turns, and levels the gun at me.

In the light from the hall the gun looks even more real. When I stare at the barrel, it *sparkles* with reality because the flashback I've felt coming all day has finally arrived. The gun starts singing to me, "Come with us, Chip, come with us now. We've got everything you want and all you need to know." And the music walks me toward the white door, which I finally realize opens onto the flash that never ends. "Can't let you go," sings the gun. "We love you so." And it sounds just like Mister Jimmy so I have to, I have to except that Angela kicks the door shut.

There's a sound like a gunshot that shatters my flashback. I stagger and Angela catches me and I put my arm around her. Maybe it's only the other door slamming.

I watch as everybody in line moves up one, and then I peel Mister Jimmy's contact lens from my right eye and drop it into the pouch with the plugs and the system unit.

Angela steers me toward the street. "Anyone want to buy a ThinkMate?" I go to the suits still waiting in line. "Hey, genuine Matshushita!"

THE DARK
. . . .
Karen Joy Fowler

With her 1991 novel, *Sarah Canary*, Karen Joy Fowler brought off a remarkable feat: a work that the sometimes prissy literary world and the somewhat paranoid science fiction enclave embraced with equal ardor. While mainstream reviewers were perfectly content to discuss *Sarah Canary* as an exemplar of North American magical realism, SF critic John Clute hailed it as "the best First Contact novel ever written." (The plot concerns the relationship between a Chinese laborer and a mysterious wild woman in the Pacific Northwest during the last century.) As I write these words, the *Nebula Awards Report* informs me that *Sarah Canary* has made the preliminary ballot for 1992; and so, even as she heads toward wider recognition, it appears that Fowler, like Ursula K. Le Guin before her, has retained the affections of her native community.

To date, Fowler has given us two short story collections, *Peripheral Vision*, from Pulphouse Publishing, and *Artificial Things*, from Bantam. In 1987 her work earned her the John W. Campbell Award as best new writer, and the following year she received a National Endowment for the Arts grant. *Sarah Canary* won the San Francisco Commonwealth Club medal for best first novel. It was my pleasure to reprint Fowler's moving, poetic story "Lieserl" in *Nebula Awards 26*.

"This is one of those things a writer should never confess," notes Fowler, "but 'The Dark' began as a fleas-in-space story. I was impressed with the durability of fleas and thought that if we shot a dog or monkey to Mars, instead of simply sending it into orbit, and there was a tragic mishap, the dog or monkey would die, but the fleas would colonize the planet. The title of the original story was 'The Oral Tradition,' and a wonderful title it is, too.

"Fleas are not only durable, they are dangerous. I began to consider the possibilities of a new superhero—Flea Man—a sort of Spider Man, but able to leap tall buildings in a single bound and wipe out half of Europe. And then I suddenly stumbled over the accusation that fleas were used as a military weapon in the tunnel war in Vietnam. This rumor shaped 'The Dark' into the story it is now. Tragically, during many rewrites, the fleas were almost completely removed from the story. They remain only as shadowy figures manipulating the plot from the background. You have to look closely to see them. Then you realize they control everything."

In the summer of 1954, Anna and Richard Becker disappeared from Yosemite National Park along with Paul Becker, their three-year-old son. Their campsite was intact; two paper plates with half-eaten frankfurters remained on the picnic table, and a third frankfurter was in the trash. The rangers took several black-and-white photographs of the meal, which, when blown up to eight by ten, as part of the investigation, showed clearly the words *love bites*, carved into the wooden picnic table many years ago. There appeared to be some fresh scratches as well; the expert witness at the trial attributed them, with no great assurance, to raccoon.

The Beckers' car was still backed into the campsite, a green De Soto with a spare key under the right bumper and half a tank of gas. Inside the tent, two sleeping bags had been zipped together marital style and laid on a large tarp. A smaller flannel bag was spread over an inflated pool raft. Toiletries included three toothbrushes; Ipana toothpaste, squeezed in the middle; Ivory soap; three washcloths; and one towel. The newspapers discreetly made no mention of Anna's diaphragm, which remained powdered with talc, inside its pink shell, or of the fact that Paul apparently still took a bottle to bed with him.

Their nearest neighbor had seen nothing. He had been in his hammock, he said, listening to the game. Of course, the reception in Yosemite was lousy. At home he had a shortwave set; he said he had once pulled in Dover, clear as a bell. "You had to really concentrate to hear the game," he told the rangers. "You could've dropped the bomb. I wouldn't have noticed."

Anna Becker's mother, Edna, received a postcard postmarked a day earlier. "Seen the firefall," it said simply. "Home Wednesday. Love." Edna identified the bottle. "Oh yes, that's Paul's bokkie," she told the police. She dissolved into tears. "He never goes anywhere without it," she said.

In the spring of 1960, Mark Cooper and Manuel Rodriguez went on a fishing expedition in Yosemite. They set up a base camp in Tuolumne Meadows and went off to pursue steelhead. They were gone from camp approximately six hours, leaving their food and a six-pack of beer zipped inside their backpacks zipped inside their tent. When they returned, both beer and food were gone. Canine footprints circled the tent, but a small and mysterious handprint remained on the tent flap. "Raccoon," said the rangers who hadn't seen it. The tent and packs were undamaged. Whatever had taken the food had worked the zippers. "Has to be raccoon."

The last time Manuel had gone backpacking, he'd suspended his pack from a tree to protect it. A deer had stopped to investigate, and when Manuel shouted to warn it off the deer hooked the pack over its antlers in a panic, tearing the pack loose from the branch and carrying it away. Pack and antlers were so entangled, Manuel imagined the deer must have worn his provisions and clean shirts until antler-shedding season. He reported that incident to the rangers, too, but what could anyone do? He was reminded of it, guiltily, every time he read *Thidwick, the Big-hearted Moose* to his four-year-old son.

Manuel and Mark arrived home three days early. Manuel's wife said she'd been expecting him.

She emptied his pack. "Where's the can opener?" she asked.

"It's there somewhere," said Manuel.

"It's not," she said.

"Check the shirt pocket."

"It's not here." Manuel's wife held the pack upside down and shook it. Dead leaves fell out. "How were you going to drink the beer?" she asked.

In August of 1962, Caroline Crosby, a teenager from Palo Alto, accompanied her family on a forced march from Tuolumne Meadows to Vogelsang. She carried fourteen pounds in a pack with an aluminum frame—and her father said it was the lightest pack on the market, and she should be able to carry one-third her weight, so fourteen pounds was nothing, but her pack stabbed her continuously in one coin-sized spot just below her right shoulder, and it still hurt the next morning. Her boots left a blister on her right heel, and her pack straps had rubbed. Her father had bought her a mummy bag with no zipper so as to minimize its weight; it was stiflingly hot, and she sweated all night. She missed an overnight at Ann Watson's house, where Ann showed them her sister's Mark Eden bust developer, and her sister retaliated by freezing all their bras behind the twin-pops. She missed "The Beverly Hillbillies."

Caroline's father had quit smoking just for the duration of the trip, so as to spare himself the weight of cigarettes, and made continual comments about nature, which were laudatory in content and increasingly abusive in tone. Caroline's mother kept telling her to smile.

In the morning her father mixed half a cup of stream water into a packet of powdered eggs and cooked them over a Coleman stove. "Damn fine breakfast," he told Caroline intimidatingly as she stared in horror at her plate. "Out here in God's own country. What else could you ask for?" He turned to Caroline's mother, who was still trying to get a pot of water to come to a boil. "Where's the goddamn coffee?" he asked. He went to the stream to brush his teeth with a toothbrush he had sawed the handle from in order to save the weight. Her mother told her to please make a little effort to be cheerful and not spoil the trip for everyone.

One week later she was in Letterman Hospital in San Francisco. The diagnosis was septicemic plague.

Which is finally where I come into the story. My name is Keith Harmon. B.A. in history with a special emphasis on epidemics. I probably know as much as anyone about the plague of Athens. Typhus. Tarantism. Tsutsugamushi fever. It's an odder historical specialty than it ought to be. More battles have been decided by disease than by generals—and if you don't believe me, take a closer look at the Crusades or the fall of the Roman Empire or Napoleon's Russian campaign.

My M.A. is in public administration. Vietnam veteran, too, but in 1962 I worked for the state of California as part of the plague-monitoring team. When Letterman's reported a plague victim, Sacramento sent me down to talk to her.

Caroline had been moved to a private room. "You're going to be fine," I told her. Of course, she was. We still lose people to the pneumonic plague, but the slower form is easily cured. The only tricky part is making the diagnosis.

"I don't feel well. I don't like the food," she said. She pointed out Letterman's Tuesday menu. "Hawaiian Delight. You know what that is? Green Jell-O with a canned pineapple ring on top. What's delightful about that?" She was feverish and lethargic. Her hair lay limply about her head, and she kept tangling it in her fingers as she talked. "I'm missing a lot of school." Impossible to tell if this last was a complaint or a boast. She raised her bed to a sitting position and spent most of the rest of the interview looking out the window, making it clear that a view of the Letterman parking lot was more arresting than a conversation with an old man like me. She seemed younger than fifteen. Of course, everyone in a hospital bed feels young. Helpless. "Will you ask them to let me wash and set my hair?"

I pulled a chair over to the bed. "I need to know if you've been anywhere unusual recently. We know about Yosemite. Anywhere else. Hiking out around the airport, for instance." The plague is endemic in the San Bruno Mountains by the San Francisco Airport. That particular species of flea doesn't bite humans, though. Or so we'd always thought. "It's kind of a romantic spot for some teenagers, isn't it?"

I've seen some withering adolescent stares in my time, but this one was practiced. I still remember it. I may be sick, it said, but at least I'm not an idiot. "Out by the airport?" she said. "Oh, right. Real romantic. The radio playing and those 727s overhead. Give me a break."

"Let's talk about Yosemite, then."

She softened a little. "In Palo Alto we go to the water temple," she informed me. "And, no, I haven't been there, either. My parents *made* me go to Yosemite. And now I've got bubonic plague." Her tone was one of satisfaction. "I think it was the powdered eggs. They *made* me eat them. I've been sick ever since."

"Did you see any unusual wildlife there? Did you play with any squirrels?"

"Oh, right," she said. "I always play with squirrels. Birds sit on my fingers." She resumed the stare. "My parents didn't tell you what I saw?"

"No," I said.

"Figures." Caroline combed her fingers through her hair. "If I had a brush, I could at least rat it. Will you ask the doctors to bring me a brush?"

"What did you see, Caroline?"

"Nothing. According to my parents. No big deal." She looked out at the parking lot. "I saw a boy."

She wouldn't look at me, but she finished her story. I heard about the mummy bag and the overnight party she missed. I heard about the eggs. Apparently, the altercation over breakfast had escalated, culminating in Caroline's refusal to accompany her parents on a brisk hike to Ireland Lake. She stayed behind, lying on top of her sleeping bag and reading the part of *Green Mansions* where Abel eats a fine meal of anteater flesh. "After the breakfast I had, my mouth was watering," she told me. Something made her look up suddenly from her book. She said it wasn't a sound. She said it was a silence.

A naked boy dipped his hands into the stream and licked the water from his fingers. His fingernails curled toward his palms like claws. "Hey," Caroline told me she told him. She could see his penis and everything. The boy gave her a quick look and then backed away into the trees. She went back to her book.

She described him to her family when they returned. "Real dirty," she said. "Real hairy."

"You have a very superior attitude," her mother noted. "It's going to get you in trouble someday."

"Fine," said Caroline, feeling superior. "Don't believe me." She made a vow never to tell her parents anything again. "And I never will," she told me. "Not if I have to eat powdered eggs until I die."

At this time there started a plague. It appeared not in one part of the world only, not in one race of men only, and not in any particular season; but it spread over the entire earth, and afflicted all without mercy of both sexes and of every age. It began in Egypt, at Pelusium; thence it spread to Alexandria and to the rest of Egypt; then went to Palestine, and from there over the whole world. . . .

In the second year, in the spring, it reached Byzantium and began in the following manner: to many there appeared phantoms in human form. Those who were so encountered were struck by a blow from the phantom, and so contracted the disease. Others locked themselves into their houses. But then the phantoms appeared to them in dreams, or they heard voices that told them that they had been selected for death.

This comes from Procopius's account of the first pandemic. A.D. 541, *De Bello Persico*, Chapter XXII. It's the only explanation I can give you for why Caroline's story made me so uneasy, why I chose not to mention it to anyone. I thought she'd had a fever dream, but thinking this didn't settle me any. I talked to her parents briefly and then went back to Sacramento to write my report.

We have no way of calculating the deaths in the first pandemic. Gibbon says that during three months, five to ten thousand people died daily in Constantinople, and many Eastern cities were completely abandoned.

The second pandemic began in 1346. It was the darkest time the planet has known. A third of the world died. The Jews were blamed, and, throughout Europe, pogroms occurred wherever sufficient health remained for the activity. When murdering Jews provided no alleviation, a committee of doctors at the University of Paris concluded the plague was the result of an unfortunate conjunction of Saturn, Jupiter, and Mars.

The third pandemic occurred in Europe during the fifteenth to eighteenth centuries. The fourth began in China in 1855. It reached Hong Kong in 1894, where Alexandre Yersin of the Institut Pasteur at least identified the responsible bacilli. By 1898 the disease had killed six million people in India. Dr. Paul-Louis Simond, also working for the Institut Pasteur, but stationed in Bombay, finally identified fleas as the primary carriers. "On June 2, 1898, I was overwhelmed," he wrote. "I had just unveiled a secret which had tormented man for so long."

His discoveries went unnoticed for another decade or so. On June 27, 1899, the disease came to San Francisco. The governor of California, acting in protection of business interests, made it a felony to publicize the presence of the plague. People died instead of *syphilitic septicemia*. Because of this deception, thirteen of the Western states are still designated plague areas.

The state team went into the high country in early October. Think of us as soldiers. One of the great mysteries of history is why the plague finally disappeared. The rats are still here. The fleas are still here. The disease is still here; it shows up in isolated cases like Caroline's. Only the epidemic is missing. We're in the middle of the fourth assault. The enemy is elusive. The war is unwinnable. We remain vigilant.

The Vogelsang Camp had already been closed for the winter. No snow yet, but the days were chilly and the nights below freezing. If the plague was present, it wasn't really going to be a problem until spring. We amused ourselves poking sticks into warm burrows looking for dead rodents. We set out some traps. Not many. You don't want to decrease the rodent population. Deprive the fleas of their natural hosts, and they just look for replacements. They just bring the war home.

We picked up a few bodies, but no positives. We could have dusted the place anyway as a precaution. *Silent Spring* came out in 1962, but I hadn't read it.

I saw the coyote on the fourth day. She came out of a hole on the bank of Lewis Creek and stood for a minute with her nose in the air. She was grayed with age around her muzzle, possibly a bit arthritic. She shook out one hind leg. She shook out the other. Then, right as I watched, Caroline's boy climbed out of the burrow after the coyote.

I couldn't see the boy's face. There was too much hair in the way. But his body was hairless, and even though his movements were peculiar and inhuman, I never thought that he was anything but a boy. Twelve years old or maybe thirteen, I thought, although small for thirteen. Wild as a wolf, obviously. Raised by coyotes maybe. But clearly human. Circumcised, if anyone is interested.

I didn't move. I forgot about Procopius and stepped into the *National Enquirer* instead. Marilyn was in my den. Elvis was in my rinse cycle. It was my lucky day. I was amusing myself when I should have been awed. It was a stupid mistake. I wish now that I'd been someone different.

The boy yawned and closed his eyes, then shook himself awake and followed the coyote along the creek and out of sight. I went back to camp. The next morning we surrounded the hole and netted them coming out. This is the moment it stopped being such a lark. This is an uncomfortable memory. The coyote was terrified, and we let her go. The boy was terrified, and we kept him. He scratched us and bit and snarled. He cut me, and I thought it was one of his nails, but he turned out to be holding a can opener. He was covered with fleas, fifty or sixty of them visible at a time, which jumped from him to us, and they all bit, too. It was like being attacked by a cloud. We sprayed the burrow and the boy and ourselves, but we'd all been bitten by then. We took an immediate blood sample. The boy screamed and rolled his eyes all the way through it. The reading was negative. By the time we all calmed down, the boy really didn't like us.

Clint and I tied him up, and we took turns carrying him down to Tuolumne. His odor was somewhere between dog and boy, and worse than both. We tried to clean him up in the showers at the ranger station. Clint and I both had to strip to do this, so God knows what he must have thought we were about. He reacted to the touch of water as if it burned. There was no way to shampoo his hair, and no one with the strength to cut it. So we settled for washing his face and hands, put our clothes back on, gave him a sweater that he dropped by the drain, put him in the backseat of my Rambler, and drove to Sacramento. He cried most of the way, and when we went around curves he allowed his body to be flung unresisting from one side of the car to the other, occasionally knocking his head against the door handle with a loud, painful sound.

I bought him a ham sandwich when we stopped for gas in Modesto, but he wouldn't eat it. He was a nice-looking kid, had a normal face, freckled, with blue eyes, brown hair, and if he'd had a haircut you could have imagined him in some Sears catalog modeling raincoats.

One of life's little ironies. It was October 14. We rescue a wild boy from isolation and deprivation and winter in the mountains. We bring him civilization and human contact. We bring him straight into the Cuban Missile Crisis.

Maybe that's why you don't remember reading about him in the paper. We turned him over to the state of California, which had other things on its mind.

The state put him in Mercy Hospital and assigned maybe a hundred doctors to the case. I was sent back to Yosemite to continue looking for fleas. The next time I saw the boy about a week had passed. He'd been cleaned up, of course. Scoured of parasites, inside and out. Measured. He was just over four feet tall and weighed seventy-five pounds. His head was all but shaved so as not to interfere with the various neurological tests, which had turned out normal and were being redone. He had been observed rocking in a seated position, left to right and back to front, mouth closed, chin up, eyes staring at nothing. Occasionally he had small spasms, convulsive movements, which suggested abnormalities in the nervous system. His teeth needed extensive work. He was sleeping under his bed. He wouldn't touch his Hawaiian Delight. He liked us even less than before.

About this time I had a brief conversation with a doctor whose name I didn't notice. I was never able to find him again. Red-haired doctor with glasses. Maybe thirty, thirty-two years old. "He's got some unusual musculature," this red-haired doctor told me. "Quite singular. Especially the development of the legs. He's shown us some really surprising capabilities." The boy started to howl, an unpleasant, inhuman sound that started in his throat and ended in yours. It was so unhappy. It made me so unhappy to hear it. I never followed up on what the doctor had said.

I felt peculiar about the boy, responsible for him. He had such a *boyish* face. I visited several times, and I took him little presents, a Dodgers baseball cap and an illustrated *Goldilocks and the Three Bears* with the words printed big. Pretty silly, I suppose, but what would you have gotten? I drove to Fresno and asked Manuel Rodriguez if he could identify the can opener. "Not with any assurance," he said. I talked personally to Sergeant Redburn, the man from Missing Persons. When he told me about the Beckers, I went to the state library and read the newspaper articles for myself. Sergeant Redburn thought the boy might be just about the same age as Paul Becker, and I thought so, too. And I know the sergeant went to talk to Anna Becker's mother about it, because he told me she was going to come and try to identify the boy.

By now it's November. Suddenly I get a call sending me back to Yosemite. In Sacramento they claim the team has reported a positive, but when I arrive in Yosemite the whole team denies it. Fleas are astounding creatures. They can be frozen for a year or more and then revived to full activity. But November in the mountains is a stupid time to be out looking for them. It's already snowed once, and it snows again, so that I can't get my team back out. We spend three weeks in the ranger station at Vogelsang huddled around our camp stoves while they air-drop supplies to us. And when I get back a doctor I've never seen before, a Dr. Frank Li, tells me the boy, who was not Paul Becker, died suddenly of a seizure while he slept. I have to work hard to put away the sense that it was my fault, that I should have left the boy where he belonged.

And then I hear Sergeant Redburn has jumped off the Golden Gate Bridge.

Non gratum anus rodentum. Not worth a rat's ass. This was the unofficial motto of the tunnel rats. We're leaping ahead here. Now it's 1967. Vietnam. Does the name Cu Chi mean anything to you? If not, why not? The district of Cu Chi is the most bombed, shelled, gassed, strafed, defoliated, and destroyed piece of earth in the history of warfare. And beneath Cu Chi runs the most complex part of a network of tunnels that connects Saigon all the way to the Cambodian border.

I want you to imagine, for a moment, a battle fought entirely in the dark. Imagine that you are in a hole that is too hot and too small. You cannot stand up; you must move on your hands and knees by touch and hearing alone through a terrain you can't see toward an enemy you can't see. At any moment you might trip a mine, put your hand on a snake, put your face on a decaying corpse. You know people who have done all three of these things. At any moment the air you breathe might turn to gas, the tunnel become so small you can't get back out; you could fall into a well of water and drown; you could be buried alive. If you are lucky, you will put your knife into an enemy you may never see before he puts his knife into you. In Cu Chi the Vietnamese and the Americans created, inch by inch, body part by body part, an entirely new type of warfare.

Among the Vietnamese who survived are soldiers who lived in the tiny underground tunnels without surfacing for five solid years. Their eyesight was permanently damaged. They suffered constant malnutrition, felt lucky when they could eat spoiled rice and rats. Self-deprivation was their weapon; they used it to force the soldiers of the most technically advanced army in the world to face them with knives, one on one, underground, in the dark.

On the American side, the tunnel rats were all volunteers. You can't force a man to do what he cannot do. Most Americans hyperventilated, had attacks of claustrophobia, were too big. The tunnel rats could be no bigger than the Vietnamese, or they wouldn't fit through the tunnels. Most of the tunnel rats were Hispanics and Puerto Ricans. They stopped wearing after-shave so the Vietcong wouldn't smell them. They stopped chewing gum, smoking, and eating candy because it impaired their ability to sense the enemy. They had to develop the sonar of bats. They had, in their own words, to become animals. What they did in the tunnels, they said, was unnatural.

In 1967 I was attached to the 521st Medical Detachment. I was an old man by Vietnamese standards, but then, I hadn't come to fight in the Vietnam War. Remember that the fourth pandemic began in China. Just before he died, Chinese poet Shih Tao-nan wrote:

> *Few days following the death of the rats,*
> *Men pass away like falling walls.*

Between 1965 and 1970, 24,848 cases of the plague were reported in Vietnam.

War is the perfect breeding ground for disease. They always go together, the trinity: war, disease, and cruelty. Disease was my war. I'd been sent to Vietnam to keep my war from interfering with everybody else's war.

In March we received by special courier a package containing three dead rats. The rats had been found—already dead, but leashed—inside a tunnel in Hau Nghia province. Also found—but not sent to us—were a syringe, a phial containing yellow fluid, and several cages. I did the test myself. One of the dead rats carried the plague.

There has been speculation that the Vietcong were trying to use plague rats as weapons. It's also possible they were merely testing the rats prior to eating them themselves. In the end, it makes little difference. The plague was there in the tunnels whether the Vietcong used it or not.

I set up a tent outside Cu Chi town to give boosters to the tunnel rats. One of the men I inoculated was David Rivera. "David has been into the tunnels so many times, he's a legend," his companions told me.

"Yeah," said David. "Right. Me and Victor."

"Victor Charlie?" I said. I was just making conversation. I could see David, whatever his record in the tunnels, was afraid of the needle. He held out one stiff arm. I was trying to get him to relax.

"No. Not hardly. Victor is the one." He took his shot, put his shirt back on, gave up his place to the next man in line.

"Victor can see in the dark," the next man told me.

"Victor Charlie?" I asked again.

"No," the man said impatiently.

"You want to know about Victor?" David said. "Let me tell you about Victor. Victor's the one who comes when someone goes down and doesn't come back out."

"Victor can go faster on his hands and knees than most men can run," the other man said. I pressed cotton on his arm after I withdrew the needle; he got up from the table. A third man sat down and took off his shirt.

David still stood next to me. "I go into this tunnel. I'm not too scared, because I think it's cold; I'm not *feeling* anybody else there, and I'm maybe a quarter of a mile in, on my hands and knees, when I can almost see a hole in front of me, blacker than anything else in the tunnel, which is all black, you know. So I go into the hole, feeling my way, and I have this funny sense like I'm not moving into the hole; the hole is moving over to me. I put out my hands, and the ground moves under them."

"Shit," said the third man. I didn't know if it was David's story or the shot. A fourth man sat down.

"I risk a light, and the whole tunnel is covered with spiders, covered like wallpaper, only worse, two or three bodies thick," David said. "I'm sitting on them, and the spiders are already inside my pants and inside my shirt and covering my arms—and it's fucking Vietnam, you know; I don't even know if they're poisonous or not. Don't care, really, because I'm going to die just from having them on me. I can feel them moving toward my face. So I start to scream, and then this little guy comes and pulls me back out a ways, and then he sits for maybe half an hour, calm as can be, picking spiders off me. When I decide to live after all, I go back out. I tell everybody. 'That was Victor,' they say. 'Had to be Victor.' "

"I know a guy says Victor pulled him from a hole," the fourth soldier said. "He falls through a false floor down maybe twelve straight feet into this tiny little trap with straight walls all around and no way up, and Victor comes down after him. *Jumps* back out, holding the guy in his arms. Twelve feet; the guy swears it."

"Tiny little guy," said David. "Even for V.C., this guy'd be tiny."

"He just looks tiny," the second soldier said. "I know a guy saw Victor buried under more than a ton of dirt. Victor just digs his way out again. No broken bones, no nothing."

Inexcusably slow, and I'd been told twice, but I had just figured out that Victor wasn't short for V.C. "I'd better inoculate this Victor," I said. "You think you could send him in?"

The men stared at me. "You don't get it, do you?" said David.

"Victor don't report," the fourth man says.

"No C.O.," says the third man. "No unit."

"He's got the uniform," the second man tells me. "So we don't know if he's special forces of some sort or if he's AWOL down in the tunnels."

"Victor lives in the tunnels," said David. "Nobody up top has ever seen him."

I tried to talk to one of the doctors about it. "Tunnel vision," he told me. "We get a lot of that. Forget it."

In May we got a report of more rats—some leashed, some in cages—in a tunnel near Ah Nhon Tay village in the Ho Bo woods. But no one wanted to go in and get them, because these rats were alive. And somebody got the idea this was my job, and somebody else agreed. They would clear the tunnel of V.C. first, they promised me. So I volunteered.

Let me tell you about rats. Maybe they're not responsible for the plague, but they're still destructive to every kind of life-form and beneficial to none. They eat anything that lets them. They breed during all seasons. They kill their own kind; they can do it singly, but they can also organize and attack in hordes. The brown rat is currently embroiled in a war of extinction against the black rat. Most animals behave better than that.

I'm not afraid of rats. I read somewhere that about the turn of the century a man in western Illinois heard a rustling in his fields one night. He got out of bed and went to the back door, and behind his house he saw a great mass of rats that stretched all the way to the horizon. I suppose this would have frightened me. All those naked tails in the moonlight. But I thought I could handle a few rats in cages, no problem.

It wasn't hard to locate them. I was on my hands and knees, but using a flashlight. I thought there might be some loose rats, too, and that I ought to look at least; and I'd also heard that there was an abandoned V.C. hospital in the tunnel that I was curious about. So I left the cages and poked around in the tunnels a bit; and when I'd had enough, I started back to get the rats, and I hit a water trap. There hadn't been a water trap before, so I knew I must have taken a wrong turn. I went back a bit, took another turn, and then another, and hit the water trap again. By now I was starting to panic. I couldn't find anything I'd ever seen before except the damn water. I went back again, farther without turning, took a turn, hit the trap.

I must have tried seven, eight times. I no longer thought the tunnel was cold. I thought the V.C. had closed the door on my original route so that I wouldn't find it again. I thought they were watching every move I made, pretty easy with me waving my flashlight about. I switched it off. I could hear them in the dark, their eyelids closing and opening, their hands tightening on their knives. I was sweating, head to toe, like I was ill, like I had the mysterious English sweating sickness or the *suette des Picards*.

And I knew that to get back to the entrance I had to go into the water. I sat and thought that through, and when I finished I wasn't the same man I'd been when I began the thought.

It would have been bad to have to crawl back through the tunnels with no light. To go into the water with no light, not knowing how much water there was, not knowing if one lungful of air would be enough or if there were underwater turns so you might get lost before you found air again, was something you'd have to be crazy to do. I had to do it, so I had to be crazy first. It wasn't as hard as you might think. It took me only a minute.

I filled my lungs as full as I could. Emptied them once. Filled them again and dove in. Someone grabbed me by the ankle and hauled me back out. It frightened me so much I swallowed water, so I came up coughing and kicking. The hand released me at once, and I lay there for a bit, dripping water and still sweating, too, feeling the part of the tunnel that was directly below my body turn to mud, while I tried to convince myself that no one was touching me.

Then I was crazy enough to turn my light on. Far down the tunnel, just within range of the light, knelt a little kid dressed in the uniform of the rats. I tried to get closer to him. He moved away, just the same amount I had moved, always just in the light. I followed him down one tunnel, around a turn, down another. Outside, the sun rose and set. We crawled for days. My right knee began to bleed.

"Talk to me," I asked him. He didn't.

Finally he stood up ahead of me. I could see the rat cages, and I knew where the entrance was behind him. And then he was gone. I tried to follow with my flashlight, but he'd jumped or something. He was just gone.

"Victor," Rat Six told me when I finally came out. "Goddamn Victor."

Maybe so. If Victor was the same little boy I put a net over in the high country in Yosemite.

When I came out, they told me less than three hours had passed. I didn't believe them. I told them about Victor. Most of them didn't believe me. Nobody outside the tunnels believed in Victor. "We just sent home one of the rats," a doctor told me. "He emptied his whole gun into a tunnel. Claimed there were V.C. all around him, but that he got them. He shot every one. Only, when we went down to clean it up, there were no bodies. All his bullets were found in the walls.

"Tunnel vision. Everyone sees things. It's the dark. Your eyes no longer impose any limit on the things you can see."

I didn't listen. I made demands right up the chain of command for records: recruitment, AWOLs, special projects. I wanted to talk to everyone who'd ever seen Victor. I wrote Clint to see what he remembered of the drive back from Yosemite. I wrote a thousand letters to Mercy Hospital, telling them I'd uncovered their little game. I demanded to speak with the red-haired doctor with glasses whose name I never knew. I wrote the Curry Company and suggested they conduct a private investigation into the supposed suicide of Sergeant Redburn. I asked the CIA what they had done with Paul's parents. That part was paranoid. I was so unstrung I thought they'd killed his parents and given him to the coyote to raise him up for the tunnel wars. When I calmed down, I knew the CIA would never be so farsighted. I knew they'd just gotten lucky. I didn't know what happened to the parents; still don't.

There were so many crazy people in Vietnam, it could take them a long time to notice a new one, but I made a lot of noise. A team of three doctors talked to me for a total of seven hours. Then they said I was suffering from delayed guilt over the death of my little dog-boy and that it surfaced, along with every other weak link in my personality, in the stress and the darkness of the tunnels. They sent me home. I missed the moon landing, because I was having a nice little time in a hospital of my own.

When I was finally and truly released, I went looking for Caroline Crosby. The Crosbys still lived in Palo Alto, but Caroline did not. She'd started college at Berkeley, but then she'd dropped out. Her parents hadn't seen her for several months.

Her mother took me through their beautiful house and showed me Caroline's old room. She had a canopy bed and her own bathroom. There was a mirror with old pictures of some boy on it. A throw rug with roses. There was a lot of pink. "We drive through the Haight every weekend," Caroline's mother said. "Just looking." She was pale and controlled. "If you should see her, would you tell her to call?"

I would not. I made one attempt to return one little boy to his family, and look what happened. Either Sergeant Redburn jumped from the Golden Gate Bridge in the middle of his investigation or he didn't. Either Paul Becker died in Mercy Hospital or he was picked up by the military to be their special weapon in a special war.

I've thought about it now for a couple of decades, and I've decided that, at least for Paul, once he'd escaped from the military, things didn't work out so badly. He must have felt more at home in the tunnels under Cu Chi than he had under the bed in Mercy Hospital.

There is a darkness inside us all that is animal. Against some things—untreated or untreatable disease, for example, or old age—the darkness is all we are. Either we are strong enough animals or we are not. Such things pare everything that is not animal away from us. As animals we have a physical value, but in moral terms we are neither good nor bad. Morality begins on the way back from the darkness.

The first two plagues were largely believed to be a punishment for man's sinfulness. "So many died," wrote Agnolo di Tura the Fat, who buried all five of his own children himself, "that all believed that it was the end of the world." This being the case, you'd imagine the cessation of the plague must have been accompanied by out-breaks of charity and godliness. The truth was just the opposite. In 1349, in Erfurt, Germany, of the three thousand Jewish residents there not one survived. This is a single instance of a barbarism so marked and so pervasive it can be understood only as a form of mass insanity.

Here is what Procopius said: *And after the plague had ceased, there was so much depravity and general licentiousness that it seemed as though the disease had left only the most wicked.*

When men are turned into animals, it's hard for them to find their way back to themselves. When children are turned into animals, there's no self to find. There's never been a feral child who found his way out of the dark. Maybe there's never been a feral child who wanted to.

You don't believe I saw Paul in the tunnels at all. You think I'm crazy or, charitably, that I was crazy then, just for a little while. Maybe you think the CIA would never have killed a policeman or tried to use a little child in a black war, even though the CIA has done everything else you've ever been told and refused to believe.

That's okay. I like your version just fine. Because if I made him up, and all the tunnel rats who ever saw him made him up, then he belongs to us, he marks us. Our vision, our Procopian phantom in the tunnels. Victor to take care of us in the dark.

Caroline came home without me. I read her wedding announcement in the paper more than twenty years ago. She married a Stanford chemist. There was a picture of her in her parents' backyard with gardenias in her hair. She was twenty-five years old. She looked happy. I never did go talk to her.

So here's a story for you, Caroline:

A small German town was much plagued by rats who ate the crops and the chickens, the ducks, the cloth and the seeds. Finally the citizens called in an exterminator. He was the best; he trapped and poisoned the rats. Within a month he had deprived the fleas of most of their hosts.

The fleas then bit the children of the town instead. Hundreds of children were taken with a strange dancing and raving disease. Their parents tried to control them, tried to keep them safe in their beds, but the moment their mothers' backs were turned the children ran into the streets and danced. The town was Erfurt. The year was 1237.

Most of the children danced themselves to death. But not all. A few of them recovered and lived to be grown-ups. They married and worked and had their own children. They lived reasonable and productive lives.

The only thing is that they still twitch sometimes. Just now and then. They can't help it.

Stop me, Caroline, if you've heard this story before.

THEY'RE MADE OUT OF MEAT

. . . .

Terry Bisson

Terry Bisson's first appearance in this series was occasioned by "Bears Discover Fire," which won not only the Nebula Award but also the Hugo Award, the Theodore Sturgeon Memorial Award, the *Asimov's* Readers' Poll, the *Locus* Poll, the Golden Pagoda, and several prizes invented expressly for the purpose of honoring that particular story (or so it seemed at the time).

But Bisson's reputation rests on far more than one shot. Among his acclaimed novels are *Talking Man*, a World Fantasy Award nominee that tells of the first auto trip to the North Pole; *Fire on the Mountain*, which dramatizes what might have happened if John Brown's raid on Harpers Ferry had succeeded; and *Voyage to the Red Planet*, an idiosyncratic space adventure. Bisson's stories have graced most of the major SF magazines, and, to save us the trouble of hunting through back issues, Tor Books is about to release *Bears Discover Fire and Other Stories*.

Originally published in *Omni*, "They're Made Out of Meat" was subsequently accorded a reprint in *Harper's* and a successful dramatization in the basement theater of the West Bank Cafe in New York City. Invited to explain the story's origins, Bisson observed: "Allen Ginsberg once corrected a pompous TV interviewer, who was prating on about their souls communicating, by saying, 'We're just meat talking to meat.' That stuck in my mind (which is made out of meat) for years. I wrote this story to amuse my family and only afterward realized that I had come rather late to a theme that has been explored in SF by Fred Pohl, among others, and that I was digging in SF's richest if most-worked lode, the First Contact tale. I followed 'TMOM' with several other all-dialogue short-shorts, which have been, without exception, fun to write but hard to sell. I don't think a story can be too short. I think the magazines should pay us a flat $1,000, then *deduct* five cents a word. But I digress. . . ."

"They're made out of meat."

"Meat?"

"Meat. They're made out of meat."

"Meat?"

"There's no doubt about it. We picked up several from different parts of the planet, took them aboard our recon vessels, and probed them all the way through. They're completely meat."

"That's impossible. What about the radio signals? The messages to the stars?"

"They use the radio waves to talk, but the signals don't come from them. The signals come from machines."

"So who made the machines? That's who we want to contact."

"*They* made the machines. That's what I'm trying to tell you. Meat made the machines."

"That's ridiculous. How can meat make a machine? You're asking me to believe in sentient meat."

"I'm not asking you. I'm telling you. These creatures are the only sentient race in that sector, and they're made out of meat."

"Maybe they're like the orfolei. You know, a carbon-based intelligence that goes through a meat stage."

"Nope. They're born meat and they die meat. We studied them for several of their life spans, which didn't take long. Do you have any idea of the life span of meat?"

"Spare me. Okay, maybe they're only part meat. You know, like the weddilei. A meat head with an electron plasma brain inside."

"Nope. We thought of that, since they do have meat heads, like the weddilei. But I told you, we probed them. They're meat all the way through."

"No brain?"

"Oh, there's a brain all right. It's just that the brain is *made out of meat!* That's what I've been trying to tell you."

"So . . . what does the thinking?"

"You're not understanding, are you? You're refusing to deal with what I'm telling you. The brain does the thinking. The meat."

"Thinking meat! You're asking me to believe in thinking meat!"

"Yes, thinking meat! Conscious meat! Loving meat. Dreaming meat. The meat is the whole deal! Are you beginning to get the picture, or do I have to start all over?"

"Omigod. You're serious, then. They're made out of meat."

"Thank you. Finally. Yes. They are indeed made out of meat. And they've been trying to get in touch with us for almost a hundred of their years."

"Omigod. So what does this meat have in mind?"

"First it wants to talk to us. Then I imagine it wants to explore the universe, contact other sentiences, swap ideas and information. The usual."

"We're supposed to talk to meat."

"That's the idea. That's the message they're sending out by radio, 'Hello. Anyone out there? Anybody home?' That sort of thing."

"They actually do talk, then. They use words, ideas, concepts?"

"Oh, yes. Except they do it with meat."

"I thought you just told me they used radio."

"They do, but what do you think is *on* the radio? Meat sounds. You know how when you slap or flap meat, it makes a noise? They talk by flapping their meat at each other. They can even sing by squirting air through their meat."

"Omigod. Singing meat. This is altogether too much. So what do you advise?"

"Officially or unofficially?"

"Both."

"Officially, we are required to contact, welcome, and log in any and all sentient races or multibeings in this quadrant of the universe, without prejudice, fear, or favor. Unofficially, I advise that we erase the records and forget the whole thing."

"I was hoping you would say that."

"It seems harsh, but there is a limit. Do we really want to make contact with meat?"

"I agree one hundred percent. What's there to say? 'Hello, meat. How's it going?' But will this work? How many planets are we dealing with here?"

"Just one. They can travel to other planets in special meat containers, but they can't live on them. And being meat, they can only travel through C space. Which limits them to the speed of light and makes the possibility of their ever making contact pretty slim. Infinitesimal, in fact."

"So we just pretend there's no one home in the universe."

"That's it."

"Cruel. But you said it yourself, who wants to meet meat? And the ones who have been aboard our vessels, the ones you probed? You're sure they won't remember?"

"They'll be considered crackpots if they do. We went into their heads and smoothed out their meat so that we're just a dream to them."

"A dream to meat! How strangely appropriate, that we should be meat's dream."

"And we marked the entire sector *unoccupied*."

"Good. Agreed, officially and unofficially. Case closed. Any others? Anyone interesting on that side of the galaxy?"

"Yes, a rather shy but sweet hydrogen core cluster intelligence in a class nine star in G445 zone. Was in contact two galactic rotations ago, wants to be friendly again."

"They always come around."

"And why not? Imagine how unbearably, how unutterably cold the universe would be if one were all alone. . . ."

PRECESSING THE SIMULACRA FOR FUN AND PROFIT

· · · · · · · ·

Bruce Sterling

Like a middle child being ignored by his parents, the author of a best-novel Nebula finalist has little chance of appearing in this series unless he actually takes the prize. It's hard enough figuring out how to represent the winning novelist each year; forget the runners-up.

When I came upon the following essay in *Monad*, Pulphouse Publishing's classy little irregular journal of SF criticism, I realized that reprinting it would, among other things, help remedy the injustice typically suffered by best-novel nominees. I strongly suspect that, in the final tally, William Gibson and Bruce Sterling's *The Difference Engine* gave Michael Swanwick's *Stations of the Tide* a run for its money (indeed, in delineating a Victorian world in which Charles Babbage's computer has taken hold, the novel emerged as one of the most persuasive "alternate histories" in recent memory), but mostly I wanted to share with you Sterling's wry odyssey through the inhospitable terrain contemporary critical theory has become. Maybe it's because I live in a college town and hear people say things like "poststructuralism" and "a rival hermeneutic" right out in public that I was particularly taken with this piece. I'm quite confident, however, that it will please anyone who delights in pondering the nature of the SF beast.

In the space that remains to me here, I shall point out that to Bruce Sterling can be credited such mind-boggling novels as *Involution Ocean*, *The Artificial Kid*, *Schismatrix*, and *Islands in the Net*, that he edited *Mirrorshades: The Cyberpunk Anthology*, that his *Crystal Express* quickly became one of the most coveted collections in the field, and that he is some sort of genius. His new collection is called *Globalhead*, and he has also recently published *The Hacker Crackdown: Law and Disorder on the Electronic Frontier*, a nonfiction book on computer crime and civil liberties. Sterling commonly finds himself called a cyberpunk, a label to which he acquiesces several times in "Precessing the Simulacra."

This essay describes my two-year explorations in the recherché hinterlands of contemporary literary theory. I undertook this expedition with a bold swagger and a stout heart, but my once-proud propeller

topee is now mere tatters of canvas and cork. Reduced nigh to madness by privation and suffering, I now pluck at people's sleeves like
the Ancient Mariner, to tell my sorry tale.

In my rash youth, I sniggered aloud at "academics"—to my shame,
I once made public fun of Ursula K. Le Guin for daring to employ
the term "semiotics"! How little I knew.

In 1988, *Mississippi Review* 47/48, the "Cyberpunk Controversy"
issue, was assembled and published. This was my first real contact
with postmodernist theory. It wasn't the first time I had heard tell
of the notion, but it was definitely the first time that it occurred to
me to pay any attention to it.

I had three basic motives for this literary expedition. The first was
my absurdly pleased realization that academics existed who took a
genuine interest in what I said and thought. The second was my dim
understanding that these postmodern guys were bitterly opposed to
the academic litterateurs I had always distrusted—that they were
the enemy's enemy and might therefore be a source of useful ideo-
logical mischief. And, last, I hoped to learn something from theory
that might have a practical application to my work—writing science
fiction.

I've always been distrustful of the standards of mainstream literary criticism as they impinge on SF—that nexus of convictions my
generation loosely calls "humanist"—because it seemed to me to
interfere with what I considered SF's legitimate ends. Much of this
unease was simple ignorance on my part. And it was not unmixed
with the traditional SF attitudes toward "the mainstream": pugna-
cious defensiveness, sneaking suspicions of inferiority, chest-pound-
ing overcompensation, *und so weiter*. As time has passed, and I've
looked long and deliberately upon the objects of my loathing, I've
come to see mainstream literary criticism as something of a paper
tiger. There doesn't seem to be a lot of solemn mandarin authority
left in mainstream criticism, for modern fiction grows more eclectic
and decentralized by the day. Today, when I worry about demonized
phantoms who might want to smother SF in its ghetto, I sensibly
direct my paranoia toward megapublishers and bookstore chains.

But still—while I'm ready to use any literary tool if it will serve
my purposes, and I'm quite willing to steal the clothes of "human-
ists" to cyberpunk ends—my basic literary catechism remains firm.

My central dogma is that science fiction is not by nature a "genre"— it is not a delimited category that can be safely assigned to a shady spot under the tree of literature. Instead, SF is, and should be, something violative and monstrous. SF is a violent break with the cultural legacy of Western literature—even popular literature.

SF is not a way to "tell stories." SF is a way to discuss the havoc wreaked on our culture by technological advance and the truths we have learned through the scientific method. SF exists in the chasm between the crumbling ramparts of literary culture and the similarly crumbling ramparts of scientific culture. True SF, while it can be written with clarity and elegance, must always reek somewhat of the monograph. It is didactic. SF always bears the Quasimodo hump of a hidden agenda.

One of the most attractive aspects of deconstructive criticism is its bold proclamation that all forms of writing bear a hidden agenda. This levels the playing field for SF and makes it, like all other prose forms, simply a species of "text." I very much enjoy this wicked notion of "text" and find it highly useful in provoking panicked spasms of reflexive denial from other authors. Admittedly, this mischief cannot actually make SF more readable. Basically, it's just the old "Well, you're another" argument, gussied up with intimidating jargon. But it does set bulldozers at the ramparts of the high-lit ivory tower and wakes its denizens from their dogmatic slumbers. And the notion of "text," as opposed to, say, "story" or "narrative," has expanded my own ideas of what is possible and legitimate within SF.

Along with "text" comes the useful notion of "subtext," a rather vague and waffling term that I take to mean the nexus of social convictions conveyed by the story (sorry, uh, "text"). The subtext (as explicated by the people who invented the term) almost always has something to do with power relationships. Political, economic, sexual—"class struggle" is a favorite motif, since these critics are generally Marxists, or have at least stolen their clothes.

Examining power relationships within a text can be quite a useful SF technique. The centers of power change as society changes: the means of production, the means of information, the marks of political legitimacy, the arbiters of style and etiquette all change. To miss this is to remain naively rooted in one's own era, accepting local historical accidents as the natural order of the universe. Open any issue of *Asimov's,* and count the number of protagonists in it who are "artists" of some description, menaced by soulless mechanical forces that threaten even their minor niche in the status quo. In *Analog,* count the rocket jockeys and Competent Men, equally muddleheaded, but identifying with unleashed and unexamined technological power in an unbecoming ecstasy.

The drawback to this technique is that an obsession with power relationships makes one clinically paranoid. Always hunting to see the money trail, where the bodies are buried, who's up and who's down, makes every coincidence or passing remark seem a dark plot of the oppressive capitalist ruling-class patriarchy. In literary terms this is goofy; in political terms it's counterproductive or actively dangerous. Marxist societies *are* paranoid societies; they *do* have oppressive and conspiratorial ruling classes; they create everything in fact that they were originally afraid of. The Marxist habit of mind seems to engender monsters.

Twentieth-century high litcrit is a very weird realm. Much like SF, it seems monolithic from the outside, but once inside the teacup it's a constant storm. Structuralists, poststructuralists, modernists, postmodernists, deconstruction, semiotics, hermeneutics. People whom outsiders can't distinguish with a spectrograph have made careers out of attacking and refuting one another. Many are quite loony.

This guy Ferdinand de Saussure (1857–1913), for instance. He was a Swiss linguist and seems to have been more or less the founder of "semiotics." I can't say he offers much in the way of useful loot for an SF writer. Saussure's major contribution seems to be that he discovered that words bear no tangible relationship to the objects—"referents"—they supposedly describe. Instead words—"signs"—bear relationships only to other "signs," which float like a kind of tangled verbal seaweed over the unknowable depths of whatever "the real" is. Many thousands of words (uh, sorry, "signs") have been devoted to the exploration of these "signs," and the result is a jargon of quite astonishing impenetrability.

Saussure, toward the end of his career, became obsessed with anagrams and used to pick Renaissance poetry apart vowel by vowel, trying to reveal what cats like Dante were really saying. The bolder of Saussure's followers (and of course most of his enemies) will grant that at this point the old boy had cracked.

Michel Foucault, a major figure in modern French thought, was into Freud and Marx and the study of madness. Some say Foucault got a little too close to his material. His stuff's supposedly pretty good, but Jean Baudrillard, a guy who actually *is* of genuine interest to SF writers, wrote a book called *Forget Foucault*, so I figured I could save a lot of pain and energy by not reading much Foucault in the first place. Whew.

Roland Barthes wrote a lot of stuff about semiotics and Japan and proclaimed "the death of the author." He got run over by a laundry truck. Terry Eagleton, a post-Althusserian who used to spend a lot of time on British TV throwing left-handed spitballs at Margaret Thatcher, wrote "Myths of Power: A Marxist Study of the Brontes." I may be a hopeless troglodyte, but this seems to me an innately hilarious title. Jacques Lacan was into the "split subject" and ended up writing "split texts," in which two separate columns of text wander down the page quarreling with one another. But wait—was that somebody else? Not Jacques Lacan? My brain's beginning to throb again. I can't begin to convey to you how stifling this stuff can be. Maybe a random quote from postmodernist doyen Fredric Jameson will serve:

> The assertion of a political unconscious proposes that we undertake just such a final analysis and explore the multiple paths that lead to the unmasking of cultural artifacts as socially symbolic acts. It projects a rival hermeneutic to those already enumerated; but it does so, as we shall see, not so much by repudiating their findings as by arguing its ultimate philosophical and methodological priority over more specialized interpretative codes whose insights are strategically limited as much by their own situational origins as by the narrow or local ways in which they construe or construct their objects of study.

> —"On Interpretation: Literature as a Socially Symbolic Act"

Still with me? Get up if you need to, walk around the room a bit, take a deep breath. And this was the mild stuff from good ol' Fredric Jameson, an American born 'n' bred, a guy whose first language was purportedly English, a professor at Duke who wrote the actually quite interesting and useful (though legendarily unreadable) "Postmodernism, or the Cultural Logic of Late Capitalism." Much exists that is almost unimaginably worse.

I cannot pretend to understand this stuff. I've blundered around it, trying unlocked windows and doors, but my brain blisters easily. Perhaps you, my reader, *do* understand it. If so, I beg you, don't attempt to enlighten my ignorance; spare me. The only way to explain this stuff satisfactorily is to put on the skin of its rhetoric and learn to talk just like it does—something one *actually begins to do* after a while, despite one's best intentions, and the effects on one's prose are horrific. Frankly, if I ever had any intention of, say, mastering the intricacies of post-Althusserian Marxism, I long ago abandoned them. Now I simply walk around with my crowbar and wheelbarrow, looking for stuff not nailed down.

The prose of '50s and '60s critics, like Barthes, Derrida, and de Man, aspired to a kind of droning hypnosis. But the language of "postmodernist" critics—Baudrillard, Arthur Kroker, Paul Virilio— frankly aspires to the condition of *hallucination.* I find this considerably more intriguing, and can whack my way through a Baudrillard essay in a matter of mere hours.

Having vanished years ago into an impenetrable muddle, postmodern theory emerges from the far end of the sump as a monstrous thing, almost completely free of the intention to make any kind of rational sense. In fact, this theory doesn't even have a delineated field of study: it's not anthropology, or psychology, or political science, or literary criticism; it has elements of all this and more, but mostly it's just, well, "theory." Baudrillard's work has the basic structure of an acid-rap, a kind of hallucinatory free association where a dual menace/promise of deep dread and sublime insight lies snuffling at the doors of perception.

Baudrillard's central thesis, like that of "postmodernism" generally, is that there has been a *rupture,* that things have become terribly and irretrievably *different,* in a basic way that is both vast and intimate. Modernity has ended; classic capitalism is over, replaced by a turbocharged information-capitalism that markets data and imagery, not mere physical product. Our society now spins empty images in a kind of dizzy gyroscopic limbo, in a process that Baudrillard calls "the precession of simulacra."

Baudrillard taught sociology at Nanterre University in 1968, the year of the Paris uprisings, and like a lot of his generation he has never put things back together. Greil Marcus describes this syndrome brilliantly in his recent book *Lipstick Traces;* the sensation of having touched or witnessed some kind of terrific raw potential whose disruption of one's psyche is permanent, even if the eggshell of a normal life is successfully reassembled. Reading Baudrillard, one draws the conclusion that Western civilization as a workable social construct ended in the summer of '68, and the ghastly *thing* that has replaced it must forever be some kind of weightless and repellent fraud. Not "reality," but, in Baudrillard's own famous term, "hyperreality." We dwell amid media-ghosts, permanently divorced from the physical. These "simulacra" are not even the remnants of the once living, but self-generating ghosts that multiply entirely on their own, a filmy species of self-replicating fictions, an endless hall of intangible mirrors where "image" means more than reality ever did. It is a basically nightmarish vision, Lovecraftian in its intensity.

Baudrillard is a true voice of the 1980s. Unlike the clunking and buzzing Fredric Jameson, Baudrillard is an excellent writer; something of his swift winging lunacy comes across even in English translation. Here Baudrillard describes an American mirror-glass skyscraper:

> The glass façades merely reflect the environment, sending back its own image. This makes them much more formidable than any wall of stone. It's just like people who wear dark glasses. Their eyes are hidden and others see only their own reflection. Everywhere the transparency of interfaces ends in internal refraction. Everything pretentiously termed "communication" and "interaction"—the Sony Walkman, dark glasses, automatic household appliances, hi-tech cars, even the perpetual dialogue with the computer—ends up with each monad retreating into the shade of its own formula, into its self-regulating little corner and its artificial immunity.
>
> It is the same outside.
>
> A camouflaged individual, with a long beak, feathers, and a yellow cagoule, a madman in fancy dress, wanders along the sidewalks downtown, and nobody, but nobody, looks at him. They do not look at other people here. They are much too afraid they will throw themselves upon them with unbearable sexual demands, requests for money or attention. Everything is charged with a somnambulic violence and you must avoid contact to escape its potential discharge. Now that the mad have been let out of the asylums everyone is seen as a potential madman.
>
> —Jean Baudrillard, *America*

This particular litany of topics: mirrorshades, madmen, computers and Walkmans, a vague terror/resentment of the mysterious commercial entities dwelling in huge skyscrapers; an intense but chilly interest in the anomic wretches who caper in the streets, a world where community has disintegrated amid a constant subliminal threat of violence—this litany makes it very clear why critics like Larry McCaffery consider "cyberpunk" an "apotheosis of postmodernism."

Baudrillard and his fellow travelers are especially entertaining when discussing another cyberpunk obsession, media. Like Marshall McLuhan's, their basic philosophical notions may be suspect; but they are among the few cultural critics willing to talk about media in terms that are as basically *weird* as media actually *are*. Here Baudrillard discusses American television:

> . . . the television, with its twenty-four-hour schedules, often to be seen functioning like an hallucination in the empty rooms of houses or vacant hotel rooms. . . . There is nothing more mysterious than a TV set left on in an empty room. . . . It is as if another planet is communicating with you. Suddenly the TV reveals itself for what it really is: a video of another world, ultimately addressed to no one at all, delivering its images indifferently, indifferent to its own messages (you can easily imagine it still functioning after humanity has disappeared).
>
> —*America*

Here's a smooth bit of rhetorical glibness on Baudrillard's part, since such a dire hallucination is by no means "easily imagined"; it takes a real gift to imagine that sort of thing; it takes a science-fictional gift. Baudrillard often buttresses his arguments with parables from science fiction. Science fiction is in fact the Ur-literature of the Baudrillardian worldview. Science fiction is the form of fiction which offers a portrait of a world that technological advance has rendered surreal. There is much to be gained in reading Jean Baudrillard; what he writes is in fact SF that is all "Quasimodo hump," SF essays without plot, character, denouement, or human interest. He's wild and hilarious, and his writing is original and often strikingly beautiful.

And, like a science fiction writer imagining the future, Baudrillard can't really escape the historical moment in which he is embedded. His very surreality, his probing detachment, paradoxically makes him a true '80s cultural artifact. To declare that "modernity" has ended in convulsion freezes you forever in the moment in which you made that declaration, and as time passes it tends to render you silly. Society may well have suffered a sea change, but the human race isn't extinct; children are still being born, we're still eating; developments that blew the last generation's mind become mere wallpaper to the young. And, of course, the postindustrialized West isn't the whole story; for the vast majority of the world's population, Baudrillard's most trenchant insights have little relevance. Things are still things. People are still people. (Actually, they're slightly less "people," what with the transplants and the prosthetics and the Retin-A and the growth hormones and such; but most of the old hungers and reflexes are still ticking over.)

I suspect the cultural tone of the '90s will differ markedly from the hallucinatory vibes of the '80s postmodernists. They're certainly right to take an interest in the topics they tackle, but their fervors have a limited appeal. Most people in the '90s—in America, at least—will live with the unspoken conviction that The Party's Over. Earth-shaking sociotechnical transformations will occur: human genes will be transplanted into animals, bacteria, other people; horrific insults to the environment will multiply, with spreading deserts and a deteriorating climate; disasters will kill millions and AIDS tens of millions; our definitions of "human" will mutate, as computers take over more and more management of our surroundings and we learn to hack the human brain and nervous system; but the reaction to these shakings of the earth will be quite muted. Most people don't bother to define "human"; they leave that sort of discourse to SF writers and abortion fanatics and pointy-headed intellectuals. What's the big deal, anyhow? Whatever works, man.

The cultural anomalies that Baudrillard and Jameson indicate with such fascinated disdain will likely occur and intensify, but very few will get particularly excited about it. The demographic majority of the American populace in the '90s will be broke and middle-aged and overworked; really busy with day care and mortgages and such; too busy to notice, as in *Neuromancer*, that a capering artificial intelligence has taken over the world. So what? That's progress. Pragmatic, nonideological resignation will reign. Modernity's dead. History marches on.

That's how I figure it, anyhow. It's certainly not how I used to think, and talk, and write, two years ago; so maybe I've learned something useful. I like to think that my autodidactic meanderings have expanded my limits as a writer; that I'm less narrow and fervent now, more sophisticated. Could be. Or maybe I just flatter myself. The proof will be found, not in the elaborated rhetoric of my literary theorizing—not in essays like this one—but in my science fiction. The SF I wrote in the past ten years was, all unwitting, "an apotheosis" of something I was deeply embedded in, but only partly able to see. If I do any more apotheosizing, I hope to do it with a full deck—of stolen cards.

Bibliography

America, by Jean Baudrillard, trans. Chris Turner. Verso, 1988.

Simulations and Simulacra, by Jean Baudrillard. Semiotext(e), 1983.

Selected Writings, by Jean Baudrillard. Polity Press, Oxford, 1988.

Postmodernist Culture: An Introduction to Theories of the Contemporary, by Steven Connor. Blackwell, 1989.

Postmodernist Fiction, by Brian McHale. Methuen, 1987.

The Panic Encyclopedia, by Arthur Kroker and Marilouise Kroker. St. Martin's, 1989.

Lipstick Traces: A Secret History of the Twentieth Century, by Greil Marcus. Harvard, 1989.

Critical Practice, by Catherine Belsey. Methuen, 1980.

Hiding in the Light: On Images and Things, by Dick Hebdige. Routledge, 1988.

Mississippi Review 47/48, Larry McCaffery, ed. University of Southern Mississippi, 1988.

Semiotext(e) SF, Rudy Rucker, Peter Lamborn Wilson, and Robert Anton Wilson, eds. Autonomedia, 1989.

Across the Wounded Galaxies: Interviews with Contemporary Science Fiction Writers, Larry McCaffery, ed. University of Illinois Press, 1990.

Twentieth Century Literary Theory: A Reader, K. M. Newton, ed. St. Martin's, 1988.

"Deconstructing the Starships," by Gwyneth Jones, *New York Review of Science Fiction*, July 1989.

"Postmodernism, or the Cultural Logic of Late Capitalism," by Fredric Jameson, *New Left Review* 146 (1984).

AUTEURS AT WORK? THE FANTASTIC FILMS OF 1991

Bill Warren

Although SFWA declined to bestow a Nebula for Best Dramatic Presentation in 1991, Ben Bova inaugurated a special President's Award for Best Dramatic Script, naming it after Ray Bradbury, a writer whose successes in motion pictures, TV, radio, and live theater almost match his achievements on the printed page. Three dozen screenplays were submitted to five SFWA members with frontline Hollywood experience, and, after narrowing the field to three choices, the panel ultimately decided to give the first Bradbury Award to James Cameron and William Wisher for *Terminator 2: Judgment Day*.

But what about the rest of the film industry's output for 1991? For the eighth year in a row, this series looks to Bill Warren for a rapid-fire succession of crisp, intelligent, informed reviews. Breezing through the following survey, you may find yourself thinking, as I did, hmmm, maybe David Cronenberg *(Naked Lunch)* should have gotten the Bradbury Award—or Wim Wenders and Peter Carey *(Until the End of the World)*—or Linda Woolverton *(Beauty and the Beast)* . . .

Warren's reviews and articles have appeared in *Starlog, Fangoria, Cinefantastique, American Film,* and other magazines. He was the American correspondent for the French TV series *Fantasy,* and he is now the system operator for the "Show Biz Round Table" on General Electric's computer service, GEnie. Anyone who loves the classic SF movies of the fifties cannot afford to be without *Keep Watching the Skies!,* Warren's two-volume, encyclopedic account of the phenomenon.

The *auteur* theory is much misunderstood in the United States. It was initially proposed by French film critics who, in the early 1950s, were suddenly treated to an almost-decade-long backlog of American films and then struggled to get a critical handle on them. The word *auteur* came to be applied to the director more than to any other figure associated with the creation of a movie. It does literally mean "author"—but, with a few exceptions, these French commentators were not claiming that the director was the *sole* author, only that the best directors were the primary creative influences on their films.

Virtually all directors admit they can't make a good movie from a bad script, but the French critics were talking less about quality than about a distinctive, analyzable artistic vision. Some people maintain that the writer is the primary creator of a film—and when it comes to plot, structure, and dialogue, this is generally true. But the films of good—and many bad—directors tend to look, sound, and "feel" much more like each other than do the films of even very powerful, distinctive writers. This is the case even when the ultimate source of a movie is a novel, play, or short story.

The year 1991 brought a variety of genre films from directors with distinctive visions (for better or worse). In this essay, I shall start out covering the movies with the strongest directorial influence, moving toward those studio products and low-budget outings that necessarily have the least. But don't expect what follows to be a journey from "good" to "bad." A cheap film like *The Dark Backward* is unquestionably the work of its director, Adam Rifkin, but it's far less satisfying than any number of movies, such as *Prayer of the Rollerboys*, that have no individual style.

And, in fact, I conclude this year's essay with a commentary on the best genre movie of the year—one that has no "sole creator" at all. It is the product of one branch of a studio, and yet it is a work of art—a work of art without an "artist."

David Cronenberg's *Naked Lunch*, loosely based on the famous William S. Burroughs novel, presents a dark, twisted world full of intrigue, drugs, black humor, insects, paranoia, and monsters. The movie is deeply and playfully intellectual, an amazing effort of the imagination—and, alas, it is painfully slow. The comic elements are dry and remote, dragged down further by the general lethargy.

Though Cronenberg cites William S. Burroughs as one of the greatest influences on him when he was an aspiring novelist himself, he dares *not* to follow the story line of Burroughs's novel. The movie is, instead, about the writing of the novel, and about writing itself.

Visually, it's astounding, as might be expected from the man who gave us *Scanners*, *The Fly*, and *Dead Ringers*, among other brilliantly imaginative films. As with *Videodrome*, in *Naked Lunch* Cronenberg slides from reality into fantasy without clarifying the transitions, very unusual in movies aimed at mainstream audiences. *Naked Lunch* is partly an allegory about drug use and how it affects a writer; it's almost entirely set within the drug-induced hallucinations of the central figure, Bill Lee (Peter Weller). He's an exterminator in the New York of 1953 who, as he tells his friends Hank (Nicholas Campbell) and Martin (Michael Zelniker), gave up writing when he was ten—"too dangerous," he mutters. A former addict himself, Bill isn't shocked when he learns his wife, Joan (Judy Davis), is addicted to his powdered cockroach poison. But he *is* shocked when, called to a police station, he meets a huge talking bug that tells him he's really a secret agent working against the other side, the mysterious Interzone (in North Africa, it turns out). And when Bill accidentally kills his wife the dissolution of reality speeds up.

A green, scaly creature called a Mugwump gives him a ticket to Interzone, and soon Bill is there, banging away on his portable typewriter in a bar full of other writers, but somehow also a spy. The strangeness escalates: his typewriter turns into an insectlike creature that has orgasms when he types on it. He meets expatriate American writers Tom (Ian Holm) and Joan Frost (Judy Davis again), encounters the evil Fadela (Monique Mercure), sends dispatches back to Hank and Martin (based on Allen Ginsberg and Jack Kerouac), wonders if he's really homosexual, and finds a web of intrigue closing around him.

Initially, all this seems literal, but Cronenberg occasionally gives us flashes of consensus reality: the ticket to Interzone is briefly seen in the form of drugs; we catch glimpses of New York City down the arched, sandy streets of Interzone; frequently the insect typewriters become real typewriters in quick cuts; and so on. But it's never clear what's happening to Bill in "reality," only what befalls him in the hallucinatory Interzone. *Did* he kill Joan? *Is* he writing a remarkable novel called *Naked Lunch*, as Martin and Hank insist? Who are the real-world equivalents of Tom, Joan, and Fadela (played not only by Mercure but also, surprisingly, by Roy Scheider), and what do they really want? Does every character and every event in Interzone have some real-world parallel?

These questions may very well be beside the point. Perhaps *Naked Lunch* should be taken at face value. The moody photography and the slightly theatrical production design teeter on the verge of naturalism most of the time; Cronenberg is making no *concessions* to fantasy; he posts no glaring *Dr. Caligari* signs saying "This Is All a Hallucination." It's a surrealistic story, but it doesn't look surrealistic; *Naked Lunch* simply *is,* like it or not. We're forced to deal with Bill's mysterious adventures on *his* terms, despite the bursts of "reality."

Cronenberg wrote the script solo, which he doesn't often do; the dialogue is astonishing at certain times, disturbing at others, but carefully crafted throughout. When Bill surprises his wife, Joan, injecting the roach powder into her breast, she grins and says, "It's a very literary high. A Kafka high—you feel like a bug." Someone comments that another character "marks all those he has met like a lemur pissing on a liana vine." Tom assures Bill that "no American should find himself in a foreign land without a pistol." As the character based on Burroughs himself, Peter Weller (who's excellent) has two great riffs of description. In the first, he tells how he considered being a homosexual, helped by an elderly queen who met a horrible death: riding in a Hispano-Suiza, his hemorrhoids became wrapped around the rear wheel, and his innards were pulled out. The second is the chronicle of a talking rectum. Both are dry, sardonic, and hilarious, perfectly delivered by Weller in a voice just this side of a monotone.

The film's wryness does not extend to its treatment of writers. As anyone who's tried to write seriously knows, it's one of the most demanding and frustrating jobs imaginable. But when you're really tapping into your subconscious, and the words pour out almost of their own volition, it's intoxicating—but it can become frightening. This partly explains why Bill denies he's been writing *Naked Lunch:* it's just too revealing. The most telling line about writing is as true in Interzone as it is in reality: "A writer leads a sad existence like everyone else. . . . The only difference is he files a report on it."

To a certain degree, writing is the act of a paranoid. The writer assumes not only that he or she is important enough to be read, but that forces are conspiring to prevent the expression of these ideas. Lee's drug-soaked mind, possibly shocked out of reality by the accidental killing of his wife, constructs a parallel delusional world.

The movie is crammed with details, allusions, and fascinating characters; it's going to be picked apart and examined for years by Cronenberg commentators—it's easily his densest work yet. But it's also his pokiest, hardest to like, and least involving. It's full of mind games and madness, but it's lacking in excitement and tension. If Cronenberg had managed to make *Naked Lunch* as fast paced as *The Fly*, it probably would be his masterpiece. What we get is a vivid, imaginative attempt at something no one else would have dreamed of trying; if he didn't build in much commercial appeal, that's too bad for his investors, but the project was worth doing. Of all those making SF and horror films today, Cronenberg is easily the most brilliant thinker. He's not always the most brilliant filmmaker, technically or creatively, but his work is so rich intellectually that he deserves to be ranked among the greatest movie fantasists.

Kenneth Branagh is also a true cinema virtuoso. He made his movie directorial and acting debut with his splendid, robust version of Shakespeare's *Henry V* two years ago, and now he's followed it up with a movie that could hardly be more different. It's a romantic private-eye thriller with comic overtones, set in Los Angeles and involving a decades-old murder, reincarnation, hypnotism, antiques, and amnesia. If it's not as splendid as *Henry V,* and if it has a few plot holes, too many closeups, and a vague air of sportive inconsequentiality, these weaknesses hardly matter. *Dead Again* (great title) is intensely engrossing, is blessedly free of wisecracks, and winds up with a gleefully bravura, even baroque, climax. Maybe Branagh really *can* do anything. (He is currently working on a new version of *Frankenstein.*)

The movie begins in the 1940s, when symphony conductor Roman Strauss (Branagh) is executed for the murder of his wife (Emma Thompson). In the present, a screaming woman (also Thompson) awakens in the Strauss manor, now an orphanage, without any memory of her past. Private eye Mike Church (also Branagh) is hired to help her find out who she is. He runs her photo in the paper, and soon a slightly shady antique dealer named Franklyn Madson (Derek Jacobi) arrives, offering to help. And we learn that the woman, whom Mike has dubbed "Grace," is a reincarnate: in a previous life, she was Margaret (also Thompson), the murdered wife of Roman Strauss. Or was she?

It's clear what attracted Branagh to this material: not only is it wildly different from *Henry V*, but it embodies a classic genre while simultaneously boasting enough novelty—the reincarnation angle—to make the resulting film unpredictable. And the script gives him not just one good role but two; Roman Strauss and Mike Church are as different from one another as each is from Henry V.

Branagh is clearly having a wonderful time in both parts, and, as Church, not only does this British actor do a perfect American accent, he goes one better—he does a perfect *Los Angeles* accent. Jacobi is delightful and seems to be giving a sly impersonation of the late, sorely missed James Mason. Best known on this side of the Atlantic for the title role in "I, Claudius," Jacobi is suave, faintly sinister, and always a bit arch and sardonic.

As Grace, Emma Thompson has to create a role out of almost nothing, for her character has no clue to her identity (and, in fact, never regains her memory), but she's still salty, humorous, and intelligent. As Margaret, the concert pianist, she becomes sexy and playful, in love with her husband but willing to flirt with an attractive younger man. Thompson, married to Branagh in real life, is as convincing as he in her dual role.

The supporting player who makes the strongest impact, Robin Williams, isn't even billed in the opening credits (a contractual amenity sometimes granted to major stars in secondary roles). He's a sour, cynical psychiatrist who gave up his profession to run a grocery store and who feeds Mike and Grace useful insights from time to time. He readily accepts the concept of past lives; by putting this belief in the mouth of the one character most deeply sunk in "reality," Branagh and the writer, Scott Frank, deftly lead us down the road of belief as well.

Branagh has fun alluding to other movies and actors; as Strauss, he does a bit of a take on Laurence Olivier. The black-and-white scenes perfectly evoke the classic *film noir* style. The wedding of Roman and Margaret cleverly quotes some scenes from *The Philadelphia Story*. There are a couple of visual references to *Citizen Kane*, such as the low-angle views of the gate and manor.

In a time when private-eye movies are scarce and their substitutes—cop movies—are crammed with glib wisecracks and facile action, the simple honesty of Frank's script is gratifying and refreshing, even daring. The dialogue is intelligent and often very amusing, particularly Jacobi's speeches, but no one tosses off cheap one-liners.

Dead Again is at heart rather silly, but because the filmmakers insist we care about the characters, we happily set aside disbelief and become involved in its strange, gothic twists and turns. Yes, there are plot holes, yes, it's a bit over the top, but, more important, the whole thing is a hell of a lot of fun. Can we doubt that Kenneth Branagh will be both one of the major actors and one of the major directors of this decade, and well into the next century?

Tom Stoppard's 1967 play *Rosencrantz and Guildenstern Are Dead* is one of the cheekiest theatrical stunts of all time. The play takes place *inside* Shakespeare's *Hamlet:* it tells how Rosencrantz and Guildenstern spend their time in Elsinore while the bard's tragedy goes on around them and sometimes with them—Stoppard included about 250 lines from Shakespeare. But he went beyond this clever conceit, turning his play into a wonderful intellectual game, a surreal comedy of chance, fate, causality, and slapstick. In the movie, directed by Stoppard, Rosencrantz (Gary Oldman) and Guildenstern (Tim Roth) are roughly modeled on Laurel and Hardy, and the poor shlumps are so ephemeral that not only are the other characters unable to tell them apart, but *they* can't either. The film, which also features Richard Dreyfuss in a robust, playful, and uncharacteristic performance as the Player King, is a delight.

Not only are Rosencrantz and Guildenstern simpletons; they don't really *exist.* They can't remember anything that happened before they found themselves on the road to Elsinore. Sometimes they're caught in the middle of big scene changes; at one point, they're standing on the stage of the traveling players' wagon, and then suddenly they're in an Elsinore hallway. But they have to take all this as it comes, because they just can't figure out what all this *is.* The strutting, glib Player King knows *his* role. "We're actors!" he declares ringingly. "We're the opposite of people!" He has no problem with being tossed around by fate (or perhaps by Shakespeare himself—occasionally manuscript pages flutter through the scenes, blown by an offstage wind).

This is the first movie directed by Stoppard, but he's done his homework. It's smooth and elegant, with impressive locations that belie the relatively low budget. There's a wonderful dreamlike sequence in which the Player King, atop his traveling stage, spots Rosencrantz and Guildenstern, sitting dopily on their horses. "An audience!" the Player King cries, and he and his troupe unfold the stage and start zestfully performing their repertoire for this audience of two. "Love, blood, and rhetoric" are what he offers, and in this brief interlude Stoppard captures the essential magic of both theater and movies: not only does the scene tell us why entertainers love to perform, it also tells us why *we* love to watch them perform. This is the best surrealistic slapstick intellectual comedy in a long time, maybe ever.

If you'd heard the rumors that the cost of *Terminator 2: Judgment Day*, budgeted at $60 million going in, was climbing up to $88 million, even to $110 million—making it easily the most expensive movie ever produced in English—you probably expected the result to be a colossal superspectacular, an eye-popping, jaw-dropping epic of unprecedented proportions.

Well, it is that—but it's basically a mammoth-scale remake of *The Terminator,* spectacular but hollow.

Undeniably, it's viscerally entertaining, and there are some awesome special effects and big, noisy stunts, but we've already seen awesome special effects and big, noisy stunts. The original was better overall; it had a stronger plot, a deeper level of emotion, and more originality. A genuine sleeper hit, *The Terminator* was tremendously influential, virtually creating a subgenre (science fiction blended with action) and establishing both star Arnold Schwarzenegger and writer-director James Cameron as major forces in pop moviemaking.

At the end of *The Terminator,* after defeating the flesh-covered, unstoppable robot from the future (Arnold Schwarzenegger), Sarah Connor (Linda Hamilton) goes off to hide in the desert, knowing she's the mother of the next century's savior. In the coming era, glimpsed briefly at the beginning of both films, humankind is pitted against intelligent, implacable machines bent on wiping us out. The machines had sent the Terminator back in time to kill Sarah before her son could be born; meanwhile, the Terminator's intended victim has dispatched an agent to protect Sarah, and that warrior—who was ultimately killed—became John Connor's father.

In *Terminator 2: Judgment Day,* fourteen-year-old John (Edward Furlong) is living with foster parents and roaring around on a small motorcycle, stealing money from automatic teller machines. His mother, Sarah, is in an insane asylum; she knows that on August 29, 1997, nuclear war will break out, killing three billion people. She has recurring nightmares of the destruction of Los Angeles (vividly depicted), but of course no one believes her tale of time-traveling killer robots. She's hardened, bitter, and desperate to escape from the asylum.

Cameron and cowriter William Wisher try some complex juggling at the beginning, but they drop a ball or two. For one thing, Sarah Connor is narrating, so we know she's destined to survive *whatever* happens. She tells us that another Terminator has been dispatched to our time, to kill John, and that a defender has been sent to protect him. Sure enough, there's naked Arnold Schwarzenegger materializing in a time bubble; he swipes clothes and a cycle from a biker and roars off into the night to the tune of "Bad to the Bone." This is, to say the least, misleading.

Elsewhere, we see another voyager (Robert Patrick) arrive; he appropriates the clothes and car of a passing cop, and then he, too, sets out after the boy. This guy is smaller and friendlier looking than Schwarzenegger—but the bogus cop is the Evil Terminator, a T-1000, snazzier than the Arnold model. This time, the Arnold Terminator is programmed to *defend* John Connor as implacably as the T-1000 is to destroy him.

The T-1000 is made of "liquid metal," which means it's a shape shifter: it can look like anything, or anyone, it touches. When not impersonating, it's a mirrored-surface humanoid (uncannily resembling the Silver Surfer or a chrome Oscar). These effects are amazing, employing computer animation that immediately establishes a new standard.

Most of Schwarzenegger's scenes are with the boy, John, who wants to make the Terminator behave like a real person. At one point, Sarah muses that this killing machine is more of a father to her son than any of the men she's known in the past ten years. This is a potentially promising story line; if Cameron and Wisher had followed it up, the film might have been truly dramatic.

But exploring the human dimension of *Terminator 2* obviously wasn't Cameron's goal. He instead focuses most of his energies on the stunning T-1000 special effects and on the colossal, explosive stunts. The problem is that we see virtually everything the silver robot can do in the first forty minutes; two-thirds of the way through the film, we become surfeited with action; we long for some quiet dialogue.

But instead Cameron doggedly carries on, a Terminator himself, destroying cars, motorcycles, buildings, trucks, the world itself, anything to awe us. Along the way, like the machines of his bleak future, he loses the simple humanity the first film evoked so well.

Epic in scale, intimate in detail, Wim Wenders's *Until the End of the World* is an impressive achievement, more accessible than his *Wings of Desire,* telling a clear, uncomplicated story with humor, tenderness, and fond irony. Given its two-and-a-half-hour length, sitting through *Until the End of the World* might seem daunting, but it's light and graceful from beginning to end, as rich in detail as a novel. I seem to be in the minority here; most reviewers were deeply disappointed.

It's 1999. An armed nuclear satellite is dropping out of orbit, and as the world sweats out where it will land, bored, aimless Claire Tonneur (Solveig Dommartin) leaves Venice and heads back to Paris. A car accident brings her into contact with a pair of amiable bank robbers, Chico (Chick Ortega) and Raymond (Eddy Mitchell), who persuade her to take their loot to Paris in exchange for a percentage. En route, she meets mysterious Trevor (William Hurt), an American fleeing from an Australian detective, Burt (Ernie Dingo). He steals some money from her, but she's also attracted to him, and so the chase begins. Trevor keeps eluding her, further arousing her interest; her former lover, writer Eugene (Sam Neill), is still sufficiently in love with her to help with the pursuit, even though its object is his potential rival.

Claire's obsession with Trevor (whose real name, she eventually learns, is Sam) takes her from Paris to Berlin and then on around the world: Lisbon, Moscow, Siberia, China, Japan, San Francisco, finally Australia. Sam and Claire eventually team up and begin to fall in love, while they're pursued by Burt, Eugene, and German private eye Winter (Rudiger Vogler) and joined by the always cheerful Chick. In Australia, they meet with Sam's scientist father, Dr. Henry Farber (Max von Sydow), and Sam's blind mother, Edith (Jeanne Moreau), and all face what might in fact be the end of the world.

The original story is by Wenders and his star, Dommartin, with the final script by Wenders and Peter Carey (who wrote *Bliss*). It's surprisingly solid science fiction. Except for a couple of matte paintings of familiar cityscapes with new buildings added, the futuristic aspects are not emphasized, but they're there in almost every scene, often very wittily presented. Pay videophones are readily available, for example, and they've been defaced with graffiti.

Sam Farber's quest springs from intelligent technological speculation. His father had developed a device that might help the blind see; when Dr. Farber learned his invention was going to be misused by the U.S. government, he fled into hiding in the outback, hoping to re-create the machine he left behind. Out of touch with his family for years, Sam has stolen the prototype from the government and is traveling around the world gathering up images for possible replay to his blind mother. The project endangers Sam's own eyesight, but he's willing to take the risk because he loves his mother and wants his father's love.

The story is not about the technology. It's about the idea that love, however important, is not always enough: we're distracted by outside events, pulled apart by the forces we hope will bring us together. Dr. Farber uses the image-visualization equipment to explore dreams, and his family becomes addicted to this potential, drifting into worlds of their own making.

This inner reality is more attractive than the outer—for all of us, it seems. When Wenders's characters begin employing the vision device to probe the unconscious, he gives us one of the most haunting ideas of this haunting film, as everyone begins to look at what Farber calls "the human soul, singing to itself."

These people are presented realistically. Wenders doesn't try to win us over in obvious ways; he allows the characters to earn what sympathy they can, honestly. Ultimately, not all of them prove endearing, but we do care about them, and the last scene, aboard a space station in orbit, is gently comic and tender, very moving. I may be alone in my fondness, but I think *Until the End of the World* is one of the best films of 1991, romantic, realistic, and truthful.

The public eagerly awaited the Steven Spielberg–directed *Hook*— but I can't recall another movie that divided audiences as sharply. Some loathed it; I've even seen it referred to as "the worst movie ever made," but it was a hit worldwide, one of the largest grossing of 1991's movies. And, to me, *Hook* is an unalloyed delight, a daring concept that works awesomely well. Not only is Spielberg back on track with a finely tuned sense of wonder, but Robin Williams again shows that, given the right material, he's a superb actor, and Dustin Hoffman delivers a charming, goofily villainous performance.

For years, Spielberg had been wanting to direct a live-action version of Sir James M. Barrie's *Peter Pan,* but he couldn't work out a satisfying approach. Meanwhile, Jim V. Hart had an idea: what if Peter finally did grow up? With Nick Castle, Hart wrote the story, then a screenplay on his own, subsequently rewritten by Malia Scotch Marmo. The rumor is that many other hands contributed to the final script.

Peter Banning (Robin Williams) is a forty-year-old lawyer and corporate executive whose obsession with his work has created a gulf between him and his wife, Moira (Caroline Goodall), and two children, Jack (the talented Charlie Korsmo) and Maggie (Amber Scott, in her film debut). In two recent films with similar themes, *The Doctor* and *Regarding Henry,* medical problems restore the protagonist to his family. But for Peter Banning, redemption requires the intrusion of the grandest pirate in all children's fiction, Captain James Hook (Hoffman). Peter doesn't merely have to reconcile with his family; he has to rediscover that he himself is the living embodiment of youthful joy: Peter Pan.

After Hook kidnaps Banning's children, neither Wendy (a luminous Maggie Smith) nor Tinkerbell (Julia Roberts) can convince Peter that he is Pan, so Tink flies him back to Neverland and tosses him into conflict with a puzzled Hook. Frightened and confused, Peter is filled with self-disgust when he can't rescue Jack and Maggie, and winds up a captive of the Lost Boys. Their new leader, the exuberant Rufio (Dante Basco, magnetic and dashing), doesn't believe—and doesn't *want* to believe—this pudgy grown-up is really Peter Pan, but Tink has made a deal with Hook, who yearns for one last battle with Pan: she has three days to make Peter understand who he is.

The weakest element of the film is the protracted sequence in which Peter regains his memory. The Lost Boys put him through an ordeal suggesting a fraternity hazing conducted in an amusement park, but instead of giving him bits and pieces of his fairy-tale heritage, each incident merely leaves Peter shaken and disturbed. The truth dawns on him all at once; I would have preferred to see him remember snatches of his past as the Boys torment him. It's more fun watching the pompous, posturing, but truly dangerous Hook trying to talk a steadfast Maggie and a weakening Jack into becoming *his* children.

Hook is Robin Williams's film from beginning to end, and he's never been better. The difficulty in casting Williams has always been to find roles in which he can display his abilities as an actor and his astonishing talents as an improvisational stand-up comic. He must have worked exceptionally hard on *Hook* and enjoyed the support of a sympathetic director and an understanding costar, because he absolutely glows. Not only does he virtually erupt from the screen when he finally becomes Peter Pan again, he also makes us care about the uptight yuppie Banning *before* the transformation. At the end, he's an amalgam of the two, a whole person at last, and we share his joy in rejoining his family and in rejoining himself.

Dustin Hoffman's accent, the press kit claims, is Etonian, but his curved smile, gapped teeth, and general attitude derive from the late Terry-Thomas. Hook is a poseur and something of a phony; when frustrated, he threatens to commit suicide, always assuming faithful, overworked Smee (Bob Hoskins) will rescue him. All he really wants is one last battle with his long-lost nemesis, Peter Pan. Recognizing himself as Pan's great opposite, he frequently claims that the world *needs* a Captain Hook.

Hoffman has made only a few period films, and most of his comedies have been realistic in tone. Captain Hook is an extravagant costume character and totally fantastic, but Hoffman seems to have been liberated by the role. He has never been less "realistic"—and rarely better.

The dialogue is surprisingly good. When Tinkerbell first confronts Banning she spouts off in a colorful, delightful barrage of challenges that lifted me right out of my seat. Hook's speeches to his men are rich and funny, and there's a colorful insult duel between Rufio and Peter. And after Banning is restored to Panhood we see that Pan is not only carefree but *uncaring*. He must become an amalgam of both, Pan and Banning, before he can save the children from Hook, and he ultimately accomplishes this for the same reason Pan finally grew up: he wants to be a father. "You are," he tells his son, "my happy thought."

Spielberg has always been at his best when expressing a childlike rapture in fantasy and adventure; he's something of a Peter Pan himself, a great big little boy who can make us share his delight in the things of childhood. He makes toy-movies, it's true; when he tries for psychological complexity, as in *The Color Purple* and *Empire of the Sun,* he seems embarrassed, and the results feel a little forced. He'd rather be *playing* with movies than teaching us the meaning of life. And that's fine. Alfred Hitchcock once said that other directors' movies were slices of life; his were slices of cake. Spielberg's best movies—and *Hook* is one—are hot-fudge sundaes served over peanut-butter sandwiches on a bed of cotton candy.

The Addams Family owes more to Charles Addams himself than to anyone else, but he was dead long before the movie went into production. The story goes that producer Scott Rudin grabbed the movie rights when, traveling back from a movie location, a group of people of varying ages joined right in when somebody began humming and snapping Vic Mizzy's clever theme song to *The Addams Family* (the TV series). The movie struggled toward the screen, gaining a top-notch cast headed by Raul Julia, Anjelica Huston, and Christopher Lloyd, with respected cinematographer Barry Sonnenfeld making his directorial debut and Orion selling the film-in-progress to Paramount.

The movie easily transcends the small-screen original. As Gomez and Morticia Addams, Julia and Huston are furlongs more sophisticated than John Astin and the late Carolyn Jones were ever allowed to be. At Sonnenfeld's urging, writers Caroline Thompson *(Edward Scissorhands)* and Larry Wilson took their cues more from Addams's elegant old *New Yorker* cartoons than from the TV series (which Addams did help create).

The gags are broad and silly, mostly Addamslike reversals on clichés. "Are you unhappy, dear?" "Oh yes, perfectly!" That kind of thing. But the cast is so adept with timing and delivery they transcend the frequent predictability of the punch lines. And some elements, such as the Shakespearean scene that the children, Pugsley (Jimmy Workman) and Wednesday (Christina Ricci), stage at their school, are wildly beyond anything even the wittily black-hearted Charles Addams might have conceived. In front of an aghast audience of mommies and daddies, the kids slaughter each other, sending fountains of blood spraying across the stage.

The film might have been better off *without* a plot, and certainly would have been better off without *this* plot. The Addams family lawyer, Tully Alford (Dan Hedaya), in desperate need of money, decides to fleece Gomez, who he knows is incredibly rich, and so Tully and his partner, Abigail, set out to pass off her son, Gordon (Christopher Lloyd), as Gomez's long-lost brother, Fester.

All this is simply too much plot. The Addamses themselves are so delightful we want to see as much of them as possible. We don't like being dragged back to Tully and Abigail and their scheme to get the Addams millions; we don't want to see Gordon/Fester agonizing over where his loyalties lie. Nor do we need to see the Addamses ousted from their home and forced to live in a (shudder) motel. We just want more of Gomez, Morticia, Gordon *as* Fester, and the entire household.

The Addams Family is not all it could have been—but then, who was expecting anything from a movie based on a musty old TV series? I wasn't, and I was pleasantly surprised. If you enjoy mildly black humor in a wacky setting, with an oddball family and plenty of corny jokes, you'll have a goofily good time with this handsome film and its fine performances by Julia, Huston, and Lloyd.

Ever since 1962's *Experiment in Terror*, writer-director Blake Edwards has been fooling around with story elements involving homosexuality and cross-dressing. With *Switch*, in which a man turns into a woman, he may have reached a stopping point. If the movie were as good as Ellen Barkin's funny, sexy leading performance, it would be dynamite. But it's not. It's dreary.

Womanizing cad Steve Brooks (Perry King) is killed by three of the many ladies he's gleefully wronged in his scurrilous career, and then he meets God. He's given one last chance: he'll be restored to life, and if he can find one woman who truly likes him he can go to heaven. He wakes up back in his apartment, transformed into a beautiful, busty blonde (Ellen Barkin), soon dubbed Amanda Brooks, Steve's half sister.

This is certainly a story for today, when gender roles are in tremendous flux, and if Edwards had been impish, daring, and imaginative, *Switch* could have been a real delight. Instead, whenever he comes up to a potentially interesting turn in the plot he chooses the least imaginative, least daring twist. We become peripherally involved with one male/female issue after another, but Edwards takes no serious stands, other than to point out the obvious fact that in the business world men take advantage of women. The clumsy vehicle rattles on, trapping Ellen Barkin's wonderful performance in its wheels and gears, concluding in just about the most unsatisfactory way possible: Amanda dies in childbirth. *Switch* sent its meager audiences out confused and angry.

Despite being a comedy, the movie doesn't contain much that's funny. Edwards avoids wit and slapstick as adroitly and consistently as Amanda avoids agreeing to have sex. Now, I don't know about you, but if I woke up one morning to find my gender switched, I do believe I'd involve myself in sexual experimentation in no time flat.

Switch called for the talents of a latter-day Billy Wilder; it needed someone who understands both sexuality and sensuality and who delights in both. The movie shouldn't have taken place in bars and boardrooms but in resorts and bedrooms. The protagonist's search for vindication is finally beside the point and makes a poor pretext for a plot. Not only is *Switch* no more daring than Vincente Minnelli's very similar (and very lame) *Goodbye, Charlie* of twenty-seven years ago; it isn't even funnier, despite Barkin's heroic efforts. If only Edwards had shown some spunk, some raunch, some skin, and some imagination; the last thing we want in a sex-switch movie is good taste.

Although *The Dark Backward* is every bit as distinctively the work of its writer-director as *Naked Lunch,* this ambitious film is an utter failure. Adam Rifkin wrote it at the age of nineteen—he was twenty-five when the film was made—and he should have abandoned the project as a youthful fantasy. He must be a pretty persuasive guy (perhaps the script reads a lot better than it plays), because he assembled a surprisingly strong cast, all of whom enter into things with great enthusiasm. But enthusiasm isn't enough. There's something unpleasantly smug about this clunky movie, as if Rifkin were serenely confident he's a genius aborning.

In an urban setting of ghastly squalor and hopelessness, garbageman Marty Malt (Judd Nelson) wishes to be a stand-up comedian, but he's wretched. His exuberant, filthy friend Gus (Bill Paxton), a fellow garbageman, keeps telling Marty he's really good, however, so Marty persists. A boil on his back, more or less ignored by the incompetent Dr. Scurvy (James Caan), grows into a third arm and hand. Low-class agent Jackie Chrome (Wayne Newton), who initially despised Marty's act, now sees possibilities and agrees to take the three-armed comic on as a client.

The Dark Backward not only fails to make any point—it's hard to see what point it could be making—it's also drearily dull and wearily overlong. It has the pacing of Eraserhead without that movie's true, mesmerizing oddness. Sure, a third arm growing out of someone's back is mighty strange, but there's no metaphorical connection between this anomaly and Marty's desire to be a comic. The arm disappears at the moment Marty is about to achieve real fame; it's the cheapest sort of irony, perverse rather than mythic. Marty doesn't undergo any self-awakening until the film's final sixty seconds.

The Dark Backward is cynical and satirical, but there's no discernible target for these attitudes. It's obvious Rifkin longs to enter David Lynch/John Waters territory, but both Lynch and Waters have very clear, very specific visions—even if you don't always know what's going on in their films, it's clear *they* do. Rifkin's "style" consists of swiping images wholesale from Lynch and Waters and tossing them up on the screen to see if any stick. The problem, of course, is that, other than being equally eccentric, Lynch and Waters have little in common. Lacking his own vision, Rifkin cannot reconcile the discordant elements he's borrowed from these two directors to whom he wants so desperately to be compared.

After this low point in *auteurism*, the rest of 1991's genre movies are all basically cut-to-order outings, movies made to suit the market; they are not the products of personal artistic visions. From bad to better to great, the following films can all be considered "standard Hollywood output."

Child's Play was a clever, creepy thriller about the spirit of a dead serial killer, Charles Lee Ray, inhabiting a highly unlikely body: a "Good Guy" talking mechanical doll called Chucky. The movie played fair by its premise; the doll succeeded (for a while) because no one believed he could walk, talk, and kill, which enabled him to pursue his goal of switching spirits with a little boy. *Child's Play 2* veered from the unlikely to the absurd; *Child's Play 3* follows the same downhill slope and crashes at the bottom.

If they last long enough, monster-movie series eventually shade off into the comic, but the makers of *Child's Play 3* have jumped the gun, turning the monster into a clown the third time out. Virtually every line Chucky has (in Brad Dourif's voice) is a sarcastic, black-hued joke. The moviemakers go for the cheap comic contrast between Chucky's cuddly-doll face and his torrent of vulgar language. But once your villain has become a buffoon, it's almost impossible for him to function as a menace. Would that were the movie's only serious flaw.

Ever since the overpraised *Halloween*, horror movies have tended to go for sheer impact, logical causes be damned. *Child's Play 3* doesn't even pretend to logic; it's *all* effect. No coherent explanation is offered for Chucky's actions or powers—nor is any explanation possible for much of what he does. Even worse, until the end, every single coincidence in a movie bursting with them helps Chucky; at the climax, every single coincidence works against him. On and on, again and again, writer Don Mancini and director Jack Bender cynically ignore rationality because it's easier to just go "boo" or have Chucky mouth off.

At first I thought *Child's Play 3* was a stupid movie made by stupid people, but after thinking about it I came to the sour conclusion that it's a stupid movie made by *smart* people. They show some cleverness, but they feel superior to it all; they can't take the premise seriously, so they've turned their film into a send-up of itself—a foredoomed enterprise when you're working with this kind of material. A walking, talking, self-aware doll *is* absurd; making him more absurd alienates the horror-movie audience, so who is the intended market? Jaded cynics like the people who made it, I presume, but they're not likely to see the film in the first place.

But maybe these *reductio ad absurdum* projects are inevitable; horror movies, in their current repetitive, sequel-driven mode, have overstayed their welcome. Boredom has set in among both the moviemakers and the audience, and with it has come parody, cynicism, and sloppiness. The genre needs to be reinvented once again.

Teenage Mutant Ninja Turtles made a mint; it is, in fact, the largest-grossing independent film ever—and was a lot of fun in its goony way. It was surprisingly gritty, with good characterizations for the Turtles and a tightly knitted plot, but both the original and its sequel are just entertainment machines. *Teenage Mutant Ninja Turtles II: The Secret of the Ooze* has its moments, but the story line is so shapeless, and the thrills are so compromised by fear of giving offense, that even hard-core Turtle fans may find this picture a chore to sit through.

Teenage Mutant Ninja Turtles II: The Secret of the Ooze does open well, and the Turtles themselves are very amusing creations, but this is the kind of movie that demands a sharp, witty script and a stylish director with a flair for comedy and action. But *Teenage Mutant Ninja Turtles II: The Secret of the Ooze* was written by Todd W. Langren and directed by Michael Pressman; neither is up to the task. While Langren did devise some nice quips for his brash and appealing heroes, his plot is weak and aimless. David Warner, playing a scientist, is more than capable of dealing with wacky fantasy (as he showed in *Time Bandits*), but he needs something to work with beyond the amusing bemusement that defines his character.

Pressman's direction is efficient. Period. There's no sense of style, certainly no feeling of comic-book style; he keeps things moving, but that's about it. It's a shame the producers were afraid to be as spunky as the Turtles themselves. They made a chunk of change, and the inevitable *Teenage Mutant Ninja Turtles III* will be along soon. *Teenage Mutant Ninja Turtles II: The Secret of the Ooze* reached its ready-made audience, but it didn't win any converts to Turtle Power.

Not that the world has been waiting for such a thing, but *Prayer of the Rollerboys* plays like a more accomplished version of *Surf Nazis Must Die!* Of movies with the word "roller" in the title, it's the first one since *Rollerball* that isn't downright embarrassing to sit through. You get the feeling that to finance the movie (a U.S.-Japanese coproduction), writer W. Peter Iliff and director Rick King were forced to make annoying compromises, and what starts out as a clever, creepily convincing tale of the near future turns into a standard infiltrate-the-gang cop action picture on rollerskates.

The date isn't specified, for obvious reasons. *Prayer of the Rollerboys* was made on a low budget, which meant the filmmakers couldn't depict much futuristic technology. Imaginatively, Iliff and King have instead given us a futuristic *society*. All the foreign investors have called in America's debts, the economy has been badly crippled, and crime has become even more rampant—concepts all wittily linked to the plot. Our late-teenage hero, Griffin (Corey Haim), drives an armored pizza delivery truck; his boss warns him not to take dollars—yen are okay. Gary Lee (Christopher Collet) is the head of the Rollerboys, a cultlike gang who skate around Venice, California, in Clockwork Orange derbies and long Jesse James dusters.

We can believe that in an America with its spirit and economy broken, a charismatic figure like Gary Lee could emerge. He is clearly an incipient Hitler, who arose amid similar chaos in post–World War I Germany. Gary Lee is a racist, but he soft-pedals that side of himself and instead emphasizes his cult-leader attractiveness; he vows America will again become the world's number-one power.

When Griffin is forced to infiltrate Gary Lee's group, *Prayer of the Rollerboys* begins to fall apart, becoming just another gang action picture. The convincing future, Gary Lee's status as the new führer, and the appeal of the Rollerboys to the masses are all shunted aside and pointedly ignored. It's a shame, really, because the material had potential.

Warlock was conceived as a supernatural variation on *The Terminator:* a powerful, villainous time traveler arrives in the present and begins battling a foe from his own era, who's helped by a modern-day woman. In this case, however, the villain is a warlock (Julian Sands)—a male witch—who is whisked from imprisonment in 1691, where he awaits execution. The Warlock's time tripping receives scant explanation, which is more than can be said for the journey of Giles Redferne (Richard E. Grant), whose arrival here from 1691 gets no explanation whatsoever.

Written by D. T. Twohy, produced and directed by Steve Miner, *Warlock* is a brisk, entertaining thriller, with adequate effects, a knockout score by Jerry Goldsmith, and acting—by the two male leads—that's above average for this kind of thing. The script is occasionally amusing, but the overtly comic lines given Lori Singer (Redferne's helper, who's steadily aging, thanks to the Warlock) are weak and obvious.

On the other hand, Twohy seems to have researched witchcraft with admirable thoroughness. The story requires the Warlock to gather the pages of the *Grand Grimoire*, the ultimate witchcraft book, which has been separated into three parts, each located in a different place around the country. So to get where he has to go, the Warlock needs to fly—and to fly he needs the rendered fat of an unbaptized male child. Which he obtains.

Miner's direction is snappy and avoids shocking images; while Sands and, particularly, Grant play their roles absolutely straight, Miner keeps his tongue slightly in cheek throughout. Occasionally he bites it; the straight scenes play well, but those that are intended to be comic fall flat. The brisk pace means that the "scary stuff" goes unemphasized, making the film routine and rote when it should be dynamic and frightening (though it's only nominally a horror film). Nevertheless, *Warlock* surprised me—and others—by being reasonably entertaining.

Star Trek VI: The Undiscovered Country, the publicity proclaimed, is the last, the ultimate, the final adventure of the original crew of the starship *Enterprise.* Leonard Nimoy (Mr. Spock) and William Shatner (Captain Kirk) have each solemnly informed interviewers there will be no more voyages (which began twenty-five years ago, when Gene Roddenberry's TV series made its debut). If *VI* had made more money, though, *Star Trek VII* would be a certainty.

The youngest of the crew, Walter Koenig, is in his fifties, and, sad to say, everyone looks a little weary. And so does the movie, as directed by *Trek* movie veteran Nicholas Meyer. (The screenplay is by Meyer and Denny Martin Flinn, from a story by Nimoy himself, Lawrence Konner, and Mark Rosenthal.) It's a pretty good *Star Trek* adventure but not the grand farewell the occasion demanded. It feels compromised, muffled, low on action and special effects. Too often the story feels perfunctory, as though everyone just wanted to get the damned thing out of the way.

There's a good supporting cast of strong character actors, including Christopher Plummer as Klingon General Chang, so tough his eyepatch is *riveted* on, David Warner, Kurtwood Smith, and others. The script makes a noble attempt to bridge the eighty-year-plus gap between the original series (and movies) and the current TV hit, *Star Trek: The Next Generation.* There's even an ancestor of that show's Worf on hand, played by Worf himself, Michael Dorn, whose role as a defense attorney goes strangely unexplained.

Kirk and most of the rest of the *Enterprise* crew are assigned to meet with Klingon Chancellor Gorkon (David Warner), who has good reasons to seek peace with the Federation at last. But there are forces that don't want this détente—there must be, or the movie wouldn't have a plot. Unfortunately, there really isn't much for any-one to *do*. Kirk and McCoy (DeForest Kelley) are isolated from the rest of the crew for about a third of the film; Spock and the others still on the *Enterprise* spend a lot of time looking for clues to solve a murder. This lets us glimpse areas of the ship we hadn't seen before (including the galley), but it's not very dramatic.

Throughout the movie, we keep wanting more, more, more. But *Star Trek V* didn't make anywhere near as much money as people expected, and so *VI* wasn't budgeted for spectacle; instead we get a set-bound, talky valediction. It's watchable and pleasant when it should be dynamic and delightful.

Long ago, the crew of the *Enterprise* transcended mere fiction. They moved into the realm of folktales, and now they're teetering on the edge of myth. They deserved a great, cosmic send-off, but when the moment of departure finally comes it's muted. The finale is sincere, and probably coaxes a tear or two from even the margin-ally sentimental, but these guys (and one gal) deserved a skyrocket full of tears, a giant explosion of sentiment, something more than just a wistful good-bye.

But I'm sure that even if we've seen the last of *this* crew of the *Enterprise*, Paramount will eventually provide big-screen adventures featuring the current cast of *Star Trek: The Next Generation*. And when those actors in turn grow old, wrinkled, and weary, a new company can be slipped in behind them. Somehow, Gene Rodden-berry and his writers tapped into something archetypal with *Star Trek*, giving us the most popular space saga yet told.

It's rare for movies to use science fiction ideas—killer robots, spaceships, aliens, time travel, and so on—for anything other than sensationalism. A neat, quiet little science fiction comedy-drama like *Late for Dinner* is therefore most unusual. Those who love SF for its own sake will enjoy this sweet film despite its flaws. The story seems to be missing one of its three acts: there's an undropped shoe—it's "shave and a haircut six . . ." without the "bits." But the movie's virtues are so tangible and its characters so winning that the lapses are easily forgiven.

Late for Dinner starts in May 1962 as slightly retarded Frank Lovegren (Peter Berg) and his best friend, Willie Husband (Brian Wimmer), are in Willie's car, fleeing the law, Willie with a bullet in him. In his voice-over narration, Frank admits it was "hard to read the road signs all by myself, but that wasn't so bad because I didn't know where I was going."

A flashback not only shows us the peculiarly complex reasons they're on the lam—the situation involves a conflict with investor Bob Freeman (Peter Gallagher, in a funny cameo)—but, more importantly, it establishes Willie's deeply loving relationship with his wife, Joy (Marcia Gay Harden), and his young daughter, Jessica (Cassy Friel). We also learn that Joy is Frank's sister, and very fond of him.

The fugitives are befriended by a peculiar doctor (Bo Brundin) who almost immediately places them in cryonic tanks and freezes them. Willie is unconscious during all this, and Frank can't really understand it, so when an accident revives them in May 1991, neither knows that twenty-nine years have passed. Willie eventually catches on and resolves to return to Santa Fe and Joy, even though he realizes his return will shock her.

Late for Dinner was written by Mark Andrus and seems to have been intended as a raucous *Back to the Future* type of comedy, with people sporting names like Husband (for a husband) and Dr. Chilblains (for an expert on cold), plus various stock characters (such as Bostitch, your standard cop). But director W. D. Richter (*Buckaroo Banzai*) has, surprisingly, given the film a tone of sweet melancholy; we feel a sense of loss throughout, as it becomes likely that poor, time-displaced Frank and Willie really won't be able to put their lives back together. Frank's fatal illness adds another note of sadness; he's dying of a kidney disease, which is what prompts Chilblains to freeze him in the first place. This idea is never central to the story but underlies many of Frank's actions.

The whole film builds to the reunion of Willie and Joy. She has married, has gotten a divorce, and now has a new lover: can Willie, with his 1962 mind and attitudes, even fit into her life again? The answer is satisfying emotionally but not fleshed out dramatically.

Evidently the makers of *Late for Dinner* fell in love with the characters of Willie and Frank—very easy to do, especially as so endearingly acted by Wimmer and Berg, but this affection led

Andrus and Richter to downplay the comedy and to skip over the potential dramatic tension. The result is a film at once moving and frustrating. We want nothing more than to see Willie and Frank happily reunited with those who love them, but we also want more of their struggles to comprehend a world in which they've been late for dinner for twenty-nine years. At the end, some home videos are employed in an attempt to resolve matters quickly, but it seems as if the key issues are being swept under the rug. Had the filmmakers trusted the material as much as they trusted their actors, the film might have been a small gem.

The Rocketeer is a bright, shiny toy-movie, full of action, black-hearted villains, big stunts, colorful explosions, and a hero who flies through the sky with a rocket on his back. It's such a pleasant film, with nothing on its busy little mind but entertainment, that I feel almost churlish complaining that it could have been *more* fun in the hands of another director. Joe Johnston is competent enough, but too few of his scenes sing and soar.

The whole thing looks sensational, always a virtue of immense importance in movies like this. It's based on a wonderful graphic novel written and drawn by Dave Stevens. He took his inspiration from some classic Republic serials of the fifties (*King of the Rocket Men,* for instance) but had the clever idea of setting his story further back in time, in the Los Angeles of the thirties. Impeccably designed by Jim Bissell, the movie follows Stevens's lead. The story takes place in a dream-world Los Angeles: no smog, lots of orange groves, beautiful tan hills, with people who love living in this paradise of sunshine and fun. To the immense credit of Johnston and writers Danny Bilson and Paul De Meo (the pair behind the almost-had-it-right "Flash" TV series), they insisted on retaining the Rocketeer's distinctive helmet and snazzy leather jacket.

When Cliff Secord (Bill Campbell), the devil-may-care test pilot, first dons the Rocketeer helmet, his mechanic and best friend, Peevy (Alan Arkin, rarely better), comments glumly that he looks like a hood ornament. Well, yes, of course he does. Stevens was influenced by the same movement, art deco, that shaped those classic ornaments, and the overall effect is undeniably 1930s.

Cliff and Peevy wind up with the rocket gear (invented by Howard Hughes, no less), which is being sought by a passel of Nazis, including dashing, Errol Flynnesque movie star Neville Sinclair (Timothy Dalton). There are snarling FBI guys, a bunch of ultimately patriotic hoodlums, and a zeppelin full of Nazis cruising awesomely over the Griffith Park Planetarium. At the climax, we see how—in this version of reality, anyway—the HOLLYWOOD-LAND realty sign got truncated to a mere, but more appropriate, HOLLYWOOD.

The Rocketeer had the potential to be as rousing and wonderful as *Star Wars,* but it falls short. Johnston is good with design, necessary for a film meant to suck you into an alternate reality, but he doesn't give individual scenes the drive and dynamism they demand. In Johnston's directorial debut, *Honey, I Shrunk the Kids,* the performances were all over the place; here, at least, everyone seems to be in the same movie. Newcomer Bill Campbell looks exactly right as dashing Cliff Secord; not only does he resemble the character Dave Stevens originally drew, but his gestures and style of acting seem appropriate for the period. He's not especially engaging as a screen presence; the character, not the actor, wins us over.

The actor having—and giving—the most fun is Timothy Dalton as Sinclair. As written, the character is a pretty standard swashbuckling movie star—a seducer, a cad, a man with a smooth line, imperious, egocentric, and so on—but Dalton gives him an extra edge of irony.

A film like this stands or falls on its special effects. What a pity the Disney company didn't spend enough money to make the tricks truly dazzling—or numerous. The Rocketeer just doesn't get off the ground often enough, and when he does we generally see him from too great a distance.

This movie deserved a sequel. As with all stories of comic-book origin, it exists largely to introduce the characters and define the hero's powers; now that we know this likable bunch, we're ready to see the Rocketeer zip off to new adventures. But, partly due to a poorly planned advertising campaign, the film was a financial disappointment, and no further chapters are planned.

Something wonderful has happened at the Disney studio in the last few years, and it has happened in the animation department. Although we'll never again see new films with the lushness of *Bambi, Pinocchio,* or *Fantasia,* a fresh wind has blown away the tired, repetitious elements, and the company has turned out some amazing work. I was very impressed by *The Little Mermaid*—but I am awe-struck by *Beauty and the Beast*, the first animated film ever nomi-nated for a best-picture Oscar. *Beauty and the Beast* is a tribute to the enormous staff who worked on it, from directors Gary Trousdale and Kirk Wise, to producer Don Hahn, all the way down to "Addi-tional Voices."

The script follows the traditional story line. As usual, a handsome prince has been changed into a ferocious Beast (voice of, believe it or not, Robby Benson); he must remain ensorcelled until he truly loves someone and that person loves him in return. The Beast cap-tures an old gentleman, Maurice (voice of Rex Everhart); to set her father free, Maurice's daughter, Belle (voice of Paige O'Hara), agrees to take his place as the Beast's prisoner in his gigantic mountaintop castle. And, as in Jean Cocteau's masterpiece, *La Belle et la Bête,* Belle's human suitor, the dashing, egocentric Gaston, tries to rescue her for his own selfish ends.

The fearsome Beast is the most brilliantly animated of the char-acters. Glen Keane did the job, and the result is a masterwork. We absolutely have to believe that the Beast has a decent soul but also that he *is* a beast, with a furious, tyrannical nature that must be conquered—by himself. Keane has created an indelible hero (some-thing lacking in *The Little Mermaid*), with a personality so strong that his *inaction* in the face of danger is at once melancholy, tragic, and noble. The Beast is one of the most memorable achievements in all of Disney animation history, part villain, part hero, but a com-plex, believable, fully realized character. I've never seen anything quite like this before.

The key to any telling of "Beauty and the Beast" is romance, and this version is unquestionably the most romantic movie ever made by the Disney studio, surpassing even *Lady and the Tramp. Beauty and the Beast* touches the heart's core; we must, absolutely must, believe that Belle and her Beast *can* fall in love, even as we fear that his grotesque appearance and nature will prove too great an obstacle.

The script by Linda Woolverton, from a story by ten other people (Charles Perrault is not credited), is charming and well written, though it's not the dialogue that will lead you to rent and re-rent the home video. It's the entirety of the film, a movie that has, as far as I could see, only one weak scene (when the overly cute teacup rescues Belle and her father) and almost nothing but magical ones. There are now two great movies of "Beauty and the Beast," two superlative works from one classical fairy tale. But, unlike Jean Cocteau's version of 1946, the work of one brilliant filmmaker-poet, the Disney *Beauty and the Beast* has no single artist to credit. It is a vivid example of the only great collaborative art: the movies.

RHYSLING AWARD WINNERS

....

Joe Haldeman
David Memmott

The last time I read Robert Heinlein's 1947 story "The Green Hills of Earth," I couldn't tell whether Rhysling, "the Blind Singer of the Spaceways," was supposed to be an artist or a hack. Heinlein seems to take the fellow pretty seriously, giving him a hero's death and informing us he was ultimately accorded "scholarly evaluations." But from the evidence of the verses in the story, Rhysling was at best capable of Kiplingesque ditties. . .

> Let the sweet fresh breezes heal me
> As they rove around the girth
> Of our lovely mother planet,
> Of the cool green hills of Earth

That sort of thing. And so, as I rove through previous Nebula anthologies and read the striking verses that took the top honors in the Science Fiction Poetry Association's annual competition—it has become traditional to reprint them in this series—I am struck by an irony. Rhysling could never have won a Rhysling Award.

The 1990 Rhysling for Best Short Poem (under fifty lines) went to Joe Haldeman for "Eighteen Years Old, October Eleventh." Although Haldeman is an accomplished poet—in 1984 he received a Rhysling for "Saul's Death"—he is known primarily for his amazing prose works, including the Nebula-winning (and Hugo-winning) novel, *The Forever War,* and the Hugo-winning story, "Tricentennial." In *Nebula Awards 26,* I was pleased to anthologize Haldeman's tour-de-force novella, "The Hemingway Hoax."

"I'm almost embarrassed to recount the origin of 'Eighteen Years Old, October Eleventh,'" Haldeman tells me. "People will think that writing poetry is *easy*.

"Every fall I attend a poetry workshop that Ottone Riccio conducts in Boston. Now and then he gives assignments, sometimes truly quirky, as in 'Write three related poems of seven syllables each.' This one was simply thematic: 'Write a poem about a girl who loses an earring on her birthday.'

"I just made it a little cosmic."

The 1990 Rhysling for Best Long Poem (over fifty lines) went to David Memmott for "The Aging Cryonicist in the Arms of His Mistress Contemplates the Survival of the Species While the Phoenix Is Consumed by Fire." Born in Grand Rapids, Michigan, in 1948, Memmott came of age in Astoria, Oregon, where he spent long hours "as a self-consciously brooding poet sitting on the docks watching the Columbia River flow into the Pacific Ocean." After his best friend was killed in Vietnam, he felt duty bound to join the Air Force, where he served as a radio operator until honorably discharged two years later as a conscientious objector. Memmott's verse has appeared in *The Magazine of Speculative Poetry, Poets of the Fantastic,* and *The Year's Best Fantasy and Horror.* His first collection, *House on Fire,* was recently published by Jazz Police Books (imprint of Wordcraft of Oregon).

" 'The Aging Cryonicist . . .' evolved from my desire to write a first-person poem in which the 'I' was a character outside myself, someone with a different way of seeing things," Memmott reports. "For some time, a line from my journal— 'They were already dead when I got there'— kept running through my mind. It occurred to me that it might make a good line in a poem about extinct species. Then I read an article in *Cryonics* about a young ALCOR 'Suspension Member' who committed suicide and was cremated before the organization could freeze his remains. The ALCOR logo is, ironically, a phoenix rising from the ashes— the one thing a cryonic suspendee can never do. The final inspiration came when I happened upon a *National Geographic* piece covering the five great extinctions of natural history and was struck by certain parallels with the five worlds of Mayan myth.

"I envision the persona as a scientifically minded, married man who is cynical about life and afraid of death. His rational tradition cannot comfort him, and eventually his loneliness and sense of emptiness drive him to a mistress, who he hopes will commit to the same plan of cryonic suspension as he."

Eighteen Years Old, October Eleventh
JOE HALDEMAN

Drunk for the first time in her life,
She tossed her head in a horsy laugh
and that new opal gift sailed off her sore earlobe,
in a graceful parabola,
pinged twice on the stone porch floor,
and rolled off to hide behind the rose bushes.

It gathered dust and silt for two centuries.
The mansion came down in a war.

For twelve hundred years
the opal hid in the dark rubble, unmoving.
An arctic chill worked down through it, and deeper,
and glaciers pushed the rubble thousands of miles,
very fast, as opals measure time.

After millions of years (the Sun just measurably cooler)
a female felt the presence of a stone,
and waved away yards of snow and ice;
waved away dozens of yards
of frozen dirt and crushed rock,
and held, in what resembled a hand,
this bauble of gold and rainbow stone:

felt a sense of loss in the silly girl,
dead as a trilobite;
felt the pain that had gone into penetrating
the soft hyperbolic paraboloid of cartilage
that then displayed the decoration;
felt its sexual purpose:
to attract a dissimilar pattern of genes
to combine and recombine a trillion trillion times,
and become herself.

She briefly cherished the stone,
and returned it to its waiting.

The Aging Cryonicist in the Arms of His Mistress Contemplates the Survival of the Species While the Phoenix Is Consumed by Fire

DAVID MEMMOTT

". . . a 23-year-old ALCOR Suspension Member took his own life by a self-inflicted shotgun wound to the head. . . . After the father was notified that his son was dead, he did not call ALCOR. Instead he allowed his son to be autopsied without any intervention by ALCOR, made arrangements for pickup of his son's remains by a mortician who was a friend of the family, and had his son's remains cremated. . . . For the first time in our history one of our Suspension Members has been lost beyond recall."

— Mike Darwin, "Beyond Recall," *Cryonics*, June 1987

1.

They were already dead when we found them,
the trilobites, ammonoids and dinosaurs.
Their passing left not tracks of tears
on cheeks of activists stalled in the halls
of congress, awaiting the passing of bills.
Each shred of evidence recovered from thin layers of earth
recalls some episode, a piece of the great puzzle, polarity shifts,
climate changes, meteor impacts. Five mass exterminations
fracture the fossil record
roughly corresponding to the five suns of Mayan myth,
Four already plunged into darkness as even now the fifth fades.
The first world was the era of dark earth
and it died from oxygen, destroyed by wind.
The Sun of Air, the second world, sank under a fiery rain.
The Sun of the Rain of Fire drowned in a fourth world flood,
The flood waters then receded and the age of man was born.
Earth, air, fire, water, all balanced in man, the fifth sun,
symbolized by the equilateral cross with man at its juncture.
So fragile this thing called life,
depending on how you define it.

2.

They were already dead when I got there,
the ancient ones, sculptors of immense plazas,
engineers of temples and pyramids
astronomers extraordinaire.
I am humble as a Paiute in this low canyon
aware of my own smallness in the shadow of their works.
Carrying my heart in my hand, I mount the sacred stairway
and mark the movement of the Sun with their calendars.
What we bring back cannot compare to what was lost beyond recall,
looted legacies in a thousand private collections,
whole cultures scattered like burning embers
until every last spark dies in the wind.
Tenuous this thing called culture,
depending on who defines it.

3.

They were already gone when I got there;
all the saviors gone, their words written down in books.
I crack their bodies for light, but no light comes.
I try to strike the stars from cold stone
and alone put back into the heavens
what the measure of science brought down to earth
and placed fluttering so fragile in my fist.
I beat the shimmering dust of old myths from my palms,
ignite a conflagration in the friction of skin against skin.
So precious this thing called faith,
so dangerous when it closes a mind.
We kill the god in man.
Osiris, Orpheus, Quetzalcoatl, Christ!
Rise, my beautiful birds, rise from the ashes
with iridescent plumage of scarlet and gold.

4.

They were already dead when we got there,
the victims of the holocaust,
their ashes still warm
when we liberated the camps,

billowing black pillars of smoke from chimneys
still suspended over all of Europe
when we found mountains of shoes and eyeglasses
that failed to help them run or see
what was happening in those showers.
Bodies, all bone, stacked up for the crematoriums
and those we saved from the cool bureaucracy of death
were uncounted casualties wearing numbers on their flesh.
We kill the earth with our numbers.
Precarious this thing called man,
so dependent on who defines him.
Now man dreams his own successor—the machine—
and how, we wonder, will machine define itself?

5.

They were already dead when I got there,
the American mastodon,
Flightless ibis,
Carolina parakeet,
the Passenger pigeon,
Giant lemur,
the great auk.
The bleached bones of six million buffalo
animate my dreams and what remains of dying breeds
chide me as I have made no difference.
The California condor,
the Hawaiian o'o-a'a' sings to himself,
for he is the last of his kind,
blue whale,
the Costa Rican spinner dolphin,
mountain gorilla,
snow leopard,
black rhinoceros,
the spotted owl.
They cry out from their homes, overrun by necessity,
and I stop my ears with music.
I go to work and sit entranced,
each day a day closer to joining the march to extinction.

We leave our record in wet cement,
a good impression of our mastering digits
mastering even ourselves.

6.

He was already dead when they found him.
We cannot raise this Phoenix from ashes.
We will never know why he pulled the trigger
or whether he'd given up any thought of immortality
so chose to sabotage even a neurosuspension
by a shotgun wound to the head.
We would have saved him, you know, this once vital Phoenix.
After a total blood washout and full body perfusion,
no doubt complicated by the headwound,
he would have been submerged in liquid nitrogen
and slowly cooled to -196 degrees centigrade
and placed in a cryocapsule to complete his first life cycle.
One day he would have been resurrected from this biostasis.
Nano-machines would have repaired the brain damage
and we could have asked him why?
Why did he give up so much so soon?
He would have had much time to think about it,
if, upon awakening, he could recall.
But now he is lost beyond recall.

7.

I was already dead when you found me, my dear,
dead but not buried, not lost beyond recall.
I was resurrected in your eyes, reborn in your arms—
so you see, I've already lived twice.
My name when formed on your lips is a lethal weapon;
it pierces the armor I'd so carefully forged.
You found a breach in my defenses and reached in
to heal me, your living touch better than any machine.
What I want now is for both of us to live forever.
So please, my love, sign here.

The Milky Way galaxy would be a better place, I think, if it contained more authors like John Kessel, a scholar who is prepared to defend the merits of science fiction even as he bemoans the many and maddening ways the genre infantalizes itself. When not busy teaching fiction writing and literature at North Carolina State University, Kessel enriches the field with his precise, layered, literate prose. *Good News from Outer Space,* a baroque and biting satire, was a 1989 Nebula finalist and the runner-up for the John W. Campbell Memorial Award. "Another Orphan," a Nebula-winning novella about a commodities broker who awakens one morning to find himself a character in *Moby Dick,* began life, believe it or not, as part of Kessel's doctoral dissertation at the University of Kansas. A short-story collection, *Meeting in Infinity,* recently appeared from Arkham House.

Asked to explain the origins of "Buffalo," Kessel replied: "When Anne Jordan first asked me to write about my hometown for *Fires of the Past,* I had an entirely different story in mind. Eight months passed, the deadline loomed, and I had gotten nowhere. Then in H. G. Wells's *Experiment in Autobiography* I read that he had visited Washington in 1934, the same time my father was there. The juxtaposition struck sparks, and Buffalo went from a setting to a metaphor.

"Duke Ellington started as a background detail but refused to keep in his place; just when I needed him, he played the story's resolution for me.

"A couple of months after it was published, I realized that 'Buffalo' is about my two fathers, and my two homes. John Kessel and Buffalo, New York, were the ones I had consciously in mind, but Wells (as he is for many of us) was my spiritual father, and science fiction is my spiritual home.

"Like our father H. G., most of us SF writers want to change the world. Like my own father, we don't have much direct power to do so. And so, as Wells said, 'We who are Citizens of the Future wander about this present scene like passengers on a ship overdue, in plain sight of a port which only some disorder in the chart room prevents us from entering.' This painful paradox has, lately, driven my fiction."

In April of 1934 H. G. Wells made a trip to the United States, where he visited Washington, D.C., and met with President Franklin

Delano Roosevelt. Wells, sixty-eight years old, hoped the New Deal might herald a revolutionary change in the U.S. economy, a step forward in an "Open Conspiracy" of rational thinkers that would culminate in a world socialist state. For forty years he'd subordinated every scrap of his artistic ambition to promoting this vision. But by 1934 Wells's optimism, along with his energy for saving the world, was waning.

While in Washington he requested to see something of the new social welfare agencies, and Harold Ickes, Roosevelt's Interior Secretary, arranged for Wells to visit a Civilian Conservation Corps camp at Fort Hunt, Virginia.

It happens that at that time my father was a CCC member at that camp. From his boyhood he had been a reader of adventure stories; he was a big fan of Edgar Rice Burroughs, and of H. G. Wells. This is the story of their encounter, which never took place.

In Buffalo it's cold, but here the trees are in bloom, the mockingbirds sing in the mornings, and the sweat the men work up clearing brush, planting dogwoods, and cutting roads is wafted away by warm breezes. Two hundred of them live in the Fort Hunt barracks high on the bluff above the Virginia side of the Potomac. They wear surplus army uniforms. In the morning, after a breakfast of grits, Sergeant Sauter musters them up in the parade yard, and they climb onto trucks and are driven by Forest Service men out to wherever they're to work that day.

For several weeks Kessel's squad has been working along the river road, clearing rest stops and turnarounds. The tall pines have shallow root systems, and spring rain has softened the earth to the point where wind is forever knocking trees across the road. While most of the men work on the ground, a couple are sent up to cut off the tops of the pines adjoining the road, so if they do fall they won't block it. Most of the men claim to be afraid of heights. Kessel isn't. A year or two ago back in Michigan he worked in a logging camp. It's hard work, but he is used to hard work. And at least he's out of Buffalo.

The truck rumbles and jounces out the river road, which is going to be the George Washington Memorial Parkway in our time, once the WPA project that will build it gets started. The humid air is cool now, but it will be hot again today, in the eighties. A couple of the guys get into a debate about whether the feds will ever catch Dillinger. Some others talk women. They're planning to go into Washington on the weekend and check out the dance halls. Kessel likes to dance; he's a good dancer. The fox-trot, the lindy hop. When he gets drunk he likes to sing, and has a ready wit. He talks a lot more, kids the girls.

When they get to the site the foreman sets most of the men to work clearing the roadside for a scenic overlook. Kessel straps on a climbing belt, takes an ax, and climbs his first tree. The first twenty feet are limbless, then climbing gets trickier. He looks down only enough to estimate when he's gotten high enough. He sets himself, cleats biting into the shoulder of a lower limb, and chops away at the road side of the trunk. There's a trick to cutting the top so that it falls the right way. When he's got it ready to go he calls down to warn the men below. Then a few quick bites of the ax on the opposite side of the cut, a shove, a crack, and the top starts to go. He braces his legs, ducks his head, and grips the trunk. The treetop skids off, and the bole of the pine waves ponderously back and forth, with Kessel swinging at its end like an ant on a metronome. After the pine stops swinging he shinnies down and climbs the next tree.

He's good at this work, efficient, careful. He's not a particularly strong man—slender, not burly—but even in his youth he shows the attention to detail that, as a boy, I remember seeing when he built our house.

The squad works through the morning, then breaks for lunch from the mess truck. The men are always complaining about the food, and how there isn't enough of it, but until recently a lot of them were living in Hoovervilles—shack cities—and eating nothing at all. As they're eating, a couple of the guys rag Kessel for working too fast. "What do you expect from a Yankee?" one of the southern boys says.

"He ain't a Yankee. He's a Polack."

Kessel tries to ignore them.

"Whyn't you lay off him, Turkel?" says Cole, one of Kessel's buddies.

Turkel is a big blond guy from Chicago. Some say he joined the CCC to duck an armed-robbery rap. "He works too hard," Turkel says. "He makes us look bad."

"Don't have to work much to make you look bad, Lou," Cole

says. The others laugh, and Kessel appreciates it. "Give Jack some credit. At least he had enough sense to come down out of Buffalo." More laughter.

"There's nothing wrong with Buffalo," Kessel says.

"Except fifty thousand out-of-work Polacks," Turkel says.

"I guess you got no out-of-work people in Chicago," Kessel says. "You just joined for the exercise."

"Except he's not getting any exercise, if he can help it!" Cole says.

The foreman comes by and tells them to get back to work. Kessel climbs another tree, stung by Turkel's charge. What kind of man complains if someone else works hard? It only shows how even decent guys have to put up with assholes dragging them down. But it's nothing new. He's seen it before, back in Buffalo.

Buffalo, New York, is the symbolic home of this story. In the years preceding the First World War it grew into one of the great industrial metropolises of the United States. Located where Lake Erie flows into the Niagara River, strategically close to cheap electricity from Niagara Falls and cheap transportation by lake boat from the Midwest, it was a center of steel, automobiles, chemicals, grain milling, and brewing. Its major employers—Bethlehem Steel, Ford, Pierce-Arrow, Gold Medal Flour, the National Biscuit Company, Ralston Purina, Quaker Oats, National Aniline—drew thousands of immigrants like Kessel's family. Along Delaware Avenue stood the imperious and stylized mansions of the city's old money, ersatz-Renaissance homes designed by Stanford White, huge Protestant churches, and a Byzantine synagogue. The city boasted the first modern skyscraper, designed by Louis Sullivan in the 1890s. From its productive factories to its polyglot work force to its class system and its boosterism, Buffalo was a monument to modern industrial capitalism. It is the place Kessel has come from—almost an expression of his personality itself—and the place he, at times, fears he can never escape. A cold, grimy city dominated by church and family, blinkered and cramped, forever playing second fiddle to Chicago, New York, and Boston. It offers the immigrant the opportunity to find steady work in some factory or mill, but, though Kessel could not have put it into these words, it also puts a lid on his opportunities. It stands for all disappointed expectations, human limitations, tawdry compromises, for the inevitable choice of the expedient over the beautiful, for an American economic system that turns all things into commodities and measures men by their bank accounts. It is the home of the industrial proletariat.

It's not unique. It could be Youngstown, Akron, Detroit. It's the place my father, and I, grew up.

The afternoon turns hot and still; during a work break Kessel strips to the waist. About two o'clock a big black De Soto comes up the road and pulls off onto the shoulder. A couple of men in suits get out of the back, and one of them talks to the Forest Service foreman, who nods deferentially. The foreman calls over to the men.

"Boys, this here's Mr. Pike from the Interior Department. He's got a guest here to see how we work, a writer, Mr. H. G. Wells from England."

Most of the men couldn't care less, but the name strikes a spark in Kessel. He looks over at the little potbellied man in the dark suit. The man is sweating; he brushes his mustache.

The foreman sends Kessel up to show them how they're topping the trees. He points out to the visitors where the others with rakes and shovels are leveling the ground for the overlook. Several other men are building a log-rail fence from the treetops. From way above, Kessel can hear their voices between the thunks of his ax. H. G. Wells. He remembers reading "The War of the Worlds" in *Amazing Stories*. He's read *The Outline of History*, too. The stories, the history, are so large, it seems impossible that the man who wrote them could be standing not thirty feet below him. He tries to concentrate on the ax, the tree.

Time for this one to go. He calls down. The men below look up. Wells takes off his hat and shields his eyes with his hand. He's balding and looks even smaller from up here. Strange that such big ideas could come from such a small man. It's kind of disappointing. Wells leans over to Pike and says something. The treetop falls away. The pine sways like a bucking bronco, and Kessel holds on for dear life.

He comes down with the intention of saying something to Wells, telling him how much he admires him, but when he gets down the sight of the two men in suits and his awareness of his own sweaty chest make him timid. He heads down to the next tree. After another ten minutes the men get back in the car, drive away. Kessel curses himself for the opportunity lost.

That evening at the New Willard Hotel, Wells dines with his old friends Clarence Darrow and Charles Russell. Darrow and Russell are in Washington to testify before a congressional committee on a report they have just submitted to the administration concerning the monopolistic effects of the National Recovery Act. The right wing is trying to eviscerate Roosevelt's program for large-scale industrial management, and the Darrow Report is playing right into their hands. Wells tries, with little success, to convince Darrow of the shortsightedness of his position.

"Roosevelt is willing to sacrifice the small man to the huge corporations," Darrow insists, his eyes bright.

"The small man? Your small man is a romantic fantasy," Wells says. "It's not the New Deal that's doing him in—it's the process of industrial progress. It's the twentieth century. You can't legislate yourself back into 1870."

"What about the individual?" Russell asks.

Wells snorts. "Walk out into the street. The individual is out on the street corner selling apples. The only thing that's going to save him is some coordinated effort, by intelligent, selfless men. Not your free market."

Darrow puffs on his cigar, exhales, smiles. "Don't get exasperated, H. G. We're not working for Standard Oil. But if I have to choose between the bureaucrat and the man pumping gas at the filling station, I'll take the pump jockey."

Wells sees he's got no chance against the American mythology of the common man. "Your pump jockey works for Standard Oil. And the last I checked, the free market hasn't expended much energy looking out for his interests."

"Have some more wine," Russell says.

Russell refills their glasses with the excellent Bordeaux. It's been a first-rate meal. Wells finds the debate stimulating even when he can't prevail; at one time that would have been enough, but as the years go on the need to prevail grows stronger in him. The times are out of joint, and when he looks around he sees desperation growing. A new world order is necessary—it's so clear that even a fool ought to see it—but if he can't even convince radicals like Darrow, what hope is there of gaining the acquiescence of the shareholders in the utility trusts?

The answer is that the changes will have to be made over their objections. As Roosevelt seems prepared to do. Wells's dinner with the president has heartened him in a way that his debate cannot negate.

Wells brings up an item he read in the *Washington Post*. A lecturer for the Communist party—a young Negro—was barred from speaking at the University of Virginia. Wells's question is, was the man barred because he was a Communist or because he was Negro?

"Either condition," Darrow says sardonically, "is fatal in Virginia."

"But students point out the university has allowed Communists to speak on campus before, and has allowed Negroes to perform music there."

"They can perform, but they can't speak," Russell says. "This isn't unusual. Go down to the Paradise Ballroom, not a mile from here. There's a Negro orchestra playing there, but no Negroes are allowed inside to listen."

"You should go to hear them anyway," Darrow says. "It's Duke Ellington. Have you heard of him?"

"I don't get on with the titled nobility," Wells quips.

"Oh, this Ellington's a noble fellow, all right, but I don't think you'll find him in the peerage," Russell says.

"He plays jazz, doesn't he?"

"Not like any jazz you've heard," Darrow says. "It's something totally new. You should find a place for it in one of your utopias."

All three of them are for helping the colored peoples. Darrow has defended Negroes accused of capital crimes. Wells, on his first visit to America almost thirty years ago, met with Booker T. Washington and came away impressed, although he still considers the peaceable coexistence of the white and colored races problematical.

"What are you working on now, Wells?" Russell says. "What new improbability are you preparing to assault us with? Racial equality? Sexual liberation?"

"I'm writing a screen treatment based on *The Shape of Things to Come*," Wells says. He tells them about his screenplay, sketching out for them the future he has in his mind. An apocalyptic war, a war of unsurpassed brutality that will begin, in his film, in 1939. In this war, the creations of science will be put to the services of destruction in ways that will make the horrors of the Great War pale in comparison. Whole populations will be exterminated. But then, out of the ruins will arise the new world. The orgy of violence will purge the human race of the last vestiges of tribal thinking. Then will come the organization of the directionless and weak by the intelligent and purposeful. The new man. Cleaner, stronger, more rational. Wells can see it. He talks on, supplely, surely, late into the night. His mind is fertile with invention, still. He can see that Darrow and Russell, despite their Yankee individualism, are caught up by his vision. The future may be threatened, but it is not entirely closed.

Friday night, back in the barracks at Fort Hunt, Kessel lies on his bunk reading a secondhand *Wonder Stories*. He's halfway through the tale of a scientist who invents an evolution chamber that progresses him through fifty thousand years of evolution in an hour, turning him into a big-brained telepathic monster. The evolved scientist is totally without emotions and wants to control the world. But his body's atrophied. Will the hero, a young engineer, be able to stop him?

At a plank table in the aisle a bunch of men are playing poker for cigarettes. They're talking about women and dogs. Cole throws in his hand and comes over to sit on the next bunk. "Still reading that stuff, Jack?"

"Don't knock it until you've tried it."

"Are you coming into D.C. with us tomorrow? Sergeant Sauter says we can catch a ride in on one of the trucks."

Kessel thinks about it. Cole probably wants to borrow some money. Two days after he gets his monthly pay he's broke. He's always looking for a good time. Kessel spends his leave more quietly; he usually walks into Alexandria—about six miles—and sees a movie or just strolls around town. Still, he would like to see more of Washington. "Okay."

Cole looks at the sketchbook poking out from beneath Kessel's pillow. "Any more hot pictures?"

Immediately Kessel regrets trusting Cole. Yet there's not much he can say—the book is full of pictures of movie stars he's drawn. "I'm learning to draw. And at least I don't waste my time like the rest of you guys."

Cole looks serious. "You know, you're not any better than the rest of us," he says, not angrily. "You're just another Polack. Don't get so high-and-mighty."

"Just because I want to improve myself doesn't mean I'm high-and-mighty."

"Hey, Cole, are you in or out?" Turkel yells from the table.

"Dream on, Jack," Cole says, and returns to the game.

Kessel tries to go back to the story, but he isn't interested anymore. He can figure out that the hero is going to defeat the hyper-evolved scientist in the end. He folds his arms behind his head and stares at the knots in the rafters.

It's true, Kessel does spend a lot of time dreaming. But he has things he wants to do, and he's not going to waste his life drinking and whoring like the rest of them.

Kessel's always been different. Quieter, smarter. He was always going to do something better than the rest of them; he's well-spoken, he likes to read. Even though he didn't finish high school, he reads everything: *Amazing, Astounding, Wonder Stories.* He believes in the future. He doesn't want to end up trapped in some factory his whole life.

Kessel's parents emigrated from Poland in 1911. Their name was Kisiel, but his got Germanized in Catholic school. For ten years the family moved from one to another middle-sized industrial town, as Joe Kisiel bounced from job to job. Springfield. Utica. Syracuse. Rochester. Kessel remembers them loading up a wagon in the middle of night with all their belongings in order to jump the rent on the run-down house in Syracuse. He remembers pulling a cart down to the Utica Club brewery, a nickel in his hand, to buy his father a keg of beer. He remembers them finally settling in the First Ward of Buffalo. The First Ward, at the foot of the Erie Canal, was an Irish neighborhood as far back as anybody could remember, and the Kisiels were the only Poles there. That's where he developed his chameleon ability to fit in, despite the fact he wanted nothing more than to get out. But he had to protect his mother, sister, and little brothers from their father's drunken rages. When Joe Kisiel died in 1924 it was a relief, despite the fact that his son ended up supporting the family.

For ten years Kessel has strained against the tug of that responsibility. He's sought the free and easy feeling of the road, of places different from where he grew up, romantic places where the sun shines and he can make something entirely American of himself.

Despite his ambitions, he's never accomplished much. He's been essentially a drifter, moving from job to job. Starting as a pinsetter in a bowling alley, he moved on to a flour mill. He would have stayed in the mill only he developed an allergy to the flour dust, so he became an electrician. He would have stayed an electrician except he had a fight with a boss and got blacklisted. He left Buffalo because of his father; he kept coming back because of his mother. When the Depression hit he tried to get a job in Detroit at the auto factories, but that was plain stupid in the face of the universal collapse, and he ended up working up in the peninsula as a farmhand, then as a logger. It was seasonal work, and when the season was over he was out of a job. In the winter of 1933, rather than freeze his ass off in northern Michigan, he joined the CCC. Now he sends twenty-five of his thirty dollars a month back to his mother and sister in Buffalo. And imagines the future.

When he thinks about it, there are two futures. The first is the one from the magazines and books. Bright, slick, easy. We, looking back on it, can see it to be the fifteen-cent utopianism of Hugo Gernsback's *Science and Mechanics,* which flourished in the midst of the Depression. A degradation of the marvelous inventions that made Wells his early reputation, minus the social theorizing that drove Wells's technological speculations. The common man's boosterism. There's money to be made telling people like Jack Kessel about the wonderful world of the future.

The second future is Kessel's own. That one's a lot harder to see. It contains work. A good job, doing something he likes, using his skills. Not working for another man, but making something that would be useful for others. Building something for the future. And a woman, a gentle woman, for his wife. Not some cheap dance-hall queen.

So when Kessel saw H. G. Wells in person, that meant something to him. He's had his doubts. He's twenty-nine years old, not a kid anymore. If he's ever going to get anywhere, it's going to have to start happening soon. He has the feeling that something significant is going to happen to him. Wells is a man who sees the future. He moves in that bright world where things make sense. He represents something that Kessel wants.

But the last thing Kessel wants is to end up back in Buffalo.

He pulls the sketchbook, the sketchbook he was to show me twenty years later, from under his pillow. He turns past drawings of movie stars: Jean Harlow, Mae West, Carole Lombard—the beautiful, unreachable faces of his longing—and of natural scenes: rivers, forests, birds—to a blank page. The page is as empty as the future, waiting for him to write upon it. He lets his imagination soar. He envisions an eagle, gliding high above the mountains of the West that he has never seen but that he knows he will visit someday. The eagle is America; it is his own dreams. He begins to draw.

Kessel does not know that Wells's life has not worked out as well as he planned. At that moment Wells is pining after the Russian émigrée Moura Budberg, once Maxim Gorky's secretary, with whom Wells has been carrying on an off-and-on affair since 1920. His wife of thirty years, Amy Catherine "Jane" Wells, died in 1927. Since that time Wells has been adrift, alternating spells of furious pamphleteering with listless periods of suicidal depression. Meanwhile, all London is gossiping about the recent attack published in *Time and Tide* by his vengeful ex-lover Odette Keun. Have his mistakes followed him across the Atlantic to undermine his purpose? Does Darrow think him a jumped-up cockney? A moment of doubt overwhelms him. In the end, the future depends as much on the open-mindedness of men like Darrow as it does on a reorganization of society. What good is a guild of samurai if no one arises to take the job?

Wells doesn't like the trend of these thoughts. If human nature lets him down, then his whole life has been a waste.

But he's seen the president. He's seen those workers on the road. Those men climbing the trees risk their lives without complaining, for minimal pay. It's easy to think of them as stupid or desperate or simply young, but it's also possible to give them credit for dedication to their work. They don't seem to be ridden by the desire to grub and clutch that capitalism rewards; if you look at it properly, that may be the explanation for their ending up wards of the state. And is Wells any better? If he hadn't got an education he would have ended up a miserable draper's assistant.

Wells is due to leave for New York Sunday. Saturday night finds him sitting in his room, trying to write, after a solitary dinner in the

New Willard. Another bottle of wine, or his age, has stirred some-thing in Wells, and despite his rationalizations he finds himself near despair. Moura has rejected him. He needs the soft, supportive em-brace of a lover, but instead he has this stuffy hotel room in a heat wave.

He remembers writing *The Time Machine,* he and Jane living in rented rooms in Sevenoaks with her ailing mother, worried about money, about whether the landlady would put them out. In the drawer of the dresser was a writ from the court that refused to grant him a divorce from his wife, Isabel. He remembers a warm night, late in August—much like this one—sitting up after Jane and her mother went to bed, writing at the round table before the open window, under the light of a paraffin lamp. One part of his mind was caught up in the rush of creation, burning, following the Time Traveler back to the Sphinx, pursued by the Morlocks, only to discover that his machine is gone and he is trapped without escape from his des-perate circumstance. At the same moment he could hear the land-lady, out in the garden, fully aware that he could hear her, complaining to the neighbor about his and Jane's scandalous habits. On the one side, the petty conventions of a crabbed world; on the other, in his mind—the future, their peril and hope. Moths fluttering through the window beat themselves against the lampshade and fell onto the manuscript; he brushed them away unconsciously and continued, furiously, in a white heat. The Time Traveler, battered and hungry, returning from the future with a warning, and a flower.

He opens the hotel windows all the way, but the curtains aren't stirred by a breath of air. Below, in the street, he hears the sound of traffic, and music. He decides to send a telegram to Moura, but after several false starts he finds he has nothing to say. Why has she refused to marry him? Maybe he is finally too old, and the magne-tism of sex or power or intellect that has drawn women to him for forty years has finally all been squandered. The prospect of spending the last years remaining to him alone fills him with dread.

He turns on the radio, gets successive band shows: Morton Dow-ney, Fats Waller. Jazz. Paging through the newspaper, he comes across an advertisement for the Ellington orchestra Darrow men-tioned: it's at the ballroom just down the block. But the thought of a smoky room doesn't appeal to him. He considers the cinema. He has never been much for the "movies." Though he thinks them an unrivaled opportunity to educate, that promise has never been properly seized—something he hopes to do in *Things to Come*. The newspaper reveals an uninspiring selection: *Twenty Million Sweethearts,* a musical, at the Earle, *The Black Cat,* with Boris Karloff and Bela Lugosi, at the Rialto, and *Tarzan and His Mate* at the Palace. To these Americans he is the equivalent of this hack, Edgar Rice Burroughs. The books I read as a child, that fired my father's imagination and my own, Wells considers his frivolous apprentice work. His serious work is discounted. His ideas mean nothing.

Wells decides to try the Tarzan movie. He dresses for the sultry weather—Washington in spring is like high summer in London—and goes down to the lobby. He checks his street guide and takes the streetcar to the Palace Theater, where he buys an orchestra seat, for twenty-five cents, to see *Tarzan and His Mate*.

It is a perfectly wretched movie, comprised wholly of romantic fantasy, melodrama, and sexual innuendo. The dramatic leads perform with wooden idiocy surpassed only by the idiocy of the screenplay. Wells is attracted by the undeniable charms of the young heroine, Maureen O'Sullivan, but the film is devoid of intellectual content. Thinking of the audience at which such a farrago must be aimed depresses him. This is art as fodder. Yet the theater is filled, and the people are held in rapt attention. This only depresses Wells more. If these citizens are the future of America, then the future of America is dim.

An hour into the film the antics of an anthropomorphized chimpanzee, a scene of transcendent stupidity that nevertheless sends the audience into gales of laughter, drives Wells from the theater. It is still mid-evening. He wanders down the avenue of theaters, restaurants, and clubs. On the sidewalk are beggars, ignored by the passersby. In an alley behind a hotel Wells spots a woman and child picking through the ashcans beside the restaurant kitchen.

Unexpectedly, he comes upon the marquee announcing DUKE ELLINGTON AND HIS ORCHESTRA. From within the open doors of the ballroom wafts the sound of jazz. Impulsively, Wells buys a ticket and goes in.

Kessel and his cronies have spent the day walking around the Mall, which the WPA is relandscaping. They've seen the Lincoln Memorial, the Capitol, the Washington Monument, the Smithsonian, the

White House. Kessel has his picture taken in front of a statue of a soldier—a photo I have sitting on my desk. I've studied it many times. He looks forthrightly into the camera, faintly smiling. His face is confident, unlined.

When night comes they hit the bars. Prohibition was lifted only last year, and the novelty has not yet worn off. The younger men get plastered, but Kessel finds himself uninterested in getting drunk. A couple of them set their minds on women and head for the Gayety Burlesque; Cole, Kessel, and Turkel end up in the Paradise Ballroom listening to Duke Ellington.

They have a couple of drinks, ask some girls to dance. Kessel dances with a short girl with a southern accent who refuses to look him in the eyes. After thanking her he returns to the others at the bar. He sips his beer. "Not so lucky, Jack?" Cole says.

"She doesn't like a tall man," Turkel says.

Kessel wonders why Turkel came along. Turkel is always complaining about "niggers," and his only comment on the Ellington band so far has been to complain about how a bunch of jigs can make a living playing jungle music while white men sleep in barracks and eat grits three times a day. Kessel's got nothing against the colored, and he likes the music, though it's not exactly the kind of jazz he's used to. It doesn't sound much like Dixieland. It's darker, bigger, more dangerous. Ellington, resplendent in tie and tails, looks like he's enjoying himself up there at his piano, knocking out minimal solos while the orchestra plays cool and low.

Turning from them to look across the tables, Kessel sees a little man sitting alone beside the dance floor, watching the young couples sway in the music. To his astonishment he recognizes Wells. He's been given another chance. Hesitating only a moment, Kessel abandons his friends, goes over to the table, and introduces himself.

"Excuse me, Mr. Wells. You might not remember me, but I was one of the men you saw yesterday in Virginia working along the road. The CCC?"

Wells looks up at a gangling young man wearing a khaki uniform, his olive tie neatly knotted and tucked between the second and third buttons of his shirt. His hair is slicked down, parted in the middle. Wells doesn't remember anything of him. "Yes?"

"I—I been reading your stories and books a lot of years. I admire your work."

Something in the man's earnestness affects Wells. "Please sit down," he says.

Kessel takes a seat. "Thank you." He pronounces "th" as "t" so that "thank" comes out "tank." He sits tentatively, as if the chair is mortgaged, and seems at a loss for words.

"What's your name?"

"John Kessel. My friends call me Jack."

The orchestra finishes a song, and the dancers stop in their places, applauding. Up on the bandstand, Ellington leans into the microphone. "Mood Indigo," he says, and instantly they swing into it: the clarinet moans in low register, in unison with the muted trumpet and trombone, paced by the steady rhythm guitar, the brushed drums. The song's melancholy suits Wells's mood.

"Are you from Virginia?"

"My family lives in Buffalo. That's in New York."

"Ah—yes. Many years ago I visited Niagara Falls, and took the train through Buffalo." Wells remembers riding along a lakefront of factories spewing waste water into the lake, past heaps of coal, clouds of orange and black smoke from blast furnaces. In front of dingy row houses, ragged hedges struggled through the smoky air. The landscape of laissez-faire. "I imagine the Depression has hit Buffalo severely."

"Yes, sir."

"What work did you do there?"

Kessel feels nervous, but he opens up a little. "A lot of things. I used to be an electrician until I got blacklisted."

"Blacklisted?"

"I was working on this job where the super told me to set the wiring wrong. I argued with him, but he just told me to do it his way. So I waited until he went away, then I sneaked into the construction shack and checked the blueprints. He didn't think I could read blueprints, but I could. I found out I was right and he was wrong. So I went back and did it right. The next day, when he found out, he fired me. Then the so-and-so went and got me blacklisted."

Though he doesn't know how much credence to put in this story, Wells finds that his sympathies are aroused. It's the kind of thing that must happen all the time. He recognizes in Kessel the immigrant stock that, when Wells visited the United States in 1906, made him skeptical about the future of America. He'd theorized that these

Italians and Slavs, coming from lands with no democratic tradition, unable to speak English, would degrade the already corrupt political process. They could not be made into good citizens; they would not work well when they could work poorly and, given the way the economic deal was stacked against them, would seldom rise high enough to do better.

But Kessel is clean, well-spoken despite his accent, and deferential. Wells realizes that this is one of the men who was topping trees along the river road.

Meanwhile, Kessel detects a sadness in Wells's manner. He had not imagined that Wells might be sad, and he feels sympathy for him. It occurs to him, to his own surprise, that he might be able to make *Wells* feel better. "So—what do you think of our country?" he asks.

"Good things seem to be happening here. I'm impressed with your President Roosevelt."

"Roosevelt's the best friend the workingman ever had." Kessel pronounces the name "Roozvelt." "He's a man that"—he struggles for the words—"that's not for the past. He's for the future."

It begins to dawn on Wells that Kessel is not an example of a class, or a sociological study, but a man like himself with an intellect, opinions, dreams. He thinks of his own youth, struggling to rise in a class-bound society. He leans forward across the table. "You believe in the future? You think things can be different?"

"I think they have to be, Mr. Wells."

Wells sits back. "Good. So do I."

Kessel is stunned by this intimacy. It is more than he had hoped for, yet it leaves him with little to say. He wants to tell Wells about his dreams and at the same time ask him a thousand questions. He wants to tell Wells everything he has seen in the world and to hear Wells tell him the same. He casts about for something to say.

"I always liked your writing. I like to read scientifiction."

"Scientifiction?"

Kessel shifts his long legs. "You know—stories about the future. Monsters from outer space. The Martians. *The Time Machine.* You're the best scientifiction writer I ever read, next to Edgar Rice Burroughs." Kessel pronounces "Edgar" as "Eedgar."

"Edgar Rice Burroughs?"

"Yes."

"You *like* Burroughs?"

Kessel hears the disapproval in Wells's voice. "Well—maybe not as much as, as *The Time Machine*," he stutters. "Burroughs never wrote about monsters as good as your Morlocks."

Wells is nonplussed. "Monsters."

"Yes." Kessel feels something's going wrong, but he sees no way out. "But he does put more romance in his stories. That princess— Dejah Thoris?"

All Wells can think of is Tarzan in his loincloth on the movie screen, and the moronic audience. After a lifetime of struggling, a hundred books written to change the world, in the service of men like this, is this all his work has come to? To be compared to the writer of pulp trash? To "Eedgar" Rice Burroughs? He laughs aloud.

At Wells's laugh, Kessel stops. He knows he's done something wrong, but he doesn't know what.

Wells's weariness has dropped down onto his shoulders again like an iron cloak. "Young man—go away," he says. "You don't know what you're saying. Go back to Buffalo."

Kessel's face burns. He stumbles from the table. The room is full of noise and laughter. He's run up against that wall again. He's just an ignorant Polack after all; it's his stupid accent, his clothes. He should have talked about something else—*The Outline of History*, politics. But what made him think he could talk like an equal with a man like Wells in the first place? Wells lives in a different world. The future is for men like him. Kessel feels himself the prey of fantasies. It's a bitter joke.

He clutches the bar, orders another beer. His reflection in the mirror behind the ranked bottles is small and ugly.

"Whatsa matter, Jack?" Turkel asks him. "Didn't he want to dance neither?"

And that's the story, essentially, that never happened.

Not long after this, Kessel did go back to Buffalo. During the Second World War he worked as a crane operator in the forty-inch rolling mill of Bethlehem Steel. He met his wife, Angela Giorlandino, during the war, and they married in June 1945. After the war he quit the plant and became a carpenter. Their first child, a girl, died in infancy. Their second, a boy, was born in 1950. At that time Kessel began building the house that, like so many things in his life, he was never entirely to complete. He worked hard, had two more children. There were good years and bad ones. He held a lot of jobs. The recession of 1958 just about flattened him; our family had to go on welfare. Things got better, but they never got good. After the 1950s, the economy of Buffalo, like that of all U.S. industrial cities caught in the transition to a postindustrial age, declined steadily. Kessel never did work for himself and as an old man was little more prosperous than he had been as a young one.

In the years preceding his death in 1946, Wells was to go on to further disillusionment. His efforts to create a sane world met with increasing frustration. He became bitter, enraged. Moura Budberg never agreed to marry him, and he lived alone. The war came, and it was, in some ways, even worse than he had predicted. He continued to propagandize for the socialist world state throughout, but with increasing irrelevance. The new leftists like Orwell considered him a dinosaur, fatally out of touch with the realities of world politics, a simpleminded technocrat with no understanding of the darkness of the human heart. Wells's last book, *Mind at the End of Its Tether,* proposed that the human race faced an evolutionary crisis that would lead to its extinction unless humanity leapt to a higher state of consciousness; a leap about which Wells speculated with little hope or conviction.

Sitting there in the Washington ballroom in 1934, Wells might well have understood that, for all his thinking and preaching about the future, the future had irrevocably passed him by.

But the story isn't quite over yet. Back in the Washington ballroom Wells sits humiliated, a little guilty for sending Kessel away so harshly. Kessel, his back to the dance floor, stares humiliated into his glass of beer. Gradually, both of them are pulled back from dark thoughts of their own inadequacies by the sound of Ellington's orchestra.

Ellington stands in front of the big grand piano, behind him the band: three saxes, two clarinets, two trumpets, trombones, a drummer, guitarist, bass. "Creole Love Call," Ellington whispers into the microphone, then sits again at the piano. He waves his hand once, twice, and the clarinets slide into a low wavering theme. The trumpet, muted, echoes it. The bass player and guitarist strum ahead at a deliberate pace, rhythmic, erotic, bluesy. Kessel and Wells, separate across the room, each unaware of the other, are alike drawn in. The trumpet growls eight bars of raucous solo. The clarinet follows, wailing. The music is full of pain and longing—but pain controlled, ordered, mastered. Longing unfulfilled, but not overpowering.

As I write this, it plays on my stereo. If anyone has a right to bitterness at thwarted dreams, a black man in 1934 has that right. That such men can, in such conditions, make this music opens a world of possibilities.

Through the music speaks a truth about art that Wells does not understand, but that I hope to: that art doesn't have to deliver a message in order to say something important. That art isn't always a means to an end but sometimes an end in itself. That art may not be able to change the world, but it can still change the moment.

Through the music speaks a truth about life that Kessel, sixteen years before my birth, doesn't understand, but that I hope to: that life constrained is not life wasted. That despite unfulfilled dreams, peace is possible.

Listening, Wells feels that peace steal over his soul. Kessel feels it too.

And so they wait, poised, calm, before they move on into their respective futures, into our own present. Into the world of limitation and loss. Into Buffalo.

for my father

GETTING REAL

· · · · · · · · ·

Susan Shwartz

"For me, one world and one vision of that world have never been enough," Susan Shwartz explains in an autobiographical essay. "I've spent a lifetime looking over my shoulder, into a mirror, or glancing quickly down a side street for glimpses of the other worlds that I sense surround us all. . . . I look forward to spending the rest of my productive life linking unlikelinesses—Wall Street and academia, military science fiction and feminism, fantasy and *Realpolitik*, life as a New York City chauvinist and travel to as many places as funds, suitcases, and available transport will allow."

Born in Youngstown, Ohio, in 1949, Shwartz has a Ph.D. in medieval English from Harvard University and currently makes her living as a financial editor and assistant vice president for Prudential Securities in Manhattan. Since entering the SF field, she has edited five anthologies, among them *Arabesques: More Tales of the Arabian Nights* and *Moonsinger's Friends: An Anthology in Honor of Andre Norton*. Her novels include *Byzantium's Crown, The Woman of Flowers, Queensblade, Silk Roads and Shadows,* and *Mistress of the Grail.* "Loose Cannon," a novelette about a T. E. Lawrence who survives his 1935 motorcycle accident, was a Nebula finalist for 1990.

Of "Getting Real," Shwartz writes: "Up until the time I moved to New York in 1980, I always hated the order to 'get real.' Then I worked temp for a while and began to understand it.

" 'Write what you know about,' they tell you. I know about *The Velveteen Rabbit.* I know about working temp. I know how brokerage houses use their employees. And God knows, I know the E-train to the World Trade Center, where the subway violinist greets me with Vivaldi and the street people are all regulars."

Someone had scrawled the usual dirty joke on the Temp Fugit Employment Agency sign, I noticed as I dodged the dawn trucking shift down Fulton Street. And dirty puns are bad for business, so I smeared off the graffiti with the front page of the *New York Post.* The sign's edge slashed open the sketch a police artist had made of the Subway Slasher, who scared commuters to death—when he didn't stab them.

In the ladies', I reached for the pink tubes of Realité. Once I got my fresh ID assignment, I'd fine-tune, but I could apply the base

coats right now. I started spraying and painting and injecting Réalité—think of it as a sort of psychic steroid that lets temps register
on the eyes of Real employers and coworkers.

Up front, Temp Fugit looks a whole lot like any other midrange
temp agency: Cosmopolitan, Apple, Irene Cohen—anywhere they
sell word-processing staff. The lobby has machine-tooled chairs,
assembly-line artwork, and AMA publications and self-help mags up
our hypothetical wazoos.

If Reals do stumble into the office, they sit around tapping their
manicures till they get disgusted when no receptionists or counselors
may-I-help them. Then they stamp out. So they never see the dressing rooms where we become the people in our ID envelopes.

One of the other temps had a *New York Daily News* with a sketch
of the Subway Slasher and photos of his victims on it, but no one
really looked at that or one another. Temps aren't likely to be mugged.
And we really don't like one another much.

You thought it was just actors who temped, didn't you? Actors do
work temp between gigs, but there's all the difference in the world
between people who work temporary jobs and temporary people.

New York's cruddy with us. Employers use us for the scut work.
After all, do you think anyone cares what a goddamned temp feels?
You'd walk into us on the street if we didn't dodge you; you try to
take the seats we're already in; and you only really talk to us in the
instant you pick up more work and go, "Wouldja mind . . ." If you're
being very formal, you go, "Hey, wouldja mind."

Mostly, we temps forget our real names and families. Fair enough:
they forgot us long ago. Check it out, if you don't believe me. Get
any nice big family in the burbs to show you its scrapbook. Make
sure you pick a big one; there's never enough life in big families to
go around.

Just you look. There's always one kid, a little scrawny, a little pale,
a little shadowy even then, usually half cut off by bad camera angles
or glare. Once you know how to look, you can always tell who's
going to turn temp once it hits puberty. School makes it even easier.
Usually the temp doesn't have a photo in the yearbook. Even if it
does, there's no nice list of college-impressing clubs and activities
under the photo, either. College simply means anonymous B minus,
C plus in the big lecture courses where the teachers and T.A.s don't

look at anyone. Mostly, temps mark time, years of never understanding why they're not called on, why people damned near walk through them on the street, why what they say just doesn't seem to register.

Don't ask me what temps do who can't make it to New York. This city needs us. It's got all sorts of jobs that people only do if they've halfway fallen through the cracks already. Temps fit right in; and since no one notices us, we can live safe from the mob, muggers, crackheads, and homeboys gone wilding.

Sure, it's tough. But it's tough for the Reals, too. Much we care about them. All we care about is getting and keeping enough life to keep on dreaming, pretending that one day we'll figure it out and we'll be real, too.

Because New York's the most alive place there is, with its electrifying street dance of cars and horses and bikers dodging, and walkers doing that broken-field walk, rising on their toes to dodge someone, swearing ("Hey ouddatowna, moveit why doncha!"), or turning to "checkitout," whatever *it* is, never breaking stride.

Shoppers prowl like hunters in sneaks and walking shoes. The men stalk ahead, clearing unnecessary room for the women, who even dress like predators in black leather or long, long black fur. They walk heads up, their eyes glazed, and they don't see anything but the perfection of their grooming in the windows as they strut past.

Simple Reaganomics. This city's so damned alive that some of that life's got to trickle down even to us.

Mostly, we live on the street. It's kind of hard to bribe supers and realtors when they can't see the hand that holds the cash. You learn after one or two tries—out of sight, out of mind. The bastards pocket the bribes and rent the place to someone else.

I've moved up (or underground) in the world. Got a place in one of the caves off the E-train terminus at the World Trade Center. There's always a crowd there, and you can usually find papers and boxes and food in the garbage from the stores and restaurants. There've been lots of papers lately. Mostly about this slasher.

Sure, you have to share papers with the crazies, but there's so much stuff thrown out, there's enough to go around. I had to learn to share with the Reals who make their homes among the urine-smelling blue posts of the E-train terminus. At first I just used to take what I wanted, till Tink called me on it.

"You mustn't think we don't see you," she told me in that voice of hers. Once it was soft and careful; now it's cracked from screaming and her last run-in with pneumonia, or maybe it's TB. "You have to share," she told me, wagging an index finger, and I got to see the children's librarian under the rags, the caked makeup, and the sores.

Tink used to be a children's librarian till budget cuts closed her school and finished the job of driving her around the bend that kids, parents, and school boards started. For a while, she read her books aloud to herself in Bellevue, Thorazined to the max, but budget cuts—Reaganomics again, see?—made them stop warehousing crazies. They call it mainstreaming. What it means is that they turn crazies loose on the streets.

Mostly crazies and temps don't get along much. They're real—so what? We're sane, but who gives a shit? Crazies like Tink, that's who. It's short for Tinkerbell. Sometimes she hasn't got change for Thunderbird, but she always manages to curl her hair, and it's still a rusty blond. Usually, she wears a straw hat with flowers on it, and she carries her stuff in a neat wire cart. The transies and rentacops don't chase her off the benches, and all the winos know her.

Tink even has a cat, a black-and-white thing we call Rabbit on account of he's so skinny his ears look too big for his head. Tink runs this stop. Not even the kids who sleep in the trains bully her. Tink's the one who made the other crazies like Sailor fall in line. I pay back by bringing back things from places that crazies can't get into: food, sometimes; pills; books for Tink when I can.

I glanced around Temp Fugit. Anything there that Tink might like? I glanced at the self-help books on the table. Never mind them. Besides, Tink had a new book some kid must have dropped and boohooed about all last night. Something about a velveteen rabbit. She was muttering to herself as she read it, folding each page back real careful, and her smile really made her look like Tinkerbell. She looked up as I passed, and I'll swear that part of that smile was even for me.

"This is going to be a good day," I muttered at the roomful of temps, who sat flexing their fingers. Real computer operators and typists are klutzy; 65 wpm and they're good, they think. Most of us go over 100 without kicking into second gear.

My sense that today would be the day I'd get a really choice assignment grew. It wasn't just that Tink had smiled at me. Today, the Apostle to the E-train had been playing by the turnstiles; and it's always a good day when he's there.

Now, I know you've seen the Apostle. He's not temp or crazy; he's real, and he's a celebrity—he's even been on the *Tonight* show. Went to Juilliard; I've heard that he's played in Carnegie Hall. Sometimes, he finishes a concert and heads straight to the E-train, where he does an instant replay of his program. When the trains howl in, he stops and chats, and always wows the out-of-towners with flashy sweeps of his bow and tosses of his little Dutch-boy haircut. His cards say he's James Graseck, but Tink calls him the Apostle, and the name's stuck.

Anyhow, the Apostle was playing as I walked by, and I could almost swear he winked at me. I wanted to ask him, but a woman walked by in her little Reeboks and sox with the cuff stripe to match her coat and suit, and tipped him a buck. He bowed like an old-style cavalier and launched into Vivaldi's *Four Seasons*. A regular. I liked the look of her and followed her up Fulton on my way to Temp Fugit. Pretending I was her, had a job and an apartment and all.

Nice dreams, I thought as I waited for my turn at the tape machine. Temp Fugit keeps its tapes in the booths that other agencies use for typing tests. Like *Mission Impossible*. If caught, Temp Fugit will deny all knowledge of your existence.

Tape told me I'd hit the jackpot this time, all right. Long-term temp assignment at Seaport Securities, the big firm by the East River. Even now, after the Crash—which was a real-person event that really registered with the temps; brokerages cut way back on hiring when the market went China Syndrome—Wall Street is happy hunting ground for temps. The yups want their work done like *now*, and they treat clericals like Handi Wipes. Well, temps are used to that shit.

And there's always the chance that even a temp might get lucky and get a full-time job. Once you're in the pipeline, New York rules apply: climb, get your Series Seven, make enough money, and you get to be real.

Believe me, there's a lot of people in this city who'd be temps if they didn't have money.

My assignment ID told me I was Debbie Goldman. The capsule bio said she was staying with people while she looked for an apartment; she'd majored in Bus. Admin. Most secretarial and computer-ops types major in "something practical" while they keyboard through school and dream of being Melanie Griffith in *Working Girl*.

I looked at the picture again. By the time I applied Realité-based mascara, I'd polished a characterization of Ms. Goldman—me as I'd be when I headed to Seaport. Good skills —which I had; corporate dresser—thank you, Temp Fugit, for your nice wardrobe.

I walked down Fulton to the harbor, a real nice place with tall ships at anchor and the kind of expensive stores that temps shouldn't even dream of. After you've bounced from assignment to assignment for a few years, it gets so you can tell how a place is going to be the instant you walk into it. Seaport Securities has its own building, glossy red stone, aluminum, and lots of glass. Point one for Seaport.

The lobby rated another point. It had fresh flowers that looked like they're changed every week whether they need to be or not. And mega-corporate art: Frank Stella, I thought, expensive arcs and rainbows high overhead. The elevators were another plus: shiny paint, no graffiti or scratches, and fresh carpeting. I used the glossy walls to check my persona. The door purred open and I faced the final test: staff.

"M'elpyou," said the receptionist, her gold earrings jangling as she set down the phone. "I mean," she corrected herself, "may I help you?"

"I'm Debbie Goldman," I told her. "I was told to report to Lisa Black, she's your—" I didn't want to say office manager or head secretary; corporate women get really defensive of their titles.

"Administrative V.P.," the receptionist supplied. "She's real nice. But she's in a meeting. You just sit here and read the paper, and when she comes down I'll tell her you're here."

Under cover of the *Wall Street Journal*, I checked the place out. More corporate art. Flowers even up here, and I didn't think that this floor was where the real senior people were—too many cubicles and not enough offices with doors. I liked the way that people came off the elevators, walking in groups, men and women, veterans and kids together. That's a good sign, that people get along when they talk like that. I checked my clothes against what the other women were wearing. The others wore nice coats and sneakers, with their sox matching the coats, trimlike.

Someone came out to relieve the receptionist. "New girl here,

Debbie," said the receptionist who was going off shift. "She's here to see Lisa."

Not "Ms. Black." Friendly place.

"Where is she?"

"Breakfast with the research director. They must be crying about the way the analysts go through secretaries again."

The first receptionist snorted and eyed me for longevity value. So, this might be a test? Assign me to an analyst and see if I could take the pressure before trying me on a real job? Temps pray, and I prayed really hard right then.

The elevator purred open. "There's Lisa now. Lisa, Debbie Goldman's here to see you."

It was the woman from the subway, the one who'd tipped the Apostle and whose look I'd liked. She'd traded her Reeboks for pumps, and she looked even better than she had on the street. Nice suit, and a silk blouse with a soft bow rather than a shirt with a severe neckline. That's always good; the hard-tailored ones can be a real bitch to work for.

Laying the paper aside—neatly, Debbie, dammit!—I stood up politely and came forward, waiting for her handshake. Mine, thanks to the Realité, would be nice and warm, too.

"Am I glad to see you, Debbie," she said. "One of our gals just left, and there's an analyst who's got a report that has to get out. I'm always glad to deal with Temp Fugit; it always tests its people on Lotus and WordPerfect, which is just what we need."

"I'll do my best, Ms. Black," I said. Always a good thing to say, and it keeps you from asking the other questions, like, what're the people I'll be working with like, where's lunch, are the regular secretaries friendly, and please, will you keep me? I glanced around, a shall-I-get-started look that I've been told makes me seem eager to work hard.

"People call me Lisa," said Lisa. "We're all on first names here. Of course, if the president comes down from thirty-six, that's different." She laughed, and I laughed dutifully back to show I understood the decencies of chain of command. "Would you like to use the ladies' room before I take you in?"

She glanced over at the off-shift receptionist, who had lingered by the desk. "Daniella, want to do me a big favor?" she asked. "Debbie's going to be working with Rick Grimaldi."

Daniella grinned real fast, then wiped it before Lisa Black had to shake her head. After all, you don't tell outsiders who's a real bastard to work with. "Now, Rick's going to want to get to work right away. I'll bet that Debbie here hasn't had any coffee yet this morning, and if I know Rick she won't have any chance to get any, either."

Lisa fished in her handbag and came up with a pretty wallet. Mark Cross, no less. Hmm. Seaport paid well, then. She pulled out a dollar.

"How you take it?" Daniella asked me.

"Regular," I said.

When I came out of the ladies' (I'd done a good job on my makeup), Lisa Black led me over to a work station where a cup of coffee steamed.

"We call Rick 'the Prince,'" she told me, and waited for me to get the joke.

"Because he's named Grimaldi, like the Prince of Monaco? Any relation?" I wouldn't have been surprised if she'd said yes, but she laughed.

"No. Because he's very demanding. But you can handle that, can't you?"

Two women passing her grinned and shook their heads.

"I hope so," I said. At that point, he could have had horns, a tail, and a whip, and I'd have tried my damnedest.

Instead, he had a fast handshake, a this-is-the-best-you-could-do glare at Lisa, and what looked like half the papers and disks in the office. Which promptly got dumped perilously close to the coffee, and I rescued them. "Let's see you enter these numbers," he demanded, and stood over me while I worked. The woman at the next work station grimaced. If I were real, I suppose I'd have a right to have a fit. As it was, I was there to type, and I typed.

Thanks to Realité, my fingers didn't chill and cramp as he stared at them, tapping his foot and lamenting that nobody, nobody at all, cared whether his work got done and how sharper than a serpent's tooth it was to have a thankless secretary, typical boss ratshit; and I typed while my coffee got cold. Finally, he humphed and dumped more paper right on my keyboard. I managed not to sigh as I disentangled myself. This wad included a take-out menu.

"Want me to order in for you?" I asked. Now, look, I know real secretaries don't have to get coffee and sandwiches anymore. I know

that. I also know that execs—male and female M.B.A. created them—
are just dying for someone who isn't wise to the fact that times have
changed. It's not that they actually need the goddamned sandwiches
and coffee; they just like giving orders and being served. Besides,
sandwiches in the Seaport area are a good four dollars each, plus
coffee and cole slaw or whatever. He might say, "Order for yourself,
too."

He did. Bingo. Hey, if I worked late, maybe he'd tell me to order
dinner, too.

When I left for the day, half wobbling from exhaustion, I walked
by Lisa Black's desk, and she flashed thumbs up at me. She looked
relieved, and I wondered how many temps Prince Grimaldi had gone
through.

I had half a sandwich and a piece of carrot cake for Tink, who let
me feed Rabbit some scraps of smoked turkey. Rabbit purred and
licked my hand.

Grimaldi's quarterly report dragged on. Gradually, the secretaries
smiled and called me Debbie. After all, there's no use in wasting
friendliness on someone who might be fired an hour from now. But
for the long-term temp who looks like she's working out—her, you
say "good morning" to. Her, you smile at in the mirror in the ladies'
room. All those Kimberlys and Theresas and Carols and Heathers,
fussing with their moussed hair and their nails, chirping at one another; and they talked to me, too, including me in the babble of
What He Did, What I Said About It, and How I Fixed That Bitch.

It was hard to pretend I cared about Challenge, Career Opportunities, Learning Experiences, and all the other upwardly mobile
jargon that staff chants to reassure itself. It was hard to contribute
to the discussions of the best way to climb the ladder when all I
wanted to do was survive. And it was hard to believe that that was
all the Reals seemed to want to do, either. Funny, if I were real I
probably wouldn't do it any different.

Unlike me, the Reals were scared of the slasher. So I had to act
scared, too.

"Make the Prince send you home in a cab," Carol told me, the
day that the *Daily News* ran a think piece about the slasher. "You're
entitled if you work after seven P.M."

I decided I'd wait till Grimaldi offered. Days passed, and the slasher managed to sneak past the cops and chalk up more victims; still, Grimaldi never thought to ask if I wanted help getting home. Again, typical. Execs know the Rules, just as well as us temps, but they just love getting something for nothing—an extra hour or so of work or maybe just the petty thrill of watching someone get off the phone just because they walk up. Or not having to put car service on an expense account.

I knew I was fitting in after a couple of weeks when Heather asked me to contribute to Carvel cake and champagne for Kimberly. I know they just did it because they needed extra money, but all the same I was pleased.

The next day, the transit cops found another one in the Canal Street subway tunnel—dead, this time, and cut bad. Kimberly was there when they took it out. I found her in the ladies', gurgling and sobbing, holding a piece of paper towel to the careful lines she had painted under her eyes so they wouldn't smudge as she wept. She was surrounded by the usual throng, patting her shoulder and crooning as she shuddered.

I was washing my hands alone at the other sink when Lisa Black came in. "The analysts are complaining that no one's picking up the phones," she announced as she entered. Then, seeing Kimberly, "What's wrong?"

"I . . . I saw . . . My boyfriend wants me to quit and find a job in Brooklyn, and we need the money . . ." She burst into tears, ruining her eyeliner and her precautions, and the light winked off the tiny diamond on her shaking left hand.

"That tears it," Lisa declared. "I'm calling car service to take you all home tonight. Are any of you afraid to go by yourselves? I can poll the guys and see who's going where."

Headshakes and sheepish laughs. I dried my hands.

"This means you, too," she told me. "Where do you live, Debbie?"

"I'm staying with friends for now," I said. "I get on at World Trade; it's pretty safe there if I stay in the center of the platform."

Lisa nodded. "That's my stop, too. All the same, if it gets late you take a cab home, you hear?"

Sure, I'd take a cab home to the E-train. Sure. The one time I'd been put into a taxi, the man took off down the street, shaking his head as if he couldn't understand why his signal light was off. Three blocks later, he picked up a fare, and I slipped out. Never saw me.

I nodded obedience. "What're you going to do?" I asked.

"Me?" Lisa said. "I'm not worried. Stories say that the slasher picks on young girls. I'm too old."

She was about my age, maybe younger, I thought, if you allow for the fact that temps seem to age more slowly than Reals—the result, probably, of less connection to the world. But her comment brought protests from the women she supervised, even a reluctant gurgle of a laugh from Kimberly.

I ducked past as the women trooped out, heading for the phones and the analysts and the piled-up work. Lisa must have thought I'd left, too, or she wouldn't have done what she did then. Leaning forward, she stared at herself in the mirror, one hand stroking the soft skin beneath her eyes as if she were brushing dry ashes from her face with her ringless left hand. She stroked the corners of her eyes where a few wrinkles were starting. For all that, though, her face was surprisingly youthful.

"Old," she whispered, her voice hollow and almost breaking. "So old." With that, she fumbled in her bag, pulled out a pillbox, and grimaced as she swallowed something and washed it down with water from the tap.

She must not have seen me. I applied more Realité at lunch.

Prince Grimaldi let me out at five that day. I huddled near Tink on the bench right by the stairs and wiped the makeup from my face as she read her book at me: the story of a velveteen toy that a child loved and cherished, but that knew it was never real and would never be real, unless someone loved it enough to make it real.

No one would ever, no one had ever loved me that much, I thought, and felt a whimper in my throat. "Old, so old," I remembered Lisa saying. At least people could see her.

"What good is it?" I scoffed at Tink, who scowled at me, the upper layers of her makeup cracking as she scowled.

"What else is there?" she asked. This must have been one of her good days, when her thoughts were clear and she could talk without spitting and swearing. "You want to live, you have to be real. But real's more 'n sitting clean and pretty. You want to be real, someone has to give you life. Someone has to care. And then you have to believe you're real, real enough to care about."

When I tried to ask questions, Tink picked up the book again, humming. Shortly afterward she nodded off. When I covered her with warm, dry papers, Rabbit leapt up and didn't even hiss at me for once. Must have been all the leftovers I'd been feeding him.

"Stop chirping," one of the temps snapped in the dressing room at Temp Fugit the next day. "Can't you just put on your Réalité and leave me alone? You talk talk talk. Like you think you're real. Like you're really fooling yourself."

That was a longer speech than I'd gotten out of anyone in all the years I'd worked out of Temp Fugit, and the anger in it startled me. Of course, I talked in the ladies'. You always had to talk in the ladies' at Seaport. That was where you heard the news, where you got the company Rules explained.

I finished up my sprays and paints real fast and left, to a mutter of "Thinks she's people, just because she's got a long-term job."

Later that morning, Grimaldi called me in and told me he had a full-time secretary starting Monday. "I wish I'd seen you when I was interviewing," he said.

So this was good-bye. Well, I couldn't say it was nice knowing him, but there were people here I'd miss.

"You've worked well for me," he told me. (News to me.) "And that's rare these days. So I've recommended you to Whittington. His secretary's going on maternity leave and might not come back. By that time, if you work out, who knows? Let me have your résumé, will you?"

I printed him a copy, gave it to him, and he grunted approval at the math minor. Sure, I was good at math. You don't need to be real to do equations. "I've spoken to Lisa Black," he told me before he headed off to a company meeting. "She'll get your paperwork from personnel. Go talk to her when you finish pasting up the tables, will you?"

I nodded, thanked him, and headed out.

"You want to remember that lots of your junior analysts start as secretaries," he told me. "Think about it."

I never had an order I liked better. Even Lisa looked pleased. Politics said it was because her decision had paid off, and now Grimaldi owed her, but I thought part of her satisfaction was for me. If I played my cards right . . . I could see myself angling for sponsorship to take the Series Seven for broker right now.

And was that the best thing I could think of to do with being real? Would I walk through people, not seeing them, real or temp, except as things to do what I needed them to? Would I run scared? Was it better to be someone like Grimaldi, who used people, or Tink, who'd been used up?

"I saw you in World Trade Center," Lisa Black told me. "You were talking to one of the street people, the woman who wears those hats, you know who I mean?"

"Tink?" The name slipped out before I could stop myself.

"That's her name?"

"What they call her."

"James"—she meant the Apostle—"warned me that some of these people can turn on you. You want to watch them," Lisa warned me. "Is this some sort of volunteer work for your church or something? Wouldn't Meals on Wheels be a safer bet?"

I hated to lie to her, so I muttered something.

Lisa reached for her purse and hauled out a twenty. "I noticed that her legs are pretty badly ulcerated. This would buy some Mercurochrome and bandages, maybe some vitamins. Do you accept donations from outsiders?"

I started to shake my head no, but she insisted, and I took the money.

After Tink finished bandaging her legs, she presided over a feast of junk food. I'd told her she needed gloves, but potato chips and rotgut it was.

I left halfway through and went to sleep. A cold nose woke me hours later. It was Rabbit. I didn't know we were on that good of terms.

"What is it, cat?" I asked.

Rabbit meowed, almost a howl.

So I got up and had a look. God, I wished I hadn't. Now I was glad that Tink had had her party. It was the last one she'd ever have. Sometime during the night the Subway Slasher had got her. Blood from the grin under her chin had drenched her tatty parka and splashed down onto the bandages, which were still clean where the blood hadn't soaked them. She'd been too drunk to run or scream. Please God, she'd been too drunk to know what hit her.

I screamed, but nothing answered: no voices, no footsteps, no whistle. I'd have been glad of anyone, but Sailor was God knows where, and even the men who sleep on cardboard by the token booths seemed to have vanished. So I sat there for what had to be hours, Rabbit with me. After a while I put my arms about my shoulders, remembering dimly that when I was a child, before I'd temped out, hugs had helped. Rabbit crawled up next to me and scrambled onto my lap. To my surprise, he licked my face; to my greater surprise, I had been crying.

"Sweet Jesus," came a new voice. Rabbit yowled and beat it. I looked up, and it was James the Apostle, just standing there, clutching his violin case and music stand. No point taking Tink's pulse, he saw that straight off. Instead, he covered her face with Bach and ran to call 911.

When he came back, he circled Tink gingerly. His foot hit something, and he rescued it from a puddle I didn't want to look at. Tink's last book, *The Velveteen Rabbit*. Shaking his head, the Apostle tucked it into his music.

"They'll be here soon," he remarked. He was an artist, and with his mission to the subways, he had to be slightly mad himself. I thought he really could see me. "Did Tink tell you about the book, about being real? I read it to my son. This is what I think. It takes life to be real. And if there's been a death, stands to reason that there's space for another real live person. Tink had a lot of heart. And I think she cared about you. Why not take the chance? Be real."

He gestured, and I suddenly knew that all I had to do was uncover her face, touch it, and believe, just like Tink and the Apostle said, and I'd be real. "Lord, I believe," they say in church. "Help Thou mine unbelief."

To be real. To care. To be cared about. To hurt the way I'd hurt when I saw that slash in Tink's wrinkled throat. To see Sailor lurking in the shadows, still afraid to come out, though Tink had been his buddy, tears pouring from ganja-reddened eyes, but afraid to come near the cops. Did he run? Was that why he looks so sad?

Courage, like danger and grief, was not a temp's concern; we were safe from that kind of pain. Why let myself in for it if I didn't have to? I was being smart, practical, I told myself.

What a damned liar.

I didn't have the guts. Or anything else.

The Apostle watched the space where I was—all right, let's say he watched me—until he realized I wasn't going to try. "Too frightened?" he asked. "What a shame."

The cops arrived in a blare of whistles and a clatter of heavy, important shoes and walkie-talkies. Two of them almost ran right through where I stood. I headed back to my little cache of treasures—clothes of my own, Reeboks just like Lisa's, nail polish the color of Kimberly's—I'd collected since starting at Seaport. My eyes burned as if Realité had spilled into them or I'd poked myself with a mascara wand, and my shoulders shook.

At Temp Fugit, it took twice the usual dose of Realité to get me looking human. I had a sink to myself, and none of the temps spoke to me. They flicked glances at me, but I found it easy to read the expressions in their eyes. Go away.

By the time I got to Seaport, I had the shakes, good and proper. But I managed to hide them until I made the morning trip to the ladies'. Lisa was there, listening as two of the girls whispered about the slasher's latest.

"The violinist found her," Heather said. "You know him."

"I saw James," Lisa said. "He's really upset. I told him to go home, but he just stood there crying and playing something Hebrew and wailing that made the violin cry, too. Then some more cops came to talk with him."

She must have seen my face because she gestured them to shut up, a down slash of her hand, real haughty and not at all like her. "You're white as a sheet," she told me. "Debbie, what's . . . Oh, Debbie," she breathed as it sank in. (Smart woman, our Lisa.) "Did you know the woman they're talking about? Was that—"

"Tink," I said, and my voice husked. From someplace in my eyes I didn't know I had, tears burst out, smearing my eyeliner and smudging the Realité I'd applied that morning. I put my hands over my face and just sobbed. For the first time in my life, I was the center of a comforting circle. Hands patted my shoulders (the comfort I'd sought in wrapping arms about myself), and voices crooned sorrow as Lisa explained that I'd done volunteer work in the World Trade Center and I knew the woman who'd been killed.

"Just last night," I said, "I bought her bandages and Mercuro-

chrome, and then gave her the rest of your money. She used it . . ."
I gasped because it hurt to get the words out. "She said she'd use it
to buy booze and potato chips for the other people there. One last
party . . ."

I swear, I wasn't the only one crying by then.

Tears rolled down Lisa's face, but she ignored them. "I'm glad
she did that. I'm glad she had that. Maybe this won't be wasted.
Maybe she'll give the police some more clues. But you, Debbie,
what do we do with you? If you go home, will there be anyone there
to take care of you?"

Home was the E-train. Home used to be Tink. It was better to
be here. I shook my head. A wet towel patted my face. It would
wash away the Realité, and no one would see me. I jerked away.

"Easy there. It's just water. Debbie, you're dead white. Do you
feel dizzy? I'm taking you to the nurse. The rest of you, scoot. Back
to work."

As she led me to the elevator, I got a glimpse of myself in the
big mirrors. Tears and that towel had washed off all the Realité. Yet
Lisa and the other women could see me. The nurse who let me lie
down on a real mattress could see me, too.

To my shock, when Lisa led me to a cab and shut the door on
me with "You go to bed early and call me if you need anything,"
the driver glanced into the backseat. "Where to, miss?"

Miss. Not "hey wouldja." But I wasn't real. I'd denied the gift. I
tucked the scrap of paper with Lisa's phone number on it away. I'd
keep it, but I'd never use it.

"World Trade," I said.

The cab drove me straight there. When I paid, the driver even
thanked me for his tip.

Rush hour was over by the time I reached the E-train. Casual,
too-clean loungers hung out by Papillon Boutique and the news-
stand at the entrance; others held newspaper props: no chance I'd
get my hands on those papers, was there? They knit their brows as
I passed, as if something troubled them. Not me, surely.

I could hear the Apostle playing in a far corner of the station.
Funny, I'd have thought he'd clear out. I gave him a wide berth and
wished I didn't have to be here, either.

The bench where I'd found Tink bore a WET PAINT sign, and the cement floor had been scrubbed even of the chalk marks cops draw around a body. Someone had already left a crumpled pizza box on the bench. I whistled under my breath, then called softly, "Here, Rabbit. Nice kitty."

Sailor emerged, not a black-and-white cat. For a miracle, his gray eyes were clear of grass fumes, though they were still reddened.

"You, girl. You come 'ere. I wants to talk to you," he said.

Passersby swerved to avoid the street person in dirty clothes and dreadlocks, his feet bare, talking to himself in the subway. If they'd seen me, they'd done more than swerve. They'd have run so they wouldn't get involved.

"You get yo'self out of heah," he told me.

"Tink said I could stay," I protested. I felt my eyes get hot again and saw tears well up in Sailor's.

"Tink . . . ain't heah no more! I says you cain't stay. This ain' no place for you now, Tink bein' gone and all dat. You different, girl. You be live now, you be young lady. You go with yo' kind now, not talk to old Sailor 'cept'n he ax you fo' any change."

"But I don't have any place—"

"You get!"

"But I'm tired."

"Hokay, then," Sailor grudged me, a vast concession. "But to-morra, fo' sure!"

It had been stupid even to try to argue with Sailor. After all these years of smoking and rotten living, he didn't have enough logic left to appeal to. I'd have to move. Maybe Temp Fugit would let me store my things in the wardrobe? The way temps there had been glaring at me, I didn't like that idea at all, but it was the best I could come up with right now.

I headed toward the tunnels where I'd stashed my stuff. A rustling ahead of me . . . My head came up. "Rabbit? C'mere, kitty."

I hadn't brought Rabbit anything. Poor cat must be starving, unless someone had dropped a Big Mac.

"Rabbit," I coaxed. More rustling, as if he'd burrowed into the papers of my bed. "Rabbit, it's okay. I'll get you something. You just wait, kitty."

I half turned to go back into the light.

Hands grabbed me, slammed across my chest, across my chin and mouth. My eyes bulged as light from the never-to-be-reached corridor glanced off a thin knife, held right at throat level. I planted my feet and tried to scream, but the knife pressed in, and I felt warmth trickle down my collar. Damn, that thing would have to be cleaned.

Words in three languages, one of them sewer, hissed and gurgled in my ears. What he was going to do to me. Slut. *Puta.* Piece of meat. Like the old witch. Thought I was so great.

I was a goddamned temp! Why'd the slasher pick on me?

From far off, I could hear the Apostle's violin. And voices. If I could get free, just a little, I could scream. Why would anyone hear a temp?

Same reason that the slasher had picked one as a victim. He was a crazy; he could see temps. Maybe he hadn't seen a temp, though. Maybe he'd seen a damned fool suicidal out-of-town woman, checking out the tunnels. Someone as real as she was real stupid.

All it took, Tink and the Apostle had said, was belief. Belief and life. And mine was in danger now.

Mine. My life. But I was a temp. I didn't have a life, I reminded myself.

Then why'd my body tense? Why'd I worry that people in the office would hate it if I got killed? Why'd I draw the deepest breath I'd ever drawn in my miserable excuse for a life—and why'd my voice die in my throat?

I tried to tear free of the grip that was dragging me back into the darkness of the tunnels, darkness he knew better than the cops, even.

His arm tightened around me, fingers groping, and I tried to break away. The cut on my neck deepened, and I flinched. My mouth bumped against the slasher's hand—more suggestions there—and I bit as hard as I could. God, I hoped he didn't have AIDS, but I had to do something.

"Stop it," he hissed, but the knife fell for a moment.

I stomped where I hoped his instep might be, just as the girls in the ladies' said you should. He howled, and his grip dropped for just a minute. I was out of that tunnel so fast . . . But he ran after me, grabbed my arm, and whirled me around.

After seeing him, I don't know why anyone would want to see

horror films, either. He had eyes and breath like a werewolf or something.

His hand was bleeding. I had marked him. I could register on someone.

He was stronger than I, he could drag me back into the tunnel, and once I was back there . . . I hadn't hurt him bad enough. You either fight to kill or not at all, they say in the ladies'; because if you fight just hard enough to make them mad, you won't come out of it.

Now I heard voices coming after me, and I screamed again, trying to jerk free. A yowling hiss came from the tunnel, and Rabbit launched himself at the slasher's face, claws out and switchblading. He yelled like someone splashed a vampire with holy water and slammed the cat off him and into the concrete wall.

"Rabbit!" The cat's pain freed my voice. Real weird thing to yell, isn't it, Debbie, when you're fighting for your life. Even then, I realized I'd called myself my ID name. Guess I'd be stuck with it if I lived.

"Stop that! Cops! Help!" A voice I remembered panted as the Apostle ran toward me. The slasher had me off balance; in a minute, he'd slam my head against a wall. If I was real lucky, I'd never feel what would happen next.

"Fire!" some woman shrieked. People always do something about fire.

The Apostle put on a burst of speed. His right hand grasped his violin by the delicate neck, like a baseball bat he was going to slam down on the slasher's head.

Not the violin. Not the music. Tink had loved the music. Lisa loved it. And so, I realized, did I. As much as anything else, it had called me to life.

I summoned all my strength and threw my weight against the slasher. My legs tangled up, and I went down.

But so did he. As he stumbled, my adrenaline spiked up, and I heaved him off me, almost into the air. He saw where he was falling, and he had time to scream once before he hit the third, the electrified rail, and bounced, stiffening, fingers spasming, as a smell of singed hair, burning, dirty clothes, and something like rotted food made me gag.

If there's been a death, stands to reason there's space for another real live person.

I didn't want life if it meant dealing with the Subway Slasher.

Oh, no? Then why'd you fight, dummy? You had to fight. He was so horrible, he made you see that even your life was worth something.

The temps don't want you around anymore, and neither does Sailor. Lisa saw you. The girls saw you. The nurse saw you. Even the taxi driver and James . . . and the slasher.

You damned well bet you're alive, girl. I felt the life in the air, rising from the tracks, the concrete, the people around me—even from myself. And I grabbed it and made it mine. Made it me.

It burned like hell, and I thought I'd never felt or tasted anything so fine.

James the violinist hugged me. "Did he hurt you?" he asked. Man was better at playing than talking, that was for sure. From the corner of my eye, I saw Rabbit sit, lick a paw, then limp away.

"I couldn't let you break your violin," I whimpered. "Not for me."

"You're people," said the Apostle. "What else could I have done?" Then I cried like a baby when the doctor spanks it. Cried all the way to the precinct, where a female cop took charge of me, stayed in the room while a doctor patched up my neck. Then she called Lisa to come and get me.

Here's the miracle. She did.

Somehow—Sailor, maybe? he'd had brains once, before he scrambled them—my stuff turned up at Seaport. So did I, and they had cake and champagne and a senior vice president to shake my hand and say that Seaport was proud of me. So I never went back to Temp Fugit, after all. Lisa said that personnel would handle the agency fee, now that I was going full-time. I spent part of my first morning back at Seaport checking the bulletin board for roommates.

Lucky for me that Heather's roommate moved in with her boyfriend about then. Heather's another one like Lisa and James the violinist. Not just real, but real people. And she likes cats.

So I'm down here in the E-train again with this stupid basket and some roast beef from the corner deli. I saw James and tried to give him a dollar, but he waved it away with a sweep of his bow. "First time's on the house," he said. Someone else framed the front page of an old *Post*. "Hero Subway Violinist Foils Slasher." He pretends to wince when he sees it, but he props it against his music stand.

A cat with a bad paw, a cat that knows my voice—how hard can it be to catch?

An old man in dreadlocks, his eyes red, points. "You lookin' for a little cat, miss?"

My God, it's Sailor, and I never noticed. But he winks at me, holds out his hand for a buck (I give him ten), and I know he understands.

Here, Rabbit. Nice Rabbit. Look what I've got for you. Come on out, Rabbit.

Woman in a suit, calling to a cat on the subway platform—I must look as crazy as Sailor.

Rabbit. Come on, cat.

There you are, kitty. Into the basket.

Rabbit's going to have a real home now. Just like me.

THE BUTTON, AND WHAT YOU KNOW

· · · · · · · · ·

W. Gregory Stewart

W. Gregory Stewart's work has been published in *Amazing Stories*, *Z Miscellaneous*, and, as he puts it, "various alphabetical entries in between." His last appearance in this series occurred with his Rhysling Award–winning poem, "Daedalus," reprinted in *Nebula Awards 23*. He is a computer programmer for the phone company, lives in Los Angeles with his wife and new son, and collects armadillos.

"Actually the title came to me first," Stewart replied when asked to account for his nominated story. " 'The button and what you know.' Don't know how, don't know why. But there it was. Right after that I got a mental image of a button, floating—disembodied, and disenfixtured. So I sat down at the word processor and went with that. From there on, it was just having fun with how and why and whatnot—and inventories. Then freezing up and not being able to get back to it for weeks. Finally, though, I did get back to it. . . .

"When I had finished it, I sent it off to Patrick Price at *Amazing Stories*. I knew a decision had been made not to carry poetry when the magazine went into its new format, but I nevertheless wanted to solicit Patrick's opinion—he had always been encouraging and kind. I had had fun writing the piece, and I hoped that, at the least, he might have fun reading it. Kim Mohan had by that time taken over *Amazing* and intercepted 'the button,' and evidently liked it. He decided to take a chance on this thing that was neither fish nor fowl, poetry nor prose. . . ."

I   this is the button and
      what you know about it:

     1. that it is a button—
        you know this.

     2. that it has suddenly
        appeared before you.

     3. that the button is
        attached to a plate;
        that the plate is attached to nothing else—
        that it floats.

4. that this floating is taking place 2 feet or
   half a meter in front of your immediate face.

5. wait—there is more.
   the button and the plate are gray,
   but not the same gray, each.
   these are strange grays, matte and yet translucent,
   and fading, dark to light and back again.
   first the button is darker, and then
   the plate is darker, and although
   the color changes are gradual and shifting,
   the button and the plate are somehow *never*
   the same gray at the same time.

   it may be that this is important.

   but it probably isn't.

6. beneath the plate, and likewise floating,
   and having appeared just as suddenly,
   and appearing just as oddly two-toned,
   is a plaque bearing the words
   ALL OR NOTHING.

7. oh, yes, a cylinder—there is a cylinder
   floating vertically beside
   the button and its plate
   and the plaque beneath. it is light gray
   at its bottom-most, and darker above;
   you will notice over the next hour
   that the light gray grows in extent—tomorrow
   at this time you will notice
   that the light gray takes up 1/7
   of the total length of the cylinder,
   and this will tell you something.
   or should, at any rate.

8. here is something else
    that may—or may not—be important:
    the button has appeared to you
    on a crowded city street, and although
    you are not alone, no one else
    seems to notice the sudden appearance
    of disenfixtured plates and buttons
    and plaques and cylinders. or else
    they do, but do not find it strange—
    you yourself choose not to ask
    anyone if they see these things,
    even though you *do* find them strange.

9. and this, too—the gray configuration
    remains before you no matter what direction
    you go. this makes it all seem personal, somehow.
    you do not dwell on this right now, but
    within two hours you will find it fairly annoying.

10. one more thing—the cylinder floats to the left
    of plaque and plate.

    it may be that *this* is important.

    but it probably isn't.

II this is a part of what you do *not* know
    that might help:

1. a similar assemblage has appeared
    to each of 26 other individuals.
    no two of these
    live on the same world,
    and of course no two worlds
    are within the same galaxy.

2. note the use of the word 'similar'
   in section II.1 above—in some cases,
   what has appeared
   is indeed a button, while
   in certain others,
   it is a toggle switch,
   or a rocker switch,
   or a touch pad. in two instances
   it appears as things that I cannot describe.
   I take on faith
   that the function remains the same,
   but I cannot guarantee this—
   it *looks* like it, though.

3. although different languages—and
   representations—are involved
   the message stays the same: ALL OR NOTHING.

   sometimes the concept is a single word.

   sometimes it is not written
   as you understand writing,
   but is nonetheless transliterated
   or recorded—audially, telepathically,
   or psychotactilely. in any case—
   ALL OR NOTHING.

4. none of you 27 is a leader of any kind.

5. no one of you is a scientist or theologian.

6. you are all unexceptional, and you have all
   just recently lost your jobs. (coincidentally?)

7. here are the races of the rest of you.
   a. saurian.
   b. cetacean.

c. canine, but unfortunately
   too similar to the Chihuahua
   to ever be made welcome at a Ho-Jo's.
d. bat. pink. and it swims.
e. rodent. hamsteroid, actually—its kind might
   eat a disobedient child simply to make a point
   to its surviving siblings.
f. molluscan (octopuscan).
g. lemur.
h. elephant.
i. cetacean—this one is smaller, similar
   to a narwhale, but the tusk
   spirals in the *other* direction.
j. arachnid.
k. arachnid.
l. arachnoid. (note: there are too many
   spiders in the universe. I say this
   entirely without prejudice.)
m. Daffy Duck. (you never even suspected,
   did you?)

next are those one step removed
from your own biologic.

n. an intelligent hollyhock whose greatest fear is
   premature pollination by a rogue bee.
o. a rogue bee.
p. manticore.
q. a streetcar actually named Desire.
r. a collective intelligence,
   the individual components of which
   look remarkably like spiders.
   (sigh . . .)
s. a bad attitude looking for
   a place to land—but it may be that you
   are more familiar with this than I suppose.
t. star maggot.
u. tuna surprise.

v. robo-droid, programmed to sell
life insurance.

with the last you will have no common ground
or basis at all for understanding:

w. a silicate lump with career goals.
x. a rock, aging.
y. a pool of industrial waste that has outlived
its creators.
z. something else.

8. each cylinder is calibrated
to the local time appropriate
to the place/space/displacement
in which it has materialized
yet all are so synchronized
that, when one finally becomes
uniformly gray, all 27 will have become
uniformly gray . . .

9. . . . which might suggest that time is running out.

10. the last thing that has anything to do with this
that you do not know
is what to do.

III apparently you must make a decision:

1. whether to push the button
2. or not. to push. the button.

IV you decide that you really need
to think about what you know, and you are right.
here are what you think about.

1. ALL OR NOTHING. is that NOTHING
   if you push the button—
   or NOTHING if you don't?

2. does NOTHING mean that nothing will happen—
   whatever you do—
   or that the universe as you know it
   will cease to exist? or something in between?
   or . . . (just give it a rest, will you?
   it's in there somewhere.)

3. ALL presents similar problems; but at least
   you think you have a pretty good handle on OR.

4. is all of this really happening, and if so,
   does it really *mean* anything—
   anything at all—
   let alone justify the cosmic paranoia
   that you are now just beginning to entertain?

5. oh yeah—and why *you*, assuming sanity?

6. but even assuming anything else
   (and on the other hand), why not?

7. and, hey—who the hell is responsible for this,
   anyway? and are they sure
   they really want you? (and isn't *that* just
   'why you' again?)

8. well. maybe a decision isn't really required—
   perhaps you can just sidestep the issue.
   (and don't you believe it, Roscoe.)

9. what's the point?

10. what's for dinner?

V after nearly a week of this, you finally decide
that you *will* push the button, and you suppose
that you must push it at the end of the week,
at precisely the same instant that the cylinder
goes uniformly gray. (yes—absolutely correct!
a good call on your part, by the way.)

you have decided to do this thing
because either you have gone entirely Bozoid and
it will therefore make no difference whatsoever
to universal cause and effect,
or you are entirely sane, and it might.

further,
you have decided that only a benevolent entity
would have set up the game this way—
evil as you know it would have forced the issue
at the first appearance, rather than giving you
a week to decide. well, you think—benevolent,
or *incredibly* indifferent; nearly the same thing.
as it happens, you are spang-on
about the benevolent bit (but entirely wrong
to generalize about evil
as you have, given your limited experience; still,
no matter—the lucky guess is still correct).

but you are not home free, not yet and not
by a long shot—because here's another thing
you don't know:

each of the 27 of you will have to push its button
at the same time as the others.
or else NOTHING, you see—
ALL OR NOTHING. (yes, I grant that a comma
after ALL would not have been amiss . . . but, then,
I didn't make the rules. did I?)

ok, ok—I'll tell you what the NOTHING part is.
the big NOTHING. the end. over, out, squat, kaput,

that's a wrap. time, space and all points between,
done. that's all. auf flipping wiedersehen.

at any rate,
it is a good thing, that you decided as you have.

(now, at this point,
you may be wondering about the nature
of benevolence, given what I said before about evil.
let us address this:
benevolence within this context is giving you
the choice of allowing the universe to continue,
or of packing it in.
you see, at this end of things,
quite a number of potential neo-universes
and eager little possible creations
are shoving and crowding and elbowing their way
to the front of the line, blinking
in and out of existence and waiting for the next
Big Bang—but nobody else gets a turn until
whoever is IT is done. you see?
you don't? no, of course you don't—well,
it doesn't matter, anyway.)

VI each of you has come to this same decision
(although of course you do not know this, because
you are unaware of each other's existence)—

each of you, that is, except
for one of the damned spiders (see—I *told* you!),
who is still waffling through it all . . .

VII . . . while time is running out.

VIII all right, all right, all right—
to make an interminable story less so,
the spider—at the last possible instant—
decides to hit its touch pad (and so
throw in with the rest of you, although

it doesn't know this), and the known
and unknown universes are saved.
at least for now.

IX you know none of this, however. having pushed
your button, you only know that nothing
on your little planet and nothing
in your sorry little life
has changed. and you are right. (and that
was the point of the exercise.) here are some things
that have not happened:

1. planets falling into their suns—
   any more often than usual.

2. Planck time.

3. the sudden appearance of a transgalactic
   black hole looking for a party.

4. the immediate and universal total decrease
   of entropy.

5. or the opposite.

6. new age accordion recitals.

7. or anything much else out of the ordinary
   for a vast and unencompassed creation.

X but as I say—you know nothing of this. go home.
go to sleep. the button is gone.
you might find work tomorrow. or you might not.

BEGGARS IN SPAIN

. . . .

Nancy Kress

I am periodically haunted by the scene from Kurt Vonnegut's *God Bless You, Mr. Rosewater* in which the title character crashes the Milford Science Fiction Writers Workshop, cheerfully informing the assembled authors that, while they "couldn't write for sour apples," it doesn't matter. "To hell with the talented sparrowfarts who write delicately of one small piece of one mere lifetime," says Eliot Rosewater, "when the issues are galaxies, eons, and trillions of souls yet to be born." This is, of course, Vonnegut himself speaking, expressing his appreciation for SF's epic agenda even as he vents his frustration at the field's lamentable tendency to mistrust talent and rationalize bad writing (or, worse, not even notice it).

The scene makes me flail about for counterexamples, and invariably I come up with the name Nancy Kress, an SF author who *can* write for sour apples (and sweet apples and golden apples and Nebulas and other prizes) and who, as you're about to see, intuitively senses that writing powerfully about "the issues" *means* having talent, it *means* caring about style.

Kress's fifth novel, *Brain Rose,* a stunning mélange of reincarnation, memory theory, and the Gaia hypothesis, was one of the most critically acclaimed SF works of 1990. Her most recent book, *Beggars in Spain,* is based on the Nebula-winning—and Hugo-winning—novella you are about to read. Her short fiction appears regularly in, as she puts it, "all the usual places," and Arkham House has just published her first collection. Kress won the 1985 short-story Nebula for "Out of All Them Bright Stars." She lives in Brockport, New York, with her husband (SF writer Marcos Donnelly) and two sons.

" 'Beggars in Spain' represents thirteen years of on-again, off-again effort," Kress comments. "I first tried in 1977 to write about people who didn't sleep. During the next three years the result was rejected by a whole host of eminent editors: Robert Silverberg, who took the time to write a thoughtful critique to a neophyte; Ed Ferman; George Scithers; and Ben Bova twice, at two different magazines. (I save and date rejection slips. Sicilian melancholy flourishes so much better on concrete objects.) Five years later I tried again. This time the story was so bad I didn't even send it out. But the idea wouldn't leave me. Finally, in 1990, I left my corporate job to become a full-time writer, and 'Beggars in Spain' was the first story I wrote. It took one week for research and two for writing.

"Why did this particular idea grip me so firmly, for so long? I think

244 · NEBULA AWARDS 27

it's because I'm one of those people who need nine hours of sleep a night. I bitterly envy all you short sleepers out there, blithely filling your extra hours with scintillating conversation, deeply meaningful work, and meditation that opens the soul. Or maybe not. At any rate, out of envy came a desire to get this story written. Eventually."

"With energy and sleepless vigilance go forward and give us victories."

—Abraham Lincoln, to Major General Joseph Hooker, 1863

I

They sat stiffly on his antique Eames chairs, two people who didn't want to be here, or one person who didn't want to and one who resented the other's reluctance. Dr. Ong had seen this before. Within two minutes he was sure: the woman was the silently furious resister. She would lose. The man would pay for it later, in little ways, for a long time.

"I presume you've performed the necessary credit checks already," Roger Camden said pleasantly. "So let's get right on to details, shall we, doctor?"

"Certainly," Ong said. "Why don't we start by your telling me all the genetic modifications you're interested in for the baby."

The woman shifted suddenly on her chair. She was in her late twenties—clearly a second wife—but already had a faded look, as if keeping up with Roger Camden was wearing her out. Ong could easily believe that. Mrs. Camden's hair was brown, her eyes were brown, her skin had a brown tinge that might have been pretty if her cheeks had had any color. She wore a brown coat, neither fashionable nor cheap, and shoes that looked vaguely orthopedic. Ong glanced at his records for her name: Elizabeth. He would bet people forgot it often.

Next to her, Roger Camden radiated nervous vitality, a man in late middle age whose bullet-shaped head did not match his careful haircut and Italian-silk business suit. Ong did not need to consult his file to recall anything about Camden. A caricature of the bullet-shaped head had been the leading graphic of yesterday's on-line edition of the *Wall Street Journal*: Camden had led a major coup in cross-border data-atoll investment. Ong was not sure what cross-border data-atoll investment was.

"A girl," Elizabeth Camden said. Ong hadn't expected her to speak first. Her voice was another surprise: upper-class British. "Blond. Green eyes. Tall. Slender."

Ong smiled. "Appearance factors are the easiest to achieve, as I'm sure you already know. But all we can do about 'slenderness' is give her a genetic disposition in that direction. How you feed the child will naturally—"

"Yes, yes," Roger Camden said, "that's obvious. Now: intelligence. *High* intelligence. And a sense of daring."

"I'm sorry, Mr. Camden—personality factors are not yet understood well enough to allow genet—"

"Just testing," Camden said, with a smile that Ong thought was probably supposed to be lighthearted.

Elizabeth Camden said, "Musical ability."

"Again, Mrs. Camden, a disposition to be musical is all we can guarantee."

"Good enough," Camden said. "The full array of corrections for any potential gene-linked health problem, of course."

"Of course," Dr. Ong said. Neither client spoke. So far theirs was a fairly modest list, given Camden's money; most clients had to be argued out of contradictory genetic tendencies, alteration overload, or unrealistic expectations. Ong waited. Tension prickled in the room like heat.

"And," Camden said, "no need to sleep."

Elizabeth Camden jerked her head sideways to look out the window.

Ong picked a paper magnet off his desk. He made his voice pleasant. "May I ask how you learned whether that genetic-modification program exists?"

Camden grinned. "You're not denying it exists. I give you full credit for that, doctor."

Ong held onto his temper. "May I ask how you learned whether the program exists?"

Camden reached into an inner pocket of his suit. The silk crinkled and pulled; body and suit came from different social classes. Camden was, Ong remembered, a Yagaiist, a personal friend of Kenzo Yagai himself. Camden handed Ong hard copy: program specifications.

"Don't bother hunting down the security leak in your data banks, doctor—you won't find it. But if it's any consolation, neither will anybody else. Now." He leaned suddenly forward. His tone changed. "I know that you've created twenty children so far who don't need to sleep at all. That so far nineteen are healthy, intelligent, and psychologically normal. In fact, better than normal—they're all unusually precocious. The oldest is already four years old and can read in two languages. I know you're thinking of offering this genetic modification on the open market in a few years. All I want is a chance to buy it for my daughter *now*. At whatever price you name."

Ong stood. "I can't possibly discuss this with you unilaterally, Mr. Camden. Neither the theft of our data—"

"Which wasn't a theft—your system developed a spontaneous bubble regurgitation into a public gate, have a hell of a time proving otherwise—"

"—*nor* the offer to purchase this particular genetic modification lies in my sole area of authority. Both have to be discussed with the Institute's board of directors."

"By all means, by all means. When can I talk to them, too?"

"You?"

Camden, still seated, looked at him. It occurred to Ong that there were few men who could look so confident eighteen inches below eye level. "Certainly. I'd like the chance to present my offer to whoever has the actual authority to accept it. That's only good business."

"This isn't solely a business transaction, Mr. Camden."

"It isn't solely pure scientific research, either," Camden retorted. "You're a for-profit corporation here. *With* certain tax breaks available only to firms meeting certain fair-practice laws."

For a minute Ong couldn't think what Camden meant. "Fair-practice laws . . ."

". . . are designed to protect minorities who are suppliers. I know, it hasn't ever been tested in the case of customers, except for redlining in Y-energy installations. But it could be tested, Dr. Ong. Minorities are entitled to the same product offerings as nonminorities. I know the Institute would not welcome a court case, doctor. None of your twenty genetic beta-test families is either black or Jewish."

"A court . . . but you're not black *or* Jewish!"

"I'm a different minority. Polish-American. The name was Kaminsky." Camden finally stood. And smiled warmly. "Look, it is preposterous. You know that, and I know that, and we both know what a grand time journalists would have with it anyway. And you know that I don't want to sue you with a preposterous case, just to use the threat of premature and adverse publicity to get what I want. I don't want to make threats at all, believe me I don't. I just want this marvelous advancement you've come up with for my daughter." His face changed, to an expression Ong wouldn't have believed possible on those particular features: wistfulness. "Doctor—do you know how much more I could have accomplished if I hadn't had to *sleep* all my life?"

Elizabeth Camden said harshly, "You hardly sleep now."

Camden looked down at her as if he had forgotten she was there. "Well, no, my dear, not now. But when I was young . . . college, I might have been able to finish college and still support . . . well. None of that matters now. What matters, doctor, is that you and I and your board come to an agreement."

"Mr. Camden, please leave my office now."

"You mean before you lose your temper at my presumptuousness? You wouldn't be the first. I'll expect to have a meeting set up by the end of next week, whenever and wherever you say, of course. Just let my personal secretary, Diane Clavers, know the details. Any time that's best for you."

Ong did not accompany them to the door. Pressure throbbed behind his temples. In the doorway Elizabeth Camden turned. "What happened to the twentieth one?"

"What?"

"The twentieth baby. My husband said nineteen of them are healthy and normal. What happened to the twentieth?"

The pressure grew stronger, hotter. Ong knew that he should not answer; that Camden probably already knew the answer even if his wife didn't; that he, Ong, was going to answer anyway; that he would regret the lack of self-control, bitterly, later.

"The twentieth baby is dead. His parents turned out to be unstable. They separated during the pregnancy, and his mother could not bear the twenty-four-hour crying of a baby who never sleeps."

Elizabeth Camden's eyes widened. "She killed it?"

"By mistake," Camden said shortly. "Shook the little thing too hard." He frowned at Ong. "Nurses, doctor. In shifts. You should have picked only parents wealthy enough to afford nurses in shifts."

"That's horrible!" Mrs. Camden burst out, and Ong could not tell if she meant the child's death, the lack of nurses, or the Institute's carelessness. Ong closed his eyes.

When they had gone, he took ten milligrams of cyclobenzaprine-III. For his back—it was solely for his back. The old injury hurting again. Afterward he stood for a long time at the window, still holding the paper magnet, feeling the pressure recede from his temples, feeling himself calm down. Below him Lake Michigan lapped peacefully at the shore; the police had driven away the homeless in another raid just last night, and they hadn't yet had time to return. Only their debris remained, thrown into the bushes of the lakeshore park: tattered blankets, newspapers, plastic bags like pathetic trampled standards. It was illegal to sleep in the park, illegal to enter it without a resident's permit, illegal to be homeless and without a residence. As Ong watched, uniformed park attendants began methodically spearing newspapers and shoving them into clean self-propelled receptacles.

Ong picked up the phone to call the president of Biotech Institute's board of directors.

Four men and three women sat around the polished mahogany table of the conference room. *Doctor, lawyer, Indian chief*, thought Susan Melling, looking from Ong to Sullivan to Camden. She smiled. Ong caught the smile and looked frosty. Pompous ass. Judy Sullivan, the Institute lawyer, turned to speak in a low voice to Camden's lawyer, a thin, nervous man with the look of being owned. The owner, Roger Camden, the Indian chief himself, was the happiest-looking person in the room. The lethal little man—what did it take to become that rich, starting from nothing? She, Susan, would certainly never know—radiated excitement. He beamed, he glowed, so unlike the usual parents-to-be that Susan was intrigued. Usually the prospective daddies and mommies—especially the daddies—sat there looking as if they were at a corporate merger. Camden looked as if he were at a birthday party.

Which, of course, he was. Susan grinned at him and was pleased when he grinned back. Wolfish, but with a sort of delight that could only be called innocent—what would he be like in bed? Ong frowned majestically and rose to speak.

"Ladies and gentlemen, I think we're ready to start. Perhaps introductions are in order. Mr. Roger Camden, Mrs. Camden are of course our clients. Mr. John Jaworski, Mr. Camden's lawyer. Mr. Camden, this is Judith Sullivan, the Institute's head of legal; Samuel Krenshaw, representing Institute director Dr. Brad Marsteiner, who unfortunately couldn't be here today; and Dr. Susan Melling, who developed the genetic modification affecting sleep. A few legal points of interest to both parties—"

"Forget the contracts for a minute," Camden interrupted. "Let's talk about the sleep thing. I'd like to ask a few questions."

Susan said, "What would you like to know?" Camden's eyes were very blue in his blunt-featured face; he wasn't what she had expected. Mrs. Camden, who apparently lacked both a first name and a lawyer, since Jaworski had been introduced as her husband's but not hers, looked either sullen or scared, it was difficult to tell which.

Ong said sourly, "Then perhaps we should start with a short presentation by Dr. Melling."

Susan would have preferred a Q&A, to see what Camden would ask. But she had annoyed Ong enough for one session. Obediently she rose.

"Let me start with a brief description of sleep. Researchers have known for a long time that there are actually three kinds of sleep. One is 'slow-wave sleep,' characterized on an EEG by delta waves. One is 'rapid-eye-movement sleep' or REM sleep, which is much lighter sleep and contains most dreaming. Together, these two make up 'core sleep.' The third type of sleep is 'optional sleep,' so-called because people seem to get along without it with no ill effects, and some short sleepers don't do it at all, sleeping naturally only three or four hours a night."

"That's me," Camden said. "I trained myself into it. Couldn't everybody do that?"

Apparently they were going to have a Q&A after all. "No. The actual sleep mechanism has some flexibility, but not the same amount for every person. The raphe nuclei on the brain stem—"

Ong said, "I don't think we need that level of detail, Susan. Let's stick to basics."

Camden said, "The raphe nuclei regulate the balance among neurotransmitters and peptides that lead to a pressure to sleep, don't they?"

Susan couldn't help it; she grinned. Camden, the laser-sharp ruthless financier, sat trying to look solemn, a third-grader waiting to have his homework praised. Ong looked sour. Mrs. Camden looked away, out the window.

"Yes, that's correct, Mr. Camden. You've done your research."

Camden said, "This is my *daughter*," and Susan caught her breath. When was the last time she had heard that note of reverence in anyone's voice? But no one in the room seemed to notice.

"Well, then," Susan said, "you already know that the reason people sleep is because a pressure to sleep builds up in the brain. Over the last twenty years, research has determined that's the *only* reason. Neither slow-wave sleep nor REM sleep serves functions that can't be carried on while the body and brain are awake. A lot goes on during sleep, but it can go on awake just as well, if other hormonal adjustments are made.

"Sleep once served an important evolutionary function. Once Clem Pre-mammal was done filling his stomach and squirting his sperm around, sleep kept him immobile and away from predators. Sleep was an aid to survival. But now it's a leftover mechanism, like the appendix. It switches on every night, but the need is gone. So we turn off the switch at its source, in the genes."

Ong winced. He hated it when she oversimplified like that. Or maybe it was the lightheartedness he hated. If Marsteiner were making this presentation, there'd be no Clem Pre-mammal.

Camden said, "What about the need to dream?"

"Not necessary. A leftover bombardment of the cortex to keep it on semialert in case a predator attacked during sleep. Wakefulness does that better."

"Why not have wakefulness instead, then? From the start of the evolution?"

He was testing her. Susan gave him a full, lavish smile, enjoying his brass. "I told you. Safety from predators. But when a modern predator attacks—say, a cross-border data-atoll investor—it's safer to be awake."

Camden shot at her, "What about the high percentage of REM sleep in fetuses and babies?"

"Still an evolutionary hangover. Cerebrum develops perfectly well without it."

"What about neural repair during slow-wave sleep?"

"That does go on. But it can go on during wakefulness, if the DNA is programmed to do so. No loss of neural efficiency, as far as we know."

"What about the release of human growth enzyme in such large concentrations during slow-wave sleep?"

Susan looked at him admiringly. "Goes on without the sleep. Genetic adjustments tie it to other changes in the pineal gland."

"What about the—"

"The *side effects?*" Mrs. Camden said. Her mouth turned down. "What about the bloody side effects?"

Susan turned to Elizabeth Camden. She had forgotten she was there. The younger woman stared at Susan, mouth turned down at the corners.

"I'm glad you asked that, Mrs. Camden. Because there *are* side effects." Susan paused; she was enjoying herself. "Compared to their age mates, the nonsleep children—who have *not* had IQ genetic manipulation—are more intelligent, better at problem solving, and more joyous."

Camden took out a cigarette. The archaic, filthy habit surprised Susan. Then she saw that it was deliberate: Roger Camden drawing attention to an ostentatious display to draw attention away from what he was feeling. His cigarette lighter was gold, monogrammed, innocently gaudy.

"Let me explain," Susan said. "REM sleep bombards the cerebral cortex with random neural firings from the brainstem; dreaming occurs because the poor besieged cortex tries so hard to make sense of the activated images and memories. It spends a lot of energy doing that. Without that energy expenditure, nonsleep cerebrums save the wear and tear and do better at coordinating real-life input. Thus—greater intelligence and problem solving.

"Also, doctors have known for sixty years that antidepressants, which lift the mood of depressed patients, also suppress REM sleep entirely. What they have proved in the last ten years is that the reverse is equally true: suppress REM sleep and people don't *get*

depressed. The nonsleep kids are cheerful, outgoing . . . *joyous.*
There's no other word for it."

"At what cost?" Mrs. Camden said. She held her neck rigid, but
the corners of her jaw worked.

"No cost. No negative side effects at all."

"So far," Mrs. Camden shot back.

Susan shrugged. "So far."

"They're only four years old! At the most!"

Ong and Krenshaw were studying her closely. Susan saw the moment the Camden woman realized it; she sank back into her chair,
drawing her fur coat around her, her face blank.

Camden did not look at his wife. He blew a cloud of cigarette
smoke. "Everything has costs, Dr. Melling."

She liked the way he said her name. "Ordinarily, yes. Especially
in genetic modification. But we honestly have not been able to find
any here, despite looking." She smiled directly into Camden's eyes.
"Is it too much to believe that just once the universe has given us
something wholly good, wholly a step forward, wholly beneficial?
Without hidden penalties?"

"Not the universe. The intelligence of people like you," Camden
said, surprising Susan more than anything that had gone before. His
eyes held hers. She felt her chest tighten.

"I think," Dr. Ong said dryly, "that the philosophy of the universe
may be beyond our concerns here. Mr. Camden, if you have no
further medical questions, perhaps we can return to the legal points
Ms. Sullivan and Mr. Jaworski have raised. Thank you, Dr. Melling."

Susan nodded. She didn't look again at Camden. But she knew
what he said, how he looked, that he was there.

The house was about what she had expected, a huge mock Tudor
on Lake Michigan north of Chicago. The land heavily wooded between the gate and the house, open between the house and the
surging water. Patches of snow dotted the dormant grass. Biotech
had been working with the Camdens for four months, but this was
the first time Susan had driven to their home.

As she walked toward the house, another car drove up behind
her. No, a truck, continuing around the curved driveway to a service
entry at the side of the house. One man rang the service bell; a

second began to unload a plastic-wrapped playpen from the back of the truck. White, with pink and yellow bunnies. Susan briefly closed her eyes.

Camden opened the door himself. She could see the effort not to look worried. "You didn't have to drive out, Susan—I'd have come into the city."

"No, I didn't want you to do that, Roger. Mrs. Camden is here?"

"In the living room." Camden led her into a large room with a stone fireplace. English country-house furniture; prints of dogs or boats, all hung eighteen inches too high: Elizabeth Camden must have done the decorating. She did not rise from her wing chair as Susan entered.

"Let me be concise and fast," Susan said. "I don't want to make this any more drawn out for you than I have to. We have all the amniocentesis, ultrasound, and Langston test results. The fetus is fine, developing normally for two weeks, no problems with the implant on the uterus wall. But a complication has developed."

"What?" Camden said. He took out a cigarette, looked at his wife, put it back unlit.

Susan said quietly, "Mrs. Camden, by sheer chance both your ovaries released eggs last month. We removed one for the gene surgery. By more sheer chance the second fertilized and implanted. You're carrying two fetuses."

Elizabeth Camden grew still. "Twins?"

"No," Susan said. Then she realized what she had said. "I mean, yes. They're twins, but nonidentical. Only one has been genetically altered. The other will be no more similar to her than any two siblings. It's a so-called 'normal' baby. And I know you didn't want a so-called normal baby."

Camden said, "No. I didn't."

Elizabeth Camden said, "I did."

Camden shot her a fierce look that Susan couldn't read. He took out the cigarette again, lit it. His face was in profile to Susan, thinking intently; she doubted he knew the cigarette was there or that he was lighting it. "Is the baby being affected by the other one's being there?"

"No," Susan said. "No, of course not. They're just . . . coexisting."

"Can you abort it?"

"Not without risk of aborting both of them. Removing the unaltered fetus might cause changes in the uterus lining that could lead to a spontaneous miscarriage of the other." She drew a deep breath. "There's that option, of course. We can start the whole process over again. But, as I told you at the time, you were very lucky to have the in vitro fertilization take on only the second try. Some couples take eight or ten tries. If we started all over, the process could be a lengthy one."

Camden said, "Is the presence of this second fetus harming my daughter? Taking away nutrients or anything? Or will it change anything for her later on in the pregnancy?"

"No. Except that there is a chance of premature birth. Two fetuses take up a lot more room in the womb, and if it gets too crowded birth can be premature. But the—"

"How premature? Enough to threaten survival?"

"Most probably not."

Camden went on smoking. A man appeared at the door. "Sir, London calling. James Kendall for Mr. Yagai."

"I'll take it." Camden rose. Susan watched him study his wife's face. When he spoke, it was to her. "All right, Elizabeth. All right." He left the room.

For a long moment the two women sat in silence. Susan was aware of disappointment; this was not the Camden she had expected to see. She became aware of Elizabeth Camden watching her with amusement.

"Oh, yes, doctor. He's like that."

Susan said nothing.

"Completely overbearing. But not this time." She laughed softly, with excitement. "Two. Do you . . . do you know what sex the other one is?"

"Both fetuses are female."

"I wanted a girl, you know. And now I'll have one."

"Then you'll go ahead with the pregnancy."

"Oh, yes. Thank you for coming, doctor."

She was dismissed. No one saw her out. But as she was getting into her car, Camden rushed out of the house, coatless. "Susan! I wanted to thank you. For coming all the way out here to tell us yourself."

"You already thanked me."

"Yes. Well. You're sure the second fetus is no threat to my daughter?"

Susan said deliberately, "Nor is the genetically altered fetus a threat to the naturally conceived one."

He smiled. His voice was low and wistful. "And you think that should matter to me just as much. But it doesn't. And why should I fake what I feel? Especially to you?"

Susan opened her car door. She wasn't ready for this, or she had changed her mind, or something. But then Camden leaned over to close the door, and his manner held no trace of flirtatiousness, no smarmy ingratiation. "I better order a second playpen."

"Yes."

"And a second car seat."

"Yes."

"But not a second night-shift nurse."

"That's up to you."

"And you." Abruptly he leaned over and kissed her, a kiss so polite and respectful that Susan was shocked. Neither lust nor conquest would have shocked her; this did. Camden didn't give her a chance to react; he closed the car door and turned back toward the house. Susan drove toward the gate, her hands shaky on the wheel until amusement replaced shock: it *had* been a deliberately distant, respectful kiss, an engineered enigma. And nothing else could have guaranteed so well that there would have to be another.

She wondered what the Camdens would name their daughters.

Dr. Ong strode the hospital corridor, which had been dimmed to half-light. From the nurse's station in Maternity a nurse stepped forward as if to stop him—it was the middle of the night, long past visiting hours—got a good look at his face, and faded back into her station. Around a corner was the viewing glass to the nursery. To Ong's annoyance, Susan Melling stood pressed against the glass. To his further annoyance, she was crying.

Ong realized that he had never liked the woman. Maybe not any women. Even those with superior minds could not seem to refrain from being made damn fools by their emotions.

"Look," Susan said, laughing a little, swiping at her face. "Doctor—*look*."

Behind the glass Roger Camden, gowned and masked, was

holding up a baby in white undershirt and pink blanket. Camden's blue eyes—theatrically blue, a man really should not have such garish eyes—glowed. The baby had a head covered with blond fuzz, wide eyes, pink skin. Camden's eyes above the mask said that no other child had ever had these attributes.

Ong said, "An uncomplicated birth?"

"Yes," Susan Melling sobbed. "Perfectly straightforward. Elizabeth is fine. She's asleep. Isn't she beautiful? He has the most adventurous spirit I've ever known." She wiped her nose on her sleeve; Ong realized that she was drunk. "Did I ever tell you that I was engaged once? Fifteen years ago, in med school? I broke it off because he grew to seem so ordinary, so boring. Oh, God, I shouldn't be telling you all this I'm sorry I'm sorry."

Ong moved away from her. Behind the glass Roger Camden laid the baby in a small wheeled crib. The nameplate said BABY GIRL CAMDEN #1. 5.9 POUNDS. A night nurse watched indulgently.

Ong did not wait to see Camden emerge from the nursery or to hear Susan Melling say to him whatever she was going to say. Ong went to have the OB paged. Melling's report was not, under the circumstances, to be trusted. A perfect, unprecedented chance to record every detail of gene alteration with a nonaltered control, and Melling was more interested in her own sloppy emotions. Ong would obviously have to do the report himself, after talking to the OB. He was hungry for every detail. And not just about the pink-cheeked baby in Camden's arms. He wanted to know everything about the birth of the child in the other glass-sided crib: BABY GIRL CAMDEN #2. 5.1 POUNDS. The dark-haired baby with the mottled red features, lying scrunched down in her pink blanket, asleep.

II

Leisha's earliest memory was of flowing lines that were not there. She knew they were not there because when she reached out her fist to touch them, her fist was empty. Later she realized that the flowing lines were light: sunshine slanting in bars between curtains in her room, between the wooden blinds in the dining room, between the crisscross lattices in the conservatory. The day she realized the golden flow was light she laughed out loud with the sheer joy of discovery, and Daddy turned from putting flowers in pots and smiled at her.

The whole house was full of light. Light bounded off the lake, streamed across the high white ceilings, puddled on the shining wooden floors. She and Alice moved continually through light, and sometimes Leisha would stop and tip back her head and let it flow over her face. She could feel it, like water.

The best light, of course, was in the conservatory. That's where Daddy liked to be when he was home from making money. Daddy potted plants and watered trees, humming, and Leisha and Alice ran between the wooden tables of flowers with their wonderful earthy smells, running from the dark side of the conservatory where the big purple flowers grew to the sunshine side with sprays of yellow flowers, running back and forth, in and out of the light. "Growth," Daddy said to her. "Flowers all fulfilling their promise. Alice, be careful! You almost knocked over that orchid." Alice, obedient, would stop running for a while. Daddy never told Leisha to stop running.

After a while the light would go away. Alice and Leisha would have their baths, and then Alice would get quiet, or cranky. She wouldn't play nice with Leisha, even when Leisha let her choose the game or even have all the best dolls. Then Nanny would take Alice to "bed," and Leisha would talk with Daddy some more until Daddy said he had to work in his study with the papers that made money. Leisha always felt a moment of regret that he had to go do that, but the moment never lasted very long, because Mamselle would arrive and start Leisha's lessons, which she liked. Learning things was so interesting! She could already sing twenty songs and write all the letters in the alphabet and count to fifty. And by the time lessons were done, the light had come back, and it was time for breakfast.

Breakfast was the only time Leisha didn't like. Daddy had gone to the office, and Leisha and Alice had breakfast with Mommy in the big dining room. Mommy sat in a red robe, which Leisha liked, and she didn't smell funny or talk funny the way she would later in the day, but, still, breakfast wasn't fun. Mommy always started with the Question.

"Alice, sweetheart, how did you sleep?"

"Fine, Mommy."

"Did you have any nice dreams?"

For a long time Alice said no. Then one day she said, "I dreamed about a horse. I was riding him." Mommy clapped her hands and kissed Alice and gave her an extra sticky bun. After that Alice always had a dream to tell Mommy.

Once Leisha said, "I had a dream, too. I dreamed light was coming in the window and it wrapped all around me like a blanket and then it kissed me on my eyes."

Mommy put down her coffee cup so hard that coffee sloshed out of it. "Don't lie to me, Leisha. You did not have a dream."

"Yes, I did," Leisha said.

"Only children who sleep can have dreams. Don't lie to me. You did not have a dream."

"Yes, I did! I did!" Leisha shouted. She could see it, almost: the light streaming in the window and wrapping around her like a golden blanket.

"I will not tolerate a child who is a liar. Do you hear me, Leisha— I won't tolerate it!"

"You're a liar!" Leisha shouted, knowing the words weren't true, hating herself because they weren't true but hating Mommy more, and that was wrong, too, and there sat Alice stiff and frozen with her eyes wide. Alice was scared and it was Leisha's fault.

Mommy called sharply, "Nanny! Nanny! Take Leisha to her room at once. She can't sit with civilized people if she can't refrain from telling lies."

Leisha started to cry. Nanny carried her out of the room. Leisha hadn't even had her breakfast. But she didn't care about that; all she could see while she cried was Alice's eyes, scared like that, reflecting broken bits of light.

But Leisha didn't cry long. Nanny read her a story and then played Data Jump with her, and then Alice came up and Nanny drove them both into Chicago to the zoo, where there were wonderful animals to see, animals Leisha could not have dreamed—nor Alice *either*. And by the time they came back Mommy had gone to her room, and Leisha knew that she would stay there with the glasses of funny-smelling stuff the rest of the day, and Leisha would not have to see her.

But that night she went to her mother's room.

"I have to go to the bathroom," she told Mamselle. Mamselle

said, "Do you need any help?" maybe because Alice still needed help in the bathroom. But Leisha didn't, and she thanked Mamselle. Then she sat on the toilet for a minute even though nothing came, so that what she had told Mamselle wouldn't be a lie.

Leisha tiptoed down the hall. She went first into Alice's room. A little light in a wall socket burned near the "crib." There was no crib in Leisha's room. Leisha looked at her sister through the bars. Alice lay on her side with her eyes closed. The lids of the eyes fluttered quickly, like curtains blowing in the wind. Alice's chin and neck looked loose.

Leisha closed the door very carefully and went to her parents' room.

They didn't "sleep" in a crib but in a huge enormous "bed," with enough room between them for more people. Mommy's eyelids weren't fluttering; she lay on her back making a hrrr-hrrr sound through her nose. The funny smell was strong on her. Leisha backed away and tiptoed over to Daddy. He looked like Alice, except that his neck and chin looked even looser, folds of skin collapsed like the tent that had fallen down in the backyard. It scared Leisha to see him like that. Then Daddy's eyes flew open so suddenly that Leisha screamed.

Daddy rolled out of bed and picked her up, looking quickly at Mommy. But she didn't move. Daddy was wearing only his underpants. He carried Leisha out into the hall, where Mamselle came rushing up saying, "Oh, sir. I'm sorry, she just said she was going to the bathroom—"

"It's all right," Daddy said. "I'll take her with me."

"No!" Leisha screamed, because Daddy was only in his underpants and his neck had looked all funny and the room smelled bad because of Mommy. But Daddy carried her into the conservatory, set her down on a bench, wrapped himself in a piece of green plastic that was supposed to cover up plants, and sat down next to her.

"Now, what happened, Leisha? What were you doing?"

Leisha didn't answer.

"You were looking at people sleeping, weren't you?" Daddy said, and because his voice was softer Leisha mumbled, "Yes." She immediately felt better; it felt good not to lie.

"You were looking at people sleeping because you don't sleep and you were curious, weren't you? Like Curious George in your book?"

"Yes," Leisha said. "I thought you said you made money in your study all night!"

Daddy smiled. "Not all night. Some of it. But then I sleep, although not very much." He took Leisha on his lap. "I don't need much sleep, so I get a lot more done at night than most people. Different people need different amounts of sleep. And a few, a very few, are like you. You don't need any."

"Why not?"

"Because you're special. Better than other people. Before you were born, I had some doctors help make you that way."

"Why?"

"So you could do anything you want to and make manifest your own individuality."

Leisha twisted in his arms to stare at him; the words meant nothing. Daddy reached over and touched a single flower growing on a tall potted tree. The flower had thick white petals like the cream he put in coffee, and the center was a light pink.

"See, Leisha—this tree made this flower. Because it *can*. Only this tree can make this kind of wonderful flower. That plant hanging up there can't, and those can't either. Only this tree. Therefore the most important thing in the world for this tree to do is grow this flower. The flower is the tree's individuality—that means just *it*, and nothing else—made manifest. Nothing else matters."

"I don't understand, Daddy."

"You will. Someday."

"But I want to understand *now*," Leisha said, and Daddy laughed with pure delight and hugged her. The hug felt good, but Leisha still wanted to understand.

"When you make money, is that your indiv . . . that thing?"

"Yes," Daddy said happily.

"Then nobody else can make money? Like only that tree can make that flower?"

"Nobody else can make it just the ways I do."

"What do you do with the money?"

"I buy things for you. This house, your dresses, Mamselle to teach you, the car to ride in."

"What does the tree do with the flower?"

"Glories in it," Daddy said, which made no sense. "Excellence is what counts, Leisha. Excellence supported by individual effort. And that's *all* that counts."

"I'm cold, Daddy."

"Then I better bring you back to Mamselle."

Leisha didn't move. She touched the flower with one finger. "I want to sleep, Daddy."

"No, you don't, sweetheart. Sleep is just lost time, wasted life. It's a little death."

"Alice sleeps."

"Alice isn't like you."

"Alice isn't special?"

"No. You are."

"Why didn't you make Alice special, too?"

"Alice made herself. I didn't have a chance to make her special."

The whole thing was too hard. Leisha stopped stroking the flower and slipped off Daddy's lap. He smiled at her. "My little questioner. When you grow up, you'll find your own excellence, and it will be a new order, a specialness the world hasn't ever seen before. You might even be like Kenzo Yagai. He made the Yagai generator that powers the world."

"Daddy, you look funny wrapped in the flower plastic." Leisha laughed. Daddy did, too. But then she said, "When I grow up, I'll make my specialness find a way to make Alice special, too," and Daddy stopped laughing.

He took her back to Mamselle, who taught her to write her name, which was so exciting she forgot about the puzzling talk with Daddy. There were six letters, all different, and together they were *her name*. Leisha wrote it over and over, laughing, and Mamselle laughed, too. But later, in the morning, Leisha thought again about the talk with Daddy. She thought of it often, turning the unfamiliar words over and over in her mind like small hard stones, but the part she thought about most wasn't a word. It was the frown on Daddy's face when she told him she would use her specialness to make Alice special, too.

Every week Dr. Melling came to see Leisha and Alice, sometimes alone, sometimes with other people. Leisha and Alice both liked Dr. Melling, who laughed a lot and whose eyes were bright and warm.

Often Daddy was there, too. Dr. Melling played games with them, first with Alice and Leisha separately and then together. She took their pictures and weighed them. She made them lie down on a table and stuck little metal things to their temples, which sounded scary but wasn't because there were so many machines to watch, all making interesting noises, while you were lying there. Dr. Melling was as good at answering questions as Daddy. Once Leisha said, "Is Dr. Melling a special person? Like Kenzo Yagai?" And Daddy laughed and glanced at Dr. Melling and said, "Oh, yes, indeed."

When Leisha was five, she and Alice started school. Daddy's driver took them every day into Chicago. They were in different rooms, which disappointed Leisha. The kids in Leisha's room were all older. But from the first day she adored school, with its fascinating science equipment and electronic drawers full of math puzzlers and other children to find countries on the map with. In half a year she had been moved to yet a different room, where the kids were still older, but they were nonetheless nice to her. Leisha started to learn Japanese. She loved drawing the beautiful characters on thick white paper. "The Sauley School was a good choice," Daddy said.

But Alice didn't like the Sauley School. She wanted to go to school on the same yellow bus as cook's daughter. She cried and threw her paints on the floor at the Sauley School. Then Mommy came out of her room—Leisha hadn't seen her for a few weeks, although she knew Alice had—and threw some candlesticks from the mantelpiece on the floor. The candlesticks, which were china, broke. Leisha ran to pick up the pieces while Mommy and Daddy screamed at each other in the hall by the big staircase.

"She's my daughter, too. And I say she can go!"

"You don't have the right to say anything about it! A weepy drunk, the most rotten role model possible for both of them . . . and I thought I was getting a fine English aristocrat."

"You got what you paid for. Nothing! Not that you ever needed anything from me or anybody else."

"Stop it!" Leisha cried. "Stop it!" and there was silence in the hall. Leisha cut her fingers on the china; blood streamed onto the rug. Daddy rushed in and picked her up. "Stop it," Leisha sobbed, and didn't understand when Daddy said quietly, "*You* stop it, Leisha. Nothing *they* do should touch you at all. You have to be at least that strong."

Leisha buried her head in Daddy's shoulder. Alice transferred to Carl Sandburg Elementary School, riding there on the yellow school bus with cook's daughter.

A few weeks later Daddy told them that Mommy was going away for a few weeks to a hospital, to stop drinking so much. When Mommy came out, he said, she was going to live somewhere else for a while. She and Daddy were not happy. Leisha and Alice would stay with Daddy, and they would visit Mommy sometimes. He told them this very carefully, finding the right words for truth. Truth was very important, Leisha already knew. Truth was being true to your self, your specialness. Your individuality. An individual respected facts, and so always told the truth.

Mommy, Daddy did not say but Leisha knew, did not respect facts.

"I don't want Mommy to go away," Alice said. She started to cry. Leisha thought Daddy would pick Alice up, but he didn't. He just stood there looking at them both.

Leisha put her arms around Alice. "It's all right, Alice. It's all right! We'll make it all right! I'll play with you all the time we're not in school so you don't miss Mommy."

Alice clung to Leisha. Leisha turned her head so she didn't have to see Daddy's face.

III

Kenzo Yagai was coming to the United States to lecture. The title of his talk, which he would give in New York, Los Angeles, Chicago, and Washington, with a repeat in Washington as a special address to Congress, was "The Further Political Implications of Inexpensive Power." Leisha Camden, eleven years old, was going to have a private introduction after the Chicago talk, arranged by her father.

She had studied the theory of cold fusion at school, and her Global Studies teacher had traced the changes in the world resulting from Yagai's patented, low-cost applications of what had, until him, been unworkable theory. The rising prosperity of the Third World, the last death throes of the old communist systems, the decline of the oil states, the renewed economic power of the United States. Her study group had written a news script, filmed with the school's professional-quality equipment, about how a 1985 American family lived with expensive energy costs and a belief in tax-supported help, while a 2019 family lived with cheap energy and a belief in the contract as the basis of civilization. Parts of her own research puzzled Leisha.

"Japan thinks Kenzo Yagai was a traitor to his own country," she said to Daddy at supper.

"No," Camden said. "*Some* Japanese think that. Watch out for generalizations, Leisha. Yagai patented and marketed Y-energy first in the United States because here there were at least the dying embers of individual enterprise. Because of his invention, our entire country has slowly swung back toward an individual meritocracy, and Japan has slowly been forced to follow."

"Your father held that belief all along," Susan said. "Eat your peas, Leisha." Leisha ate her peas. Susan and Daddy had only been married less than a year; it still felt a little strange to have her there. But nice. Daddy said Susan was a valuable addition to their household: intelligent, motivated, and cheerful. Like Leisha herself.

"Remember, Leisha," Camden said. "A man's worth to society and to himself doesn't rest on what he thinks other people should do or be or feel, but on himself. On what he can actually do, and do well. People trade what they do well, and everyone benefits. The basic tool of civilization is the contract. Contracts are voluntary and mutually beneficial. As opposed to coercion, which is wrong."

"The strong have no right to take anything from the weak by force," Susan said. "Alice, eat your peas, too, honey."

"Nor the weak to take anything by force from the strong," Camden said. "That's the basis of what you'll hear Kenzo Yagai discuss tonight, Leisha."

Alice said, "I don't like peas."

Camden said, "Your body does. They're good for you."

Alice smiled. Leisha felt her heart lift; Alice didn't smile much at dinner anymore. "My body doesn't have a contract with the peas."

Camden said, a little impatiently, "Yes, it does. Your body benefits from them. Now eat."

Alice's smile vanished. Leisha looked down at her plate. Suddenly she saw a way out. "No, Daddy, look—Alice's body benefits, but the peas don't. It's not a mutually beneficial consideration—so there's no contract. Alice is right!"

Camden let out a shout of laughter. To Susan he said, "Eleven years old . . . *eleven*." Even Alice smiled, and Leisha waved her spoon triumphantly, light glinting off the bowl and dancing silver on the opposite wall.

But, even so, Alice did not want to go hear Kenzo Yagai. She was going to sleep over at her friend Julie's house; they were going to curl their hair together. More surprisingly, Susan wasn't coming, either. She and Daddy looked at each other a little funny at the front door, Leisha thought, but Leisha was too excited to think about this. She was going to hear *Kenzo Yagai*.

Yagai was a small man, dark and slim. Leisha liked his accent. She liked, too, something about him that took her awhile to name. "Daddy," she whispered in the half-darkness of the auditorium, "he's a joyful man."

Daddy hugged her in the darkness.

Yagai spoke about spirituality and economics. "A man's spirituality—which is only his dignity as a man—rests on his own efforts. Dignity and worth are not automatically conferred by aristocratic birth—we have only to look at history to see that. Dignity and worth are not automatically conferred by inherited wealth—a great heir may be a thief, a wastrel, cruel, an exploiter, a person who leaves the world much poorer than he found it. Nor are dignity and worth automatically conferred by existence itself—a mass murderer exists, but is of negative worth to his society and possesses no dignity in his lust to kill.

"No, the only dignity, the only spirituality, rests on what a man can achieve with his own efforts. To rob a man of the chance to achieve, and to trade what he achieves with others, is to rob him of his spiritual dignity as a man. This is why communism has failed in our time. *All* coercion—all force to take from a man his own efforts to achieve—causes spiritual damage and weakens a society. Conscription, theft, fraud, violence, welfare, lack of legislative representation—*all* rob a man of his chance to choose, to achieve on his own, to trade the results of his achievement with others. Coercion is a cheat. It produces nothing new. Only freedom—the freedom to achieve, the freedom to trade freely the results of achievement—creates the environment proper to the dignity and spirituality of man."

Leisha applauded so hard her hands hurt. Going backstage with Daddy, she thought she could hardly breathe. Kenzo Yagai!

But backstage was more crowded than she had expected. There

were cameras everywhere. Daddy said, "Mr. Yagai, may I present my daughter Leisha," and the cameras moved in close and fast—on *her*. A Japanese man whispered something in Kenzo Yagai's ear, and he looked more closely at Leisha. "Ah, yes."

"Look over here, Leisha," someone called, and she did. A robot camera zoomed so close to her face that Leisha stepped back, startled. Daddy spoke very sharply to someone, then to someone else. The cameras didn't move. A woman suddenly knelt in front of Leisha and thrust a microphone at her. "What does it feel like to never sleep, Leisha?"

"What?"

Someone laughed. The laugh was not kind. "Breeding geniuses . . ."

Leisha felt a hand on her shoulder. Kenzo Yagai gripped her very firmly, pulled her away from the cameras. Immediately, as if by magic, a line of Japanese men formed behind Yagai, parting only to let Daddy through. Behind the line, the three of them moved into a dressing room, and Kenzo Yagai shut the door.

"You must not let them bother you, Leisha," he said in his wonderful accent. "Not ever. There is an old Oriental proverb: 'The dogs bark but the caravan moves on.' You must never let your individual caravan be slowed by the barking of rude or envious dogs."

"I won't," Leisha breathed, not sure yet what the words really meant, knowing there was time later to sort them out, to talk about them with Daddy. For now she was dazzled by Kenzo Yagai, the actual man himself, who was changing the world without force, without guns, with trading his special individual efforts. "We study your philosophy at my school, Mr. Yagai."

Kenzo Yagai looked at Daddy. Daddy said, "A private school. But Leisha's sister also studies it, although cursorily, in the public system. Slowly, Kenzo, but it comes. It comes." Leisha noticed that he did not say why Alice was not here tonight with them.

Back home, Leisha sat in her room for hours, thinking over everything that had happened. When Alice came home from Julie's the next morning, Leisha rushed toward her. But Alice seemed angry about something.

"Alice—what is it?"

"Don't you think I have enough to put up with at school already?"

Alice shouted. "Everybody knows, but at least when you stayed quiet it didn't matter too much. They'd stopped teasing me. Why did you have to do it?"

"Do what?" Leisha said, bewildered.

Alice threw something at her: a hard-copy morning paper, on newsprint flimsier than the Camden system used. The paper dropped open at Leisha's feet. She stared at her own picture, three columns wide, with Kenzo Yagai. The headline said, YAGAI AND THE FUTURE: ROOM FOR THE REST OF US? Y-ENERGY INVENTOR CONFERS WITH 'SLEEP-FREE' DAUGHTER OF MEGA-FINANCIER ROGER CAMDEN.

Alice kicked the paper. "It was on TV last night, too—on *TV*. I work hard not to look stuck-up or creepy, and you go and do this! Now Julie probably won't even invite me to her slumber party next week." She rushed up the broad curving stairs toward her room.

Leisha looked down at the paper. She heard Kenzo Yagai's voice in her head: "The dogs bark but the caravan moves on." She looked at the empty stairs. Aloud she said, "Alice—your hair looks really pretty curled like that."

IV

"I want to meet the rest of them," Leisha said. "Why have you kept them from me this long?"

"I haven't kept them from you at all," Camden said. "Not offering is not the same as denial. Why shouldn't you be the one to do the asking? You're the one who now wants it."

Leisha looked at him. She was fifteen, in her last year at the Sauley School. "Why didn't you offer?"

"Why should I?"

"I don't know," Leisha said. "But you gave me everything else."

"Including the freedom to ask for what you want."

Leisha looked for the contradiction and found it. "Most things that you provided for my education I didn't ask for, because I didn't know enough to ask and you, as the adult, did. But you've never offered the opportunity for me to meet any of the other sleepless mutants—"

"Don't use that word," Camden said sharply.

"—so either you must think it was not essential to my education or else you had another motive for not wanting me to meet them."

"Wrong," Camden said. "There's a third possibility. That I think meeting them is essential to your education, that I do want you to, but this issue provided a chance to further the education of your self-initiative by waiting for *you* to ask."

"All right," Leisha said, a little defiantly; there seemed to be a lot of defiance between them lately, for no good reason. She squared her shoulders. Her new breasts thrust forward. "I'm asking. How many of the Sleepless are there, who are they, and where are they?"

Camden said, "If you're using that term—'the Sleepless'—you've already done some reading on your own. So you probably know that there are 1,082 of you so far in the United States, a few more in foreign countries, most of them in major metropolitan areas. Seventy-nine are in Chicago, most of them still small children. Only nineteen anywhere are older than you."

Leisha didn't deny reading any of this. Camden leaned forward in his study chair to peer at her. Leisha wondered if he needed glasses. His hair was completely gray now, sparse and stiff, like lonely broomstraws. The *Wall Street Journal* listed him among the hundred richest men in America; *Women's Wear Daily* pointed out that he was the only billionaire in the country who did not move in the society of international parties, charity balls, and personal jets. Camden's jet ferried him to business meetings around the world, to the chairmanship of the Yagai Economics Institute, and to very little else. Over the years he had grown richer, more reclusive, and more cerebral. Leisha felt a rush of her old affection.

She threw herself sideways into a leather chair, her long slim legs dangling over the arm. Absently she scratched a mosquito bite on her thigh. "Well, then, I'd like to meet Richard Keller." He lived in Chicago and was the beta-test Sleepless closest to her own age. He was seventeen.

"Why ask me? Why not just go?"

Leisha thought there was a note of impatience in his voice. He liked her to explore things first, then report on them to him later. Both parts were important.

Leisha laughed. "You know what, Daddy? You're predictable."

Camden laughed, too. In the middle of the laugh Susan came in. "He certainly is not. Roger, what about that meeting in Buenos Aires

Thursday? Is it on or off?" When he didn't answer, her voice grew shriller. "Roger? I'm talking to you!"

Leisha averted her eyes. Two years ago Susan had finally left genetic research to run Camden's house and schedule; before that she had tried hard to do both. Since she had left Biotech, it seemed to Leisha, Susan had changed. Her voice was tighter. She was more insistent that cook and the gardener follow her directions exactly, without deviation. Her blond braids had become stiff sculptured waves of platinum.

"It's on," Roger said.

"Well, thanks for at least answering. Am I going?"

"If you like."

"I like."

Susan left the room. Leisha rose and stretched. Her long legs rose on tiptoe. It felt good to reach, to stretch, to feel sunlight from the wide windows wash over her face. She smiled at her father and found him watching her with an unexpected expression.

"Leisha—"

"What?"

"See Keller. But be careful."

"Of what?"

But Camden wouldn't answer.

The voice on the phone had been noncommittal. "Leisha Camden? Yes, I know who you are. Three o'clock on Thursday?" The house was modest, a thirty-year-old Colonial on a quiet suburban street where small children on bicycles could be watched from the front window. Few roofs had more than one Y-energy cell. The trees, huge old sugar maples, were beautiful.

"Come in," Richard Keller said.

He was no taller than she, stocky, with a bad case of acne. Probably no genetic alterations except sleep, Leisha guessed. He had thick dark hair, a low forehead, and bushy black brows. Before he closed the door Leisha saw him stare at her car and driver, parked in the driveway next to a rusty ten-speed bike.

"I can't drive yet," she said. "I'm still fifteen."

"It's easy to learn," Keller said. "So, you want to tell me why you're here?"

Leisha liked his directness. "To meet some other Sleepless."

"You mean you never have? Not any of us?"

"You mean the rest of you know each other?" She hadn't expected that.

"Come to my room, Leisha."

She followed him to the back of the house. No one else seemed to be home. His room was large and airy, filled with computers and filing cabinets. A rowing machine sat in one corner. It looked like a shabbier version of the room of any bright classmate at the Sauley School, except there was more space without a bed. She walked over to the computer screen.

"Hey—you working on Boesc equations?"

"On an application of them."

"To what?"

"Fish migration patterns."

Leisha smiled. "Yeah—that would work. I never thought of that."

Keller seemed not to know what to do with her smile. He looked at the wall, then at her chin. "You interested in Gaea patterns? In the environment?"

"Well, no," Leisha confessed. "Not particularly. I'm going to study politics at Harvard. Prelaw. But of course we had Gaea patterns at school."

Keller's gaze finally came unstuck from her face. He ran a hand through his dark hair. "Sit down, if you want."

Leisha sat, looking appreciatively at the wall posters, shifting green on blue, like ocean currents. "I like those. Did you program them yourself?"

"You're not at all what I pictured," Keller said.

"How did you picture me?"

He didn't hesitate. "Stuck-up. Superior. Shallow, despite your IQ."

She was more hurt than she had expected to be.

Keller blurted, "You're the only one of the Sleepless who's really rich. But you already know that."

"No, I don't. I've never checked."

He took the chair beside her, stretching his stocky legs straight in front of him, in a slouch that had nothing to do with relaxation. "It makes sense, really. Rich people don't have their children genetically modified to be superior—they think any offspring of theirs is already superior. By their values. And poor people can't afford it.

We Sleepless are upper-middle class, no more. Children of professors, scientists, people who value brains and time."

"My father values brains and time," Leisha said. "He's the biggest supporter of Kenzo Yagai."

"Oh, Leisha, do you think I don't already know that? Are you flashing me or what?"

Leisha said with great deliberateness, "I'm *talking* to you." But the next minute she could feel the hurt break through on her face.

"I'm sorry," Keller muttered. He shot off his chair and paced to the computer, back. "I *am* sorry. But I don't . . . I don't understand what you're doing here."

"I'm lonely," Leisha said, astonished at herself. She looked up at him. "It's true. I'm lonely. I am. I have friends and Daddy and Alice—but no one really knows, really understands—what? I don't know what I'm saying."

Keller smiled. The smile changed his whole face, opened up its dark planes to the light. "I do. Oh, do I. What do you do when they say, 'I had such a dream last night!'?"

"Yes!" Leisha said. "But that's even really minor—it's when *I* say, 'I'll look that up for you tonight,' and they get that funny look on their face that means 'She'll do it while I'm asleep.'"

"But that's even really minor," Keller said. "It's when you're playing basketball in the gym after supper and then you go to the diner for food and then you say, 'Let's have a walk by the lake,' and they say, 'I'm really tired. I'm going home to bed now.'"

"But that's really minor," Leisha said, jumping up. "It's when you really are absorbed by the movie and then you get the point and it's so goddamn beautiful you leap up and say, 'Yes! Yes!' and Susan says, 'Leisha, really—you'd think nobody but you ever enjoyed anything before.'"

"Who's Susan?" Keller said.

The mood was broken. But not really; Leisha could say "my stepmother" without much discomfort over what Susan had promised to be and what she had become. Keller stood inches from her, smiling that joyous smile, understanding, and suddenly relief washed over Leisha so strong that she walked straight into him and put her arms around his neck, tightening them only when she felt his startled jerk. She started to sob—she, Leisha, who never cried.

"Hey," Richard said. "Hey."

"Brilliant," Leisha said, laughing. "Brilliant remark."

She could feel his embarrassed smile. "Wanta see my fish migration curves instead?"

"No," Leisha sobbed, and he went on holding her, patting her back awkwardly, telling her without words that she was home.

Camden waited up for her, although it was past midnight. He had been smoking heavily. Through the blue air he said quietly, "Did you have a good time, Leisha?"

"Yes."

"I'm glad," he said, and put out his last cigarette and climbed the stairs—slowly, stiffly, he was nearly seventy now—to bed.

They went everywhere together for nearly a year: swimming, dancing, to the museums, the theater, the library. Richard introduced her to the others, a group of twelve kids between fourteen and nineteen, all of them intelligent and eager. All Sleepless.

Leisha learned.

Tony's parents, like her own, had divorced. But Tony, fourteen, lived with his mother, who had not particularly wanted a Sleepless child, while his father, who had, acquired a red hovercar and a young girlfriend who designed ergonomic chairs in Paris. Tony was not allowed to tell anyone—relatives, schoolmates—that he was Sleepless. "They'll think you're a freak," his mother said, eyes averted from her son's face. The one time Tony disobeyed her and told a friend that he never slept, his mother beat him. Then she moved the family to a new neighborhood. He was nine years old.

Jeanine, almost as long-legged and slim as Leisha, was training for the Olympics in ice skating. She practiced twelve hours a day, hours no Sleeper still in high school could ever have. So far the newspapers had not picked up the story. Jeanine was afraid that if they did they would somehow not let her compete.

Jack, like Leisha, would start college in September. Unlike Leisha, he had already started his career. The practice of law had to wait for law school; the practice of investment required only money. Jack didn't have much, but his precise financial analyses parlayed $600 saved from summer jobs to $3,000 through stock-market investing, then to $10,000, and then he had enough to qualify for information-fund speculation. Jack was fifteen, not old enough to make legal investments; the transactions were all in the name of Kevin Baker, the oldest of the Sleepless, who lived in Austin. Jack told Leisha, "When I hit 84 percent profit over two consecutive quarters, the data analysts logged onto me. They were just sniffing. Well, that's their job, even when the overall amounts are actually small. It's the patterns they care about. If they take the trouble to cross-reference data banks and come up with the fact that Kevin is a Sleepless, will they try to stop us from investing somehow?"

"That's paranoid," Leisha said.

"No, it's not," Jeanine said. "Leisha, you don't *know.*"

"You mean because I've been protected by my father's money and caring," Leisha said. No one grimaced; all of them confronted ideas openly, without shadowy allusions. Without dreams.

"Yes," Jeanine said. "Your father sounds terrific. And he raised you to think that achievement should not be fettered—Jesus Christ, he's a Yagaiist. Well, good. We're glad for you." She said it without sarcasm. Leisha nodded. "But the world isn't always like that. They hate us."

"That's too strong," Carol said. "Not hate."

"Well, maybe," Jeanine said. "But they're different from us. We're better, and they naturally resent that."

"I don't see what's natural about it," Tony said. "Why shouldn't it be just as natural to admire what's better? We do. Does any one of us resent Kenzo Yagai for his genius? Or Nelson Wade, the physicist? Or Catherine Raduski?"

"We don't resent them because we *are* better," Richard said. "Q.E.D."

"What we should do is have our own society," Tony said. "Why should we allow their regulations to restrict our natural, honest achievements? Why should Jeanine be barred from skating against them and Jack from investing on their same terms just because we're Sleepless? Some of them are brighter than others of them. Some have greater persistence. Well, we have greater concentration, more biochemical stability, and more time. All men are not created equal."

"Be fair, Tony—no one has been barred from anything yet," Jeanine said.

"But we will be."

"*Wait.*" Leisha said. She was deeply troubled by the conversation.

"I mean, yes, in many ways we're better. But you quoted out of context, Tony. The Declaration of Independence doesn't say all men are created equal in ability. It's talking about rights and power—it means that all are created equal *under the law*. We have no more right to a separate society or to being free of society's restrictions than anyone else does. There's no other way to freely trade one's efforts, unless the same contractual rules apply to all."

"Spoken like a true Yagaiist," Richard said, squeezing her hand.

"That's enough intellectual discussion for me," Carol said, laughing. "We've been at this for hours. We're at the beach, for Chrissake. Who wants to swim with me?"

"I do," Jeanine said. "Come on, Jack."

All of them rose, brushing sand off their suits, discarding sunglasses. Richard pulled Leisha to her feet. But just before they ran into the water, Tony put his skinny hand on her arm. "One more question, Leisha. Just to think about. If we achieve better than most other people, and we trade with the Sleepers when it's mutually beneficial, making no distinction there between the strong and the weak—what obligation do we have to those so weak they don't have anything to trade with us? We're already going to give more than we get—do we have to do it when we get nothing at all? Do we have to take care of their deformed and handicapped and sick and lazy and shiftless with the products of our work?"

"Do the Sleepers have to?" Leisha countered.

"Kenzo Yagai would say no. He's a Sleeper."

"He would say they would receive the benefits of contractual trade even if they aren't direct parties to the contract. The whole world is better fed and healthier because of Y-energy."

"Come on," Jeanine yelled. "Leisha, they're dunking me. Jack, you stop that. Leisha, help me!"

Leisha laughed. Just before she grabbed for Jeanine, she caught the look on Richard's face, on Tony's: Richard frankly lustful, Tony angry. At her. But why? What had she done, except argue in favor of dignity and trade?

Then Jack threw water on her, and Carol pushed Jack into the warm spray, and Richard was there with his arms around her, laughing.

When she got the water out of her eyes, Tony was gone.

Midnight. "Okay," Carol said. "Who's first?"

The six teenagers in the bramble clearing looked at each other. A Y-lamp, kept on low for atmosphere, cast weird shadows across their faces and over their bare legs. Around the clearing Roger Camden's trees stood thick and dark, a wall between them and the closest of the estate's outbuildings. It was very hot. August air hung heavy, sullen. They had voted against bringing an air-conditioned Y-field because this was a return to the primitive, the dangerous; let it be primitive.

Six pairs of eyes stared at the glass in Carol's hand.

"Come *on*," she said. "Who wants to drink up?" Her voice was jaunty, theatrically hard. "It was difficult enough to get this."

"How *did* you get it?" said Richard, the group member—except for Tony—with the least influential family contacts, the least money. "In a drinkable form like that?"

"My cousin Brian is a pharmaceutical supplier to the Biotech Institute. He's curious." Nods around the circle; except for Leisha, they were Sleepless precisely because they had relatives somehow connected to Biotech. And everyone was curious. The glass held interleukin-1, an immune-system booster, one of many substances that as a side effect induced the brain to swift and deep sleep.

Leisha stared at the glass. A warm feeling crept through her lower belly, not unlike the feeling when she and Richard made love.

Tony said, "Give it to me!"

Carol did. "Remember—you only need a little sip."

Tony raised the glass to his mouth, stopped, looked at them over the rim from his fierce eyes. He drank.

Carol took back the glass. They all watched Tony. Within a minute he lay on the rough ground; within two, his eyes closed in sleep.

It wasn't like seeing parents sleep, siblings, friends. It was Tony. They looked away, didn't meet each other's eyes. Leisha felt the warmth between her legs tug and tingle, faintly obscene.

When it was her turn, she drank slowly, then passed the glass to Jeanine. Her head turned heavy, as if it were being stuffed with damp rags. The trees at the edge of the clearing blurred. The portable lamp blurred, too—it wasn't bright and clean anymore but squishy, blobby; if she touched it, it would smear. Then darkness

swooped over her brain, taking it away: *taking away her mind.*
"Daddy!" She tried to call, to clutch for him, but then the darkness
obliterated her.

Afterward they all had headaches. Dragging themselves back
through the woods in the thin morning light was torture, com-
pounded by an odd shame. They didn't touch each other. Leisha
walked as far away from Richard as she could. It was a whole day
before the throbbing left the base of her skull or the nausea her
stomach.

There had not even been any dreams.

"I want you to come with me tonight," Leisha said, for the tenth or
twelfth time. "We both leave for college in just two days; this is the
last chance. I really want you to meet Richard."

Alice lay on her stomach across her bed. Her hair, brown and
lusterless, fell around her face. She wore an expensive yellow jump-
suit, silk by Ann Patterson, which rucked up in wrinkles around her
knees.

"Why? What do you care if I meet Richard or not?"

"Because you're my sister," Leisha said. She knew better than to
say "my twin." Nothing got Alice angry faster.

"I don't want to." The next moment Alice's face changed. "Oh,
I'm sorry, Leisha—I didn't mean to sound so snotty. But . . . but I
don't want to."

"It won't be all of them. Just Richard. And just for an hour or so.
Then you can come back here and pack for Northwestern."

"I'm not going to Northwestern."

Leisha stared at her.

Alice said, "I'm pregnant."

Leisha sat on the bed. Alice rolled onto her back, brushed the
hair out of her eyes, and laughed. Leisha's ears closed against the
sound. "Look at you," Alice said. "You'd think it was *you* who was
pregnant. But you never would be, would you, Leisha? Not until it
was the proper time. Not you."

"How?" Leisha said. "We both had our caps put in . . ."

"I had the cap removed," Alice said.

"You wanted to get pregnant?"

"Damn flash I did. And there's not a thing Daddy can do about it. Except, of course, cut off all credit completely, but I don't think he'll do that, do you?" She laughed again. "Even to me?"

"But, Alice . . . why? Not just to anger Daddy."

"No," Alice said. "Although you would think of that, wouldn't you? Because I want something to love. Something of my *own*. Something that has nothing to do with this house."

Leisha thought of her and Alice running through the conservatory, years ago, her and Alice darting in and out of the sunlight. "It hasn't been so bad growing up in this house."

"Leisha, you're stupid. I don't know how anyone so smart can be so stupid. Get out of my room! Get out!"

"But, Alice . . . a *baby* . . ."

"Get out!" Alice shrieked. "Go to Harvard. Go be successful. Just get out!"

Leisha jerked off the bed. "Gladly! You're irrational, Alice. You don't think ahead, you don't plan a *baby* . . ." But she could never sustain anger. It dribbled away, leaving her mind empty. She looked at Alice, who suddenly put out her arms. Leisha went into them.

"You're the baby," Alice said wonderingly. "You *are*. You're so . . . I don't know what. You're a baby."

Leisha said nothing. Alice's arms felt warm, felt whole, felt like two children running in and out of sunlight. "I'll help you, Alice. If Daddy won't."

Alice abruptly pushed her away. "I don't need your help."

Alice stood. Leisha rubbed her empty arms, fingertips scraping across opposite elbows. Alice kicked the empty, open trunk in which she was supposed to pack for Northwestern and then abruptly smiled, a smile that made Leisha look away. She braced herself for more abuse. But what Alice said, very softly, was, "Have a good time at Harvard."

V

She loved it.

From the first sight of Massachusetts Hall, older than the United States by a half century, Leisha felt something that had been missing in Chicago: Age. Roots. Tradition. She touched the bricks of Widener Library, the glass cases in the Peabody Museum, as if they were the grail. She had never been particularly sensitive to myth or drama;

the anguish of Juliet seemed to her artificial, that of Willy Loman merely wasteful. Only King Arthur, struggling to create a better social order, had interested her. But now, walking under the huge autumn trees, she suddenly caught a glimpse of a force that could span generations, fortunes left to endow learning and achievement the benefactors would never see, individual effort spanning and shaping centuries to come. She stopped and looked at the sky through the leaves, at the buildings solid with purpose. At such moments she thought of Camden, bending the will of an entire genetic-research institute to create her in the image he wanted.

Within a month she had forgotten all such mega-musings.

The work load was incredible, even for her. The Sauley School had encouraged individual exploration at her own pace; Harvard knew what it wanted from her, at its pace. In the last twenty years, under the academic leadership of a man who in his youth had watched Japanese economic domination with dismay, Harvard had become the controversial leader of a return to hard-edged learning of facts, theories, applications, problem solving, intellectual efficiency. The school accepted one out of every two hundred applications from around the world. The daughter of England's prime minister had flunked out her first year and been sent home.

Leisha had a single room in a new dormitory, the dorm because she had spent so many years isolated in Chicago and was hungry for people, the single so she would not disturb anyone else when she worked all night. Her second day, a boy from down the hall sauntered in and perched on the edge of her desk.

"So you're Leisha Camden."

"Yes."

"Sixteen years old."

"Almost seventeen."

"Going to outperform us all, I understand, without even trying."

Leisha's smile faded. The boy stared at her from under lowered downy brows. He was smiling, his eyes sharp. From Richard and Tony and the others Leisha had learned to recognize the anger that presented itself as contempt.

"Yes," Leisha said coolly. "I am."

"Are you sure? With your pretty little-girl hair and your mutant little-girl brain?"

"Oh, leave her alone, Hannaway," said another voice. A tall blond boy, so thin his ribs looked like ripples in brown sand, stood in jeans and bare feet, drying his wet hair. "Don't you ever get tired of walking around being an asshole?"

"Do you?" Hannaway said. He heaved himself off the desk and started toward the door. The blond moved out of his way. Leisha moved into it.

"The reason I'm going to do better than you," she said evenly, "is because I have certain advantages you don't. Including sleeplessness. And then after I 'outperform' you I'll be glad to help you study for your tests so that you can pass, too."

The blond, drying his ears, laughed. But Hannaway stood still, and into his eyes came an expression that made Leisha back away. He pushed past her and stormed out.

"Nice going, Camden," the blond said. "He deserved that."

"But I meant it," Leisha said. "I will help him study."

The blond lowered his towel and stared. "You did, didn't you? You meant it."

"Yes! Why does everybody keep questioning that?"

"Well," the boy said, "I don't. You can help me if I get into trouble." Suddenly he smiled. "But I won't."

"Why not?"

"Because I'm just as good at anything as you are, Leisha Camden."

She studied him. "You're not one of us. Not Sleepless."

"Don't have to be. I know what I can do. Do, be, create, trade."

She said, delighted, "You're a Yagaiist!"

"Of course." He held out his hand. "Stewart Sutter. How about a fishburger in the Yard?"

"Great," Leisha said. They walked out together, talking excitedly. When people stared at her she tried not to notice. She was here. At Harvard. With space ahead of her, time to learn, and with people like Stewart Sutter who accepted and challenged her.

All the hours he was awake.

She became totally absorbed in her classwork. Roger Camden drove up once, walking the campus with her, listening, smiling. He was more at home than Leisha would have expected: he knew Stewart Sutter's father, Kate Addams's grandfather. They talked about

Harvard, business, Harvard, the Yagai Economics Institute, Harvard. "How's Alice?" Leisha asked once, but Camden said that he didn't know, she had moved out and did not want to see him. He made her an allowance through his attorney. While he said this, his face remained serene.

Leisha went to the Homecoming Ball with Stewart, who was also majoring in prelaw but was two years ahead of Leisha. She took a weekend trip to Paris with Kate Addams and two other girlfriends, taking the Concorde III. She had a fight with Stewart over whether the metaphor of superconductivity could apply to Yagaiism, a stupid fight they both knew was stupid but had anyway, and afterward they became lovers. After the fumbling sexual explorations with Richard, Stewart was deft, experienced, smiling faintly as he taught her how to have an orgasm both by herself and with him. Leisha was dazzled. "It's so *joyful*," she said, and Stewart looked at her with a tenderness she knew was part disturbance but didn't know why.

At midsemester she had the highest grades in the freshman class. She got every answer right on every single question on her midterms. She and Stewart went out for a beer to celebrate, and when they came back Leisha's room had been destroyed. The computer was smashed, the data banks wiped, hard copies and books smoldering in a metal wastebasket. Her clothes were ripped to pieces, her desk and bureau hacked apart. The only thing untouched, pristine, was the bed.

Stewart said, "There's no way this could have been done in silence. Everyone on the floor—hell, on the floor *below*—had to know. Someone will talk to the police." No one did. Leisha sat on the edge of the bed, dazed, and looked at the remnants of her homecoming gown. The next day Dave Hannaway gave her a long, wide smile.

Camden flew east again, taut with rage. He rented her an apartment in Cambridge with E-lock security and a bodyguard named Toshio. After he left Leisha fired the bodyguard but kept the apartment. It gave her and Stewart more privacy, which they used to endlessly discuss the situation. It was Leisha who argued that it was an aberration, an immaturity.

"There have always been haters, Stewart. Hate Jews, hate blacks, hate immigrants, hate Yagaiists who have more initiative and dignity than you do. I'm just the latest object of hatred. It's not new, it's not remarkable. It doesn't mean any basic kind of schism between the Sleepless and Sleepers."

Stewart sat up in bed and reached for the sandwiches on the night stand. "Doesn't it? Leisha, you're a different kind of person entirely. More evolutionarily fit, not only to survive but to prevail. Those other 'objects of hatred' you cite except Yagaiists—they were all powerless in their societies. They occupied *inferior* positions. You, on the other hand—all three Sleepless in Harvard Law are on the *Law Review*. All of them. Kevin Baker, your oldest, has already founded a successful bio-interface software firm and is making money, a lot of it. Every Sleepless is making superb grades, none have psychological problems, all are healthy—and most of you aren't even adults yet. How much hatred do you think you're going to encounter once you hit the big-stakes world of finance and business and scarce endowed chairs and national politics?"

"Give me a sandwich," Leisha said. "Here's my evidence you're wrong: you yourself. Kenzo Yagai. Kate Addams. Professor Lane. My father. Every Sleeper who inhabits the world of fair trade, mutually beneficial contracts. And that's most of you, or at least most of you who are worth considering. You believe that competition among the most capable leads to the most beneficial trades for everyone, strong and weak. Sleepless are making real and concrete contributions to society, in a lot of fields. That has to outweigh the discomfort we cause. We're *valuable* to you. You know that."

Stewart brushed crumbs off the sheets. "Yes. I do. Yagaiists do."

"Yagaiists run the business and financial and academic worlds. Or they will. In a meritocracy, they *should*. You underestimate the majority of people, Stew. Ethics aren't confined to the ones out front."

"I hope you're right," Stewart said. "Because, you know, I'm in love with you."

Leisha put down her sandwich.

"Joy," Stewart mumbled into her breasts. "You are joy."

When Leisha went home for Thanksgiving, she told Richard about Stewart. He listened tight-lipped.

"A Sleeper."

"A *person*," Leisha said. "A good, intelligent, achieving person."

"Do you know what your good intelligent achieving Sleepers have done, Leisha? Jeanine has been barred from Olympic skating.

'Genetic alteration, analogous to steroid abuse to create an unsportsmanlike advantage.' Chris Devereaux's left Stanford. They trashed his laboratory, destroyed two years' work in memory-formation proteins. Kevin Baker's software company is fighting a nasty advertising campaign, all underground, of course, about kids using software designed by 'nonhuman minds.' Corruption, mental slavery, satanic influences: the whole bag of witch-hunt tricks. Wake up, Leisha!"

They both heard his words. Moments dragged by. Richard stood like a boxer, forward on the balls of his feet, teeth clenched. Finally he said, very quietly, "Do you love him?"

"Yes," Leisha said. "I'm sorry."

"Your choice," Richard said coldly. "What do you do while he's asleep? Watch?"

"You make it sound like a perversion!"

Richard said nothing. Leisha drew a deep breath. She spoke rapidly but calmly, a controlled rush: "While Stewart is asleep I work. The same as you do. Richard—don't do this. I didn't mean to hurt you. And I don't want to lose the group. I believe the Sleepers are the same species as we are—are you going to punish me for that? Are you going to *add* to the hatred? Are you going to tell me that I can't belong to a wider world that includes all honest, worthwhile people whether they sleep or not? Are you going to tell me that the most important division is by genetics and not by economic spirituality? Are you going to force me into an artificial choice, 'us' or 'them'?"

Richard picked up a bracelet. Leisha recognized it: she had given it to him in the summer. His voice was quiet. "No. It's not a choice." He played with the gold links a minute, then looked up at her. "Not yet."

By spring break, Camden walked more slowly. He took medicine for his blood pressure, his heart. He and Susan, he told Leisha, were getting a divorce. "She changed, Leisha, after I married her. You saw that. She was independent and productive and happy, and then after a few years she stopped all that and became a shrew. A whining shrew." He shook his head in genuine bewilderment. "You saw the change."

Leisha had. A memory came to her: Susan leading her and Alice in "games" that were actually controlled cerebral-performance tests. Susan's braids dancing around her sparkling eyes. Alice had loved Susan, then, as much as Leisha had.

"Dad, I want Alice's address."

"I told you up at Harvard, I don't have it," Camden said. He shifted in his chair, the impatient gesture of a body that never expected to wear out. In January Kenzo Yagai had died of pancreatic cancer; Camden had taken the news hard. "I make her allowance through an attorney. By her choice."

"Then I want the address of the attorney."

The attorney, however, refused to tell Leisha where Alice was. "She doesn't want to be found, Ms. Camden. She wanted a complete break."

"Not from me," Leisha said.

"Yes," the attorney said, and something flickered behind his eyes, something she had last seen in Dave Hannaway's face.

She flew to Austin before returning to Boston, making her a day late for classes. Kevin Baker saw her instantly, canceling a meeting with IBM. She told him what she needed, and he set his best datanet people on it, without telling them why. Within two hours she had Alice's address from the attorney's electronic files. It was the first time, she realized, that she had ever turned to one of the Sleepless for help, and it had been given instantly. Without trade.

Alice was in Pennsylvania. The next weekend Leisha rented a hovercar and driver—she had learned to drive, but only groundcars as yet—and went to High Ridge, in the Appalachian Mountains.

It was an isolated hamlet, twenty-five miles from the nearest hospital. Alice lived with a man named Ed, a silent carpenter twenty years older than she, in a cabin in the woods. The cabin had water and electricity but no news net. In the early spring light the earth was raw and bare, slashed with icy gullies. Alice and Ed apparently worked at nothing. Alice was eight months pregnant.

"I didn't want you here," she said to Leisha. "So why are you?"

"Because you're my sister."

"God, look at you. Is that what they're wearing at Harvard? Boots like that? When did you become fashionable, Leisha? You were always too busy being intellectual to care."

"What's this all about, Alice? Why here? What are you doing?"

"Living," Alice said. "Away from dear Daddy, away from Chicago, away from drunken broken Susan—did you know she drinks? Just like Mom. He does that to people. But not to me. I got out. I wonder if you ever will."

"Got out? To *this*?"

"I'm happy," Alice said angrily. "Isn't that what it's supposed to be about? Isn't that the aim of your great Kenzo Yagai—happiness through individual effort?"

Leisha thought of saying that Alice was making no efforts that she could see. She didn't say it. A chicken ran through the yard of the cabin. Behind, the Appalachian Mountains rose in layers of blue haze. Leisha thought what this place must have been like in winter: cut off from the world where people strived toward goals, learned, changed.

"I'm glad you're happy, Alice."

"Are you?"

"Yes."

"Then I'm glad, too," Alice said, almost defiantly. The next moment she abruptly hugged Leisha, fiercely, the huge hard mound of her belly crushed between them. Alice's hair smelled sweet, like fresh grass in sunlight.

"I'll come see you again, Alice."

"Don't," Alice said.

VI

SLEEPLESS MUTIE BEGS FOR REVERSAL OF GENE TAMPERING, screamed the headline in the Food Mart. "PLEASE LET ME SLEEP LIKE REAL PEOPLE!" CHILD PLEADS.

Leisha typed in her credit number and pressed the news kiosk for a printout, although ordinarily she ignored the electronic tabloids. The headline went on circling the kiosk. A Food Mart employee stopped stacking boxes on shelves and watched her. Bruce, Leisha's bodyguard, watched the employee.

She was twenty-two, in her final year at Harvard Law, editor of the *Law Review*, ranked first in her class. The next three were Jonathan Cocchiara, Len Carter, and Martha Wentz. All Sleepless.

In her apartment she skimmed the printout. Then she accessed the Groupnet run from Austin. The files had more news stories about the child, with comments from other Sleepless, but before she could call them up Kevin Baker came on-line himself, on voice.

"Leisha. I'm glad you called. I was going to call you."

"What's the situation with this Stella Bevington, Kev? Has anybody checked it out?"

"Randy Davies. He's from Chicago, but I don't think you've met him, he's still in high school. He's in Park Ridge, Stella's in Skokie. Her parents wouldn't talk to him—were pretty abusive, in fact—but he got to see Stella face to face anyway. It doesn't look like an abuse case, just the usual stupidity: parents wanted a genius child, scrimped and saved, and now they can't handle that she *is* one. They scream at her to sleep, get emotionally abusive when she contradicts them, but so far no violence."

"Is the emotional abuse actionable?"

"I don't think we want to move on it yet. Two of us will keep in close touch with Stella—she does have a modem, and she hasn't told her parents about the net—and Randy will drive out weekly."

Leisha bit her lip. "A tabloid shitpiece said she's seven years old."

"Yes."

"Maybe she shouldn't be left there. I'm an Illinois resident, I can file an abuse grievance from here if Candy's got too much in her briefcase. . . ." *Seven years old.*

"No. Let it sit awhile. Stella will probably be all right. You know that."

She did. Nearly all of the Sleepless stayed "all right," no matter how much opposition came from the stupid segment of society. And it was only the stupid segment, Leisha argued—a small if vocal minority. Most people could, and would, adjust to the growing presence of the Sleepless, when it became clear that that presence included not only growing power but growing benefits to the country as a whole.

Kevin Baker, now twenty-six, had made a fortune in microchips so revolutionary that artificial intelligence, once a debated dream, was yearly closer to reality. Carolyn Rizzolo had won the Pulitzer Prize in drama for her play *Morning Light.* She was twenty-four. Jeremy Robinson had done significant work in superconductivity applications while still a graduate student at Stanford. William Thaine, *Law Review* editor when Leisha first came to Harvard, was now in private practice. He had never lost a case. He was twenty-six, and the cases were becoming important. His clients valued his ability more than his age.

But not everyone reacted that way.

Kevin Baker and Richard Keller had started the datanet that bound the Sleepless into a tight group, constantly aware of each other's personal fights. Leisha Camden financed the legal battles, the educational costs of Sleepless whose parents were unable to meet them, the support of children in emotionally bad situations. Rhonda Lavelier got herself licensed as a foster mother in California, and whenever possible the Group maneuvered to have small Sleepless who were removed from their homes assigned to Rhonda. The Group now had three ABA lawyers; within the next year they would gain four more, licensed to practice in five different states.

The one time they had not been able to remove an abused Sleepless child legally, they kidnapped him.

Timmy DeMarzo, four years old. Leisha had been opposed to the action. She had argued the case morally and pragmatically—to her they were the same thing—thus: if they believed in their society, in its fundamental laws and in their ability to belong to it as free-trading productive individuals, they must remain bound by the society's contractual laws. The Sleepless were, for the most part, Yagaiists. They should already know this. And if the FBI caught them, the courts and press would crucify them.

They were not caught.

Timmy DeMarzo—not even old enough to call for help on the datanet, they had learned of the situation through the automatic police-record scan Kevin maintained through his company—was stolen from his own backyard in Wichita. He had lived the last year in an isolated trailer in North Dakota; no place was too isolated for a modem. He was cared for by a legally irreproachable foster mother who had lived there all her life. The foster mother was second cousin to a Sleepless, a broad cheerful woman with a much better brain than her appearance indicated. She was a Yagaiist. No record of the child's existence appeared in any data bank: not the IRS's, not any school's, not even the local grocery store's computerized checkout slips. Food specifically for the child was shipped in monthly on a truck owned by a Sleepless in State College, Pennsylvania. Ten of the Group knew about the kidnapping, out of the total 3,428 born in the United States. Of that total, 2,691 were part of the Group via the net. Another 701 were as yet too young to use a modem. Only 36 Sleepless, for whatever reason, were not part of the Group.

The kidnapping had been arranged by Tony Indivino.

"It's Tony I wanted to talk to you about," Kevin said to Leisha. "He's started again. This time he means it. He's buying land."

She folded the tabloid very small and laid it carefully on the table. "Where?"

"Allegheny Mountains. In southern New York State. A lot of land. He's putting in the roads now. In the spring, the first buildings."

"Jennifer Sharifi still financing it?" She was the American-born daughter of an Arab prince who had wanted a Sleepless child. The prince was dead, and Jennifer, dark-eyed and multilingual, was richer than Leisha would one day be.

"Yes. He's starting to get a following, Leisha."

"I know."

"Call him."

"I will. Keep me informed about Stella."

She worked until midnight at the *Law Review*, then until four A.M. preparing her classes. From four to five she handled legal matters for the Group. At five A.M. she called Tony, still in Chicago. He had finished high school, done one semester at Northwestern, and at Christmas vacation he had finally exploded at his mother for forcing him to live as a Sleeper. The explosion, it seemed to Leisha, had never ended.

"Tony? Leisha."

"The answer is yes, yes, no, and go to hell."

Leisha gritted her teeth. "Fine. Now tell me the questions."

"Are you really serious about the Sleepless withdrawing into their own self-sufficient society? Is Jennifer Sharifi willing to finance a project the size of building a small city? Don't you think that's a cheat of all that can be accomplished by patient integration of the Group into the mainstream? And what about the contradictions of living in an armed restricted city and still trading with the Outside?"

"I would never tell *you* to go to hell."

"Hooray for you," Tony said. After a moment he added, "I'm sorry. That sounds like one of *them*."

"It's wrong for us, Tony."

"Thanks for not saying I couldn't pull it off."

She wondered if he could. "We're not a separate species, Tony."

"Tell that to the Sleepers."

"You exaggerate. There are haters out there, there are *always* haters, but to give up . . ."

"We're not giving up. Whatever we create can be freely traded: software, hardware, novels, information, theories, legal counsel. We can travel in and out. But we'll have a safe place to return *to*. Without the leeches who think we owe them blood because we're better than they are."

"It isn't a matter of owing."

"Really?" Tony said. "Let's have this out, Leisha. All the way. You're a Yagaiist—what do you believe in?"

"Tony . . ."

"*Do it*," Tony said, and in his voice she heard the fourteen-year-old Richard had introduced her to. Simultaneously, she saw her father's face: not as he was now, since the bypass, but as he had been when she was a little girl, holding her on his lap to explain that she was special.

"I believe in voluntary trade that is mutually beneficial. That spiritual dignity comes from supporting one's life through one's own efforts, and trading the results of those efforts in mutual cooperation throughout the society. That the symbol of this is the contract. And that we need each other for the fullest, most beneficial trade."

"Fine," Tony bit off. "Now what about the beggars in Spain?"

"The what?"

"You walk down a street in a poor country like Spain and you see a beggar. Do you give him a dollar?"

"Probably."

"Why? He's trading nothing with you. He has nothing to trade."

"I know. Out of kindness. Compassion."

"You see six beggars. Do you give them all a dollar?"

"Probably," Leisha said.

"You would. You see a hundred beggars and you haven't got Leisha Camden's money—do you give them each a dollar?"

"No."

"Why not?"

Leisha reached for patience. Few people could make her want to cut off a comm link; Tony was one of them. "Too draining on my own resources. My life has first claim on the resources I earn."

"All right. Now consider this. At Biotech Institute—where you and I began, dear pseudo sister—Dr. Melling has just yesterday—"

"Who?"

"Dr. Susan Melling. Oh, God, I completely forgot—she used to be married to your father!"

"I lost track of her," Leisha said. "I didn't realize she'd gone back to research. Alice once said . . . never mind. What's going on at Biotech?"

"Two crucial items, just released. Carla Dutcher has had first-month fetal genetic analysis. Sleeplessness is a dominant gene. The next generation of the Group won't sleep, either."

"We all knew that," Leisha said. Carla Dutcher was the world's first pregnant Sleepless. Her husband was a Sleeper. "The whole world expected that."

"But the press will have a windfall with it anyway. Just watch. 'Muties Breed!' 'New Race Set to Dominate Next Generation of Children!' "

Leisha didn't deny it. "And the second item?"

"It's sad, Leisha. We've just had our first death."

Her stomach tightened. "Who?"

"Bernie Kuhn. Seattle." She didn't know him. "A car accident. It looks pretty straightforward—he lost control on a steep curve when his brakes failed. He had only been driving a few months. He was seventeen. But the significance here is that his parents have donated his brain and body to Biotech, in conjunction with the pathology department at the Chicago Medical School. They're going to take him apart to get the first good look at what prolonged sleeplessness does to the body and brain."

"They should," Leisha said. "That poor kid. But what are you so afraid they'll find?"

"I don't know. I'm not a doctor. But whatever it is, if the haters can use it against us, they will."

"You're paranoid, Tony."

"Impossible. The Sleepless have personalities calmer and more reality oriented than the norm. Don't you read the literature?"

"Tony—"

"What if you walk down that street in Spain and a hundred beggars each want a dollar and you say no and they have nothing to trade you but they're so rotten with anger about what you have that they knock you down and grab it and then beat you out of sheer envy and despair?"

Leisha didn't answer.

"Are you going to say that's not a human scenario, Leisha? That it never happens?"

"It happens," Leisha said evenly. "But not all that often."

"Bullshit. Read more history. Read more *newspapers*. But the point is: what do you owe the beggars then? What does a good Yagaiist who believes in mutually beneficial contracts do with people who have nothing to trade and can only take?"

"You're not—"

"*What*, Leisha? In the most objective terms you can manage, what do we owe the grasping and nonproductive needy?"

"What I said originally. Kindness. Compassion."

"Even if they don't trade it back? Why?"

"Because . . ." She stopped.

"Why? Why do law-abiding and productive human beings owe anything to those who neither produce very much nor abide by laws? What philosophical or economic or spiritual justification is there for owing them anything? Be as honest as I know you are."

Leisha put her head between her knees. The question gaped beneath her, but she didn't try to evade it. "I don't know. I just know we do."

"*Why?*"

She didn't answer. After a moment Tony did. The intellectual challenge was gone from his voice. He said, almost tenderly, "Come down in the spring and see the site for Sanctuary. The buildings will be going up then."

"No," Leisha said.

"I'd like you to."

"No. Armed retreat is not the way."

Tony said, "The beggars are getting nastier, Leisha. As the Sleepless grow richer. And I don't mean in money."

"Tony—" she said, and stopped. She couldn't think what to say.

"Don't walk down too many streets armed with just the memory of Kenzo Yagai."

In March, a bitterly cold March of winds whipping down the Charles River, Richard Keller came to Cambridge. Leisha had not seen him for four years. He didn't send her word on the Groupnet that he was coming. She hurried up the walk to her townhouse, muffled to the eyes in a red wool scarf against the snowy cold, and he stood there blocking the doorway. Behind Leisha, her bodyguard tensed.

"Richard! Bruce, it's all right, this is an old friend."

"Hello, Leisha."

He was heavier, sturdier looking, with a breadth of shoulder she didn't recognize. But the face was Richard's, older but unchanged: dark low brows, unruly dark hair. He had grown a beard.

"You look beautiful," he said.

She handed him a cup of coffee. "Are you here on business?" From the Groupnet she knew that he had finished his master's and had done outstanding work in marine biology in the Caribbean but had left that a year ago and disappeared from the net.

"No. Pleasure." He smiled suddenly, the old smile that opened up his dark face. "I almost forgot about that for a long time. Contentment, yes, we're all good at the contentment that comes from sustained work, but pleasure? Whim? Caprice? When was the last time you did something silly, Leisha?"

She smiled. "I ate cotton candy in the shower."

"Really? Why?"

"To see if it would dissolve in gooey pink patterns."

"Did it?"

"Yes. Lovely ones."

"And that was your last silly thing? When was it?"

"Last summer," Leisha said, and laughed.

"Well, mine is sooner than that. It's now. I'm in Boston for no other reason than the spontaneous pleasure of seeing you."

Leisha stopped laughing. "That's an intense tone for a spontaneous pleasure, Richard."

"Yup," he said, intensely. She laughed again. He didn't.

"I've been in India, Leisha. And China and Africa. Thinking, mostly. Watching. First I traveled like a Sleeper, attracting no attention.

Then I set out to meet the Sleepless in India and China. There are a few, you know, whose parents were willing to come here for the operation. They pretty much are accepted and left alone. I tried to figure out why desperately poor countries—by our standards, anyway; over there Y-energy is mostly available only in big cities—don't have any trouble accepting the superiority of Sleepless, whereas Americans, with more prosperity than any time in history, build in resentment more and more."

Leisha said, "Did you figure it out?"

"No. But I figured out something else, watching all those communes and villages and kampongs. We are too individualistic."

Disappointment swept Leisha. She saw her father's face: *Excellence is what counts, Leisha. Excellence supported by individual effort. . . .* She reached for Richard's cup. "More coffee?"

He caught her wrist and looked up into her face. "Don't misunderstand me, Leisha. I'm not talking about work. We are too much individuals in the rest of our lives. Too emotionally rational. Too much alone. Isolation kills more than the free flow of ideas. It kills joy."

He didn't let go of her wrist. She looked down into his eyes, into depths she hadn't seen before: it was the feeling of looking into a mine shaft, both giddy and frightening, knowing that at the bottom might be gold or darkness. Or both.

Richard said softly, "Stewart?"

"Over long ago. An undergraduate thing." Her voice didn't sound like her own.

"Kevin?"

"No, never—we're just friends."

"I wasn't sure. Anyone?"

"No."

He let go of her wrist. Leisha peered at him timidly. He suddenly laughed. "Joy, Leisha." An echo sounded in her mind, but she couldn't place it and then it was gone and she laughed, too, a laugh airy and frothy as pink cotton candy in summer.

"Come home, Leisha. He's had another heart attack."

Susan Melling's voice on the phone was tired. Leisha said, "How bad?"

"The doctors aren't sure. Or say they're not sure. He wants to see you. Can you leave your studies?"

It was May, the last push toward her finals. The *Law Review* proofs were behind schedule. Richard had started a new business, marine consulting to Boston fishermen plagued with sudden inexplicable shifts in ocean currents, and was working twenty hours a day.

"I'll come," Leisha said.

Chicago was colder than Boston. The trees were half budded. On Lake Michigan, filling the huge east windows of her father's house, whitecaps tossed up cold spray. Leisha saw that Susan was living in the house: her brushes on Camden's dresser, her journals on the credenza in the foyer.

"Leisha," Camden said. He looked old. Gray skin, sunken cheeks, the fretful and bewildered look of men who accepted potency like air, indivisible from their lives. In the corner of the room, on a small eighteenth-century slipper chair, sat a short, stocky woman with brown braids.

"*Alice.*"

"Hello, Leisha."

"*Alice.* I've looked for you. . . ." The wrong thing to say. Leisha had looked but not very hard, deterred by the knowledge that Alice had not wanted to be found. "How are you?"

"I'm fine," Alice said. She seemed remote, gentle, unlike the angry Alice of six years ago in the raw Pennsylvania hills. Camden moved painfully on the bed. He looked at Leisha with eyes that, she saw, were undimmed in their blue brightness.

"I asked Alice to come. And Susan. Susan came a while ago. I'm dying, Leisha."

No one contradicted him. Leisha, knowing his respect for facts, remained silent. Love hurt her chest.

"John Jaworski has my will. None of you can break it. But I wanted to tell you myself what's in it. The last few years I've been selling, liquidating. Most of my holdings are accessible now. I've left a tenth to Alice, a tenth to Susan, a tenth to Elizabeth, and the rest to you, Leisha, because you're the only one with the individual ability to use the money to its full potential for achievement."

Leisha looked wildly at Alice, who gazed back with her strange remote calm. "Elizabeth? My . . . mother? Is alive?"

"Yes," Camden said.

"You told me she was dead! Years and years ago."

"Yes. I thought it was better for you that way. She didn't like what you were, was jealous of what you could become. And she had nothing to give you. She would only have caused you emotional harm."

Beggars in Spain . . .

"That was wrong, Dad. You were *wrong*. She's my *mother* . . ." She couldn't finish the sentence.

Camden didn't flinch. "I don't think I was. But you're an adult now. You can see her if you wish."

He went on looking at her from his bright, sunken eyes, while around Leisha the air heaved and snapped. Her father had lied to her. Susan watched her closely, a small smile on her lips. Was she glad to see Camden fall in his daughter's estimation? Had she all along been that jealous of their relationship, of Leisha . . .

She was thinking like Tony.

The thought steadied her a little. But she went on staring at Camden, who went on staring implacably back, unbudged, a man positive even on his deathbed that he was right.

Alice's hand was on her elbow, Alice's voice so soft that no one but Leisha could hear. "He's done now, Leisha. And after a while you'll be all right."

Alice had left her son in California with her husband of two years, Beck Watrous, a building contractor she had met while waitressing in a resort on the Artificial Islands. Beck had adopted Jordan, Alice's son.

"Before Beck there was a real bad time," Alice said in her remote voice. "You know, when I was carrying Jordan I actually used to dream that he would be Sleepless? Like you. Every night I'd dream that, and every morning I'd wake up and have morning sickness with a baby that was only going to be a stupid nothing like me. I stayed with Ed—in Pennsylvania, remember? You came to see me there once—for two more years. When he beat me, I was glad. I wished Daddy could see. At least Ed was touching me."

Leisha made a sound in her throat.

"I finally left because I was afraid for Jordan. I went to California, did nothing but eat for a year. I got up to a hundred and ninety pounds." Alice was, Leisha estimated, five-foot-four. "Then I came home to see Mother."

"You didn't tell me," Leisha said. "You knew she was alive and you didn't tell me."

"She's in a drying-out tank half the time," Alice said, with brutal simplicity. "She wouldn't see you if you wanted to. But she saw me, and she fell slobbering all over me as her 'real' daughter, and she threw up on my dress. And I backed away from her and looked at the dress and knew it *should* be thrown up on, it was so ugly. Deliberately ugly. She started screaming how Dad had ruined her life, ruined mine, all for *you*. And do you know what I did?"

"What?" Leisha said. Her voice was shaky.

"I flew home, burned all my clothes, got a job, started college, lost fifty pounds, and put Jordan in play therapy."

The sisters sat silent. Beyond the window the lake was dark, unlit by moon or stars. It was Leisha who suddenly shook, and Alice who patted her shoulder.

"Tell me . . ." Leisha couldn't think what she wanted to be told, except that she wanted to hear Alice's voice in the gloom, Alice's voice as it was now, gentle and remote, without damage anymore from the damaging fact of Leisha's existence. Her very existence as damage. ". . . tell me about Jordan. He's five now? What's he like?"

Alice turned her head to look levelly into Leisha's eyes. "He's a happy, ordinary little boy. Completely ordinary."

Camden died a week later. After the funeral, Leisha tried to see her mother at the Brookfield Drug and Alcohol Abuse Center. Elizabeth Camden, she was told, saw no one except her only child, Alice Camden Watrous.

Susan Melling, dressed in black, drove Leisha to the airport. Susan talked deftly, determinedly, about Leisha's studies, about Harvard, about the *Review*. Leisha answered in monosyllables, but Susan persisted, asking questions, quietly insisting on answers: When would Leisha take her bar exams? Where was she interviewing for jobs? Gradually Leisha began to lose the numbness she had felt since her father's casket was lowered into the ground. She realized that Susan's persistent questioning was a kindness.

"He sacrificed a lot of people," Leisha said suddenly.

"Not me," Susan said. She pulled the car into the airport parking lot. "Only for a while there, when I gave up my work to do his. Roger didn't respect sacrifice much."

"Was he wrong?" Leisha said. The question came out with a kind of desperation she hadn't intended.

Susan smiled sadly. "No. He wasn't wrong. I should never have left my research. It took me a long time to come back to myself after that."

He does that to people, Leisha heard inside her head. Susan? Or Alice? She couldn't, for once, remember clearly. She saw her father in the old conservatory, potting and repotting the dramatic exotic flowers he had loved.

She was tired. It was muscle fatigue from stress, she knew; twenty minutes of rest would restore her. Her eyes burned from unaccustomed tears. She leaned her head back against the car seat and closed them.

Susan pulled the car into the airport parking lot and turned off the ignition. "There's something I want to tell you, Leisha."

Leisha opened her eyes. "About the will?"

Susan smiled tightly. "No. You really don't have any problems with how he divided the estate, do you? It seems to you reasonable. But that's not it. The research team from Biotech and Chicago Medical has finished its analysis of Bernie Kuhn's brain."

Leisha turned to face Susan. She was startled by the complexity of Susan's expression. Determination, and satisfaction, and anger, and something else Leisha could not name.

Susan said, "We're going to publish next week, in the *New England Journal of Medicine.* Security has been unbelievably restricted—no leaks to the popular press. But I want to tell you now, myself, what we found. So you'll be prepared."

"Go on," Leisha said. Her chest felt tight.

"Do you remember when you and the other Sleepless kids took interleukin-1 to see what sleep was like? When you were sixteen?"

"How did you know about that?"

"You kids were watched a lot more closely than you think. Remember the headache you got?"

"Yes." She and Richard and Tony and Carol and Jeanine . . . after her rejection by the Olympic Committee, Jeanine had never skated again. She was a kindergarten teacher in Butte, Montana.

"Interleukin-1 is what I want to talk about. At least partly. It's one of a whole group of substances that boost the immune system. They stimulate the production of antibodies, the activity of white blood cells, and a host of other immunoenhancements. Normal people have surges of IL-1 released during the slow-wave phases of sleep. That means that they—we—are getting boosts to the immune system during sleep. One of the questions we researchers asked ourselves twenty-eight years ago was: will Sleepless kids who don't get those surges of IL-1 get sick more often?"

"I've never been sick," Leisha said.

"Yes, you have. Chicken pox and three minor colds by the end of your fourth year," Susan said precisely. "But in general you were all a very healthy lot. So we researchers were left with the alternative theory of sleep-driven immunoenhancement: that the burst of immune activity existed as a counterpart to a greater vulnerability of the body in sleep to disease, probably in some way connected to the fluctuations in body temperature during REM sleep. In other words, sleep *caused* the immune vulnerability that endogenous pyrogens like IL-1 counteract. Sleep was the problem, immune-system enhancements were the solution. Without sleep, there would be no problem. Are you following this?"

"Yes."

"Of course you are. Stupid question." Susan brushed her hair off her face. It was going gray at the temples. There was a tiny brown age spot beneath her right ear.

"Over the years we collected thousands—maybe hundreds of thousands—of Single Photon Emission Tomography scans of you and the other kids' brains, plus endless EEGs, samples of cerebrospinal fluid, and all the rest of it. But we couldn't really see inside your brains, really know what's going on in there. Until Bernie Kuhn hit that embankment."

"Susan," Leisha said, "give it to me straight. Without more buildup."

"You're not going to age."

"What?"

"Oh, cosmetically, yes. Gray hair, wrinkles, sags. But the absence of sleep peptides and all the rest of it affects the immune and tissue-restoration systems in ways we don't understand. Bernie Kuhn had a perfect liver. Perfect lungs, perfect heart, perfect lymph nodes, perfect pancreas, perfect medulla oblongata. Not just healthy or young—*perfect*. There's a tissue-regeneration enhancement that clearly derives from the operation of the immune system but is radically different from anything we ever suspected. Organs show no wear and tear—not even the minimal amount expected in a seventeen-year-old. They just repair themselves, perfectly, on and on . . . and on."

"For how long?" Leisha whispered.

"Who the hell knows? Bernie Kuhn was young—maybe there's some compensatory mechanism that cuts in at some point and you'll all just collapse, like an entire fucking gallery of Dorian Grays. But I don't think so. Neither do I think it can go on forever; no tissue regeneration can do that. But a long, long time."

Leisha stared at the blurred reflections in the car windshield. She saw her father's face against the blue satin of his casket, banked with white roses. His heart, unregenerated, had given out.

Susan said, "The future is all speculative at this point. We know that the peptide structures that build up the pressure to sleep in normal people resemble the components of bacterial cell walls. Maybe there's a connection between sleep and pathogen receptivity. We don't know. But ignorance never stopped the tabloids. I wanted to prepare you because you're going to get called supermen, *Homo perfectus,* who all knows what. Immortal."

The two women sat in silence. Finally Leisha said, "I'm going to tell the others. On our datanet. Don't worry about the security. Kevin Baker designed Groupnet; nobody knows anything we don't want them to."

"You're that well organized already?"

"Yes."

Susan's mouth worked. She looked away from Leisha. "We better go in. You'll miss your flight."

"Susan . . ."

"What?"

"Thank you."

"You're welcome," Susan said, and in her voice Leisha heard the thing she had seen before in Susan's expression and not been able to name: it was longing.

———

Tissue regeneration. A long, long time, sang the blood in Leisha's ears on the flight to Boston. *Tissue regeneration.* And, eventually: *immortal.* No, not that, she told herself severely. Not that. The blood didn't listen.

"You sure smile a lot," said the man next to her in first class, a business traveler who had not recognized Leisha. "You coming from a big party in Chicago?"

"No. From a funeral."

The man looked shocked, then disgusted. Leisha looked out the window at the ground far below. Rivers like microcircuits, fields like neat index cards. And on the horizon fluffy white clouds like masses of exotic flowers, blooms in a conservatory filled with light.

The letter was no thicker than any hard-copy mail, but hard-copy mail addressed by hand to either of them was so rare that Richard was nervous. "It might be explosive." Leisha looked at the letter on their hall credenza. MS. LIESHA CAMDEN. Block letters, misspelled.

"It looks like a child's writing," she said.

Richard stood with head lowered, legs braced apart. But his expression was only weary. "Perhaps deliberately like a child's. You'd be more open to a child's writing, they might have figured."

"'They'? Richard, are we getting that paranoid?"

He didn't flinch from the question. "Yes. For the time being."

A week earlier the *New England Journal of Medicine* had published Susan's careful, sober article. An hour later the broadcast and datanet news had exploded in speculation, drama, outrage, and fear. Leisha and Richard, along with all the Sleepless on the Groupnet, had tracked and charted each of four components, looking for a dominant reaction: speculation ("The Sleepless may live for centuries, and this might lead to the following events . . ."); drama ("If a Sleepless marries only Sleepers, he may have lifetime enough for a dozen brides—and several dozen children, a bewildering blended family . . ."); outrage ("Tampering with the law of nature has only brought among us unnatural so-called people who will live with the unfair advantage of time: time to accumulate more kin, more power, more property than the rest of us could ever know . . ."); and fear ("How soon before the Superrace takes over?").

"They're all fear, of one kind or another," Carolyn Rizzolo finally said, and the Groupnet stopped their differentiated tracking.

Leisha was taking the final exams of her last year of law school. Each day comments followed her to the campus, along the corridors, and in the classroom; each day she forgot them in the grueling exam sessions, all students reduced to the same status of petitioner to the great university. Afterward, temporarily drained, she walked silently back home to Richard and the Groupnet, aware of the looks of people on the street, aware of her bodyguard, Bruce, striding between her and them.

"It will calm down," Leisha said. Richard didn't answer.

The town of Salt Springs, Texas, passed a local ordinance that no Sleepless could obtain a liquor license, on the grounds that civil rights statutes were built on the "all men were created equal" clause of the Declaration of Independence and Sleepless clearly were not covered. There were no Sleepless within a hundred miles of Salt Springs, and no one had applied for a new liquor license there for the past ten years, but the story was picked up by United Press and by Datanet News, and within twenty-four hours heated editorials appeared, on both sides of the issue, across the nation.

More local ordinances appeared. In Pollux, Pennsylvania, the Sleepless could be denied apartment rental on the grounds that their prolonged wakefulness would increase both wear and tear on the landlord's property and utility bills. In Cranston Estates, California, Sleepless were barred from operating twenty-four-hour businesses: "unfair competition." Iroquois County, New York, barred them from serving on county juries, arguing that a jury containing Sleepless, with their skewed idea of time, did not constitute "a jury of one's peers."

"All those statutes will be thrown out in superior courts," Leisha said. "But, God, the waste of money and docket time to do it!" A part of her mind noticed that her tone as she said this was Roger Camden's.

The state of Georgia, in which some sex acts between consenting adults were still a crime, made sex between a Sleepless and a Sleeper a third-degree felony, classing it with bestiality.

Kevin Baker had designed software that scanned the newsnets at high speed, flagged all stories involving discrimination or attacks on

Sleepless, and categorized them by type. The files were available on Groupnet. Leisha read through them, then called Kevin. "Can't you create a parallel program to flag defenses of us? We're getting a skewed picture."

"You're right," Kevin said, a little startled. "I didn't think of it."

"Think of it," Leisha said, grimly. Richard, watching her, said nothing.

She was most upset by the stories about Sleepless children. Shunning at school, verbal abuse by siblings, attacks by neighborhood bullies, confused resentment from parents who had wanted an exceptional child but had not bargained on one who might live centuries. The school board of Cold River, Iowa, voted to bar Sleepless children from conventional classrooms because their rapid learning "created feelings of inadequacy in others, interfering with their education." The board made funds available for Sleepless to have tutors at home. There were no volunteers among the teaching staff. Leisha started spending as much time on Groupnet with the kids, talking to them all night long, as she did studying for her bar exams, scheduled for July.

Stella Bevington stopped using her modem.

Kevin's second program catalogued editorials urging fairness toward Sleepless. The school board of Denver set aside funds for a program in which gifted children, including the Sleepless, could use their talents and build teamwork through tutoring even younger children. Rive Beau, Louisiana, elected Sleepless Danielle du Cherney to the city council, although Danielle was twenty-two and technically too young to qualify. The prestigious medical research firm of Halley-Hall gave much publicity to their hiring of Christopher Amren, a Sleepless with a Ph.D. in cellular physics.

Dora Clarq, a Sleepless in Dallas, opened a letter addressed to her, and a plastic explosive blew off her arm.

Leisha and Richard stared at the envelope on the hall credenza. The paper was thick, cream-colored, but not expensive: the kind of paper made of bulky newsprint dyed the shade of vellum. There was no return address. Richard called Liz Bishop, a Sleepless who was majoring in criminal justice in Michigan. He had never spoken with her before—neither had Leisha—but she came on Groupnet immediately and told them how to open it, or she could fly up and do it if they preferred. Richard and Leisha followed her directions for remote detonation in the basement of the townhouse. Nothing blew up. When the letter was open, they took it out and read it:

> Dear Ms. Camden,
>   You been pretty good to me and I'm sorry to do this but I quit. They are making it pretty hot for me at the union not officially but you know how it is. If I was you I wouldn't go to the union for another bodyguard I'd try to find one privately. But be careful. Again I'm sorry but I have to live too.
>
>   Bruce

"I don't know whether to laugh or cry," Leisha said. "The two of us getting all this equipment, spending hours on this set-up so an explosive won't detonate . . ."

"It's not as if I at least had a whole lot else to do," Richard said. Since the wave of anti-Sleepless sentiment, all but two of his marine-consultant clients, vulnerable to the marketplace and thus to public opinion, had canceled their accounts.

Groupnet, still up on Leisha's terminal, shrilled in emergency override. Leisha got there first. It was Tony.

"Leisha. I'll need your legal help, if you'll give it. They're trying to fight me on Sanctuary. Please fly down here."

Sanctuary was raw brown gashes in the late-spring earth. It was situated in the Allegheny Mountains of southern New York State, old hills rounded by age and covered with pine and hickory. A superb road led from the closest town, Belmont, to Sanctuary. Low, maintenance-free buildings, whose design was plain but graceful, stood in various stages of completion. Jennifer Sharifi, looking strained, met Leisha and Richard. "Tony wants to talk to you, but first he asked me to show you both around."

"What's wrong?" Leisha asked quietly. She had never met Jennifer before, but no Sleepless looked like that—pinched, spent, *weary*— unless the stress level was enormous.

Jennifer didn't try to evade the question. "Later. First look at Sanctuary. Tony respects your opinion enormously, Leisha; he wants you to see everything."

The dormitories each held fifty, with communal rooms for cooking, dining, relaxing, and bathing, and a warren of separate offices and studios and labs for work. "We're calling them 'dorms' anyway, despite the etymology," Jennifer said, trying to smile. Leisha glanced at Richard. The smile was a failure.

She was impressed, despite herself, with the completeness of Tony's plans for lives that would be both communal and intensely private. There was a gym, a small hospital—"By the end of next year, we'll have eighteen AMA-certified doctors, you know, and four are thinking of coming here"—a day-care facility, a school, an intensive-crop farm. "Most of our food will come in from the outside, of course. So will most people's jobs, although they'll do as much of them as possible from here, over datanets. We're not cutting ourselves off from the world—only creating a safe place from which to trade with it." Leisha didn't answer.

Apart from the power facilities, self-supported Y-energy, she was most impressed with the human planning. Tony had Sleepless interested from virtually every field they would need both to care for themselves and to deal with the outside world. "Lawyers and accountants come first," Jennifer said. "That's our first line of defense in safeguarding ourselves. Tony recognizes that most modern battles for power are fought in the courtroom and boardroom."

But not all. Last, Jennifer showed them the plans for physical defense. She explained them with a mixture of defiance and pride: every effort had been made to stop attackers without hurting them. Electronic surveillance completely circled the 150 square miles Jennifer had purchased—some *counties* were smaller than that, Leisha thought, dazed. When breached, a force field a half-mile within the E-gate activated, delivering electric shocks to anyone on foot—"But only on the *outside* of the field. We don't want any of our kids hurt." Unmanned penetration by vehicles or robots was identified by a system that located all moving metal above a certain mass within Sanctuary. Any moving metal that did not carry a special signaling device designed by Donna Pospula, a Sleepless who had patented important electronic components, was suspect.

"Of course, we're not set up for an air attack or an outright army assault," Jennifer said. "But we don't expect that. Only the haters in self-motivated hate." Her voice sagged.

Leisha touched the hard copy of the security plans with one finger. They troubled her. "If we can't integrate ourselves into the world . . . free trade should imply free movement."

"Yeah. Well," Jennifer said, such an uncharacteristic Sleepless remark—both cynical and inarticulate—that Leisha looked up. "I have something to tell you, Leisha."

"What?"

"Tony isn't here."

"Where is he?"

"In Allegheny County jail. It's true we're having zoning battles about Sanctuary—zoning! In this isolated spot. But this is something else, something that just happened this morning. Tony's been arrested for the kidnapping of Timmy DeMarzo."

The room wavered. "FBI?"

"Yes."

"How . . . how did they find out?"

"Some agent eventually cracked the case. They didn't tell us how. Tony needs a lawyer, Leisha. Dana Monteiro has already agreed, but Tony wants you."

"Jennifer—I don't even take the bar exams until July."

"He says he'll wait. Dana will act as his lawyer in the meantime. Will you pass the bar?"

"Of course. But I already have a job lined up with Morehouse, Kennedy & Anderson in New York—" She stopped. Richard was looking at her hard, Jennifer gazing down at the floor. Leisha said quietly, "What will he plead?"

"Guilty," Jennifer said. "With—what is it called legally?—extenuating circumstances."

Leisha nodded. She had been afraid Tony would want to plead not guilty: more lies, subterfuge, ugly politics. Her mind ran swiftly over extenuating circumstances, precedents, tests to precedents. . . . They could use *Clements v. Voy* . . .

"Dana is at the jail now," Jennifer said. "Will you drive in with me?"

"Yes."

In Belmont, the county seat, they were not allowed to see Tony. Dana Monteiro, as his attorney, could go in and out freely. Leisha, not officially an attorney at all, could go nowhere. This was told them by a man in the D.A.'s office whose face stayed immobile while he spoke to them and who spat on the ground behind their shoes when they turned to leave, even though this left him with a smear of spittle on his courthouse floor.

Richard and Leisha drove their rental car to the airport for the flight back to Boston. On the way Richard told Leisha he was leaving her. He was moving to Sanctuary, now, even before it was functional, to help with the planning and building.

She stayed most of the time in her townhouse, studying ferociously for the bar exams or checking on the Sleepless children through Groupnet. She had not hired another bodyguard to replace Bruce, which made her reluctant to go outside very much; the reluctance in turn made her angry with herself. Once or twice a day she scanned Kevin's electronic news clippings.

There were signs of hope. The *New York Times* ran an editorial, widely reprinted on the electronic news services:

PROSPERITY AND HATRED: A LOGIC CURVE WE'D RATHER NOT SEE

The United States has never been a country that much values calm, logic, rationality. We have, as a people, tended to label these things "cold." We have, as a people, tended to admire feeling and action: we exalt in our stories and our memorials; not the creation of the Constitution but its defense at Iwo Jima; not the intellectual achievements of a Stephen Hawking but the heroic passion of a Charles Lindbergh; not the inventors of the monorails and computers that unite us but the composers of the angry songs of rebellion that divide us.

A peculiar aspect of this phenomenon is that it grows stronger in times of prosperity. The better off our citizenry, the greater their contempt for the calm reasoning that got them there, and the more passionate their indulgence in emotion. Consider, in the last century, the gaudy excesses of the Roaring Twenties and the antiestablishment contempt of the sixties. Consider, in our own century, the unprecedented prosperity brought about by Y-energy—and then consider that Kenzo Yagai, except to his followers, was seen as a greedy and bloodless logician, while our national adulation goes to neonihilist writer Stephen Castelli, to "feelie" actress Brenda Foss, and to daredevil gravity-well diver Jim Morse Luter.

But most of all, as you ponder this phenomenon in your Y-energy houses, consider the current outpouring of irrational feeling directed at the "Sleepless" since the publication of the joint findings of the Biotech Institute and the Chicago Medical School concerning Sleepless tissue regeneration.

Most of the Sleepless are intelligent. Most of them are calm, if you define that much-maligned word to mean directing one's energies into solving problems rather than to emoting about them. (Even Pulitzer Prize winner Carolyn Rizzolo gave us a stunning play of ideas, not of passions run amok.) All of them show a natural bent toward achievement, a bent given a decided boost by the one-third more time in their days to achieve in. Their achievements lie, for the most part, in logical fields rather than emotional ones: Computers. Law. Finance. Physics. Medical research. They are rational, orderly, calm, intelligent, cheerful, young, and possibly very long-lived.

And, in our United States of unprecedented prosperity, increasingly hated.

Does the hatred that we have seen flower so fully over the last few months really grow, as many claim, from the "unfair advantage" the Sleepless have over the rest of us in securing jobs, promotions, money, success? Is it really envy over the Sleepless' good fortune? Or does it come from something more pernicious, rooted in our tradition of shoot-from-the-hip American action: hatred of the logical, the calm, the considered? Hatred in fact of the superior mind?

If so, perhaps we should think deeply about the founders of this country: Jefferson, Washington, Paine, Adams—inhabitants of the Age of Reason, all. These men created our orderly and balanced system of laws precisely to protect the property and achievements created by the individual efforts of balanced and rational minds. The Sleepless may be our severest internal test yet of our own sober belief in law and order. No, the Sleepless were *not* "created equal," but our attitudes toward them should be examined with a care equal to our soberest jurisprudence. We may not like what we learn about our own motives, but our credibility as a people may depend on the rationality and intelligence of the examination.

Both have been in short supply in the public reaction to last month's research findings.

Law is not theater. Before we write laws reflecting gaudy and dramatic feelings, we must be very sure we understand the difference.

Leisha hugged herself, gazing in delight at the screen, smiling. She called the *New York Times:* who had written the editorial? The receptionist, cordial when she answered the phone, grew brusque. The *Times* was not releasing that information, "prior to internal investigation."

It could not dampen her mood. She whirled around the apartment, after days of sitting at her desk or screen. Delight demanded physical action. She washed dishes, picked up books. There were gaps in the furniture patterns where Richard had taken pieces that belonged to him; a little quieter now, she moved the furniture to close the gaps.

Susan Melling called to tell her about the *Times* editorial; they talked warmly for a few minutes. When Susan hung up, the phone rang again.

"Leisha? Your voice still sounds the same. This is Stewart Sutter."

"Stewart." She had not seen him for years. Their romance had lasted two years and then dissolved, not from any painful issue so much as from the press of both their studies. Standing by the comm terminal, hearing his voice, Leisha suddenly felt again his hands on her breasts in the cramped dormitory bed: all those years before she had found a good use for a bed. The phantom hands became Richard's hands, and a sudden pain pierced her.

"Listen," Stewart said. "I'm calling because there's some information I think you should know. You take your bar exams next week, right? And then you have a tentative job with Morehouse, Kennedy & Anderson."

"How do you know all that, Stewart?"

"Men's-room gossip. Well, not as bad as that. But the New York legal community—that part of it, anyway—is smaller than you think. And you're a pretty visible figure."

"Yes," Leisha said neutrally.

"Nobody has the slightest doubt you'll be called to the bar. But there is some doubt about the job with Morehouse, Kennedy. You've got two senior partners, Alan Morehouse and Seth Brown, who have changed their minds since this . . . flap. 'Adverse publicity for the firm,' 'turning law into a circus,' blah blah blah. You know the drill. But you've also got two powerful champions, Ann Carlyle and Michael Kennedy, the old man himself. He's quite a mind. Anyway, I wanted you to know all this so you can recognize exactly what the situation is and know whom to count on in the in-fighting."

"Thank you," Leisha said. "Stew . . . why do you care if I get it or not? Why should it matter to you?"

There was a silence on the other end of the phone. Then Stewart said, very low, "We're not all noodleheads out here, Leisha. Justice does still matter to some of us. So does achievement."

Light rose in her, a bubble of buoyant light.

Stewart said, "You have a lot of support here for that stupid zoning fight over Sanctuary, too. You might not realize that, but you do. What the parks commission crowd is trying to pull is . . . but they're just being used as fronts. You know that. Anyway, when it gets as far as the courts, you'll have all the help you need."

"Sanctuary isn't my doing. At all."

"No? Well, I meant the plural you."

"Thank you. I mean that. How are you doing?"

"Fine. I'm a daddy now."

"Really! Boy or girl?"

"Girl. A beautiful little bitch, drives me crazy. I'd like you to meet my wife sometime, Leisha."

"I'd like that," Leisha said.

She spent the rest of the night studying for her bar exams. The bubble stayed with her. She recognized exactly what it was: joy.

It was going to be all right. The contract, unwritten, between her and her society—Kenzo Yagai's society, Roger Camden's society—would hold. With dissent and strife and, yes, some hatred: she suddenly thought of Tony's beggars in Spain, furious at the strong because they themselves were not. Yes. But it would hold.

She believed that.

She did.

VII

Leisha took her bar exams in July. They did not seem hard to her. Afterward three classmates, two men and a woman, made a fakely casual point of talking to Leisha until she had climbed safely into a taxi whose driver obviously did not recognize her, or stop signs. The three were all Sleepers. A pair of undergraduates, clean-shaven blond men with the long faces and pointless arrogance of rich stupidity, eyed Leisha and sneered. Leisha's female classmate sneered back.

Leisha had a flight to Chicago the next morning. Alice was going to join her there. They had to clean out the big house on the lake, dispose of Roger's personal property, put the house on the market. Leisha had had no time to do it earlier.

She remembered her father in the conservatory, wearing an ancient flat-topped hat he had picked up somewhere, potting orchids and jasmine and passion flowers.

When the doorbell rang she was startled: she almost never had visitors. Eagerly, she turned on the outside camera—maybe it was

Jonathan or Martha, back in Boston to surprise her, to celebrate—
why hadn't she thought before about some sort of celebration?

Richard stood gazing up at the camera. He had been crying.
She tore open the door. Richard made no move to come in. Leisha
saw that what the camera had registered as grief was actually something else: tears of rage.

"Tony's dead."

Leisha put out her hand, blindly. Richard did not take it.

"They killed him in prison. Not the authorities—the other prisoners. In the recreation yard. Murderers, rapists, looters, scum of
the earth—and they thought they had the right to kill *him* because
he was different."

Now Richard did grab her arm, so hard that something, some
bone, shifted beneath the flesh and pressed on a nerve. "Not just
different—*better*. Because he was better, because we all are, we
goddamn just don't stand up and shout it out of some misplaced
feeling for *their* feelings . . . God!"

Leisha pulled her arm free and rubbed it, numb, staring at Richard's contorted face.

"They beat him to death with a lead pipe. No one even knows
how they got a lead pipe. They beat him on the back of the head
and they rolled him over and—"

"Don't!" Leisha said. It came out a whimper.

Richard looked at her. Despite his shouting, his violent grip on
her arm, Leisha had the confused impression that this was the first
time he had actually seen her. She went on rubbing her arm, staring
at him in terror.

He said quietly, "I've come to take you to Sanctuary, Leisha. Dan
Walcott and Vernon Bulriss are in the car outside. The three of us
will carry you out, if necessary. But you're coming. You see that,
don't you? You're not safe here, with your high profile and your
spectacular looks—you're a natural target if anyone is. Do we have
to force you? Or do you finally see for yourself that we have no
choice—the bastards have left us no choice—except Sanctuary?"

Leisha closed her eyes. Tony, at fourteen, at the beach. Tony, his
eyes ferocious and alight, the first to reach out his hand for the glass
of interleukin-1. Beggars in Spain.

"I'll come."

She had never known such anger. It scared her, coming in bouts throughout the long night, receding but always returning again. Richard held her in his arms, sitting with their backs against the wall of her library, and his holding made no difference at all. In the living room Dan and Vernon talked in low voices.

Sometimes the anger erupted in shouting, and Leisha heard herself and thought, *I don't know you.* Sometimes it became crying, sometimes talking about Tony, about all of them. Not the shouting nor the crying nor the talking eased her at all.

Planning did, a little. In a cold dry voice she didn't recognize, Leisha told Richard about the trip to close the house in Chicago. She had to go; Alice was already there. If Richard and Dan and Vernon put Leisha on the plane, and Alice met her at the other end with union bodyguards, she should be safe enough. Then she would change her return ticket from Boston to Belmont and drive with Richard to Sanctuary.

"People are already arriving," Richard said. "Jennifer Sharifi is organizing it, greasing the Sleeper suppliers with so much money they can't resist. What about this townhouse here, Leisha? Your furniture and terminal and clothes?"

Leisha looked around her familiar office. Law books lined the walls, red and green and brown, although most of the same information was on-line. A coffee cup rested on a printout on the desk. Beside it was the receipt she had requested from the taxi driver this afternoon, a giddy souvenir of the day she had passed her bar exams; she had thought of having it framed. Above the desk was a holographic portrait of Kenzo Yagai.

"Let it rot," Leisha said.

Richard's arm tightened around her.

"I've never seen you like this," Alice said, subdued. "It's more than just clearing out the house, isn't it?"

"Let's get on with it," Leisha said. She yanked a suit from her father's closet. "Do you want any of this stuff for your husband?"

"It wouldn't fit."

"The hats?"

"No," Alice said. "Leisha—what is it?"

"Let's just *do* it!" She yanked all the clothes from Camden's closet, piled them on the floor, scrawled FOR VOLUNTEER AGENCY on a piece of paper, and dropped it on top of the pile. Silently, Alice started adding clothes from the dresser, which already bore a taped paper scrawled ESTATE AUCTION.

The curtains were already down throughout the house; Alice had done that yesterday. She had also rolled up the rugs. Sunset glared redly on the bare wooden floors.

"What about your old room?" Leisha said. "What do you want there?"

"I've already tagged it," Alice said. "A mover will come Thursday."

"Fine. What else?"

"The conservatory. Sanderson has been watering everything, but he didn't really know what needed how much, so some of the plants are—"

"Fire Sanderson," Leisha said curtly. "The exotics can die. Or have them sent to a hospital, if you'd rather. Just watch out for the ones that are poisonous. Come on, let's do the library."

Alice sat slowly on a rolled-up rug in the middle of Camden's bedroom. She had cut her hair; Leisha thought it looked ugly, jagged brown spikes around her broad face. She had also gained more weight. She was starting to look like their mother.

Alice said, "Do you remember the night I told you I was pregnant? Just before you left for Harvard?"

"Let's do the library."

"Do you?" Alice said. "For God's sake, can't you just once listen to someone else, Leisha? Do you have to be so much like Daddy every single minute?"

"I'm not like Daddy!"

"The hell you're not. You're exactly what he made you. But that's not the point. Do you remember that night?"

Leisha walked over the rug and out the door. Alice simply sat. After a minute Leisha walked back in. "I remember."

"You were near tears," Alice said implacably. Her voice was quiet. "I don't even remember exactly why. Maybe because I wasn't going to college after all. But I put my arms around you, and for the first time in years—years, Leisha—I felt you really were my sister. Despite all of it—the roaming the halls all night and the show-off arguments with Daddy and the special school and the artificially long legs and golden hair—all that crap. You seemed to need me to hold you. You seemed to need me. You seemed to *need*."

"What are you saying?" Leisha demanded. "That you can only be close to someone if they're in trouble and need you? That you can only be a sister if I was in some kind of pain, open sores running? Is that the bond between you Sleepers? 'Protect me while I'm unconscious, I'm just as crippled as you are'?"

"No," Alice said. "I'm saying that *you* could be a sister only if you were in some kind of pain."

Leisha stared at her. "You're stupid, Alice."

Alice said calmly, "I know that. Compared to you, I am. I know that."

Leisha jerked her head angrily. She felt ashamed of what she had just said, and yet it was true, and they both knew it was true, and anger still lay in her like a dark void, formless and hot. It was the formless part that was the worst. Without shape, there could be no action; without action, the anger went on burning her, choking her.

Alice said, "When I was twelve, Susan gave me a dress for our birthday. You were away somewhere, on one of those overnight field trips your fancy progressive school did all the time. The dress was silk, pale blue, with antique lace—very beautiful. I was thrilled, not only because it was beautiful but because Susan had gotten it for me and gotten software for you. The dress was mine. Was, I thought, *me*." In the gathering gloom Leisha could barely make out her broad, plain features. "The first time I wore it a boy said, 'Stole your sister's dress, Alice? Snitched it while she was *sleeping?*' Then he laughed like crazy, the way they always did.

"I threw the dress away. I didn't even explain to Susan, although I think she would have understood. Whatever was yours was yours, and whatever wasn't yours was yours, too. That's the way Daddy set it up. The way he hard-wired it into our genes."

"You, too?" Leisha said. "You're no different from the other envious beggars?"

Alice stood up from the rug. She did it slowly, leisurely, brushing dust off the back of her wrinkled skirt, smoothing the print fabric. Then she walked over and hit Leisha in the mouth.

"Now do you see me as real?" Alice asked quietly.

Leisha put her hand to her mouth. She felt blood. The phone rang, Camden's unlisted personal line. Alice walked over, picked it up, listened, and held it calmly out to Leisha. "It's for you."

Numb, Leisha took it.

"Leisha? This is Kevin. Listen, something's happened. Stella Bevington called me, on the phone, not Groupnet, I think her parents took away her modem. I picked up the phone and she screamed, 'This is Stella! They're hitting me he's drunk—' and then the line went dead. Randy's gone to Sanctuary—hell, they've *all* gone. You're closest to her, she's still in Skokie. You better get there fast. Have you got bodyguards you trust?"

"Yes," Leisha said, although she hadn't. The anger—finally—took form. "I can handle it."

"I don't know how you'll get her out of there," Kevin said. "They'll recognize you, they know she called somebody, they might even have knocked her out . . ."

"I'll handle it," Leisha said.

"Handle what?" Alice said.

Leisha faced her. Even though she knew she shouldn't, she said, "What your people do. To one of ours. A seven-year-old kid who's getting beaten up by her parents because she's Sleepless—because she's *better* than you are—" She ran down the stairs and out to the rental car she had driven from the airport.

Alice ran right down with her. "Not your car, Leisha. They can trace a rental car just like that. My car."

Leisha screamed. "If you think you're—"

Alice yanked open the door of her battered Toyota, a model so old the Y-energy cones weren't even concealed but hung like drooping jowls on either side. She shoved Leisha into the passenger seat, slammed the door, and rammed herself behind the wheel. Her hands were steady. "Where?"

Blackness swooped over Leisha. She put her head down, as far between her knees as the cramped Toyota would allow. Two—no, three—days since she had eaten. Since the night before the bar exams. The faintness receded, swept over her again as soon as she raised her head.

She told Alice the address in Skokie.

"Stay way in the back," Alice said. "And there's a scarf in the glove compartment—put it on. Low, to hide as much of your face as possible."

Alice had stopped the car along Highway 42. Leisha said. "This isn't—"

"It's a union quick-guard place. We have to look like we have some protection, Leisha. We don't need to tell him anything. I'll hurry."

She was out in three minutes with a huge man in a cheap dark suit. He squeezed into the front seat beside Alice and said nothing at all. Alice did not introduce him.

The house was small, a little shabby, with lights on downstairs, none upstairs. The first stars shone in the north, away from Chicago. Alice said to the guard, "Get out of the car and stand here by the car door—no, more in the light—and don't do anything unless I'm attacked in some way." The man nodded. Alice started up the walk. Leisha scrambled out of the backseat and caught her sister two-thirds of the way to the plastic front door.

"Alice, what the hell are you doing? *I* have to—"

"Keep your voice down," Alice said, glancing at the guard. "Leisha, *think.* You'll be recognized. Here, near Chicago, with a Sleepless daughter—these people have looked at your picture in magazines for years. They've watched long-range holovids of you. They know you. They know you're going to be a lawyer. Me they've never seen. I'm nobody."

"Alice—"

"For Chrissake, get back in the car!" Alice hissed, and pounded on the front door.

Leisha drew off the walk, into the shadow of a willow tree. A man opened the door. His face was completely blank.

Alice said, "Child Protection Agency. We got a call from a little girl, this number. Let me in."

"There's no little girl here."

"This is an emergency, priority one," Alice said. "Child Protection Act 186. Let me in!"

The man, still blank faced, glanced at the huge figure by the car. "You got a search warrant?"

"I don't need one in a priority-one child emergency. If you don't let me in, you're going to have legal snarls like you never bargained for."

Leisha clamped her lips together. No one would believe that, it was legal gobbledygook. . . . Her lip throbbed where Alice had hit her.

The man stood aside to let Alice enter.

The guard started forward. Leisha hesitated, then let him. He entered with Alice.

Leisha waited, alone, in the dark.

In three minutes they were out, the guard carrying a child. Alice's broad face gleamed pale in the porch light. Leisha sprang forward, opened the car door, and helped the guard ease the child inside. The guard was frowning, a slow puzzled frown shot with wariness.

Alice said, "Here. This is an extra hundred dollars. To get back to the city by yourself."

"Hey . . ." the guard said, but he took the money. He stood looking after them as Alice pulled away.

"He'll go straight to the police," Leisha said despairingly. "He has to, or risk his union membership."

"I know," Alice said. "But by that time we'll be out of the car."

"*Where?*"

"At the hospital," Alice said.

"Alice, we can't—" Leisha didn't finish. She turned to the backseat. "Stella? Are you conscious?"

"Yes," said the small voice.

Leisha groped until her fingers found the rear-seat illuminator. Stella lay stretched out on the backseat, her face distorted with pain. She cradled her left arm in her right. A single bruise colored her face, above the left eye.

"You're Leisha Camden," the child said, and started to cry.

"Her arm's broken," Alice said.

"Honey, can you . . ." Leisha's throat felt thick, she had trouble getting the words out ". . . can you hold on till we get you to a doctor?"

"Yes," Stella said. "Just don't take me back there!"

"We won't," Leisha said. "Ever." She glanced at Alice and saw Tony's face.

Alice said, "There's a community hospital about ten miles south of here."

"How do you know that?"

"I was there once. Drug overdose," Alice said briefly. She drove hunched over the wheel, with the face of someone thinking furiously. Leisha thought, too, trying to see a way around the legal charge of kidnapping. They probably couldn't say the child came willingly: Stella would undoubtedly cooperate, but at her age and in her condition she was probably *non sui juris*, her word would have no legal weight . . .

"Alice, we can't even get her into the hospital without insurance information. Verifiable on-line."

"Listen," Alice said, not to Leisha but over her shoulder, toward the backseat. "Here's what we're going to do, Stella. I'm going to tell them you're my daughter and you fell off a big rock you were climbing while we stopped for a snack at a roadside picnic area. We're driving from California to Philadelphia to see your grandmother. Your name is Jordan Watrous and you're five years old. Got that, honey?"

"I'm seven," Stella said. "Almost eight."

"You're a very large five. Your birthday is March twenty-third. Can you do this, Stella?"

"Yes," the little girl said. Her voice was stronger.

Leisha stared at Alice. "Can *you* do this?"

"Of course I can," Alice said. "I'm Roger Camden's daughter."

Alice half carried, half supported Stella into the emergency room of the small community hospital. Leisha watched from the car: the short stocky woman, the child's thin body with the twisted arm. Then she drove Alice's car to the farthest corner of the parking lot, under the dubious cover of a skimpy maple, and locked it. She tied the scarf more securely around her face.

Alice's license plate number, and her name, would be in every police and rental-car databank by now. The medical banks were slower; often they uploaded from local precincts only once a day, resenting the governmental interference in what was still, despite a half century of battle, a private-sector enterprise. Alice and Stella would probably be all right in the hospital. Probably. But Alice could not rent another car.

Leisha could.

But the data file that would flash to rental agencies on Alice Camden Watrous might or might not include that she was Leisha Camden's twin.

Leisha looked at the rows of cars in the lot. A flashy luxury Chrysler, an Ikeda van, a row of middle-class Toyotas and Mercedes, a vintage '99 Cadillac—she could imagine the owner's face if that were missing—ten or twelve cheap runabouts, a hovercar with the uniformed driver asleep at the wheel. And a battered farm truck.

Leisha walked over to the truck. A man sat at the wheel, smoking. She thought of her father.

"Hello," Leisha said.

The man rolled down his window but didn't answer. He had greasy brown hair.

"See that hovercar over there?" Leisha said. She made her voice sound young, high. The man glanced at it indifferently; from this angle you couldn't see that the driver was asleep. "That's my bodyguard. He thinks I'm in the hospital, the way my father told me to, getting this lip looked at." She could feel her mouth swollen from Alice's blow.

"So?"

Leisha stamped her foot. "So I don't want to be inside. He's a shit and so's Daddy. I want out. I'll give you four thousand bank credits for your truck. Cash."

The man's eyes widened. He tossed away his cigarette, looked again at the hovercar. The driver's shoulders were broad, and the car was within easy screaming distance.

"All nice and legal," Leisha said, and tried to smirk. Her knees felt watery.

"Let me see the cash."

Leisha backed away from the truck, to where he could not reach her. She took the money from her arm clip. She was used to carrying a lot of cash; there had always been Bruce, or someone like Bruce. There had always been safety.

"Get out of the truck on the other side," Leisha said, "and lock the door behind you. Leave the keys on the seat, where I can see them from here. Then I'll put the money on the roof where you can see it."

The man laughed, a sound like gravel pouring. "Regular little

Dabney Engh, aren't you? Is that what they teach you society debs at your fancy schools?"

Leisha had no idea who Dabney Engh was. She waited, watching the man try to think of a way to cheat her, and tried to hide her contempt. She thought of Tony.

"All right," he said, and slid out of the truck.

"Lock the door!"

He grinned, opened the door again, locked it. Leisha put the money on the roof, yanked open the driver's door, clambered in, locked the door, and powered up the window. The man laughed. She put the key into the ignition, started the truck, and drove toward the street. Her hands trembled.

She drove slowly around the block twice. When she came back, the man was gone, and the driver of the hovercar was still asleep. She had wondered if the man would wake him, out of sheer malice, but he had not. She parked the truck and waited.

An hour and a half later Alice and a nurse wheeled Stella out of the emergency entrance. Leisha leaped out of the truck and yelled, "Coming, Alice!" waving both her arms. It was too dark to see Alice's expression; Leisha could only hope that Alice showed no dismay at the battered truck, that she had not told the nurse to expect a red car.

Alice said, "This is Julie Bergadon, a friend that I called while you were setting Jordan's arm." The nurse nodded, uninterested. The two women helped Stella into the high truck cab; there was no backseat. Stella had a cast on her arm and looked drugged.

"How?" Alice said as they drove off.

Leisha didn't answer. She was watching a police hovercar land at the other end of the parking lot. Two officers got out and strode purposefully toward Alice's locked car under the skimpy maple.

"My God," Alice said. For the first time she sounded frightened.

"They won't trace us," Leisha said. "Not to this truck. Count on it."

"Leisha." Alice's voice spiked with fear. "Stella's *asleep*."

Leisha glanced at the child, slumped against Alice's shoulder. "No, she's not. She's unconscious from painkillers."

"Is that all right? Normal? For . . . her?"

"We can black out. We can even experience substance-induced

sleep." Tony and she and Richard and Jeanine in the midnight woods. . . . "Didn't you know that, Alice?"

"No."

"We don't know very much about each other, do we?"

They drove south in silence. Finally Alice said, "Where are we going to take her, Leisha?"

"I don't know. Any one of the Sleepless would be the first place the police would check—"

"You can't risk it. Not the way things are," Alice said. She sounded weary. "But all my friends are in California. I don't think we could drive this rust bucket that far before getting stopped."

"It wouldn't make it anyway."

"What should we do?"

"Let me think."

At an expressway exit stood a pay phone. It wouldn't be data shielded, as Groupnet was. Would Kevin's open line be tapped? Probably.

There was no doubt the Sanctuary line would be.

Sanctuary. All of them going there or already there, Kevin had said. Holed up, trying to pull the worn Allegheny Mountains around them like a safe little den. Except for the children like Stella, who could not.

Where? With whom?

Leisha closed her eyes. The Sleepless were out; the police would find Stella within hours. Susan Melling? But she had been Alice's all-too-visible stepmother and was cobeneficiary of Camden's will; they would question her almost immediately. It couldn't be anyone traceable to Alice. It could only be a Sleeper that Leisha knew, and trusted, and why should anyone at all fit that description? Why should she risk so much on anyone who did? She stood a long time in the dark phone kiosk. Then she walked to the truck. Alice was asleep, her head thrown back against the seat. A tiny line of drool ran down her chin. Her face was white and drained in the bad light from the kiosk. Leisha walked back to the phone.

"Stewart? Stewart Sutter?"

"Yes?"

"This is Leisha Camden. Something has happened." She told the story tersely, in bald sentences. Stewart did not interrupt.

"Leisha—" Stewart said, and stopped.

"I need help, Stewart." *"I'll help you, Alice."* *"I don't need your help."* A wind whistled over the dark field beside the kiosk, and Leisha shivered. She heard in the wind the thin keen of a beggar. In the wind, in her own voice.

"All right," Stewart said, "this is what we'll do. I have a cousin in Ripley, New York, just over the state line from Pennsylvania on the route you'll be driving east. It has to be in New York, I'm licensed in New York. Take the little girl there. I'll call my cousin and tell her you're coming. She's an elderly woman, was quite an activist in her youth, her name is Janet Patterson. The town is—"

"What makes you so sure she'll get involved? She could go to jail. And so could you."

"She's been in jail so many times you wouldn't believe it. Political protests going all the way back to Vietnam. But no one's going to jail. I'm now your attorney of record, I'm privileged. I'm going to get Stella declared a ward of the state. That shouldn't be too hard with the hospital records you established in Skokie. Then she can be transferred to a foster home in New York, I know just the place, people who are fair and kind. Then Alice—"

"She's resident in Illinois. You can't—"

"Yes, I can. Since those research findings about the Sleepless life span have come out, legislators have been railroaded by stupid constituents scared or jealous or just plain angry. The result is a body of so-called 'law' riddled with contradictions, absurdities, and loopholes. None of it will stand in the long run—or at least I hope not—but in the meantime it can all be exploited. I can use it to create the most goddamn convoluted case for Stella that anybody ever saw, and in the meantime she won't be returned home. But that won't work for Alice—she'll need an attorney licensed in Illinois."

"We have one," Leisha said. "Candace Holt."

"No, not a Sleepless. Trust me on this, Leisha. I'll find somebody good. There's a man in—are you crying?"

"No," Leisha said, crying.

"Ah, God," Stewart said. "Bastards. I'm sorry all this happened, Leisha."

"Don't be," Leisha said.

When she had directions to Stewart's cousin, she walked back to the truck. Alice was still asleep, Stella still unconscious. Leisha closed the truck door as quietly as possible. The engine balked and roared, but Alice didn't wake. There was a crowd of people with them in the narrow and darkened cab: Stewart Sutter, Tony Indivino, Susan Melling, Kenzo Yagai, Roger Camden.

To Stewart Sutter she said, You called to inform me about the situation at Morehouse, Kennedy. You are risking your career and your cousin for Stella. And you stand to gain nothing. Like Susan telling me in advance about Bernie Kuhn's brain. Susan, who lost her life to Daddy's dream and regained it by her own strength. A contract without consideration for each side is not a contract: every first-year student knows that.

To Kenzo Yagai she said, Trade isn't always linear. You missed that. If Stewart gives me something, and I give Stella something, and ten years from now Stella is a different person because of that and gives something to someone else as yet unknown—it's an ecology. An *ecology* of trade, yes, each niche needed, even if they're not contractually bound. Does a horse need a fish? *Yes.*

To Tony she said, Yes, there are beggars in Spain who trade nothing, give nothing, do nothing. But there are *more* than beggars in Spain. Withdraw from the beggars, you withdraw from the whole damn country. And you withdraw from the possibility of the ecology of help. That's what Alice wanted, all those years ago in her bedroom. Pregnant, scared, angry, jealous, she wanted to help *me,* and I wouldn't let her because I didn't need it. But I do now. And she did then. Beggars need to help as well as be helped.

And, finally, there was only Daddy left. She could *see* him, bright eyed, holding thick-leaved exotic flowers in his strong hands. To Camden she said, You were wrong. Alice *is* special. Oh, Daddy— the specialness of Alice! You were *wrong.*

As soon as she thought this, lightness filled her. Not the buoyant bubble of joy, not the hard clarity of examination, but something else: sunshine, soft through the conservatory glass, where two children ran in and out. She suddenly felt light herself, not buoyant but translucent, a medium for the sunshine to pass clear through, on its way to somewhere else.

She drove the sleeping woman and the wounded child through the night, east, toward the state line.

About the Nebula Awards

Throughout the year, the members of the Science-fiction and Fantasy Writers of America read and recommend novels and stories for the annual Nebula Awards. The editor of the *Nebula Awards Report* collects the recommendations and publishes them. Near the end of the year, the *NAR* editor tallies the endorsements, draws up the preliminary ballot, and sends it to all active SFWA members. Under the current rules, each novel and story enjoys a one-year eligibility period from its date of publication. If the work fails to make the preliminary ballot during that interval, it is dropped from further Nebula consideration.

The *NAR* editor processes the results of the preliminary ballot and then compiles a final ballot listing the five most popular novels, novellas, novelettes, and short stories. For purposes of the Nebula Award, a novel is 40,000 words or more; a novella is 17,500 to 39,999 words; a novelette is 7,500 to 17,499 words; and a short story is 7,499 words or fewer. At the present time, SFWA impanels both a novel jury and a short-fiction jury to oversee the voting process and, if an outstanding work in any category was neglected by the membership at large, to supplement the five nominees with a sixth choice. Thus, the appearance of extra finalists bespeaks two distinct processes: jury discretion and ties.

Founded in 1965 by Damon Knight, the Science Fiction Writers of America began with a charter membership of seventy-eight authors. Today it boasts about a thousand members and an augmented name. Early in his tenure, Lloyd Biggle, Jr., SFWA's first secretary-treasurer, proposed that the organization periodically select and publish the year's best stories. This notion quickly evolved into the elaborate balloting process, an annual awards banquet, and a series of Nebula anthologies. Judith Ann Lawrence designed the trophy from a sketch by Kate Wilhelm. It is a block of Lucite containing a rock crystal and a spiral nebula made of metallic glitter. The prize is handmade, and no two are exactly alike.

The Grand Master Nebula Award goes to a living author for a lifetime of achievement. The membership bestows it no more than six times in a decade. In accordance with SFWA's bylaws, the president nominates a candidate, normally after consulting with past presidents and the board of directors. This nomination then goes before the officers; if a majority approves, that candidate becomes a Grand Master. Past recipients include Robert A. Heinlein (1974), Jack Williamson (1975), Clifford D. Simak (1976), L. Sprague de Camp (1978), Fritz Leiber (1981), Andre Norton (1983), Arthur C. Clarke (1985), Isaac Asimov (1986), Alfred Bester (1987), Ray Bradbury (1988), and Lester del Rey (1990).

The twenty-seventh annual Nebula Awards banquet was held at the Colony Square Hotel in Atlanta, Georgia, on April 25, 1992. Beyond the Nebulas for novel, novella, novelette, and short story, the first annual Ray Bradbury Award (Best Dramatic Script) was given to James Cameron and William Wisher for *Terminator 2: Judgment Day.*

Selected Titles from the 1991 Preliminary Nebula Ballot

The following four lists provide an overview of those works, authors, and periodicals that particularly attracted SFWA's notice during 1991. Finalists and winners are excluded from this catalog, as these are documented in the introduction.

Novels

Ring of Charon by Roger MacBride Allen (Tor)
A Woman of the Iron People by Eleanor Amason (William Morrow)
Xenocide by Orson Scott Card (Tor)
Twistor by John Cramer (William Morrow)
The Little Country by Charles de Lint (William Morrow)
Tam Lin by Pamela Dean (Tor)
Buddy Holly Is Alive and Well on Ganymede by Bradley Denton (William Morrow)
Gnome Man's Land by Esther Freisner (Ace)
The Difference Engine by William Gibson and Bruce Sterling (Bantam)

Carve the Sky by Alexander Jablokov (William Morrow)
The Silicon Man by Charles Platt (Bantam)
Soothsayer by Mike Resnick (Ace)
Pacific Edge by Kim Stanley Robinson (Tor)
Nothing Sacred by Elizabeth Ann Scarborough (Bantam)
The Dagger and the Cross by Judith Tarr (Foundation)
Days of Atonement by Walter Jon Williams (Tor)
A Roil of Stars by Don Wismer (Baen)

Novellas

"Candle" by Tony Daniel (*Isaac Asimov's Science Fiction Magazine*, June 1991)
"Frankenswine" by Janet Kagan (*Isaac Asimov's Science Fiction Magazine*, August 1991)
"Raising Cane" by Janet Kagan (*Isaac Asimov's Science Fiction Magazine*, March 1991)
"And Wild to Hold" by Nancy Kress (*Isaac Asimov's Science Fiction Magazine*, July 1991)
"Desert Rain" by Mark L. Van Name and Pat Murphy (*Full Spectrum 3*)

Novelettes

"Dispatches from the Revolution" by Pat Cadigan (*Isaac Asimov's Science Fiction Magazine*, July 1991)
"Understand" by Ted Chiang (*Isaac Asimov's Science Fiction Magazine*, August 1991)
"Living Will" by Alexander Jablokov (*Isaac Asimov's Science Fiction Magazine*, June 1991)
"Hummers" by Lisa Mason (*Isaac Asimov's Science Fiction Magazine*, February 1991)
"Traveling West" by Pat Murphy (*Isaac Asimov's Science Fiction Magazine*, February 1991)
"Over There" by Mike Resnick (*Isaac Asimov's Science Fiction Magazine*, September 1991)
"A History of the Twentieth Century, with Illustrations" by Kim Stanley Robinson (*Isaac Asimov's Science Fiction Magazine*, April 1991)

"The Bee Man" by Mary Rosenblum (*Isaac Asimov's Science Fiction Magazine*, September 1991)

Short Stories

"Bright Light, Big City" by Greg Costikyan (*Isaac Asimov's Science Fiction Magazine*, February 1991)

"Lichen and Rock" by Eileen Gunn (*Isaac Asimov's Science Fiction Magazine*, June 1991)

"Pogrom" by James Patrick Kelly (*Isaac Asimov's Science Fiction Magazine*, January 1991)

"A Walk in the Sun" by Geoffrey Landis (*Isaac Asimov's Science Fiction Magazine*, October 1991)

"For Fear of Little Men" by Terry McGarry (*Aboriginal Science Fiction*, March/April 1991)

"Daughter Earth" by James Morrow (*Full Spectrum 3*)

"One Perfect Morning, with Jackals" by Mike Resnick (*Isaac Asimov's Science Fiction Magazine*, March 1991)

"Winter Solstice" by Mike Resnick (*Fantasy and Science Fiction*, October/November 1991)

"Critical Cats" by Susan Shwartz (*Cat Two*)

"TV Time" by Mark L. Van Name (*Isaac Asimov's Science Fiction Magazine*, April 1991)

Past Nebula Award Winners

1965

Best Novel: *Dune* by Frank Herbert
Best Novella: "The Saliva Tree" by Brian W. Aldiss
"He Who Shapes" by Roger Zelazny (tie)
Best Novelette: "The Doors of His Face, the Lamps of His Mouth" by Roger Zelazny
Best Short Story: " 'Repent, Harlequin!' Said the Ticktockman" by Harlan Ellison

1966

Best Novel: *Flowers for Algernon* by Daniel Keys
Babel-17 by Samuel R. Delany (tie)

Best Novella: "The Last Castle" by Jack Vance
Best Novelette: "Call Him Lord" by Gordon R. Dickson
Best Short Story: "The Secret Place" by Richard McKenna

1967

Best Novel: *The Einstein Intersection* by Samuel R. Delany
Best Novella: "Behold the Man" by Michael Moorcock
Best Novelette: "Gonna Roll the Bones" by Fritz Leiber
Best Short Story: "Aye, and Gomorrah" by Samuel R. Delany

1968

Best Novel: *Rite of Passage* by Alexei Panshin
Best Novella: "Dragonrider" by Anne McCaffrey
Best Novelette: "Mother to the World" by Richard Wilson
Best Short Story: "The Planners" by Kate Wilhelm

1969

Best Novel: *The Left Hand of Darkness* by Ursula K. Le Guin
Best Novella: "A Boy and His Dog" by Harlan Ellison
Best Novelette: "Time Considered as a Helix of Semi-Precious Stones"
by Samuel R. Delany
Best Short Story: "Passengers" by Robert Silverberg

1970

Best Novel: *Ringworld* by Larry Niven
Best Novella: "Ill Met in Lankhmar" by Fritz Leiber
Best Novelette: "Slow Sculpture" by Theodore Sturgeon
Best Short Story: no award

1971

Best Novel: *A Time of Changes* by Robert Silverberg
Best Novella: "The Missing Man" by Katherine MacLean
Best Novelette: "The Queen of Air and Darkness" by Poul Anderson
Best Short Story: "Good News from the Vatican" by Robert Silverberg

1972

Best Novel: *The Gods Themselves* by Isaac Asimov
Best Novella: "A Meeting with Medusa" by Arthur C. Clarke
Best Novelette: "Goat Song" by Poul Anderson
Best Short Story: "When It Changed" by Joanna Russ

1973

Best Novel: *Rendezvous with Rama* by Arthur C. Clarke
Best Novella: "The Death of Doctor Island" by Gene Wolfe
Best Novelette: "Of Mist, and Grass, and Sand" by Vonda N. McIntyre
Best Short Story: "Love Is the Plan, the Plan Is Death" by James Tiptree, Jr.
Best Dramatic Presentation: *Soylent Green*

1974

Best Novel: *The Dispossessed* by Ursula K. Le Guin
Best Novella: "Born with the Dead" by Robert Silverberg
Best Novelette: "If the Stars Are Gods" by Gordon Eklund and Gregory Benford
Best Short Story: "The Day Before the Revolution" by Ursula K. Le Guin
Best Dramatic Presentation: *Sleeper*
Grand Master: Robert A. Heinlein

1975

Best Novel: *The Forever War* by Joe Haldeman
Best Novella: "Home Is the Hangman" by Roger Zelazny
Best Novelette: "San Diego Lightfoot Sue" by Tom Reamy
Best Short Story: "Catch That Zeppelin!" by Fritz Leiber
Best Dramatic Presentation: *Young Frankenstein*
Grand Master: Jack Williamson

1976

Best Novel: *Man Plus* by Frederik Pohl
Best Novella: "Houston, Houston, Do You Read?" by James Tiptree, Jr.

Best Novelette: "The Bicentennial Man" by Isaac Asimov
Best Short Story: "A Crowd of Shadows" by Charles L. Grant
Grand Master: Clifford D. Simak

1977

Best Novel: *Gateway* by Frederik Pohl
Best Novella: "Stardance" by Spider and Jeanne Robinson
Best Novelette: "The Screwfly Solution" by Raccoona Sheldon
Best Short Story: "Jeffty Is Five" by Harlan Ellison
Special Award: *Star Wars*

1978

Best Novel: *Dreamsnake* by Vonda N. McIntyre
Best Novella: "The Persistence of Vision" by John Varley
Best Novelette: "A Glow of Candles, a Unicorn's Eye" by Charles L. Grant
Best Short Story: "Stone" by Edward Bryant
Grand Master: L. Sprague de Camp

1979

Best Novel: *The Fountains of Paradise* by Arthur C. Clarke
Best Novella: "Enemy Mine" by Barry Longyear
Best Novelette: "Sandkings" by George R. R. Martin
Best Short Story: "giANTS" by Edward Bryant

1980

Best Novel: *Timescape* by Gregory Benford
Best Novella: "The Unicorn Tapestry" by Suzy McKee Charnas
Best Novelette: "The Ugly Chickens" by Howard Waldrop
Best Short Story: "Grotto of the Dancing Deer" by Clifford D. Simak

1981

Best Novel: *The Claw of the Conciliator* by Gene Wolfe
Best Novella: "The Saturn Game" by Poul Anderson
Best Novelette: "The Quickening" by Michael Bishop

Best Short Story: "The Bone Flute" by Lisa Tuttle °
Grand Master: Fritz Leiber

1982

Best Novel: *No Enemy But Time* by Michael Bishop
Best Novella: "Another Orphan" by John Kessel
Best Novelette: "Fire Watch" by Connie Willis
Best Short Story: "A Letter from the Clearys" by Connie Willis

1983

Best Novel: *Startide Rising* by David Brin
Best Novella: "Hardfought" by Greg Bear
Best Novelette: "Blood Music" by Greg Bear
Best Short Story: "The Peacemaker" by Gardner Dozois
Grand Master: Andre Norton

1984

Best Novel: *Neuromancer* by William Gibson
Best Novella: "PRESS ENTER ■" by John Varley
Best Novelette: "Bloodchild" by Octavia E. Butler
Best Short Story: "Morning Child" by Gardner Dozois

1985

Best Novel: *Ender's Game* by Orson Scott Card
Best Novella: "Sailing to Byzantium" by Robert Silverberg
Best Novelette: "Portraits of His Children" by George R. R. Martin
Best Short Story: "Out of All Them Bright Stars" by Nancy Kress
Grand Master: Arthur C. Clarke

1986

Best Novel: *Speaker for the Dead* by Orson Scott Card
Best Novella: "R & R" by Lucius Shepard
Best Novelette: "The Girl Who Fell into the Sky" by Kate Wilhelm
Best Short Story: "Tangents" by Greg Bear
Grand Master: Isaac Asimov

° This Nebula Award was declined by the author.

1987

Best Novel: *The Falling Woman* by Pat Murphy
Best Novella: "The Blind Geometer" by Kim Stanley Robinson
Best Novelette: "Rachel in Love" by Pat Murphy
Best Short Story: "Forever Yours, Anna" by Kate Wilhelm
Grand Master: Alfred Bester

1988

Best Novel: *Falling Free* by Lois McMaster Bujold
Best Novella: "The Last of the Winnebagos" by Connie Willis
Best Novelette: "Schrödinger's Kitten" by George Alec Effinger
Best Short Story: "Bible Stories for Adults, No. 17: The Deluge" by James Morrow
Grand Master: Ray Bradbury

1989

Best Novel: *The Healer's War* by Elizabeth Ann Scarborough
Best Novella: "The Mountains of Mourning" by Lois McMaster Bujold
Best Novelette: "At the Rialto" by Connie Willis
Best Short Story: "Ripples in the Dirac Sea" by Geoffrey Landis

1990

Best Novel: *Tehanu: The Last Book of Earthsea* by Ursula K. Le Guin
Best Novella: "The Hemingway Hoax" by Joe Haldeman
Best Novelette: "Tower of Babylon" by Ted Chiang
Best Short Story: "Bears Discover Fire" by Terry Bisson
Grand Master: Lester del Rey

Those who are interested in category-related awards should also consult *A History of the Hugo, Nebula, and International Fantasy Awards* by Donald Franson and Howard DeVore (Misfit Press, 1987). Periodically updated, the book is available from Howard DeVore, 4705 Weddel, Dearborn, Michigan 48125.